SHEPPERTON BABYLON

Matthew Sweet is a writer and broadcaster with a doctorate from Oxford University for work on Wilkie Collins. He has been film critic of the *Independent on Sunday*, presenter of BBC Radio 4's *The Film Programme*, and a reporter for BBC2's *The Culture Show*. His first book, *Inventing the Victorians*, is also published by Faber and Faber.

by the same author

INVENTING THE VICTORIANS

Shepperton Babylon

The Lost Worlds of British Cinema

MATTHEW SWEET

faber and faber

First published in 2005
by Faber and Faber Limited
Bloomsbury House, 74–77 Great Russell Street, London WC1B 3DA

This paperback edition first published in 2006

Typeset by Faber and Faber Ltd
Printed in England by CPI Group (UK) Ltd,
Croydon, CRO 4YY

A CIP record for this book
is available from the British Library

ISBN 978–0–571–21298–9
ISBN 0–571–21298–0

For Nicola and Gracie

Contents

Illustrations

Author's collection, *pages* 1, 11, 32, 54, 84, 113, 116, 164, 189, 194, 204, 211, 249, 305,
319; private collection, 18; courtesy of Henryetta Edwards, 37, 41, 82; courtesy
BFI, 43, 49, 66, 98, 101, 151, 174, 188, 223, 268, 275, 282; courtesy of Ernest Dudley,
45; courtesy of Nerina Shute, 73; courtesy of Ian Killick, 86, 91; Basil Dean
Collection, John Rylands Library, Manchester, 125, 129, 140, 143, 148; courtesy of
Jonathan Balcon, 160, 161, 165, 177; courtesy of Roy Ward Baker, 215, 239, 245;
courtesy of Pamela Green, 287; courtesy of John M. East, 312, 315

Acknowledgements

As this is primarily a work of oral history, I am most deeply in debt to the people who did the talking: Sir Anthony Havelock-Allan, Gerry Anderson, Avril Angers, Robin Askwith, Roy Ward Baker, Jill Balcon, Jonathan and Sally Balcon, the Rt Hon Tony Benn, Alan Birkinshaw, Derek Bond, Dora Bryan OBE, Phyllis Calvert, Judy Campbell, Geraldine, Josephine, Eugene and Michael Chaplin, Pat Coombs, Sir Tom Courtenay, Constance Cummings, Stephen Dean, Winton Dean FSA, Maurice Denham, Catherine Deneuve, Yolande Donlan, Bruce Doxatt Pratt, Betty Driver, Ernest Dudley, John M. East, Henryetta Edwards, Rupert Everett, the Rt Hon Michael Foot, Barry Foster, Stephen Frears, Stuart Freeborn, Mike Freeman, William Friedkin, Renée Gadd, Tudor Gates, Timothy Gee, Lewis Gilbert, Frank Godwin, Cora Goffin (Lady Littler), Michael Grade, Dulcie Gray CBE, Pamela Green, Val Guest, Guy and Kerima Hamilton, Ray Harryhausen, Olivia de Havilland, Sir Ian Holm, Victoria Hopper, Roy Hudd, Ruth Prawer Jhabvala, Jean Kent, Udo Kier, Sheila Keith, Jacqueline Lacey, Bryan Langley, Christopher Lee, Mike Leigh, Herschell Gordon Lewis, Herbert Lom, Lorenzo Marioni, John McCallum, Joan Morgan, Oswald Morris, Christopher Neame, Ronald Neame CBE, Sir Alan Parker, David Parsons Tree, Nicholas Parsons OBE, Anthony Perry, Sian Phillips, Barney Platts Mills, Stephen Poliakoff, Sybil Rhoda, Patricia Roc, Nicolas Roeg, Ken Russell, Margaretta Scott, Mildred Shay, Nerina Shute and Jocelyn Williams, Douglas and Muriel Slocombe, Hugh Stewart, Sylvia Syms, Tony Tenser, Betty Tetrick, Charles Tingwell, Richard Todd OBE, Harry Alan Towers, Geoffrey Toone, Sir Peter Ustinov, Pete Walker, David Warner, Alan Warren, Fay Weldon CBE, June Whitfield OBE, Hugo Williams, Googie Withers OBE, Sir Norman Wisdom, Hugh

Wooldridge and Vera Zorina. I also owe thanks to Stephen Bristow, Kay Dunbar, Nicki Foster, Antony Gormley, Alun Jones, Liz Miller, Austin and Howard Mutti-Mewse, Peter Noble, Clare Norton-Smith, Steven Pearson, Susan Picken, Jonathan Rutter, Hilary Smith and Brian Robinson for making some of these interviews and conversations possible. Robin Buss and Garth Pedler both kindly allowed me to listen to their recordings of subjects already in their graves. Invaluable information was provided by Neil Brand, Kevin Brownlow, Charlie and Julien Courtauld, Kate Guyon-varch, Tony Fletcher, Lord Healey, Peter Hennessey, Ian Killick, Peter Lieberson, Fred Lake, Simon Milner, William Nicholson, David Robinson, Jeremy Robson, Jill Salisbury, Steven Wormell and members of the BECTU history committee. Janice Headland reeled through miles of microfilm on my behalf, and gave me the benefit of her immense knowledge of British silent film – without her contribution, this book would be much the poorer. I'm also grateful to my colleagues at the *Independent* and *Independent on Sunday* – particularly Suzi Feay, Marcus Field, Simon O'Hagan, Ian Irvine and Charlotte O'Sullivan – for indulging my obsession with British cinema, to Elizabeth Burke, Lizzie Harris, Mohini Patel, Sarah Roome and Jerome Weatherald at BBC Radio Four, and to librarians and archivists at the British Library, the British Film Institute, the Bodleian Library, the Golders Green Local History Library and the John Rylands Library. Jenny Turner did me the great favour of coming up with the title. David Benedict, Bryony Dixon, Dominic Druce, Ryan Gilbey, Christine Gledhill, Joan Hills, Peter Sweasey and Melanie Williams all read the text in whole or in part – and saved me from innumerable blushes. I also owe thanks to Jon Riley; to my editor, Walter Donohue, for his patience and enthusiasm; to my agent, Simon Trewin, for lunch and encouragement; to my parents, for allowing me to stay up late to watch *Carry On* films; to Nicola, for everything, as ever; and to Gracie, who raced this book into the world, and won.

M.S.

Strange England

A satire on the amatory effects of cinema-going, *c.*1916

When cinema was young, it had no memory, no history. It told no stories of its pioneers; kept no records of its endeavours. The medium celebrated nothing but its flickering present. Past successes, when they were no longer saleable on the lowest circles of the exhibition system, became a burden and a hazard to their owners. Forgotten titles were left to moulder in back rooms and storage cupboards, where they sometimes took their revenge by bursting into flames. More often, their volatility was cured by the furnace, or by scrap merchants who juiced old reels of celluloid for the silver and camphor they contained. When the trailblazing producer Cecil Hepworth went bankrupt in 1924, his entire back catalogue of negatives was bought by a dealer who melted them down into resin for waterproofing the canvas of aircraft wings. Two thousand films, which had showcased Britain's first generation of stars, were liquefied, along with other camphor-rich trash: broken tortoiseshell spectacles, gap-toothed plastic combs, discarded Xylonite dentures. By the time that this prudence had been reconceived as a form of cultural vandalism, the damage had been done: 80 per cent of films shot in these islands between the death of Queen Victoria and the Wall Street Crash had been junked, allowed to decompose, or fed, eighteen reels at a time, into the jaws of the stripping machines. Next time you see a Hurricane in a museum, run your fingers over its skin. You might be touching a vanished masterpiece, or a pair of your great-grandmother's false teeth.

If you have ever tried to trace your family tree, opened a file of yellowed newspaper cuttings, or sifted through a box of old photographs, you'll know that the pleasure of historical research is derived as much from a shivery sense of what is missing and what has been lost or destroyed as

from the information that can be gleaned from the fragments that have
survived. The appeal is occult, not scientific. This is especially true of film,
a medium that offers a window into the lives of the dead; allows you to see
how they arranged their hair, how they buttoned their collars, how they
smiled or frowned, on an afternoon now lost in time. Light plays across
their faces; the narrative unspools; the camera's gaze meets their own and
allows their eyes to meet yours. And once the credits have rolled, you are
left wondering about the ghosts with whom you have shared an hour or
so of darkness. What kind of lives did they lead? Who did they love? What
happened to them once the studio stopped calling? Did they breathe their
last in their bed or take a bullet in the trenches? Could they still be alive,
sitting in the day-room of a provincial nursing home, telling a teenage
care-worker that they used to be in pictures? And, if so, could they be persuaded to tell their story with honesty and candour?

Shepperton Babylon is written against the cultural trend that discouraged others from answering such questions half a century ago, when the
pool of potential contributors was much deeper. If you examine the last
seventy years of writing on cinema in this country, it's easy to see why so
little work was done in this field. Celluloid has more vicious enemies than
mould and entropy. Historically, nobody has hated British film more than
British film critics. Except, perhaps, for British academics, British cultural mandarins and the editors of British film magazines.

In 1927, *Close-Up*, the first significant cinema journal to be published in
this country, inaugurated this tradition of hostility by making regular
unfavourable comparisons between continental European films and
those emanating from Elstree and Shepherd's Bush. Its contributors were
a caucus of aristocrats, activists and avant-gardists (a lover of Wyndham-
Lewis here, a millionaire banker's son there), many of whom were mistrustful of mainstream culture and none of whom realised that several of
the technical innovations for which they garlanded the Soviet directors
had been formulated by British talents a decade earlier.[1]

As few subsequent writers deviated from their critical prejudices, it is
preposterously easy to harvest grandly dismissive quotes from the record.
Let us pull out three plums of intellectual snobbery. Paul Rotha's landmark study *The Film Till Now* (1930) dismissed British cinema as a
colourless counterfeit of its European and American forms and insisted

that 'British studios are filled with persons of third rate intelligence who are inclined to condemn anything that is beyond their range.'[2] In the 1950s, Roger Manvell, the first head of the British Film Academy, compared British pictures to 'faded leaves painted in exquisite detail by a lady in Cornwall'.[3] A decade later, Victor Perkins used an editorial essay in the inaugural issue of *Movie* magazine to pronounce, in a huge typeface, 'British cinema is as dead as before. Perhaps it was never alive. Our films have improved, if at all, only in their intention. We are still unable to find evidence of artistic sensibilities in working order.'[4]

In 1969, when François Truffaut made his notorious declaration that there was 'a certain incompatibility between the words "cinema" and "Britain"',[5] nowhere were his words taken more seriously than in the country whose heritage he scorned. Contempt for British cinema was already a badge of intellectual seriousness: nascent university film courses ignored British films completely; film hacks and historians filled their work with dismissive accounts of pictures they had not taken the trouble to view; academics dizzy with auteur theory constructed a tiny canon of native work that they considered worthy of attention and suggested that the rest was strictly for Little Englanders, nostalgia bores and Bakelite-sniffers – people who felt warm and fuzzy inside when they saw John Mills in naval stripes, Jack Hawkins in an Aran sweater, or a half-remembered music-hall turn gurning innuendoes into the camera. Under this orthodoxy, British cinema was dismissed as constipated, conservative, class-ridden. It was West End theatre photographed and projected to bank clerks' wives at suburban Odeons, or end-of-the-pier routines duplicated for plebs who were suckers for musical numbers and mild smut. Any film made before 1930 was a forgotten boredom; most films made after 1970 were crass and parochial.[6]

And while this cultural estrangement was being formalised in seminar rooms and on the pages of *Films and Filming*, those veterans who had peopled cinema's images since the 1890s – those upon whom the mercury-vapour lamps had shone, and then dimmed – found themselves enclosed in a rare kind of darkness. Only a handful of researchers considered their stories of interest to posterity. In the 1940s and fifties, Rachael Low sought audiences with pioneer producers for her multi-volume *History of the British Film* (1948–85), but she did not allow her work to be polluted by their anecdotes. In the early 1960s, The film-maker and historian Kevin Brownlow, in spite of his dislike for British pictures, accumulated an invaluable archive of interviews with its practitioners, in the course of his research into American and European production. The collector and cataloguer Denis Gifford took his reel-to-reel tape-recorder to meetings with a number of British cinema's earliest practitioners: his principal interest was in establishing casting and production details that might fill the blanks in his monumental work, the *British Film Catalogue*, but he found the personal histories of his interviewees spilling on to the tape. The actress Gertie Potter told Gifford about the childhood she spent being rescued by elephants and churning up suburban lawns in a horse-drawn pantechnicon, all for the benefit of the cameras. The director Maurice Elvey narrated his rise from page boy at the Hyde Park Hotel to Britain's most prolific film director. Elvey described how, for *The Loss of the* Birkenhead (1914), he recreated the sinking of the British troop ship in a back garden in Finchley; how it took two months to fill the water tank from the kitchen tap; and how he secured shots of startling realism by neglecting to warn his gang of extras when the mocked-up boat would collapse under them.

Most productively, perhaps, a film enthusiast named Garth Pedler spent several afternoons in 1972 with Walter Summers, an elderly director known for his quasi-documentary First World War epics, his vicious temper and his predilection for persuading young hopefuls to strip naked during screen tests. Summers was dying of lung cancer by the time he met Pedler, and lodging in Roehampton with a nurse who was paid to change his dressings and administer injections through an intravenous tube sunk into his chest. On a hot July weekend thirty years after they were recorded, I listened to these taped reminiscences. I heard Summers describe his attempts to make his picture *Ypres* (1925) into 'a new kind of film [with] no heroes and no heroines . . . about a whole lot of people [and] nobody in particular' – and his interest in subsequent stabs at the same idea by Sergei Eisenstein and Ken Loach. ('You can see much the same thing in *Cathy Come Home*,' he observes.) I listened to him tell the story of the first day's filming for *Mons* (1926), on which the pyrotechnic effects killed two of his extras and robbed three more of an assortment of limbs and eyes. I heard him recall the night he spent at Balmoral Castle screening *The Bat-*

tles of Coronel and Falkland Islands (1927) to the royal family and a phalanx of kilted ghillies. He remembered how the last reel of the picture was
marred by a violent hissing noise, which he assumed was a fault in the
projector; and how the ghillies processed out of the room at the end of
the film to reveal a large lake of urine, lapping over the flagstones within
inches of the hem of the Duchess of York's gown. I listened as he boasted
of his novel solution to the problem of IRA sabotage when filming a
political thriller, *Ourselves Alone* (1936), on location in Dublin – giving
three important roles in the picture to members of Sinn Féin. With each
successive tape, his voice became more slurred, his fits of coughing more
protracted and phlegmatic, his thoughts more disordered. In the last
moments of the final reel, I heard the nurse enter the room and terminate
the meeting. She did not, recalls Pedler, consider her patient sufficiently
strong for another session in front of the microphone, and permission to
continue the interview at a later date was refused. Summers died without
completing his story. We must be grateful, however, that he was given the
opportunity to share some of his experiences with later, more curious
generations. Most of his peers died unrecognised and uninterviewed,
their memories unrecorded, their work neglected or despised. Flesh was
not so recyclable as celluloid.

What has changed since Walter Summers went to his grave? Although
the study of British film within our universities remains a marginal pursuit, a new generation of film historians has begun the process of mapping out its lesser-known territories. In 1986, an influential essay by Julian
Petley expressed the hope that the small number of British films that had
received praise from commentators such as Roger Manvell 'would look
less like isolated islands revealing themselves, and more like the peaks of
a long submerged lost continent'.[7] Year by year, more hidden regions have
been recovered as new books and essays have given serious critical con-
sideration to areas formerly languishing beneath the sea of critical contempt. A scholarly publication, the *Journal of Popular British Cinema*, was
launched in 1998. In the same year, an annual film festival celebrating
silent British cinema was inaugurated in Leicester; subsequent events
have been held in Nottingham. The crowning occasion of the 2004 weekend was a screening of *Mons*. In 1972, Walter Summers, clinging on to life,
spoke in defence of his forgotten career. Three decades after his death, his

name unknown and most of his work absent from the archive, he has been vindicated.

Shepperton earns its place in the title of this book not because this famous film studio is the main focus, but because, unlike Ealing or Pinewood, it is not strongly identified with a particular kind of picture. Its name may stand, therefore, for the British studio system as a whole. The title also plays upon *Hollywood Babylon* (1975), Kenneth Anger's *Who's Who* of the orgiasts and overdosers of the Californian hills. Although it offers the details of many of British cinema's coeval scandals, suicides, immolations and contract killings, *Shepperton Babylon* is primarily a work of oral history; an attempt to pursue the story of our native cinema to the limits of living memory. The book traces the rise of the British film studio system from the first decade of the twentieth century through the experiences of those who survived it and those who capitalised upon its eventual collapse. It aims to cast light upon forgotten areas of our cinematic heritage, and offer fresh ways of looking at films and performances rendered over-familiar by endless repetition on daytime television. It has more to offer readers who are curious about silent cinema, exploitation cinema and quota quickies than those whose interest in British pictures extends no further than Powell, Pressburger and John Grierson. It is the product of thousands of conversations with veteran performers, writers, directors, producers, cinematographers, publicists and journalists, and three years of turning every morning to the obituary pages, hoping only to see the faces of physicists and clergymen. Some of these interviewees remain celebrated to this day. Others were once household names, but lost their grip on fame with the cancellation of a contract or the coming of sound. Some toiled anonymously beyond the camera's view. I have visited them, like out-of-season seaside resorts, and gossiped with them about the lives of their dead compatriots: who got rich, who got lucky, who took to the bottle, who took pills.

Their recollections have shaped the book: the actress who remembers the day in 1912 when she slipped into the soft green velvet costume she wore for a colour film adaptation of *Little Lord Fauntleroy*; the screenwriter who, one night in 1924, watched his film idols snort cocaine from an illuminated glass dance floor on the banks of the Thames at Maidenhead; the movie columnist of the 1930s whose sense of job satisfaction

increased with every writ that landed on her editor's desk; the drama student whose resemblance to a producer's dead lover gave her four short
years of film stardom; the director whose career was undone by the
grandest gay Western ever produced; the model who escaped Soho's
gangsters to become the queen of the nudie flicks; the genteel Scottish
comedienne who, at the age of fifty-five, reinvented herself as a star of
extreme horror cinema, and fondly remembers 'the one where I drilled in
people's heads and ate their brains'. A Babel of voices from the lost worlds
of British cinema.

CHAPTER ONE

The Silent World of Lilian Hall-Davis

Lilian Hall-Davis, Hitchcock's first muse, before the gas and the razor-blade
ended her career in the movies

For most of the 1920s, the kohl-rimmed eyes of Lilian Hall-Davis gazed out from magazines, posters and double-page advertisements in the *Kinematograph Weekly*. She had been born, hyphenless, in Mile End but, for the purposes of publicity, later shifted her birthplace a few miles west to Hampstead and locked another barrel to her name. Fan publications ran cute copy about her hobbies, her pet likes and dislikes: 'Her favourite recreation is motoring,' breezed *Film Weekly*, 'and she is never so happy as when spinning along a country road, the fresh air blowing in her face.'[1] She was in demand: an eye-popping £150 was said to be her weekly wage, and producers in London, Rome and Berlin were willing to sign the cheques. Viewing her surviving work, it's easy to see why. Even when the material is flimsy, her performances are substantial. *Maisie's Marriage* (1923) is an eccentric romance of contraception, made only because the producer, G. B. Samuelson, purchased the film rights to Marie Stopes's best-seller, *Married Love*, not realising that it was a sexological tract. Hall-Davis conveys the heroine's disgust for her parents' unregulated production of children with impressive force. With more robust material, she demonstrates her instinctive understanding of screen acting. In 1927, she starred in the three most prestigious British films of the year. In Maurice Elvey's *The Roses of Picardy* – a film now lost to the archive – she is a Flemish girl whose inability to choose between two lovers is resolved by the intervention of shellfire. In Adrian Brunel's *Blighty*, she is a privileged young woman into whose life the Great War introduces a vicious dose of reality. The opening scene – a reconstruction of the assassination of the Archduke Franz Ferdinand – cuts to a shot of her at the breakfast table, buried in the *Morning Post*. Her grave expression suggests that she is about to reveal some anxiety about the coming war. 'Jack Johnson beat Moran on points!' she exclaims, establishing the complacency from which the events of the film will quickly shake her. In Alfred Hitchcock's *The Ring*, she is the ticket girl at the fairground boxing booth who marries the boyish, simple-hearted resident fighter, while consumed with desire for the big-time champion who employs him as a sparring partner. She is not one of the bleached Rhinemaidens with whom Hitchcock would later become fixated. She is fleshy and desiring: she presses a stick of chewing gum into her boyfriend's mouth, knowing that the act will excite his rival, watching from near by; when the two men clash in the ring, she urges the fairground barker to talk up the imminent destruction of her fiancé to the blood-randy crowd; after she has allowed her lover to slide his gift of a silver serpentine bracelet up her arm and past her elbow, she spends the rest of the film hiding it from her husband as if it were a love bite. It is a performance of devious sensuality; a *star* performance.

On a chilly autumn day six years later, Lilian Hall-Davis locked herself in the kitchen of her home on the Golders Green Estate, turned on the gas taps, and drew a razor across her throat. In 1933, the estate was as cheerless a neighbourhood as it is today: a dormitory development with few amenities; concentric circles of identical semi-detached houses marooned by the side of one of north London's main arterial roads. Its builders, the Laing Company, attempted to ameliorate its barrenness by holding a competition for the best-kept front garden: Lilian Hall-Davis, of 45 Cleveland Gardens, won second prize. Walk through her neighbourhood in the middle of a weekday afternoon and you will hear the same silence that she heard on 25 October 1933, just before she took her own life. She had the house to herself that day. Her brother, Charles Davis, a GPO engineer and the owner of the property, was out at work. Her husband, an actor named Walter Pemberton, was in Bristol performing in *Mother-of-Pearl*, a backstage musical starring the former Moulin Rouge chorine Alice Delysia. It was Hall-Davis's fourteen-year-old son, Grosvenor, who returned home from school to find a letter from his mother lying on the hall table, and the kitchen door bolted shut. Clutching the note in his hand, he ran across the road to the home of a neighbour, Lily Barnard, who must have quickly guessed what lay on the other side of the kitchen door. 'She told me a few days ago', Barnard informed the coroner, 'that she felt impelled to put her head in a gas-oven. I did not believe this, and talked her out of it.' Knowing that she had not argued persuasively enough, Mrs Barnard summoned the assistance of Herbert French, another resident of Cleveland Gardens, who smashed the kitchen window of number 45 with a hammer, allowing her to clamber through. The room was thick with fumes as gas continued to hiss from the oven. Lilian Hall-Davis's body lay sprawled on the floor, blood pooling from the gash in her throat, her brother's razor still clasped in her right hand.[2] Just like something from the movies.

The story of her suicide made many of the newspapers and cinema trade journals. The *Kinematograph Weekly* described her as 'one whom it was a delight to grasp by the hand and converse with', and ascribed her demise to 'ill-health and disappointment'.[3] The film correspondent of the London *Evening News* revealed that he had observed her a few weeks before her death, watching a scene being shot at one of the studios. 'She looked young and beautiful as ever,' he recalled, 'though a film star is supposed to be getting "old" at 34. To my suggestion that she should return to the screen she returned the same evasive answer as she gave to those who offered her work. "No thank you. My nerves are gone. I can't act for the films any more."'[4] She had been receiving treatment for neurasthenia at a Harley Street clinic, and was clearly in the throes of some kind of break-down. 'It is a melancholy fact', noted the *News of the World*, 'that a poignant tragedy was needed to recall to the public mind the name of Miss Lilian Hall-Davis, the lovely British screen actress, who commanded the admiration of countless "fans" in the days of the silent film.'[5] In the lengths to which they went to remind their readers who she had been, the reports of her death confirmed the anxiety that had driven her to suicide. The public had completely forgotten her.

She was not the only casualty of this cultural amnesia. The coming of sound propelled many film personnel into obscurity. Others had retired, or been abandoned by their audiences years before Jolson sang. In 1916, John Marlborough East, a leading actor and founder of the Neptune Studios at Borehamwood, received 3,640 votes in *Picturegoer* magazine's poll to determine the identity of 'the Greatest British Film Player'. In 1924, he was plugging his rotten teeth with candle wax and being paid peanuts by the *Daily Sketch* to galumph up and down the promenade at Margate, disguised as Uncle Oojah, the newspaper's cartoon elephant. Alma Taylor, whose name topped the same *Picturegoer* survey, was, by 1932, trudging around the Elstree backlot, touting for crowd work. (She successfully sued *Film Weekly* for suggesting she was washed up, but winning the case did not endear her to directors: she rarely worked in a film studio again.) Violet Hopson, who spent the 1920s offering make-up tips to her fans and awarding tennis trophies named in her honour, was also, ten years later, reduced to walk-on roles, and found better employment designing uniforms for usherettes. Ivy Duke, a silent beauty whose career took a similar downward turn, felt that cough-and-spit parts were beneath her dignity, unscrewed the gin bottle, and, by 1937, had succeeded in drinking herself to death.[6]

If these figures were forgotten only a few years after their faces had adorned billboards and broadsheets and birthday cards, they have gone to some darker oblivion now. Fire, fungus and ignorance have obliterated the majority of their work. Most British film critics have never seen a native picture of this period, and would be hard-pressed to name any of the stars who vied, successfully, with their well-remembered American rivals. Although there has been a recent upsurge in academic interest in this era, intolerance towards it runs deep. The 2004 online prospectus for a film studies course run by the University of Dundee, for example, summed up the first thirty years of British production in five words: 'cottage industry stifled by prejudice'. In fact – despite the effects of the First World War and ruthless American economic protectionism – Britain's silent years were among the most vital and productive in the history of the industry. Musical films, action flicks, weepies, detective serials, avant-garde experimenta, period dramas with casts of thousands, satirical animation, proto-fascist science fiction, star vehicles for idols such as Ivor Novello, Alma Taylor, Chrissie White, Henry Edwards: it is hard to generalise about the kind of work produced by British practitioners between the Boer War and *Blackmail*. Beyond a small circle of enthusiasts and researchers, however, its pleasures and achievements are unknown. British silent cinema is a blank space, a lost world.

A handful of survivors lived on into the twenty-first century to describe their experiences. Sybil Rhoda, born 1902, appeared opposite Ivor Novello in Hitchcock's *Downhill* (1927), but the intervening years have stolen her memories of the experience. (In 2004, however, she could still remember the £20 fee she received as the face of Players' cork-tipped cigarettes, and the desperate daily flights made from the set of *Boadicea* (1927) to her dressing room at Drury Lane.) Ernest Dudley, a screenwriter and prolific detective novelist born in 1908, recalls a sweltering afternoon spent in the garden of his father's hotel in Cookham, Berkshire, supplying restorative lemonade to Stewart Rome, as the film actor's thick Leichner No. 5 deliquesced in the heat. Ronald Neame remembers belting around the corridors of Elstree, two decades before he produced *Brief Encounter* (1945), and watching Hitchcock direct Lilian Hall-Davis on the set of *The Farmer's Wife* (1928). As a child actor, Jack Cardiff, the Oscar-laden cinematographer of *Black Narcissus* (1947) and *The Red Shoes* (1948), shared a scene with Violet Hopson in *Her Son* (1920), and can recall the words barked by the director through his long megaphone: 'Look over to Miss Hopson . . . You *love* her . . . *smile* a little . . . Take his hand, Violet . . . Jackie, look up at her and *smile* . . .'[7] Until her death in May 2004, Cora Goffin, born in 1902, could remember hurling herself from a horse on location for *Down Under Donovan* (1922), and under a red car on the streets of Paris – 'the police,' she noted, 'turned out to be rather angry to be in a film with no prior permission'.[8] A few days before her death in June 2004, the actress Joan Morgan could still see, in her mind's eye, the 'wonderful light, the sparkling glass' of the Motograph Studio, a film facility housed inside Joseph Paxton's Crystal Palace at Sydenham. She made her first film there during the First World War, under the direction of Maurice Elvey: *The Cup Final Mystery* (1914), in which the villains of the piece tied her up in a sack and hurled her from a bridge. She was the last silent British film star. And for that reason, she is the principal witness of this chapter.

Joan Morgan's Edwardian childhood encompassed a candlelit evening with Anatole France, a week on the beach with Lady Tree, and a ringside view of the only meeting that ever took place between Ellen Terry and George Bernard Shaw. In 1921, her father, Sidney Morgan, directed an adaptation of *The Mayor of Casterbridge* for which Thomas Hardy came on location. ('He can't be that great an author if he lives in such a poky little house,' her father remarked, on his return from Max Gate). While still in her teens, she played leading roles in films shot in New York and Johannesburg, and she treasured until the end of her life the memory of galloping on horseback across the South African veldt, with no human being in sight. When I made my first visit to her in the summer of 2002,

Joan Morgan, the perky British star cheated out of
a Hollywood contract by her father

her world was much more circumscribed. A small, birdlike figure, she sat in her high-backed, nursing-home chair, her hands clenched arthritically, sipping milky tea from the spout of a plastic training mug. On the chest of drawers were a number of photographs, publicity shots from her girlhood. Her published works – half-a-dozen novels and a volume of autobiography – were lined up on her bedside table. She was proud that, like Dickens, she was published by Chapman & Hall. The first page of each volume was pasted with her personal bookplate: a woodcut of Joan of Arc, the flames licking at her feet.

Her novel *Camera!* (1940) is a romance of the silent film studios that could have been written only by an eyewitness.

Here an electrician would contact the carbons of a Westminster arc, there swings a mercury-vapour [lamp] while the liquid rushed up and down its glass tubes, tubes that shone out in long perpendicular lines of greenish light, turning your face livid as the face of a drowned person, gashed with lips of deadly nightshade purple. If you looked long enough into them the lines of light photographed themselves on your retina and returned to keep you awake as soon as you closed your eyes.

Its heroine, Fay, is a thinly disguised self-portrait. A secondary character, Rosemary Shaw, suggests another original. Shaw is a popular British film star of the 1920s whom the talkies condemn to the obscurity of extra work. After a long day striking a pose in the background of a shot, she takes a cab back to her Bloomsbury flat, her eyes burned by exposure to the lights. 'She was too tired to undress. Too tired. When she had taken the aspirin she lay on the bed in her tarnished gold dress.' The following day, her lover, Gerard Pemberton – his surname echoing that of Lilian Hall-Davis's husband – sees the billboards for the London *Evening Standard*, ranged in order of importance: 'League meets'; 'Great short story'; 'Close of play'; 'Ex-film star's death'.[9]

I asked Joan Morgan what she recalled about Lilian Hall-Davis. 'Didn't she kill herself?' she replied. I confirmed this. 'Oh dear,' she mused. 'Did you know her?' I didn't tell her that I was born forty years after Hall-Davis's death. We moved on to other subjects. I scrabbled in my bag and produced a photocopied page of a 1924 edition of *Picturegoer* magazine, which reproduced an appreciative verse composed by one of her many fans. I read the poem aloud:

> Of all the British screen stars,
> The one I like the best
> Is very sweet – and who she is
> Most probably you've guessed.
> Her name? – Why Joan – Joan Morgan,
> By friends she's nicknamed 'Joe',
> I think it's quite a good one
> Because it suits her so.
> Her eyes are blue and limpid,
> Her acting is divine.
> The films I've seen her in – let's see –
> I think I've been to nine.
> She is both young and clever
> (Her age is three times six)
> With prettiness, she does abound,
> But affectation - NIX!![10]

The subject of this verse pronounced herself amazed. It was a changeable day in June, in which downpours and bright spells had alternated since lunchtime. When the sun broke through the clouds and the light fell on her face, Joan Morgan gasped with delight. She gestured towards the window, which framed a view of the Thames and a long procession of weeping willows. 'Just like a picture from one of my films,' she said.

Joan Morgan's involvement with the movies began in 1912, when she was cast in the title role of an adaptation of *Little Lord Fauntleroy*, which its producers intended to shoot in an early colour process named Prizmacolour. The day before filming was due to commence, a solicitor representing Frances Hodgson Burnett stormed into the offices of the production company and slapped a writ on the managing director, Charles Urban, who had failed to secure the rights to film the novel. Joan Morgan could remember the green velvet folds of her costume, and the eight-shilling fee she was promised for her work. She also had good recall of the long run of films she made after this first disappointment, when her father ran the Progress Film Studios on the beach at Shoreham, Sussex. She described the accommodation block, formed from two railway carriages hauled on to the narrow spit of shingle, and its saloon bar with a roulette wheel, biased towards 19 Red. She recalled her long-dead co-stars: the imperious Lady Tree, as contemptuous of the new medium as her acting style was unsuited to it; Sydney Fairbrother, whose pet white rat would sit on her belt all day, quite motionless; Alice de Winton, a melancholy lady of the nineteenth-century stage whose life had been touched by some undisclosed tragedy. But the story that Joan Morgan most wanted to relate, the story to which her thoughts continually returned, tells how, in the summer of 1920, she missed her chance of a career in Hollywood.

It begins with Bryant Washburn, a handsome American actor–producer, who came to London to make a film of David Skatts Foster's novel *The Road to London*. After seeing Joan's performance in the title role of *Little Dorrit*, he cast her as his leading lady. The rest of the story Joan conveyed as a series of vivid tableaux, as if she were narrating the plot of a silent picture. First you must imagine her father sitting in the drawing room of the Washburns' flat in Dover Street. He is dressed in one of his loudest sports jackets, listening to the American making plans: Joan's name in lights on Broadway marquees; Joan's star rising; Mary Pickford watching her back; a guaranteed five-year contract. He names a figure, and asks Sidney what he thinks of it. Then the scene changes: the young actress and her mother, Evelyn, are waiting anxiously in their suite at the Grosvenor Hotel for the news that will alter the course of their lives. The clock strikes eleven, and Sidney appears at the door. They learn his reply to Washburn's question: 'Not much.'

She repeated the phrase several times, shaking her head in disbelief, still appalled by its bluntness. I found myself imagining how it might look as a hand-painted intertitle. Eighty years after the event, the shock and disappointment were vivid in Joan Morgan's mind. 'Mother froze. What a thing to say to people. And so that was the end. That was one of the tragedies of my life, refusing that contract. I blame my father very much for that.' The next morning, instead of setting off for California, the Morgans checked out of the Grosvenor and boarded the train to Shoreham. Joan's film career lasted several more summers. A six-month shoot in South Africa raised her spirits, but when she returned to Britain she found it increasingly difficult to find work. She remembered how bereft she felt when, after ten successful years before the camera, she accepted that her acting career was over. Her last filmed performance was given for a talkie, *Her Reputation* (1931), in which she and Lilian Hall-Davis played

supporting roles to a gaggle of better-spoken theatre stars – Iris Hoey,
Maurice Braddell, Malcolm Tearle. 'I was finished at sixteen,' she mur-
mured. 'It was hopeless.'

Joan Morgan's was an extraordinary generation. Fairground whip-
crackers, scientific experimenters, hygienists, newspaper hacks, beauty
queens, music-hall turns, champagne socialists and prize-fighters: these
were the personnel of early British cinema. They built its studios, created
its stars, shot its scenes, populated its images. 'I was in at the beginning,'
asserted the veteran actor Douglas Payne, when interviewed in the 1960s,

and believe me, the British film industry developed through the efforts of the
strangest conglomerate of humanity one could imagine. Of course, there were the
visionaries, the pioneering spirits, the intellectuals, but in comparison with other
industries, more than the usual percentage of adventurers, confidence men, and
even a few of what used to be called in my youth "white slavers", who saw the casting couch as the answer to their wildest dreams. I once mistakenly lent a dress suit
to a producer. It was returned to me covered in blood, the by-product of discharging pox. Yes, you met all kinds of game in those days.[11]

Sidney Northcote was one of the wilder specimens. In the years before
the First World War, he was a legitimate practitioner, even if his choice of
subject matter was forehead-smackingly repetitive: he spent 1912 shooting *The Smuggler's Daughter of Anglesey*, *The Belle of Bettwys-y-Coed*, *A
Cornish Romance*, *The Pedlar of Penmaenmawr*, *A Tragedy of the Cornish
Coast* and *The Fisher Girl of Cornwall*, all of which featured Dorothy Foster emoting on various stretches of British coastline. Shortly after this
spurt of activity, however, it struck him that it was not absolutely necessary to make a picture in order to extract cash from its backers, and took
to touring seaside resorts, raising funds for the production of movies, and
absconding with the loot before a frame was in the can. By 1923, he had
been arrested four times on fraud charges, and spent three months in
prison for obtaining money under false pretences. His final scam was
foiled on Jersey, where he established a bogus production company
named Victory Photoplays and persuaded a local businessman named
William Condliffe to disgorge fifty pounds for the privilege of casting
Mrs Condliffe as – unsurprisingly enough – 'a "fishing maid or something" in his new film'.[12]

Elsewhere in this jungle, other odd beasts roamed. Eliot Stannard was one of the first university graduates to enter British films, a likeable eccentric who produced some of the earliest theoretical writings on cinema, scripted most of Hitchcock's silents, and – once his career as a scenario-writer had evaporated – took a job in a vehicle licensing office, where he deliberately sabotaged the filing system. Bernard Edwin Doxatt-Pratt was a trained architect who worked as a film director in Britain and Holland, making boxing pictures and movie adaptations of West End hits. He deserted two wives, disappeared with the fees of a film acting school for which he failed to teach a single class, served a short prison sentence for failing to pay a hotel bill, and was last spotted in the early 1960s when he attempted to touch his estranged brother for a loan. Percy Smith was a pioneer of time-lapse photography who shot *The Birth of a Flower* (1911), a series of breathtakingly beautiful images of lilies spreading their petals, onion-stalks groping the light and beans exploding with tendrils, and *The Strength and Agility of Insects* (1911), a macabre scientific comedy in which bluebottles, glued on to their backs, juggle champagne corks. 'Tread softly, because you tread on my stars,' he told a visiting reporter, as he led him up the garden path – a warning which he may have repeated to his wife, as their house in the London suburb of Southgate became so stuffed with horticultural and cinematographic paraphernalia that she was forced to move into the garden shed. Unlike many of his contemporaries, Smith was not forgotten by the public. This did not, however, prevent him swallowing a lethal dose of rat poison in 1945.

Cecil Milton Hepworth was also a creature of eccentricities and contradictions. He was the most important British film-maker to emerge before the First World War, yet he forbade his children to go to the cinema. He was a gloomy, taciturn, bad-tempered, socially awkward man, but he had a passion for surreal comedy, and once spent over a year designing and sewing a series of dinosaur costumes that worked on the same principle as the pantomime horse. He oversaw the production of films which were, at their best, radical, polished and popular, yet his own ideas about cinema were conservative. He was born in 1874, the son of a magic lanternist at the London Polytechnic Institute, a palace of scientific entertainment on Regent Street where families could view moving magic lantern slides such as *Man Swallowing a Rat* and then descend underwater in an indoor diving bell. (An orchestra played loudly, it was said, to muffle the screams of the drowning.) In 1899, after three years running an unsuccessful photographic processing business from Cecil Court – a paved street between St Martin's Lane and the Charing Cross Road so firmly associated with the kinematograph trade that it was known as 'Flicker Alley' – Hepworth decided to relocate the business to the Surrey village of Walton-on-Thames, and rented a villa on a suburban stretch named Hurst Grove. No clients came, so rather than waiting for production companies to bring him their material, he decided to shoot and sell his own. Actualities – films of tortoise races, street markets and donkey derbies – were his forte, but by the first years of the twentieth century, the public appetite for such work was waning. Narrative subjects provided a more complex and crafted form of entertainment.

Initially, Hepworth's dramas were acted out on a stage in the back garden, a grubby wooden platform marooned in a sea of dandelions and nettles. Twenty-five years later, the site was occupied by a studio complex roofed with sunlight-diffusing Muranese glass and powered by a series of turbines salvaged from a captured German U-boat. On this tract of land, long since obliterated by a multi-storey car park, a phase of unparalleled experimentation and progress unfolded. The company shot sound pictures with Hepworth's Vivaphone system, one-take films in which screen personalities lip-synched to popular songs. (In *The Death of Nelson* a uniformed actor expired beneath a hinged mast rigged to explode on cue. In *Are We Down-Hearted?* Chrissie White and Hay Plumb sang of their poverty, and shook their son until the farthings tumbled from his pockets. In *You Made Me Love You* Stewart Rome and Violet Hopson mimed grudgingly to Joe McCarthy's popular song, and managed to invest only one line, 'I didn't want to do it', with any degree of sincerity.)[13] The Walton studio made propaganda films about the wartime ban on poultry food, the wisdom of recycling waste paper, and the crippling economic effects of unregulated trade. (One of Hepworth's employees cared so passionately about this issue that he named his horse Tariff.) Most importantly, the firm presided over two great changes in the nature of movies and moviegoing: the formation of the star system, through which film performers evolved from anonymous faces to named personalities; and the shift from a cinema predicated upon the supply of gags, stunts, stings and sensations to the cinema of sustained narrative that we have now all been trained to expect at the multiplex.

These innovations are customarily ascribed to American practitioners. Florence Lawrence is usually identified as the first named film star – propelled to fame in 1910 when Carl Laemmle, the future head of Universal, decided that the best way to market her was to spread the rumour that she had been mangled to death in a streetcar accident. D. W. Griffith is usually saluted as the creator of the syntax of fiction film-making. As David A. Cook asserts, 'in the brief span of six years, between directing his first one-reeler in 1908 and *The Birth of a Nation* in 1914, Griffith established the narrative language of the cinema as we know it today'.[14] That, indeed, was the director's own view. After leaving the Biograph Company in December 1913, he placed an advert in the New York *Dramatic Mirror* in which he claimed credit for the invention of 'the use of large close-up figures, distant views . . . the "switchback", sustained suspense, the "fade-out", and restraint in expression, raising motion picture acting, which has won for it recognition as a genuine art'. Perhaps Griffith had forgotten that in 1908 he was a down-at-heel playwright who, unable to persuade any theatres to produce his material, had swallowed his pride and taken a day's acting work on a Biograph drama entitled *Rescued from the Eagle's Nest*. The picture was a direct imitation of one that had wowed American audiences three years previously: the Hepworth Manufacturing Company's *Rescued by Rover* (1905), a British film that contains many of Griffith's 'innovations'.

A century after it was made, *Rescued by Rover* remains a source of cinematic pleasure and a model of narrative economy. It was a phenomenal success: 395 prints were sold worldwide, necessitating two shot-by-shot remakes to replace the worn-out original negatives. (For comparison, 390 prints of a more recent British success, *The Full Monty* (1997), were struck for worldwide distribution.) *Rescued by Rover* is a comic thriller which uses brisk editing and visual repetition to create tension and satisfaction. The movie features a protagonist who, five years before Florence Lawrence was named, fits the definition of the film star. Hepworth's young, bright-eyed British performer was widely recognised by the public. Movies were constructed as vehicles for his particular talents. At his passing in 1914, he was eulogised in the papers. The posthumous revelations that his real name was Blair and that he liked to eat shaving soap should not be allowed to dim his triumph. Nor should the fact that he was a sheepdog.

Although the surviving print of *Rescued by Rover* is incomplete, it follows what, in the 1910s, would emerge as the standard pattern of narrative cinema. It opens with an establishing shot of the cheerful-looking collie and a tiny baby (Hepworth's daughter, Barbara), before initiating the action in an exterior scene shot on a country lane. A nanny spurns the attentions of an old beggar woman, and then, a little further along the track, flirts with a soldier, sharing a cigarette with him. While she is distracted, the old woman scurries out from behind a hedge, and absconds with the baby. The nanny fails to register the outrage and walks on arm-in-arm with the soldier, kissing him as they go. A small advance in time then occurs. We are in the drawing room of a well-to-do household: the mistress (Margaret Hepworth) is sitting in an armchair, sewing; Rover is perched on a wicker stool, in noble profile. The nanny rushes in and relates the calamity, crawling on the carpet in abjection. As she emotes, Rover gazes towards the camera as if to affirm his bond with the audience, licks consolingly at the nanny's face, and bounds into action. In a series of speedily edited location shots, we see him leap through the window of the house, belt down the street, hurtle around the corner, swim briskly across a river, and conduct an efficient door-to-door search of a run-down row of labourers' cottages. The action then switches to an attic room in one of these cottages – an indoor studio set in which an arc lamp simulates daylight streaming through the window – where the old woman is stripping the baby of her bonnet and petticoats. The hag settles the kidnapped child on the floor, takes a swig from a stone bottle, and lies down next to her victim – at which point Rover makes an unsuccessful attempt to intervene. The film then cuts back to the street outside, from where Rover repeats his journey across water and mud and cobblestones until he reaches home. Inside the house, Rover's master (Cecil Hepworth) is sitting, forlorn, at the parlour table. The dog implores him to exert himself, and eventually persuades him to follow him from the house. The journey sequence is repeated, this time with the master trailing Rover down the street and across the river in a rowing boat, until they reach the row of cottages. The screen then shows the squalid attic room, where

Rover licks the baby enthusiastically before her father scoops her up and flees. After they have gone, the old woman draws consolation from the bottle and the cache of saleable baby clothes. Back at the house, the family are reunited: the film cuts from a medium shot to a close-up within the same scene, reinforcing the cosy domesticity of the image.[15]

Cecil Hepworth was always happy to accept the praise for *Rescued by Rover*, though he was probably not its principal author. Hepworth was a technician, a darkroom man, a creator of special effects, a news photographer. He designed a lens for snapping solar eclipses, and went to Algiers to test it out. He made human limbs rain from the air in *The Explosion of a Motor Car* (1900), contracted and expanded the heroine of *Alice in Wonderland* (1903), attached a system of swinging weights to the camera to convey the seismic impact of *That Fatal Sneeze* (1907), and conjured the transparent wraiths of *The Ghost's Holiday* (1907). His attempts at sustained narrative film-making, however, looked more to painterly and theatrical models than the styles and structures now associated with popular cinema. *Tansy* (1921) is a pastoral sage whose panoramic exteriors alternate with domestic tableaux in which the action is viewed as if through a proscenium. *The Pipes of Pan* (1923) is like a moving version of the Cottingley Fairies photographs that duped Conan Doyle.[16] Hepworth's adaptation of *Comin' Thro' the Rye* (1923), a prestige costume drama in production when the studio went into liquidation, has none of the urgency and aggressive use of the editorial razor found in *Rescued by Rover*. But its style does seem continuous with the pictorialist approach to film editing that Hepworth expresses in his autobiography: 'Unreasoned jerkiness is very tiring and unconsciously irritating,' he complained. 'Only the direst need will form an excuse for lifting an audience up by the scruff of its neck and carrying it round to the other side, just because you suddenly want to photograph something from the south when a previous scene has been taken from the north.'[17] By the time he wrote these words, Hepworth was employed cutting trailers for other people's films – although his name still carried sufficient cachet for *Picturegoer* to serialise his memoirs. There was no mysterious process of atavism at work. Most of the pictures that went out under his corporate banner were not directly overseen by Hepworth himself: he seems to have been happy to delegate direction to a changing cast of employees – Percy Stow, Hay Plumb,

Henry Edwards and Lewin Fitzhamon – until his affair with one of the company's stars gave him an incentive to clamber back behind the camera. (Margaret Hepworth, it should be noted, never believed that her husband's countryside jaunts with Alma Taylor were the location hunts he professed them to be.)

In 1905, the clear division of labour between the work of directors, producers and camera operators had yet to emerge. But if his own testimony is to be believed, then Lewin Fitzhamon was the most energetic revolutionary in Hepworth's ranks, and the motivating force behind *Rescued by Rover*. A clergyman's son, prematurely bald with agile black eyebrows, Fitzhamon had been a professional jockey, a drama student and a villain in touring melodrama before he took up residence in Walton-on-Thames on a salary of three pounds a week. He had also appeared in some of the earliest British films, playing the latter role in *Briton vs. Boer* (1900) – 'Two Minutes of White Heat Excitement taking place on the Open Veldt' – projected to patriotic applause from audiences who did not care that the piece had actually been shot on a Home Counties golf course.[18] In temperament, employee and employer were polar opposites. Hepworth was a patrician who ran his firm like a Catholic boarding school; Fitzhamon was a louche divorcee who decorated his rented cottage with strips of clashing orange and scarlet wallpaper, moved in his manservant, a former guardsman, and established an aviary in the back garden. (He had a preternatural affinity with animals: as a child, he had trained a pig to follow him around the house; at Walton, he delighted in offering presents of cheese to the rats that lived in the tree behind his cottage.)

Fitzhamon's arrival coincided with the completion of Hepworth's adaptation of *Alice in Wonderland*. It was a landmark film for the studio, recreating the famous Tenniel illustrations with admirable accuracy and including an array of impressive set-piece special-effects. In 1903, it also had the distinction of being the longest fiction film ever shot on British soil. It struck Fitzhamon, however, as drab and crude. He was disgusted by its flimsy scenery (the company owned one stage flat, which they lugged into the kitchen and repainted according to the demands of the scenario) and by what he considered its amateurish performances (the pinafored heroine was played by the company secretary, Mabel Clark; the frog footman by Cecil Hepworth; the White Rabbit by Margaret Hep-worth, who, according to Fitzhamon, 'couldn't act for nuts'). He must also have been mistrustful of the film's loose structure, caught somewhere between a coherent literary adaptation and a discontinuous presentation of incidents from the book. (Exhibitors were given the option of pur-chasing the entire film or a selection of individual scenes, which would have been impossible with any of Fitzhamon's own films.) After the direc-tor's arrival, Hepworth movies changed their character. They became more reliant upon editing to tell their stories. The increasingly elaborate and substantial sets testified to the recruitment of a resident carpenter. Professional actors slowly colonised productions.

For *Rescued by Rover*, Fitzhamon employed Sebastian and Lindsay Smith, a pair of married stage artistes, to play the flirtatious soldier and the gypsy kidnapper. They were paid half a guinea each, a fee which included the price of their return ticket from Surbiton. They were the first of many. Fitzhamon summoned former colleagues from his touring days, or took the train to Waterloo and chose artists from the books of Den-ton's Theatrical Agency. A regular company of performers was soon established. They included Dolly Lupone, a yellow-eyed teenage actress who had played starving waifs and dying match girls on stage with Fitzhamon, and who was probably his lover; Hetty, Gertie and Bertie Pot-ter, Lupone's young cousins from Wimbledon; Gladys Sylvani, a Gaiety girl born plain Smith who became the first British film actor to negotiate a regular contract, and the first to retire from the screen on the arm of a rich American husband; Rosina White, fresh from the Seymour Hicks musical *The Gay Gordons* (1907); and her sister Chrissie, who became one of the biggest stars in Hepworth's stable.

It was not until 1910, however, that Hepworth accepted the wisdom of naming these performers in the publicity for his company's films. Before then, only dogs and horses – who tended not to have pushy agents, or receive tempting offers from rival firms – received billing above or within the title. The reason why Fitzhamon's *Black Beauty* (1906) has no dis-cernible connection with the novel of the same name is that the film is not a literary adaptation, but a star vehicle for his horse. (As Blair had become Rover for the purposes of publicity, so Tariff became Black Beau-ty.) The horse also played an important supporting role in the first British one-reel feature film, *Dick Turpin's Ride to York* (1906), teamed up with Rover to rescue Gertie Potter from drowning in *Dumb Sagacity* (1907), extracted a baby from a burning hayrick in *Baby's Playmate* (1908) and untied a miner from a powder keg in *A Friend in Need* (1909).

It was Rover, however, who was Marlene to Fitzhamon's Von Sternberg. Under the director's regime of gentle encouragement and sausagey bribery, the gallant dog saved a policeman from a watery grave in *The Detective in Peril* (1910), brought home a pair of children in *Lost in the Woods* (1912), snared criminals in *The Dog Thief* (1908) and *Plucky Little Girl* (1909), and even repaired a broken marriage in *The Dog's Devotion* (1911). In *The Dog Outwits the Kidnapper* (1908), a minor masterpiece of British surrealism, a toddling Barbara Hepworth is snatched from the drive of her home. Rover bounds off in hot pursuit, jumps into the driving seat of the abductor's car and, paws on the steering wheel, chugs his charge back to safety along the road from Shepperton to Walton. (We are prepared for this amazing sight by an opening scene in which little Barbara dresses him up in goggles and a chauffeur's cap.) An extra one-shot film, *Rover Takes a Call* (1905), in which the canine star acknowledges the praise of his admirers, could be appended to any of these productions, allowing the audience to cheer their hero.

A pack of copycat talents – ungulates and avians, particularly – stalked the star, though they were more frequently required to cause chaos than resolve it. The Clarendon Studio's sequence of sex comedies starring a performing parrot is a good example: in *Jack Spratt's Parrot Gets His Own Back* (1916), the bird smears soot on a housemaid's pillow in order to give the impression that she has become intimate with a sweep; in *Jack Spratt's Parrot as the Artful Dodger* (1916), a sailor and a servant exchange jammy kisses at the tea table as their feathered persecutor contrives to bring a dresser loaded with china crashing to the floor.

Rover's primacy, however, was confirmed at his passing. When the canine superstar shuttled off his mortal collar in February 1914, *Pictures and Picturegoer* noted that his debut still held the record for the most prints sold of any British production, and saluted him as 'the first animal to play an independent part in a cinematograph film . . . No other animal in the picture world', the magazine concluded, 'has ever attained the same amount of celebrity.'[19] By 1914, however, the dog-star had fallen. Audiences bathed in the light of a new generation of human performers. They had grown to recognise the men and women projected for their pleasure on the screen; to wonder about the details of their off-screen lives, weave fantasies around their forms and faces.

Initially, they were known only by nicknames, first generated by audiences themselves, and eventually recognised by studios as an effective way of branding their productions. Rolf Leslie, for instance, was known as the 'Man with the Crepe Hair', as a consequence of the twenty-seven different roles he played in Will Barker's historical epic, *Sixty Years a Queen* (1913); Violet Hopson was the 'Dear Delightful Villainess'. Public access to these new stars, however, was strictly regulated. In August 1916, the in-house *Hepworth Picture-Play Paper* issued a stern warning to a correspondent from Southend, whose enquiries into the private lives of the Hepworth Picture Players were considered to have gone too far. 'We really must state', rumbled the Walton publicity department, 'that we cannot answer such very intimate questions, as to whom they are married, are they divorced, how many children, their private addresses, etc.' For the most part, the studio kept such secrets. To their public, the stars of silent British cinema were fascinating phantoms: images around which official biographies were constructed to protect their real identities and enhance their marketability. Since cinema's inception, many potential middle-class patrons had been discouraged from attending their local picture house by the medium's association with groping couples, heavy breathers and lunching fleas. Hepworth answered their anxieties by using daisy-fresh virginity to sell his stars.

On the other side of the Atlantic, the approach was radically different. In Hollywood, William Fox was turning Theodosia Goodman, a brassy Jewish girl from Cincinnati, into Theda Bara, an exotic creature whose constitution required her to recline, veiled, on piles of tiger-skins in overheated Hollywood hotel rooms. In Walton-on-Thames, sincerity and naturalness were constructed with equal energy. The Hepworth girls were rural innocents. Alma Taylor was tagged the 'Girl Who Believed' after the studio circulated the story that some of her first films were shot without her knowledge. She and her publicists claimed that, rather than making pictures in the country's best-equipped film studio, she thought she was attending a party in a chemical works. Articles about her stressed her dis-

Chrissie White and Alma Taylor, the teenage anarchists of Walton-on-Thames

taste for Oxford Street shops, and even claimed that she wore her costume from *Comin' Thro' the Rye* in private life – though she and Chrissie White were, it seems, very keen on their annual luncheon at the Army and Navy

Stores, at which they were presented with a hamper of free gifts. As late as 1951 Hepworth was still insisting that his starlets never wore more make-up than a lick of mascara and a dab of Lipsyl, though the banks of mercury lamps in the studio necessitated a thick face-pack of Leichner yellow and the application of a poisonous blue rim around the mouth and eyes. This fact was quietly ignored, as were the marriages of the players – unless they decided, as Chrissie White did, to divorce an obscure first husband and marry Henry Edwards, another contract player. Hepworth stars were plucked from country orchards, not chorus lines. Hepworth films depicted an England of sun-dappled rural lanes populated by wily tramps, destructive schoolgirls, swag-bagging burglars and sagacious collies; and they were shot in a carefree, improvisational manner.[20] What saved them from dissolving into syrup was their impeccable sense of anarchy.

Fitzhamon's *Tilly* cycle is the best expression of the studio's winning formula, a series of films in which two apple-cheeked, bowed and beribboned schoolgirls – most frequently played by Alma Taylor and Chrissie White – bring mayhem to the streets of Walton-on-Thames. Fortunately, many of these have escaped destruction. In *Tilly's Party* (1911), Taylor and White beat up their servants, invite a pair of amorous sailors into their nursery and smash the furniture to matchwood. In *When Tilly's Uncle Flirted* (1911), a male relative offers the girls money to turn a blind eye to his seduction of a housemaid; instead, they pocket the cash and frustrate his desires with a barrage of kitchen utensils. In *Tilly and the Fire Engines* (1911), the girls hijack a fire engine, turn the hose on the fire-fighters and, snorting with laughter, award each other medals for gallantry. In *Tilly the Tomboy Visits the Poor* (1910), the girls commandeer a laundry van, fell their pursuers by hurling bundles of bed linen in their faces, take the fight to a bakery where everybody is pitched into the flour, and, in the final sequence, manufacture an alibi by invading the bedroom of an infirm old lady, to whom they read the Bible and dole out Bovril. Once they have persuaded the authorities that they were with their patient all along, they drag the invalid from her bed and jump up and down on her.

No such insubordination was tolerated from the teenage actresses who filled these roles. Hepworth expected his stars to put in their hours in the developing and drying rooms if they were not required for filming, to refrain from making public appearances, and to change their professional names upon arrival at the studio. He assumed that the names of his actors were company property; his to assign and reassign as he saw fit. He thought that a new arrival bore a strong resemblance to a musical comedy actress named Chrissie Bell, so Ada Constance White became Chrissie White. Ethelbert Edwards, a successful stage actor who had given over 600 performances as the hero of *Robin Hood*, appeared in Hepworth's films as Henry Edwards, and lived under the name until his death. Matthew Reginald Sheffield-Casson, who played the title role of *David Copperfield* (1913) for Hepworth, did so as Eric Desmond – although he reverted to his own name when he later became a moderately successful character actor in Hollywood. Sometimes a pseudonym was employed even when a performer had a reputation elsewhere upon which Hepworth might have capitalised. Jamie Darling, who played Daniel Peggotty in *David Copperfield*, was Thomas Dawson Walker, a famous whiteface clown who had performed his act – which incorporated a red-hot poker, a spade and a singing donkey – for Queen Victoria at Windsor Castle in 1886.[21] The public, it seems, was not fooled by this rechristening: when Walker retired to the Norfolk resort of Gorleston, he opened a rifle range on the pier and named it Peggotty's Hut.

Hepworth guarded these names so jealously that he was even prepared to take legal action against his actors to protect them. In later years, Olivia de Havilland's decision to sue Warner Brothers led to the 1945 De Havilland Law, a celebrated piece of legislation which limited studio contracts to seven years. Hepworth's day in court with Stewart Rome, one of his company's leading players, set a more fundamental precedent: it gave actors the right to their own names. Rome, born Septimus William Ryott in Newbury, Berkshire, was an engineer by trade. He abandoned his first career to become a musical comedy chorus boy, but suffered a nervous breakdown when the work dried up. He then bankrupted himself attempting to become a sheep farmer in Australia and was forced to lug bricks on a Perth building site to scrimp his fare back to England. Still keen to act, but prohibited by his doctor from taking further stage jobs, he applied for work at the studios, and played minor parts for Hepworth throughout 1913. His big break came after the collapse of the marriage of two of the studio's biggest draws, Violet Hopson and Alec Worcester, which left a vacancy for a romantic hero. A new contract was signed, and

Ryott became Rome, the studio's new seven-pound-a-week leading man, a rugged type with a slick centre parting and neat bow-tie. Hepworth's eye for a star was sure: in 1915, Rome was voted second only to Charlie Chaplin in a *Pictures* magazine popularity poll. 'We are proud to say', gushed the studio's publicists, 'that his heart is entirely in the world of pictures.' Unfortunately, it was not so firmly located in Walton-on-Thames. After completing a year of National Service, Rome accepted an offer from Broadwest Films in Walthamstow, on a weekly wage of twenty pounds. Hepworth issued a writ against Rome, arguing that the actor was profiting unfairly from the £5,000 a year invested by the studio in the marketing of its stock company of performers. Mr Justice Astbury found in favour of the defendant and ruled that cinema actors owned their own names, no matter who had concocted them. The name of Stewart Rome continued to be seen on credit rolls for a further twenty years. Today, of course, nobody remembers it.

Rome and his contemporaries are now impossibly distant figures. The cinema canned their shadows and the public forgot their names. Viewing their surviving films in the basement of the British Film Institute, loading the reels on to the Steenbeck editing machines, watching long-dead actors gazing into the lens, their mouths moving silently, these men and women appear as phantoms glimpsed at a séance, or figments from a camera's dream. Sometimes, their world is invaded by a sudden chaos of blotches, and you realise that time and mould have reduced this portion of the original negative to a chaos of frothing emulsion. Faces melt and buckle in the frame; figures flicker from positive to negative; subjects succumb to the physical collapse of the medium in which, long ago, their images were fixed. It seems impossible that they could ever really have existed, in the corporeal, fleshy way that you and I exist. Facts from their later lives – that Lewin Fitzhamon was a friend of Julie Christie, Chrissie White an avid viewer of *Neighbours*, or that Maurice Braddell lived long enough to play one of Joe Dallessandro's tricks in Andy Warhol's *Flesh* (1969) – offend historical decorum. Now they are gone, and those old enough to remember them will also soon be gone, the chance of recovering a sense of who they were is fast slipping away. Even the most celebrated British silent stars have left behind only the most partial and fragmentary details of their lives beyond the screen: mendacious and banal publicity dope about their hobbies, passions and domestic arrangements; fan magazine interviews by deferential hacks; the odd radio talk or ghost-written memoir, in which their experiences have been turned and polished until they shine like lies.

Chrissie White and Henry Edwards are now forgotten names, but at the zenith of their fame they were hailed as the British answers to Douglas Fairbanks and Mary Pickford. White was an English rose with a taste for motorbikes and fast cars; Edwards a muscular hero with tar-brush eyebrows perfect for the expression of romantic agony. (Naturally, he specialised in loping innocents, dashing naval types and the wrongfully accused.) When White and Edwards toured England in 1929, local newspapers printed the times at which their car was likely to be passing through the neighbourhood, so that their readers could wait to cheer them by. Film footage survives of a publicity visit they made to Leamington Spa: it depicts crowds waiting for them at their hotel; the mayoress presenting Chrissie White with a huge bouquet; a dark mass of people surging around the Pump Room and through the streets in their wake. Fan magazines heaped blossoms at their feet: 'British screen art is jumping ahead by leaps and bounds,' observed *Picture Show*, 'and one of the people who have played an enviable part in this happy state of affairs is winning, blue-eyed Chrissie White.' Her husband, declared the same publication, 'is one of the most popular and accomplished of all picture players, and we should feel justly proud that we can claim him as a Briton.'[22]

Their daughter, Henryetta, now in her seventies, remembers her childhood's starry quality. She recalls, at the age of ten, a visit to the Albion Hotel in Brighton, where she signed autographs for admirers and was presented with a box of chocolates by the owner, Sir Harry Preston ('Look what the waiter gave me!' she exclaimed). For a generation of cinemagoers, White and Edwards were figures from some ethereal realm: what else could they be, having fallen in love in Venice while making a picture called *The City of Beautiful Nonsense* (1919)? 'Do you know how you would feel if the characters in a fairy story stepped out on the page and spoke to you?' asked a contemporary journalist.[23] 'If you do you will know why I felt so queer when I heard the lovely voice of Chrissie White on the end of the telephone yesterday morning.' Another impressionable hack contrasted the romantic atmosphere that surrounded these stars with the sexual and narcotic scandals emerging from studios on the other side of

Chrissie White and Henry Edwards before they met, married and became
Britain's answer to Mary Pickford and Douglas Fairbanks

the Atlantic: 'There was a time when our hearts would be moved to wor-
ship at the shrine of some famous "star" as being far removed from the
average human being. But stories of unsavoury divorces and happenings
behind the scenes, emanating chiefly from America, dispel these halos.'
The great era of British film scandals was yet to come: the theatre
remained the London media's best source of tales involving cocaine and
chorus girls. In contrast, Chrissie White and Henry Edwards offered 'a
truly delightful piece of romance. Not in the fictitious sense of the word,
but the real thing.'[24]

I heard one voice, however, that dissented from this view. I got to know
John East – smut-pedlar, broadcaster, actor, screenwriter, theatre historian, night-club promoter and pimp – in the last eighteen months of his
life, when he was living in a post-war semi in Norbury, surrounded by the
artefacts of his bizarre career. Posters from his films – British sexploitation flicks of the late 1970s – were stacked on the carpet. Photographs of
his maternal grandfather, John Marlborough East, the founder of the
Neptune Studios near Elstree, were ranged upon the hearth. A letter from
Margaret Thatcher was framed on the wall, not far from a portrait of Max

Miller, the legendary music-hall comedian, into whose care East's mother surrendered him at the age of nine. John East wrote Miller's biography; Miller shaped John East's personality. He would always sign off with an innuendo plucked from his mentor's joke book. ('Donald Duck is staying in the Ritz Hotel and rings room service for a French letter. The waiter asks if he wants it to be put on his bill.') Miller also introduced East to sex, or at least to the sugar daddies with whom, as a teenager, he traded favours for pocket money, foreign holidays and the use of a flat on Jermyn Street. The life gave him a taste for gossip: whenever we met, he would delight in unwinding anecdotes about the peccadilloes and scandals of the celebrated dead. He described a visit to Gabrielle Ray, an Edwardian stage beauty who appeared with his grandfather, and whose husband slashed her with a razor from cheek to cheek. He boasted of procuring boys for Leonard Bernstein in a brothel on the King's Road. (It was depressing, somehow, that the composer had stipulated that they should be blond and German.) He reminisced about being fellated by the British porn star Mary Millington, who would visit him after a hard day in her sex shop around the corner. ('Used her tongue!' he exclaimed. 'Best blow job I ever had!') His mantelpiece was crowded with photographs of himself arm-in-arm with the figures with whom he shared his career: the flushed meringue of Dame Barbara Cartland, the smiling figure of Linda Christian – with whose husband, Tyrone Power, he claimed to have enjoyed a passionate afternoon in a field near Rottingdean. On my first visit to him, another photograph attracted my attention: a publicity shot of Henry Edwards from *The Flag Lieutenant* (1926), in a neat plastic frame. 'He was my real father, you know,' said John East, with pride.

I knew that East had made this claim on a number of occasions; that this account of his parentage had been recorded in newspaper and radio interviews, and from these had migrated to the biographical database of the British Film Institute. Although John professed that he often met Edwards during his childhood, he said that he knew nothing of their blood relationship until 1984, when his mother spilled the secret on her deathbed. East's mother, the story went, met Edwards at Elstree in her teens, and consummated the affair while her husband was away on business in Egypt. East described Edwards as a kind but volatile man, then recounted a misanthropic outburst in the Piccadilly traffic, and an incident in which he forced Wally Bosco, an old silent film actor and music-hall turn fallen on hard times, to drink half a pint of whisky. Articles about Edwards in contemporary fan magazines yield few clues as to his character: he clearly found interviews embarrassing, and on one occasion appears to have hidden from the journalist despatched to Walton to pump him for quotes. So John East's anecdotes could well have been accurate. I found myself, however, regarding his recollections with growing scepticism, particularly when he told me the details of his own miserable childhood. He would not name his mother's husband, but spoke of him in villainous terms, noting the man's enthusiasm for corporal punishment, and recalling the afternoon on which he deliberately mangled an employee's hand in an office guillotine. If the man named on my birth certificate had been so brutal, I believe I too might have fantasised myself the love child of a glamorous film actor. John died on 1 April 2003: a bout of bronchial pneumonia had caused his heart to give out. His legatees were informed separately of his passing: he wanted no funeral, no memorial, and forbade any gathering in his name. His ashes were scattered over the lawn of Streatham crematorium before most of his friends or acquaintances were aware of his demise. A few months before his death, I had encouraged him to write to Henryetta Edwards and explain his claim to share a father with her. She suggested that a DNA test might settle the matter. He declined to have one. It would be impossible to prove, but I suspect that he went to his death comforted by a cherished fiction.

In any case, East's image of Edwards as an aggressive, unpredictable figure seemed to have little in common with the man conjured by the reminiscences of Henryetta Edwards. She recalled him as a temperate, softly spoken gentleman, who raised his voice to her only once in his life. In the first of many afternoons spent with her, poring over her father's diaries and letters, I learned of Edwards's brother, Burgoyne, who ran away from home in his teens and never returned. (Edwards's film *The Bargain*, centres upon a character who does the same.) I heard of his nervous breakdown in 1921, and his therapeutic tour of the Far East. ('Dr Bakewell says sea voyage for three or four months imperative, or twelve months in nursing home later and perhaps no more films.') I read a short autobiographical note written in 1918, in which he described himself as a stubborn and obstinate child who, when slippered by his father, would

customarily threaten to throw himself from the Clifton Suspension
Bridge. ('I spent most of the afternoon thinking out suicides, and trying
to suffocate myself in the bottom of a huge chest of drawers, but of course
couldn't close the drawer after I'd got inside.')[25] I read through a commonplace book crammed with remarks and doodles: frames of a story-
board, notes for a scene played through a close-up of a pair of lovers'
hands reaching towards each other across a table, innovative ideas for
intertitles, hundreds of fragmentary ideas for plots and scenes. 'He is
about to speak the words that will save her into the phone when she pulls
the trigger [and] the Phone is Shattered'; 'He is poor but she is poorer. He
has made a little money. He puts some coins into her pocket – cautiously
– so that she shall not know – He is arrested for picking her pocket'; 'Girl's
eyes close as she feels the kiss on her hand – No she says – I can't.' At the
end of my first visit to Henryetta, I mentioned the name of John Marlborough East. She remembered that her father had directed him in *The
Bargain* (1921) and *Owd Bob* (1924). She also recalled that her mother,
Chrissie White, travelled home with him on the train from Walton-on-
Thames, on which he would tease her by asking her, in declamatory tones,
to thank Mrs White for her last basket of washing. It was clear, however,
that she had never heard the suggestion that the two families were linked
by anything deeper than professional acquaintance.

Henry Edwards's diaries are not confessional. They are, however,
extremely thorough. When he had a film in production, he gave an hour-
by-hour account of his activities. The shooting of *Owd Bob*, his last work
for Hepworth, and the film in which John Marlborough East made his
final appearance on camera, is recorded in meticulous detail. The diary
reveals that the two dogs of the story, Owd Bob and Red Wull, were much
more difficult to cast than the human characters. (Edwards describes long
car rides to audition sheepdogs that turn out to be too small, too bad-
tempered, too uncooperative, or, in one case, dead.) We know that he
found his Owd Bob on 13 May 1924, in the person of Buttons, an Old
English sheepdog that belonged to the young daughter of a Surrey
farmer, who could be persuaded to part with the animal only by being
promised two weeks on location in the Lake District. (Her father, thinking, perhaps, of the celebrity of Blair, the star of *Rescued by Rover*, initially refused to part with his dog for less than fifty pounds.) We know that

on the first day of shooting in the studios at Walton-on-Thames, the hero, played by Ralph Forbes, accidentally wrenched the bolt from the door of the cottage set. We know that Edwards had a difference of opinion with Edward Ollivant, the author of the original novel, about the breed of dog used in the film. (Ollivant insisted it must be a collie; Edwards retorted that all the collies he had spotted in Yorkshire were 'small ratlike creatures' quite incapable of knocking down a man, as the story required.) We also know that Hugh Maclean, the co-author of the screenplay, gave him some trouble, insisting on taking a sole writing credit on the picture. ('Then we got rude. He was not sure that he wanted his name in association with mine, I was sure I did not want mine in association with him. But fact was fact and we'd have the truth or leave the names of the adapters out altogether.') The only references to John Marlborough East are a handful of comments about his cantankerous behaviour on location in Kendal. If Edwards was conducting an affair with the actor's daughter, he did not entrust it to his journal.

On 28 June 1924, the exterior work for *Owd Bob* came to an end, and

Chrissie White and Henry Edwards in later years, in the Surrey garden
in which they incinerated their lives' work

Edwards returned to Walton to find Cecil Hepworth deep in negotiations with his accountant, a Mr Button. Words such as 'liquidation' and 'receivership' pepper the text. Hepworth's back catalogue was, from that moment, destined for the receiver, and for a depressingly literal form of liquidation. Many of Henry Edwards's films were destroyed. Among the survivors are: *East Is East* (1916), a sparky social comedy in which he directed himself as a working-class entrepreneur who founds his own fish-and-chip empire – shops, home delivery, branded ketchup – by capitalising on a deluge of dogfish; *The Bargain*, in which he fights for his life in the Australian gold fields, hurling himself down scree-slopes and mountain torrents; *Broken in the Wars* (1919), a cranky propaganda film in which he plays an incapacitated ex-serviceman who is helped back to prosperity by John Hodge, MP (played, appropriately, by John Hodge, MP). *Lily of the Alley* (1923), probably the world's first feature film to elucidate its narrative without recourse to intertitles, *The Amazing Quest of Mr Ernest Bliss* (1920), a romantic serial later remade as a vehicle for Cary Grant, and Edwards's pair of E. Temple Thurston fantasies, *The City of Beautiful Nonsense* and *The World of Wonderful Reality* (1924), are all lost. Edwards and White retained their own copies of these films, which they stowed in the attic of Gracious Pond, the rose-tangled Surrey cottage to which they retired. They might yet have been preserved in the archive if, during the Second World War, somebody had not pointed out to the couple that packing a thatched roof with old celluloid was like asking to be fricasseed in your sleep, and persuaded them to remedy the problem with a bonfire.

The work of most figures of British silent cinema is similarly depleted; the legacy of carelessness and critical distaste. Of Joan Morgan's films, only one survives in its entirety: *A Lowland Cinderella* (1921), the story of a Scottish girl whose father has disappeared to the gold fields of South Africa, and entrusted her to the care of an exploitative guardian who spends her fortune while she skivvies in his kitchen. As this is the Cenerentola story, there are two ugly sisters who decline, on her behalf, her invitation to a costume ball, and a Prince Charming who supplies her with a frock: a pretty confection of tulle and pearl beading. Joan, unfortunately, could recall nothing of the making of her only extant work. Her clearest memories were of *The Shadow of Egypt* (1924), an Oriental romance for which Sidney Morgan took the cast and crew to Cairo – all except Joan,

Alma Taylor gives comfort to Joan Morgan's Princess Moonface
in *The Shadow of Egypt* (1924)

who was obliged to remain at home. 'I had to commit suicide on this one,'
she volunteered as we leafed through the film's illustrated press book. 'I
was awfully good at committing suicide. I stabbed myself in the right
place and doubled up. I was always pleased if there was a part with a suicide in it.'

Something in this statement stirred another memory. Joan began to talk about Lilian Hall-Davis, and described sharing a dressing room with her on the set of *Her Reputation*. 'Lilian was one of our biggest stars, but nobody lasted,' she reflected. 'She rather told me the truth: that suddenly her career had collapsed, not for any particular reason, and she didn't know how to get it back again. I didn't know how to get mine back again, but she paid rather more for hers than I did for mine. You could in that world. It came to the point where she couldn't go on any longer.' Did she have a weak voice, a strong accent? Joan looked at me as if she considered this a peculiar question. 'I think', she said, 'it was more a question of not sleeping with the right people.'

And this was all she could recall: Joan was moving round once more to the subject of Bryant Washburn, the Hollywood contract, and her night of misery in the Grosvenor Hotel. Looking down at my notes for a prompt to my next question, my eye was caught by a quotation that I had copied out from *Backwater*, a volume of memoirs that Joan published in 1942.[26] 'Leave them all,' she wrote, 'the restless trees and the men and women who have had their day. Leave the night to the ghosts. We, in our day, have eclipsed them all, our history is history itself.' And I asked no more questions about Lilian Hall-Davis. At that moment, she seemed utterly irreclaimable.

CHAPTER TWO

The Pleasure Garden

Ernest Dudley – with toupee – in a publicity still from the 1940s

Ernest Dudley charges over the wet grass beneath Maidenhead Bridge with an alacrity unusual in a man on the home straight for his century, but perhaps not for a man who took up marathon-running in his seventies, and twenty years later jogs every day in the park near his little flat behind Broadcasting House. Today, his eagerness is a product of nostalgia. The three-mile stretch of river up- and downstream of Maidenhead – from Cookham in the north to Bray in the south – was, in Ernest's teenage years, the pleasure ground of London's film people. On summer evenings in the early 1920s he would come to this spot, park his bicycle by the wall, and stand on tiptoe to spy upon the movie stars, sportsmen and socialites who populated the riverside watering-places. On the far bank stood Skindles Hotel, the Mecca of metropolitan adulterers, where hired lovers in white-and-brown 'co-respondent' shoes helped manufacture the photographic evidence necessary to dissolve unhappy marriages. Under the bridge itself, on the Maidenhead side, was Murray's, a night-club, which to Ernest, then and now, was the epitome of glamour. 'It was here,' he exclaims, sketching the shape of the building with his arms. 'It was a white bungalow, and out here was the glass dance floor. The orchestra was inside. It was all in white. And at night, of course, it looked marvellous. And you'd see the chaps in dinner jackets and the girls dancing on the glass floor, and the river full of canoes and boats, all playing gramophone records.' His face cracks with a delighted smile. 'Bloody good stuff,' he breathes.

The proprietor of Murray's was Jack May, a former medic in the American army who settled in Britain after the Armistice and made a fortune dealing drugs under the counters of his night-clubs. Everyone came to

Jack's. There was 'Gorgeous' Georges Carpentier, the world light-heavy-weight boxing champion, whose extended stay in Britain in 1921 gave him time to floor a dozen British fighters and to play the hero in a swash-buckler entitled *A Gypsy Cavalier* (1922). There was Lady Diana Manners, the principal society beauty of the period, whose fame was enhanced when she took the lead in *The Glorious Adventure* (1922), a lavish histori-cal romance made in hallucinogenic red–green Prizmacolor. (Audiences watched her leap torrents of molten lead streaming from the burning roof of St Paul's Cathedral, and acknowledged that she was more than just a good set of bones.) The co-star of both these productions was also part of Jack May's world: Flora Le Breton, a doll-like teenage dancer who first achieved prominence on the parquet of the London branch of Mur-ray's, and from there was recruited into pictures.[1] She claimed to have narrowly escaped drowning when, on location on the river for *A Gypsy Cavalier*, the coach in which she was riding pitched into the water. *The Times* printed a photograph of her, sinking decorously from view.[2] 'A good many people have twitted me that the accident was a clever stunt, devised, at the time, to get a lot of publicity for the picture,' she told a fan magazine. 'Some people may be willing to flirt with death to get their names before the public. I am not.'[3] Le Breton was also the star of the most controversial British film of the 1920s: Graham Cutts's *Cocaine* (1922), a melodrama of the British narcotic underworld enlivened by a Chinese villain based on one of Jack May's business associates, a fellow drug-dealing club-owner known as Brilliant Chang. 'Cocaine was what people came to Jack May's club for,' declares Ernest, surveying the site of the establishment. 'It was slipped to you in packets, very quietly, when you coughed up the loot. There was one chap, a well-known actor who was a drug addict. He was pinched by the police at Cookham, had up before the magistrates at Maidenhead and sent up to Reading Gaol, where they sent Oscar Wilde. He was very tall and had been very good-looking, but his face was grey and lined. He came to stay at my father's hotel but he didn't pay the bill.'

By the time that Ernest was peering over the balustrade into Murray's, the links between Jack May, the drugs trade and the film business had already been adumbrated in the popular press, through the agency of an up-and-coming cinema actor named Lionel Belcher. As Leon Belcher, he

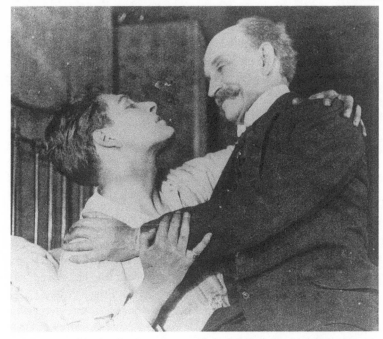

Leon Belcher's ailing hero is reconciled with his father (Jeff Barlow)
in *Bonnie Mary* (1918)

played a clean-cut army captain in *In Another Girl's Shoes* (1917); in *Love's
Old Sweet Song* (also 1917), he was the dime-straight sweetheart of a
woman attempting to conceal the fact that her mother is a murderous
adulteress who has escaped justice by taking holy orders. In *Bonnie Mary*
(1918), he played Rob MacAllister, a young Scottish composer whose love
for a local girl is forbidden by a clan antagonism dating back 300 years.[4]
The same year that he shot this picture, however, his career received a fatal
dose of publicity when he became involved in the Billie Carleton case, the
period's most notorious drugs scandal. Carleton was an actress and
cabaret star who, in December 1918, was found dead in her apartment
behind the Savoy Hotel. She was a cocaine user, but it now seems likely
that she died from an overdose of sleeping pills.[5] The inquest cast light
upon a coke-snorting culture among bohemian Londoners, and generat-

ed improbable amounts of shrill journalistic copy. 'War has increased the nervous tension of the individual to an unheard-of degree,' blared the *Daily Express.* 'Men and women alike have craved a change from the dead normal to the fantastic and rare. Men have wished to forget their shames, women to forget their broken lives, and the pander and the tempter have been ever at their elbow to introduce them to the realm of drugs.'[6]

Jack May attended the inquest into Carleton's death – a witness suggested that it was he who had introduced her to the opium pipe – but it was Belcher who became the focus of newspaper attention. The night before her body was discovered, the court heard, Carleton had met Belcher at a Victory Ball at the Albert Hall; he had then given her a sachet of cocaine. The inquest revealed that, contrary to his dashing image on the screen, Belcher had deserted his wife and was living with a girlfriend who shared his interest in narcotics. The pair supplemented his erratic earnings from film work by dealing cocaine, which he confessed to have purchased illegally from a chemist on Lisle Street, 'well-known in the theatrical and cinema world'.[7] Malvina Longfellow, who had played Lady Hamilton opposite Donald Calthrop in Maurice Elvey's *Nelson* (1918), testified that she had seen Carleton snorting a line of cocaine given to her by a dress designer named Reggie De Veulle; Belcher was an associate of De Veulle.

While the trial was still in progress, Belcher's film *The Yoke* (1915) was re-released into cinemas by enterprising managers. Now lost, it starred Belcher as a young man weaned from drugs by the love of his sweetheart. It was one of the last films to deal with narcotic themes without becoming the object of journalistic and official opprobrium. By the time that Graham Cutts produced *Cocaine*, the subject was becoming too hot to handle. T. P. O'Connor, the film censor and founding editor of the *Sun*, expressed the fear that Cutts's film would 'excite curiosity in a form of vice that is at present practically confined to a very small portion of the community'.[8] The *Evening News*, however, voiced its suspicion that the Home Office had forced O'Connor to impose the ban, in the belief that 'the authorities . . . feared a flood of films based on this subject, with consequent wide advertisement of the vice all over the country'.[9]

The Billie Carleton affair has fascinated Ernest Dudley since his teens. He keeps a thick file of newspaper cuttings on the case, on the cover of which he has pasted his own contribution – 'Pipe of Dreams', written for the *Evening News* in 1956.[10] He worked with some of the major personalities of the twenties and thirties, and knows the stories about the rest. Such celebrities as Noël Coward, Stanley Spencer, Elsa Lanchester, Erich von Stroheim and Rex Harrison populate his conversation with the giddy freedom of a balloon debate. (His favourite anecdote dates from his stint as club correspondent of the *Daily Mail* – using the byline Charles Ton – when he accosted Fred Astaire in the Burlington Arcade and persuaded him to take him back to the Palace Theatre to work out some new dance steps.) Forgotten names, too, figure in his thoughts: the playwright William Freshman, whom he knew in the writers' pool at British International Pictures, and encountered, years later, in arthritic obscurity, running a dry-cleaning business in Mayfair; Constant Lambert, the composer who, at a royal gala night at the Lyric, Hammersmith, bowed drunkenly to the wrong box; Eille Norwood, the Sherlock Holmes of the silent screen, to whose stepdaughter, Jane Grahame, Ernest was married for sixty years.

Norwood was a formidable name of the period: when the Stoll Company sold his forty-seven Holmes two-reelers to an American distributor, a giant transparency of his face was suspended across Times Square. Ernest is the only person alive who knows that his father-in-law's stage name was derived from his romantic attachment to a woman called Eily who lived in Norwood; that he shaved his head at the temples to make himself look more like the detective of Sidney Paget's illustrations; that his common-law wife, Jane's mother, a bosomy Edwardian actress named Ruth MacKay, was more interested in women than men, and more interested in drink than either. And that is partly why Ernest Dudley is, in a Zelig-like way, the principal player in this chapter.

Ernest was born Vivian Ernest Coltman-Allen in Dudley, the town from which he borrowed the professional name he has used since his teens. During his immense, haphazard career, he has been an actor, boxing correspondent, playwright, novelist, gossip columnist, screenwriter and crime reporter. In the late 1920s, he toured Shakespeare around rural Ireland, performing in church halls and sleeping in barns. In the 1930s, he jobbed around the West End, wrote freelance articles for the *Hollywood*

Reporter and knocked out scripts for British International Pictures and Fox-British. In the 1940s, he created a detective character named Dr Morelle – a sinister psychiatrist–sleuth whose diagnoses kept radio audiences enthralled during the Blitz – and hosted a crime anthology series entitled *The Armchair Detective*. (In the 1950s, indifferent films were made of both: he starred in the latter, under a preposterous toupee.) He ascribes the bewildering multiplicity of his activities to his lack of education: childhood illness prevented him from attending school until he was sixteen years old. Before that, his father, Frank Coltman-Allen, proprietor of the King's Arms at Cookham, allowed him to run wild on the banks of the Thames.

Frank bought the King's Arms in 1920. He walked into the dilapidated saloon bar, offered the landlord £70 for the freehold, and made a deal at £73. He immediately began a programme of refurbishment, aiming to draw some of Maidenhead's more discreet weekenders a couple of miles further upstream. That the painter Stanley Spencer lived next door to the hotel helped him realise his ambitions. An artistic colony soon formed at Cookham, with the King's Arms at its centre. Consequently, Ernest's childhood was bright with stars. Jack Buchanan helped him rehearse a song for an amateur concert, telegraphing him with a reminder to fasten his flies before he went out on stage. ('My father hoped that the postmistress would assume that the message was about angling,' he recalls.) Gladys Cooper stayed in the farmhouse over the road. Guy Newall and Ivy Duke drifted through the pretty garden at the back of the hotel. Flora Le Breton and her producers came to discuss filming Victor Bridges's thriller *Greensea Island* (1922). Stewart Rome and Violet Hopson used the hotel as a location base. One of the most frequent visitors was Sir Edward Marsh, an influential patron of the arts who used his money – inherited from the estate of Spencer Perceval, the assassinated British Prime Minister – to encourage the artistic efforts of young male protégés. His most significant discovery was Rupert Brooke, the Apollonian poet who wrote against the horror of war and the degradation of old age, and was prevented from suffering the latter by his experience of the former. Brooke died from the results of a septic mosquito bite on a hospital ship somewhere in the Aegean in 1915, whereupon Marsh became his mythographer-in-chief. And when he saw, later that year, on the back page of the

News of the World, a photograph of a clean-limbed young composer named Ivor Novello, he was certain that he had discovered Brooke's successor. Marsh cultivated Novello; invited him to his chambers at Gray's Inn, where he was waited upon by a conveniently deaf housekeeper; read to him from the Greek lexicon he kept on top of the wardrobe; allowed him to sleep in 'Rupert's bed'; brought him up to Cookham for weekends; and attempted to mould him in Brooke's image – to no avail. Ivor Novello was something else entirely: charming, flirtatious, vacuous, and one of cinema's great icons of agony and sex.

Novello first came to prominence in 1915, when his song 'Keep the Home Fires Burning' became one of the signature tunes of the home front. The words were written by a young American lyricist named Lena Guilbert Ford, who was killed in 1918 by a Zeppelin raid on Maida Vale, allowing Novello to take the applause alone and bank some £17,000 in royalties. Today, he is best remembered as a songwriter, thanks to the music awards that bear his name and Jeremy Northam's cute impersonation of him in *Gosford Park* (2002). The coterie of retainers who helped shape Novello's posthumous reputation would have been delighted by this emphasis – possibly even by the inaccurately sweet quality of Northam's singing. (Novello compared his voice to 'a bullfrog with a sore throat'.) The importance of his contribution to cinema was deliberately downplayed in the eulogies offered by members of his circle. W. Macqueen-Pope, his business manager and first biographer, considered that 'the film career of Ivor [was] not of vital importance in his life story'.[11] Richard Rose, another old friend and memoirist, stated that films were 'a far cry from the theatre where he longed to be'.[12] These custodians of his memory imagined, as Novello himself did, that his reputation would stand on his stage musicals – *King's Rhapsody, The Dancing Years, Perchance to Dream* and *Glamorous Night* – and could not have foreseen how comprehensively this work would be forgotten. Unlike the plays of his friend and rival Noël Coward (who wrote 'Mad About the Boy' in Novello's honour), *King's Rhapsody* and its fellows did not survive the rise of the angry young men. They have long been exiled from the repertoire – and are unlikely to re-enter it, unless gloopy Ruritanian fantasy comes back into vogue. Novello's films, however, are more promising candidates for reassessment. *The Rat* (1925) and its two sequels, *The Lodger* (1926),

Ivor Novello: drugs and homosexuality for mass-market consumption

Downhill (1927), *The Vortex* (1927) and *The Constant Nymph* (1928) made him a world-class star, the pre-eminent British matinee idol of the 1920s.

Although he owned a production and a distribution company, signed two Hollywood contracts and two with British studios, Novello, like his biographers, always insisted that his film career was a serendipitous distraction from his work in musical theatre. There were two stories he loved to tell about the effortlessness of his progress into the medium: no fan magazine hack ever went home without hearing them. The first told how the French director Louis Mercanton had spotted his photograph in the files of a talent agency in London and wired him immediately to offer him the lead role in his new picture. Without an audition or a screen test, he was cast as the moody Sicilian hero of *The Call of the Blood* (1920). The director, it seems, did not care that this young man was a composer who had never acted in his life: the boy had glossy hair, dark eyes, a great slash of a mouth and a perfect profile; that was enough. History, Novello insisted, repeated itself in 1922, when he happened to be sitting at a table in the Savoy Grill one night when D. W. Griffith was dining there with the famously toxic critic Hannen Swaffer. Griffith, so the story goes, was transfixed by Novello's divine profile, and decided to offer him a contract on the spot. (The part of a guilt-racked ordinand in *The White Rose* (1923) was the first role of the deal – upon which Griffith subsequently reneged.) When he related the story, Novello usually neglected to mention that the meeting between actor and director was a scam concocted with the assistance of Swaffer and the Savoy's head waiter: Novello was seated directly in Griffith's line of sight, and made an elegant performance of eating his main course, sipping his wine and lighting his cigarettes.

Novello was born David Ivor Davies, the son of a Welsh rate collector, but let that pass. He was his mam's boy, adopting her middle name first for billing purposes and later by deed poll, despite it not really being hers to give. (Madame Clara Novello Davies had swiped it herself from the Italian singing teacher who taught her everything she knew: it impressed the students who visited her for music lessons.) Ivor lived with his mother in a flat above the Strand Theatre from 1913 until her death, and spent much of the time between picking up the tabs for her disastrous schemes and projects. The most embarrassing of these came in 1937 when she disappeared to the continent with the intention of bringing the Nazis to their knees with the assistance of her Welsh Singing Grandmothers' Choir. ('When we sing for Hitler in the stadium,' she announced, 'we're going to change from our Welsh costumes into white angel dresses for our Grand Finale and release hundreds of pigeons, each one carrying on its leg a little message of peace.'[13]) Despite these aggravations, mother and son rarely lost an opportunity to insist upon the intensity of their relationship. She discoursed upon his loveliness in the pages of *Film Weekly* and went trolling about town with bracelets on each wrist, festooned with little cameo photographs of his face. He addressed her as 'beauty popsy darling', told interviewers that she was 'the most wonderful woman in the world' and declared himself 'particularly fond of pictures of "mother-love".'[14] He starred in one such picture – Adrian Brunel's film of Noël Coward's play *The Vortex* (1927), the story of Nicky Lancaster, a young composer driven to hysteria by his mother's relationship with a younger man. 'She's wonderful,' he gushes, showing her photograph to a young reporter who has come to profile him at his piano.

Some sections of Novello's audience derided this mutual devotion. At the disastrous opening night of Coward's play *Sirocco* (1927), Novello was required to make a dramatic exit with the line, 'I go to my mother' – at which a voice from the cheap seats called out a suggestion as to what he might do when he arrived. After Novello's death, a Sunday newspaper identified this heckle as the source of his disinclination to marry: 'If there was any hope that Novello would win his way through this mother complex to normal manhood, that nightmare experience must have killed it.'[15] A hint of the Oedipal, however, also made for good box-office returns: while Novello reserved his most passionate declarations for Madame Clara, his female fans lived in hope. (So too did his co-star Gladys Cooper, whose dearest ambition was to enlist the help of a doctor who might persuade Novello of the therapeutic value of marrying her.[16])

Everyone knew that Ivor loved his mother. But quite a few knew – and many assumed – that he loved his chauffeurs and secretaries more. The identities of these men are well documented. Bobbie Andrews, a West End actor with a practised repertoire of spontaneous anecdotes and a passionate attachment to his own good looks, was the most faithful companion. (Donald Sinden once encountered Andrews in the Charing Cross Road: 'Donald, my dear, I hardly recognised you – you're looking so young and beautiful – for a moment I thought you were Bobbie Andrews.'[17]) Lloydie Williams, a school friend for whose nose-job Novello wrote a cheque, was the longest serving. Christopher Hassall, a poet and lyricist and another discovery of Sir Edward Marsh, was the one who suffered most, losing his marriage after an entanglement with the star. ('Novello', recalled Hassall's son Nicholas, 'had no scruples about taking whom or whatever he wanted, instinctively, and possibly guilelessly, and without a qualm.'[18]) Siegfried Sassoon was another notch on the Novello bedpost. The pair met by chance in Venice in October 1922, where Novello was filming *The Man without Desire* (1923) and Sassoon was holidaying with his lover, Prince Philipp of Hesse. Sassoon, jealous of Edward Marsh's interest in Novello, cut him dead ('I despise him and all that he stands for,' he told the prince[19]). At the end of 1924, however, the two men appear to have had an affair – a note of dinner with Novello at the Savoy is followed in Sassoon's diary by three months of obliterated entries; but letters survive in which the poet commiserates with a young actor, Glen Byam Shaw, another of Novello's cast-offs. ('You must try not to feel bitter about "him",' he wrote. 'I don't, though he outraged and betrayed my decent feelings to an incredible degree.'[20]) Lastly, there is even a report – albeit from the notoriously unreliable source of Somerset Maugham's secretary–lover Alan Searle – that Winston Churchill took Novello to bed. 'Very musical' was, Searle claimed, the statesman's verdict on the experience.[21]

Novello's queerness was not an obstacle to success: indeed, it was an integral part of his appeal. It appears to have sent his audience home in a state of romantic excitement. Novello gazes into the lens, his eyes ablaze, his lashes thick with mascara, his mouth half open, his pupils hugely dilated. He is racked by hidden desires, secret passions. He is always painted, primped, pomaded. Some film stars of the orthochromatic age smeared themselves in slap until they achieved the appearance of a cadaver boat-hooked from the Seine. Novello applied his Leichner with more skill than any of his female co-stars. As Adrian Brunel admitted in his memoirs, it was a struggle to find leading ladies who were sufficiently beautiful to share a two-shot with him. Novello understood how his beauty worked, and how an audience might be wired into the circuit of his own narcissism. He looked the sort of boy for whom a Woolworth's shopgirl or a retired drill sergeant might happily squander a reputation. 'That young man would make me nod to anything,' gushed a female journalist who interviewed him in his pyjamas.[22] But, perversely, the source of Novello's power was his passivity, his willingness to submit to the punishments of a melodramatic plot. On screen, he agonised, he wept, he bled, he sighed. When he made personal appearances, mobs of fans ripped the doors from his car and the belt-buckles from his trousers.[23] And, like Betty Balfour, he knew the value of baring his legs: he adored the kilt in which he was costumed in *Bonnie Prince Charlie* (1923), and appalled Gladys Cooper by wearing it out in public; he rarely passed on an opportunity to play a part in lederhosen; he wrote a locker-room leg-washing scene into *Downhill*, eliciting squeals of delight from the audience.[24] When he gazed into the camera, he offered himself as the object of the audience's desires.

In his first film for a British director, Brunel's *The Man without Desire*, Novello's erotic passivity is an integral element of the narrative. He plays Count Vittorio Dandolo, a Venetian aristocrat placed in mesmeric suspension for three centuries and resuscitated in the Jazz Age.[25] After crawling from his sarcophagus, the Count takes up smoking, goggles at the vaporetto, bows to the telephone receiver and marries a young socialite. (The part was played by Nina Vanna. Just before filming commenced, Novello had persuaded her to abandon her real surname – Yasikova – for something that sounded less emetic.) Dandolo is incapable, however, of consummating his relationship with his new wife. He kisses her passionlessly. He stares glumly over her shoulder as they embrace. He is immobilised by ennui. He is soon cuckolded. 'Life today', he sighs, 'is savourless.' The picture is peculiar, mixing location footage filmed in Venice with the undisguised artificiality of the studio. A wall climbed by Novello is clearly composed of cardboard and cellophane; a cutaway shot of an article in an eighteenth-century copy of the *Gazzetta Veneziana* has been bashed out on an Imperial typewriter. More odd still is the casual attitude that the modern characters take to the resurrected nobleman's mental condition. They barely acknowledge that his depression might be a product of his occult preservation in the tomb: his new father-in-law regards it as a form of post-nuptial neurosis. No matter about these lapses of logic: Novello's romantic melancholia is at the centre of the frame; his mental distress is anatomised for our pleasure. 'Oh Leonora!' he cries, declaring the name of his lover. But when Brunel cuts back from the intertitle, Novello is staring into our eyes, not hers.

British cinema of the 1920s has a reputation for stolidity and conservatism, but only among those who have not troubled to investigate its pleasures. The images that have endured from my viewing of material from this period are those of passion, permissiveness and action: terrorists blowing up the Channel Tunnel rail link in *High Treason* (1928); Ivy Duke in *The Lure of Crooning Water* (1920), lounging in a hammock and teaching a baby to smoke; Betty Balfour in *The Sea Urchin* (1926), crashing down in her boyfriend's aeroplane and engaging in a vegetable-fight in a French street market; *Ultus, The Man from the Dead* (1916) battling sects of hooded criminals; Ivor Novello above all – his hair picturesquely disarranged, his eyes alive with pain. Whichever director crouched behind the camera with a megaphone, Novello's screen persona remained his own – partly because his films were frequently based upon his own material, partly because he gave the projection of his image a higher priority than the demands of a specific script. Eroticism, passivity, narcissism, hysteria – these qualities attend him throughout his film career.

During the shooting of *The Man without Desire*, Novello drafted a treatment for a film centred upon a character named Pierre Boucheron, a charismatic Parisian cutpurse, jewel-thief and club dancer. He failed to find the money to back the production, so, in collaboration with Constance Collier – a sickly, middle-aged actress whose life was saved by the discovery of insulin – he rewrote the story as a stage play for the Theatre Royal, Brighton, and found himself in possession of a phenomenal hit. Film studios began agitating for the film rights; Rudolph Valentino cabled a bid. Novello, however, had already signed a three-picture deal with Michael Balcon's Gainsborough Studios. *The Rat* presents Novello in imago form: the impossibly beautiful, morally compromised, extravagantly feminised sex object – or, as he put it, a 'curious mixed character [who] seems to have made an immediate appeal to all kinds of audiences, for it is a curious blending of child, angel and devil'.[26] For the first half of the film, Novello's anti-hero radiates bravado and confidence. (On the run from the police, he dips below a grille in the street, reaches up through the bars and slices an officer's shoelaces with his flick-knife.) The female regulars of the White Coffin – a dockside dive populated by boys with long hair and Anna May Wong eye shadow and girls sporting men's jackets and frizzed bobs – are prepared to hurl each other across the barroom to compete for his attention. When Boucheron wants to hang up his cap, he flings it at the wall and impales it against the woodwork with his flick-knife. When he wants to tango with a tart, he slits her pencil skirt from hip to hem, allowing her legs to wrap around his. He is all pouts and arched eyebrows and posturing: his masculinity is so overstated that it becomes a kind of drag act. Beyond the dance floor, however, Boucheron's power is more equivocal. As he luxuriates in the seed-pearl-and-chinchilla decor of the apartment of Zelie de Chaumet (Isabel Jeans), a glamorous aristocrat whose jewels he covets, his girlfriend Odile (Mae Marsh), back home in the slums, suffers a sexual assault from Zelie's lover, Herman (Robert Scholz). Boucheron dashes home in time to kill her attacker, but Odile takes the rap. With his girlfriend in the dock for murder, Boucheron goes to pieces, leering and thrashing and biting the hands of the gendarmes who attempt to restrain him. The first of two sequels, *The Triumph of the Rat* (1926), subjected its protagonist to deeper humiliations, forcing him to stumble, ragged, through the city streets, to steal food from dogs, to accept a strangely sensuous knife-thrust from a swaggering rival in the White Coffin: the villain presses the blade against Novello's exposed torso; blood trickles down his chest; he lopes from the room, framed in the sarcophagus-shaped doorway, and we are invited to enjoy the excess of the spectacle.

The director of these pictures, Graham Cutts, knew the value of sadism, particularly in the treatment of leading performers. A director, he insisted, when telling *Picturegoer* how he wrung emotion from his actresses, 'sets himself – dishonest fellow – to charm her gently and lead her deprecatingly, knowing all the time that soon he is going to rap out an order to her as roughly as a sergeant-major to a raw recruit, with the express intention of wounding her feelings in full view of the camera. Like a vivisector, he bares her tenderest feelings first, to make them writhe the more at the first plunge of the knife.'[27] Cutts, the principal director of Gainsborough Pictures since the company's inception in 1924, had a reputation for promiscuity as well as tyranny (Islington gossips were particularly fond of recounting the story of how he took two sisters into his dressing room in the course of one lunch break), and his surviving films bear traces of his extrovert, sensual personality. In *The Passionate Adventure* (1924), for instance, he has Marjorie Daw string up a hopelessly flimsy screen to prevent Clive Brook from ogling her as she sponges herself in a tin bath in front of the fire, and ensures that our own view remains unobscured. He packed the crowd scenes of his films with potential girlfriends, and enlisted Gainsborough colleagues to help him conceal these relationships from his wife.

By 1926, however, both his personal and professional lives were beginning to unravel. For some time he had been reliant on an ambitious protégé some fifteen years his junior, who took on increasingly wide responsibilities until he was acting as his production manager, second-unit director, costume designer, script-doctor, intertitle-writer and chief provider of the alibis Cutts required to manage the complexities of his sex life. With this increasing dependence grew resentment and depression. The mentor had first begun to feel eclipsed by his talented student as early as 1925, while shooting *The Prude's Fall*. 'We went off looking for the right locations,' recalled Alfred Hitchcock, the protégé in question, 'Paris, Saint Moritz, Venice – but Cutts's girlfriend, an Estonian he'd picked up along the route, was unhappy wherever he went. So we all came back to London without a foot of film.'[28] When Michael Balcon allocated the next Ivor Novello picture to Hitchcock, Cutts did his best to sabotage the film, and very nearly succeeded.

The Lodger turns on a question perfectly suited to the sexual ambiguities of Novello's screen persona. A killer with a penchant for garrotting girls with peroxide curls is stalking the London streets. Novello is a nameless newcomer in Mrs Bunting's boarding house, and while his bizarre behaviour marks him as a prime suspect it also makes him curiously attractive to Daisy (June Tripp), the daughter of the household. His arrival on the premises is one of the great moments of British silent cinema: the front door swings open to reveal a figure muffled in a hat and scarf, wreathed in fog, one hand pressed to his heart and the other gripping the handle of a Gladstone bag. His eyes burn brightly; his movements are as stiff and strange as those of Max Schreck in *Nosferatu*. (The critic of the *New York Times* detected homosexuality before the star was even over the threshold: 'There now enters Mr Novello, looking pale and drawn and with a manner plainly saying that he very likely doesn't care for blondes at all.'[29]) When the new arrival goes up to his room, he finds the walls hung with cheap prints of Victorian nudes – John Everett Millais's *The Knight Errant* is prominent – which he turns to face the wall. Mrs Bunting (Marie Ault) suppresses her suspicions. 'Even if he is a bit queer,' she concludes, 'he's a gentleman.' Between them, Hitchcock and Novello set about making the lodger appear as queer as possible. He disturbs the people downstairs by pacing feverishly across his room: the ceiling dissolves to a glass pane, so that we can see his feet pounding over the space. He seems transfixed by Daisy's curls, praising her 'beautiful golden hair', and reaching out to touch it. He buys a dress for her, staring furiously at the department-store mannequins as they model the latest arrivals. He glares savagely from the staircase when a flirtatious policeman claps Daisy playfully in his handcuffs. Despite this suggestive behaviour, however, Novello's character is not the killer, but the brother of one of his victims. In the final reels, Daisy assists him in escaping a mob who believe him to be the murderer: he ends the chase suspended by his cuffed hands from a set of iron railings, in a peculiar quasi-crucifixion. Just as in *The Rat*, Novello moves from being a source of suspicion to an object of pity.

Hitchcock claimed that pressure from Gainsborough forced him to reveal his protagonist as an innocent. Balcon and his business partner, C. M. Woolf, it seems, were reluctant to harm their box office by casting Novello as a misogynistic strangler. Graham Cutts increased this pressure, hugger-muggering with Hitchcock's colleagues to tell them 'that boy on the set' was about to serve up an appalling turkey. 'Hitch could not understand what he had done to offend Cutts,' wrote Michael Balcon, forty years on, 'and I had to explain to him that he had done nothing wrong; it was only that Cutts was jealous. Hitch was rising too fast for Cutts's taste and he resented him as a rival director in the same studio.'[30] Unfortunately for Hitchcock, the marginalised director found a sympathetic ear in Woolf, who owned the company through which Gainsborough's films were distributed. The studio shelved *The Lodger*, and hired an aristocratic young writer named Ivor Montagu to rewrite the intertitles. If the surviving print is anything to go by, no serious damage was done.

The second and final collaboration between Novello and Hitchcock proved less problematic, but kept the star's seductively perverse persona in its sights. In *Downhill*, Novello plays Roddy Berwick, a sixth-former expelled from school when he is wrongly accused of having paid for sex with – and impregnated – the daughter of a local confectioner. Male transgressors in silent cinema customarily volunteered for colonial service, assuaging their shame by dodging the spears of the Yoruba. They rarely went on the game. Novello's progress in *Downhill*, however, follows a road to ruin much travelled by the heroines of the period. It is a film that takes shameless delight in its hero's moral reverses, teasing its audience about their desire to see him fall. After a scene depicting Roddy's banishment from the family home, Hitchcock cuts to Novello, clean cut and dickie-bowed, in a smart resort hotel. The shot widens to reveal that he is not a patron, but a waiter attending a couple seated at a table on the terrace. The couple then rise to their feet, and disappear from the frame. The woman has left her cigarette case on the table. Novello looks shiftily from side to side, and pockets the trinket. Just as you are convinced that Roddy has become some Riviera sneak-thief, the camera moves back, disclosing that this hotel is a set on the stage of a West End show. The couple whom Roddy has been serving are the principals, who are now delivering dialogue in the glare of the footlights. Novello remains behind, an insignificant chorus boy. A line of bathing belles files on: he and his fellow actors scoot into formation, and begin bobbing half-heartedly in time to the music. The plot, however, has worse degradations in store for its hero than a minor role in musical comedy. After squandering an inheritance on a brief, disastrous marriage, Roddy ends up working as a taxi-dancer in a Parisian night-club. 'There is a nice English boy,' says the madame of the establishment, 'very cheap at fifty francs a dance.' The morning light breaking through the windows at closing-time exposes the misery of the place – hollow-eyed, rouge-smeared middle-aged women slumped drunk and doped in the detritus of the night before. It is a magnificently disgusting scene.

Ironically, Novello's next picture under the Gainsborough contract, *The Vortex*, adapted from Noël Coward's stage play, was much more timid in its depiction of narcosis – despite the dependence of Willette Kershaw, the American actress playing the female lead, upon what the film's direc-

tor, Adrian Brunel, described as 'vegetable extract pellets'. The coca plant,
I suppose, is a vegetable. 'For the first five seconds of every scene,' he
recalled, 'she would be detached and miles away, then she would come to,
performing excellently for about twenty seconds, when she would begin
to sag.'[31] No such indulgence was permitted on the screen. Novello's Nicky
Lancaster confiscates a little metal casket containing what is presumably
cocaine from a libidinous Parisian dancer (played by Julie Suedo), and,
several reels and personal disasters later, is depicted opening this 'little
box of forgetfulness' and considering whether to allay his misery by
snorting its contents up his nose. Despite the lingering close-ups of his
tormented features, Nicky resists temptation. Although the film is not as
prissy and corseted as Brunel, in later life, liked to insist, it seems that
explicit depictions of drug use would not be countenanced by Michael
Balcon. However, as Novello's next film demonstrated, the seduction of
schoolgirls posed no such problem.

Little read today, Margaret Kennedy's *The Constant Nymph* was one of
the best-selling novels of the 1920s. It tells the story of Tessa Sanger, a
fourteen-year-old raised in a wildly Bohemian household in the Austrian
Alps, and the passion she conceives for Lewis Dodd, an impoverished
composer of the highly strung, art-for-art's-sake variety, who – not inci-
dentally – is twice her age. At the climax of the novel, Dodd escapes his
wife and elopes to Brussels with the girl, who dies from the effects of a
heart condition while trying to open their hotel window. 'Sanger's Circus', as Tessa's family circle was known to the book's readers, was based
on the domestic arrangements of the artist Augustus John, which added
a gossipy *frisson* to the story. 'Millions of middle-class readers', writes
Alan Jenkins, 'were persuaded to accept the life of artists, the idea of "free
love", and a situation akin to that of Lolita and Humbert Humbert, as
romantic.'[32]

The novel had been adapted for the stage by Basil Dean, a theatrical
producer with beer-bottle specs, a high-pitched voice and a reputation
for rehearsal-room brutality that had earned him such nicknames as 'The
Terrible Turk' and 'Bloody Basil'. Dean is a significant and unfairly
neglected figure in the history of British cinema and – as Chapter 5 will
illustrate – had private reasons for being enthusiastic about a story with
such a plot. He completed his script with the co-operation, but not the

respect, of its author. 'Basil Dean', Margaret Kennedy informed the poet Flora Forster, 'is the biggest fool I think I ever met (straight face difficult). His great phrase "I didn't think about that".[33] She persevered: the play opened in September 1926 with Edna Best and Noël Coward in the principal parts and touts outside the New Theatre marking up their tickets to ten pounds. Producers hungry for marketable stories to put before the camera also took note, and Dean found himself in a powerful bargaining position when Michael Balcon came to see him about turning *The Constant Nymph* into a Gainsborough picture. Although Dean did not yet understand basic cinematographic terms such as 'long shot', 'close-up' and 'dissolve', he somehow persuaded Balcon to allow him to write the scenario and to remain with the film in a supervisory capacity, breathing down the neck of its allotted director, Adrian Brunel.

The casting of Novello as Lewis Dodd was inevitable, but a suitable Tessa proved difficult to find. The press speculated that Dorothy Gish – in Britain working through a three-picture contract with Herbert Wilcox, and spotted in the audience at the New Theatre – would take the role. Gerald du Maurier encouraged Dean to cast his daughter, Daphne, but Balcon and Brunel were unenthusiastic about her screen test, and decided to award the part to an established screen actor, Mabel Poulton. She was a sweetly pretty London secretary whose film career had been launched in 1920 when the manager of the Alhambra Theatre noted her resemblance to Lillian Gish, liberated her from the typing pool and persuaded her to wrap up in a kimono and recline on a divan as part of a tableau that preceded the theatre's screenings of D. W. Griffith's *Broken Blossoms* (1919). She is one of the few British silent stars to have written her memoirs, albeit in a slippery and eccentric form. The British Film Institute holds two typescript versions of her autobiography. One, entitled *Tessa and I*, is a straightforward rendering of her experiences, bashed out in imperfect English at some point in the 1970s: 'Suddenly without much warning the horrors of the first World War was upon them with the Zeppilin raids.' The other document is much more revealing: *Cockles and Caviare: A Story of Theatre and Film Studios* is a *roman-à-clef* about Jenny Brown, a British film actress whose career incorporates success, disappointment, alcoholism, and an attempted rape at the hands of a director. At some point during its construction, Poulton has taken a blue ballpoint pen and replaced the names of the characters with the real figures upon whom they are based, exposing Jenny's experiences as a version of her own. She writes of her jealous feelings towards Betty Balfour, describing how both were signed by the producer George Pearson, but Balfour, after her scene-stealing success as a slatternly maidservant in *Nothing Else Matters* (1920), took all the best roles at the Welsh–Pearson Studio. She writes of how the producer Thomas Bentley came to the studio and asked her to hoist her skirts, explaining that the role he had in mind for her would require her to expose her legs. Curiously, the part turned out to be Little Nell in *The Old Curiosity Shop*. Bentley was known for his fussily insincere attitude to actors – one studio correspondent listened as he 'crooned like a theme song pervert' to calm an actress whose dress had accidental-

Lewis Dodd (Ivor Novello) and Tessa Sanger (Mabel Poulton) pursue
a doomed affair in *The Constant Nymph* (1928)

ly wound around her waist during a scene: 'There, there, darling, don't you mind. Pull it down, duckie. Don't get excited. Pull it down, my sweetheart.'[34] Poulton was not treated so gently. On the last day of location work, Bentley demanded that the actress demonstrate her gratitude to him for casting her in the part. Poulton writes: 'He laughed and taking her in his arms forced a very unpleasant kiss on her. Jenny, disgusted, pulled away from him and, inflamed more by her resistance, he threw her on the bed and tried to take her in his arms again. Jenny with her blood up now and in a violent temper pushed him away scratching his face as she did so. "You little bitch," he said. "I'll see you get no more opportunities in this film."'[35] If this really was how Bentley treated Poulton, then at least other producers were more generous: Abel Gance, after seeing *The Old Curiosity Shop*, conveyed her to Paris. Dean and Brunel, however, supplied her definitive role. On location for *The Constant Nymph*, she was 'absolutely living the part' – which included falling hopelessly in love with Ivor Novello. Michael Balcon described the initial meeting between the film's stars, on location at Liverpool Street Station: 'Mabel grinned in her friendly way and said, "'Allo, 'ow are ya?" Ivor thought it was a joke and replied in equally broad Cockney, only to discover that that was Mabel's natural accent.'[36]

The shoot was not a happy one. When the cast and crew arrived in the Tyrol, Basil Dean succeeded in splitting the company into two factions. He surrounded himself with the alumni of the stage production and Novello's ever-present lieutenants, Bobbie Andrews and Lloydie Williams. He cold-shouldered Mabel Poulton, the cameraman Dave Gobbett, and Brunel and his wife Babs. Brunel coined the name 'The Basilisk' for his new overseer. 'I determined to make every sacrifice to get through the film as he wished it,' he recounted in 1949, 'without the doubtful publicity of a murder attached to the celebrity of the subject. I do not think anyone has ever been so tactful as I was – at least, I hope no one has ever had to be.'[37]

Dean's arrogance was not Brunel's only problem. The weather delayed filming for a month. A car accident on a mountain bend pitched Frances Doble, the actress playing Poulton's cousin, into a ditch. Keneth Kent, playing the impresario Jacob Birnbaum, came down with mumps: to prevent the infection spreading, Andrews and Williams, who had travelled out with Kent, put themselves under quarantine and gargled antiseptic hourly. With gritted teeth, Brunel endured Dean's egotism during the location shoot, through the studio work in Munich, during the filming of additional interior scenes in Islington, and at a final session at the Queen's Hall, in which he put seventy shots in the can during the course of a day and a night.

Basil Dean was not an immediate convert to cinema, but the medium became more attractive to him as the 1920s trickled away. On a trip to New York in 1927, he attended a programme of Warner Brothers Vitaphone shorts at the Colony Cinema on Broadway, and the implications for theatre actors and writers became immediately clear to him: the medium of film was now ready to make more use of skills associated with the stage. His interest in cinema also increased for less idealistic reasons: his theatre work in 1928 and 1929 comprised an unbroken run of flops; in Britain, at least, the silent *Nymph* was accounted a success. He revived the play and sent it out on tour – for which decision Ernest Dudley has reason to be grateful. As a poor young actor in London in the late 1920s, he spent some of his scant income taking out the secretaries of West End producers for tea and cakes, whereupon he would pump them for information about forthcoming productions. Basil Dean's personal assistant was one of the most amenable. Through her influence, he secured an audience with her employer, who granted him a minor role in a party scene in the touring production. During the tour, he found himself falling in love with the actress playing Tessa Sanger: Jane Grahame, whom he recalled having seen ten years before, playing opposite her stepfather Eille Norwood in the Sherlock Holmes two-reeler *The Solitary Cyclist* (1921).

Those around Basil Dean, meanwhile, found that praise in the British press for the film version was going to his head. When the *Picturegoer* asked if it was possible for a theatre director to jump between media, he replied that 'Michael Angelo was a sculptor as well as a painter.'[38] To be fair to him, the audience at the premiere seemed to agree with this assessment of his abilities: the Marble Arch Pavilion resounded with cheers, although – as Dean was absent and Brunel and Balcon were not on speaking terms – it was left to Mabel Poulton to take the applause. Poulton would not have attended the event herself, had she not stormed from the set of her current picture, *Not Quite a Lady* (1928). (The director was

Thomas Bentley, which may have had something to do with it.) Poulton managed to whisper her thanks to the audience. She had not yet heard that on the other side of the Atlantic, the critics were blowing raspberries: 'The English', sneered *Variety*, 'are so slow in their picture making. No lighting, no camerawork, nothing: just a dull passing through a series of slow scenes.' The showbiz paper's synopsis of *The Constant Nymph* was a classic of its poisonous kind: 'Story is of a hoydenish group, children of a great composer who dies in his studio in the Austrian Tyrol. Later his most hoydenish daughter also dies. In between the picture dies.'[39]

The summary demonstrates the fervour of anti-British prejudice in Hollywood. The worst that should be said about Brunel's film is that it might have given a few schoolgirls unrealistic expectations about the intentions of older men. The picture is actually fluent and involving. Novello takes the opportunity to shift the emphasis of his 'curious mixed character' closer to the child than the devil, gobbing plum-stones into beer-mugs, banging his knife and fork on the table to encourage his host to come downstairs, singing a daft song which requires him – as the inter-titles explain – to oink like a pig. Once the plot has transferred from the Tyrol to London, however, the film darkens considerably. Dodd's wealthy wife Florence (Frances Doble) asks her husband a point-blank question about the nature of his relationship with Tessa. 'Is she your mistress?' she demands. Novello's face registers shock. 'No, she's not!' he protests. From this moment, though, he is tormented with the knowledge of Tessa's passion for him. He is once more a passive victim of someone else's desire – a rich irony, considering that his lover is below the age of consent. What motivates him to spirit her away to Brussels? The hope that she might return the childlike qualities robbed from him by his loveless marriage? A low desire to violate her? A willingness to transgress the bourgeois values of British society? Novello's face tells you everything and nothing. It is a perfect mask of agony.

However much emotion Novello unleashed on the screen, he succeeded in turning his private life into a dazzling, sunny blankness. He was always gracious with his fans. He made a point of smiling and being polite to people, particularly those he could not bear. His Gainsborough contract included a morality clause – a customary stipulation in this kind of document – obliging him to 'comport himself with dignity and decency in private and professional life and not to commit or permit any act or thing which would bring him into notoriety or contempt or disgrace'.[40] In the face of this, it is interesting how content he and the studio were for him to take on roles which seemed to use his exotic sexuality as a point of reference. Certainly, he made little attempt to straighten his public persona. He rarely removed his stage make-up after a performance. He enthused about his love for the works of Richard Wagner – a composer strongly identified with a homosexual audience.[41] He lolled around in his trunks at Redroofs, a sprawling villa near Maidenhead which he bought in 1926, and filled the place with actresses and chorus boys. He opened a night-club on Wardour Street called the Fifty–Fifty, and covered the walls with caricatures of the stars who propped up its bar; the name, apparently, alluded to the bisexuality of the clientele. (A scene in *The First Mrs Fraser* (1932) set in a club named the 'Half-and-Half' suggests that it was a place in which 'the women look half men and the men look half nothing'.) Novello's life was almost entirely free of scandal until 1944, when he was sent to Wormwood Scrubs for contravening wartime petrol regulations and found himself doing time in a cell next door to 'Mad' Frankie Fraser. (The one-month sentence, imposed by a notoriously anti-homosexual judge, broke both his spirit and his health.) There are claims that his death – ascribed by the certificate to coronary thrombosis – was the result of suicide, that he was a frequent victim of blackmail, and that one of his more eccentric parlour games at Redroofs involved him lying naked in a specially designed glass coffin, past which his friends were required to file in rehearsal of their future woes. If there is a breath of truth in any of these stories, it expired with him.

For Mabel Poulton, who had hoped he might have reciprocated her love, he remained an untarnished idol. After Novello's death, Redroofs became a retirement home for impecunious actors: Poulton was one of its first residents. 'There was a large photograph of him just after she had played with him in their big success and she gazed at the handsome face with fond affection,' she records, in *Cockles and Caviare*. 'Sitting afterwards dozing in a chair by the river in the garden her mind began to wander and she began to relive the past when she was young and attractive.'

Ernest Dudley's childhood recollections offer an insight into the limits which Novello placed upon the projection of his sexuality into his films.

In 1926, Novello and Eddie Marsh rolled up at the King's Arms with a proposal for Stanley Spencer. Marsh had finally accepted that Novello was not a second Rupert Brooke, but that did not preclude his protégé from taking the lead role in a film about the life of the poet. Novello was enthusiastic about the project, and Spencer was persuaded to be art director on the picture, which they imagined would be shot on location in Cambridge. Then, it seems, the idea was crushed by an outside agency. Rupert Brooke's mother got wind of the film. If Marsh progressed these plans any further, she would denounce him as a corrupter of her dead son, blackening Novello's name in the process. 'That stopped them in their tracks,' explains Ernest. 'The scandal would have been terrible.'

After our tour of Maidenhead Bridge, Ernest and I make our way to Cookham. We pause at the war memorial, which he scans for familiar names. He points out the post office where he received his telegram from Jack Buchanan; the chemist's shop where local girls could buy an abortion draught under the counter; the rival hotel opposite his father's, which had to send its guests to bathe in the houses across the street. We step through the doors of the King's Arms, now owned by a catering chain which has lavished it with an expensive refurbishment. I had worried that Ernest might find a return to his childhood home disorientating, but he seems delighted to be back. We sit in the bar and toast the people who have passed this way before: Flora Le Breton, Ivy Duke, Guy Newall, Stewart Rome, Eddie Marsh, Georges Carpentier, Ivor Novello. The last above all. 'He could do it,' enthuses Ernest. 'He could really do it.'

CHAPTER THREE

Shute the Journalist

Nerina Shute, teenage gossip columnist of *Film Weekly*

Between 1928 and 1932, a movie gossip column appeared in the plush, photogravure, fan magazine *Film Weekly* that filled some of its featured subjects with pleasure, and others with rage. A few victims plied its teenage author with cocktails at the Savoy, hoping that she might toss a few approving remarks their way. The rest got on the phone to their lawyers. Madeleine Carroll took the girl into her dressing room and into her confidence. Carl Brisson took her out to lunch, and told her she was cute. Elissa Landi and Lya de Putti fought their desire to spit in her face.

Nerina Shute, the woman behind the byline, revelled in this notoriety, and watched it ignite her writing career. Lord Beaverbrook invited her up for the weekend, took her riding, quizzed her on her views on *The Well of Loneliness*, and gave her a job on the *Daily Express*. Rebecca West reviewed her first novel, *Another Man's Poison*, declaring, 'Shute writes not so much badly as barbarously, as if she had never read anything but a magazine, never seen any picture but a moving one, never heard any music except at restaurants.'[1] Seventy-five years later, Shute had not abandoned the unprissy directness of her youth. It suited her appearance: the strong jawline, the hair, marshalled into those lacquered peaks once favoured by Margaret Thatcher – and, more pertinently, by Phyllis Haylor, the ballroom-dancing champion who was the love of Nerina Shute's life. 'I'm bisexual, you see,' she explained, with gentle frankness, as her companion, Jocelyn, brought in a tray of tea and biscuits. 'Tell me, what do your generation think about such things?'

Nerina was introduced to the movies by her mother, Renie, who wrote fiction under her married name, Mrs Cameron Shute. In 1920, two men persuaded Renie to leave her husband and board the *Mauretania* and the

Twentieth Century for Hollywood. The producer Thomas Ince proposed to film her novel, *The Unconscious Bigamist* (1911); an actor named Raymond Brathwayt proposed something less professional, in fifty-two tightly argued love letters. The Shutes, mother and daughter, lived in a suite at the Hollywood Hotel on Hollywood Boulevard until Mrs Brathwayt sued for divorce, and Mr Cameron Shute arrived from England to demand an explanation. The former lost her case and her husband; the latter was dismayed to discover his wife living with another woman's husband, but more dismayed that she had squandered the last of the family money on buying a Californian gold mine that did not seem to contain any gold. Their daughter, however, adored her Hollywood life; enjoyed the crowd work, the parties, and the company of real-life cowboys, until a glut of misfortunes closed the transatlantic chapter of her life. First, Raymond Brathwayt was snagged under the wheel of an engine in the goldless gold mine. He recovered sufficiently from his injuries only to kill himself in a car crash. Seeking consolation for this catastrophe, Renie Shute then married Jack Breene, a penniless Irish film actor – without first going to the trouble of securing a divorce from her husband. Finally, Renie's chances of seeing *The Unconscious Bigamist* on screen evaporated in November 1924, when the life of Thomas Ince ended suddenly on board the *Oneida*, a yacht belonging to the media mogul William Randolph Hearst. The official reports ascribed his death to indigestion; the rumourmongers insisted that Hearst had discovered his wife, Marion Davies, in bed with Ince, whom he had shot in the back, under the impression that he was Charlie Chaplin.

Three years later, Nerina Shute, still only nineteen, returned to London, snipped off her pigtails, bought herself a wide-brimmed black hat, joined a circle of 'ambisextrous' social radicals and – through some strategy she has long since forgotten – secured the job of studio correspondent of Britain's newest and most expensive fan magazine. Her timing was impeccable. In 1927, the first Cinematograph Films Act was passed, obliging British cinemas to screen a fixed percentage of domestic productions. For the next three years, speculators surrendered their money to film companies, anticipating quick returns from this large and wholly artificial market. Offices sprang up along Wardour Street, the new administrative centre of the film business. New facilities were built around the

London suburbs. Norman Loudon established the Sound City Studios near the Surrey village of Shepperton; Alexander Korda was among his most loyal tenants. British Instructional Pictures began building at Welwyn, where Anthony Asquith, the son of the former Liberal Prime Minister, made the landmark picture *Underground* (1928). British Talking Pictures set up in Wembley and, with less success, shot a musical with Stewart Rome. The thriller writer Edgar Wallace established the British Lion Studios at Beaconsfield, which he oversaw until he was wooed to Hollywood to script *King Kong* (1933). The largest and grandest development, however, appeared on the edge of the village of Borehamwood: a sprawling new neighbour for the old Neptune Studios once owned by John Marlborough East. The name of the location did not exactly exude glamour, so a village slightly further west was adopted as the studio's nominal home.

Elstree, as it became known, was founded by James Dixon Williams and Isidore Schlesinger, two American-born entrepreneurs who liked the ring of the phrase 'British Hollywood', and thought that they might build one on the forty acres of Hertfordshire countryside that they had purchased in 1925. They enlisted the help of a native, the producer Herbert Wilcox, and formed a new company, British National Pictures. Unfortunately, the relationship between the firm's two major partners soon chilled into a blizzard of writs. In January 1927, arbitration arrived in the form of John Maxwell, an unexcitable Glaswegian solicitor who was to emerge as one of the most powerful men in the British film business. Fifteen years earlier, so the story goes, Maxwell had been surprised to learn from his accountant that he owned a substantial number of shares in 'the cinematograph theatre business'. Pleased with the discovery, he decided to expand into film distribution. By the end of the negotiations with Schlesinger and Williams, he had secured a controlling interest in the new studios and the two warring founders had gone their separate ways. Schlesinger returned to his power base in Johannesburg, where he enjoyed a virtual monopoly on public entertainment companies. Williams departed for America, where he oversaw production of *The Viking* (1931), on which the director and all but one of the crew were killed in an explosion off the coast of Newfoundland. ('Twenty-six men died to make this film!' was the publicity tag Williams used to sell the picture.)

He followed his luckless crew three years later, felled by financial worries, a nervous breakdown and two heart-attacks.[2]

With Elstree's founders out of the picture, and Wilcox settled in a new facility on an adjoining site, Maxwell began to build his empire. British National Pictures became British International Pictures. Walter Mycroft, a five-foot hunchback whose career had brought him from proto-fascist politics to the post of film critic of the London *Evening Standard*, was headhunted to take charge of the scenario department. Eager Fleet Street penny-a-liners were recruited to fill the mass of ranked desks in the screenwriters' pool. Alfred Hitchcock – one of the few directors whose name was widely known among the public – was inherited from the previous management, on a three-year, twelve-picture, £13,000 contract. Victor Saville was poached from Gainsborough and E. A. Dupont from Paramount. Lilian Hall-Davis, Betty Balfour, Anna May Wong and Sydney Chaplin – Charlie's half-brother – were wooed and won.

Stuart Paton was the most unusual new arrival. That was Nerina Shute's view, at least. She pounced on him and put his story into print. A Scottish émigré to America, Paton was a successful director of Western pictures at Universal when a silver dollar hurled at a prizefight sent twenty-three particles of spectacle lens flying into his only working eye. After eight months in the dark he emerged from hospital to find that his eyesight had been restored, and that his wife had eloped, taking all the furniture and his beloved Alsatian dog. Then, under circumstances that he never divulged, Paton was found lying inert on the floor of his lodgings, and pronounced dead by the family doctor – who was forced to revise his judgement when the body began to twitch on the mortuary slab. Being certified dead, however, did not prevent Paton returning to Britain to work alongside Walter Mycroft.[3]

This influx of talent yielded a rich period of production at Elstree. With the exception of Hitchcock's *Blackmail* (1929), however, these films have been woefully underappreciated. The prejudice against them is rooted in the hostility expressed towards BIP productions by Hugh Castle, a writer for the pioneering film journal *Close-Up*, and one of the few serious British film critics of the late 1920s. His views have proved tenacious, and are legible in those of later commentators who, in many cases, betray no sign of having troubled to view the pictures themselves. Castle gave grudging praise for the famous sequence in *Blackmail* in which Anny Ondra's heroine is tormented by the soundtrack's savage repetition of the word 'knife', but expressed little but contempt for the rest of the studio's output. E. A. Dupont's *Piccadilly* (1929), for instance, was dismissed as 'a typical British film' and consequently 'one of the world's worst'. These comments were reproduced by Rachael Low in her *History of the British Film*, the standard account of the period, unglossed by her own views and prefaced by the wider assertion that BIP films 'were not particularly interesting'.[4] The judgement is grotesque. True, the studio produced a few duds. Jean de Kucharski went to Bombay to make *Emerald of the East* (1929), and returned with footage that might have been shot on the backlot. (The sudden switches between scenes filled with Indian extras and scenes filled with turbaned white Britons signal the action's return to Elstree.) *The White Sheik* (1928) makes better use of its Egyptian locations but handles its story of a European adventurer gone native with soporific delicacy.

In contrast, though, the majority of the studio's early output remains a sure source of populist pleasure. Sydney Chaplin was given full rein to prove that he could be just as inventive as his half-brother in *A Little Bit of Fluff* (1928), an adaptation of a successful stage sex farce involving a mansion block, a gangster's moll and a diamond necklace. Betty Balfour, the googly-eyed good-time girl who was the principal comic lead of 1920s British cinema, played the champagne-swashed girl next door; Chaplin filled the golfing brogues of Bertram, a feckless newlywed whose life begins to unravel after he makes a complaint about the noise from her apartment. A scene in which he persuades a tiny dog to lick the stamps for his letters and another in which he attempts to extract a bee from his underpants demonstrate the sharpness of Chaplin's talent for physical comedy. The highlight of the picture, however, is a sequence founded upon the comedy of embarrassment. The setting is a fashionable nightclub: Sydney is sitting alone when he notices, at the next table, a person whom he takes to be a little girl. She is in fact a dwarf, whose similarly diminutive husband has just excused himself from the table. Sydney gives her a sweet little wave. She doesn't object. He forms finger puppets from a pair of table decorations and dances them about like a couple of Tiller Girls. Still more amused than confused, she explains that she doesn't speak English. Undaunted, Syd picks her up in both hands and bounces her up and down on his knee. The distress on her face indicates that she has understood his misapprehension. When her husband returns from the lavatory, Sydney also realises his mistake. It is too late to make amends. The husband leaps up on the table and assaults the man who has insulted his wife – so furiously that the waiters are forced to drag him away. 'Mail him home!' is Syd's indignant parting shot.

It is one of the great tragedies of British pictures that Chaplin's follow-up film, *The Mumming Birds*, was cancelled when his ensuing bankruptcy and a sex scandal involving an Elstree actress named Molly Wright sent him fleeing back to America to escape prosecution.[5] In Chaplin's absence, Wright sued BIP for 'assault, libel and slander'. The studio settled out of court, damning Chaplin by announcing their regret for 'an incident complained of in the statement of claim, which took place on their premises, but for which they were in no way responsible'. Ronald Neame recalls that the studio gossips insisted that Syd's outrage was committed upon an underage girl[6] – but the victim appears to have been six years over the age of consent. The physical details, however, are horrific. According to Betty Tetrick, cousin to the Chaplin brothers, Sydney raped Molly Wright and bit off one of her nipples.[7]

Other gems rolled from the Elstree production line. Arthur Robison's *The Informer* (1929) is a masterpiece by any measure, a stark melodrama on the corrosive effects of guilt in which a young Dubliner shops the IRA fugitive he believes is having an affair with his wife, then finds himself unable to live with the consequences. (A scene in which he offers his condolences to the weeping mother of the man he has helped to kill is as powerful as anything in cinema.)

Vagabond Queen (1929) parachutes Betty Balfour into the plot of *The Prisoner of Zenda*, and rewards her with a slapstick finale in which, posing as the future queen of Bolonia, she dodges a barrage of assassination attempts. Harry Lachman's *Under the Greenwood Tree* (1929) is a masterclass in the use of film music. *The Manxman* (1929) is an airy romantic drama shot by Hitchcock before he was overmastered by his predilection for the pathological. The object of Castle's contempt, *Piccadilly*, is in fact an accomplished, extravagantly sensual melodrama which conjures the British capital as a very Weimar of savage appetites. (In Dupont's film, Anna May Wong plays a kitchen scullion plucked from the grease and suds by Jameson Thomas, a club impresario who serves her up in cabaret as a shimmering confection of glamour and sex. Gilda Gray is the jilted predecessor who assuages her jealousy with murder.)

Victor Saville's *Kitty* (1929) is a full-blooded oddity that would fascinate any admirer of Douglas Sirk. It relates the attempts of a possessive aristocrat to prevent her wheelchair-bound son, Alex (John Stuart), from consummating his marriage to a tobacconist's daughter, Kitty (Estelle Brody). The couple communicate by secret messages – she holds up a placard outside his window which he reads with the use of binoculars and answers by wrapping his reply around an orange and tossing it into the street – enabling Kitty to kidnap Alex from his minders. Like *Blackmail*, *Kitty* uses sound in a strikingly intelligent way. During the bizarre climax – in which the heroine deliberately risks drowning in a holed punt in order to prove that Alex's paralysis is psychosomatic and therefore conquerable – the film bursts into sound, as if the emotions of its characters were simply too powerful to be suppressed. At the premiere at the Hippodrome, the audience erupted into spontaneous applause.

Nerina Shute's columns tracked the arrivals of the stars who populated these films and the directors who oversaw their production. Her easy relationship with Walter Mycroft was vital to the success of her work. Mycroft was widely feared and disliked at Elstree, particularly after 1930, when Maxwell promoted him to Head of Production. His autocratic manner earned him the nickname of 'the Tsar of all the Rushes'. A celebrated piece of graffiti in the Elstree gents' declared, 'Mycroft is a shit', with the words 'I'm not!' appended two feet above the floor. Shute, however, used her column to secure his favour: 'He is among the nicest people in the British studios,' she wrote, though she knew she was expressing the view of a minority of one.[8] In Shute, Mycroft recognised an efficient means of publicising BIP's output. He gave her the freedom to snoop about Elstree in search of raw material for her sweetly poisonous copy. Offending the odd actor or director, he reasoned, was a price worth paying for filling a page of *Film Weekly* with free publicity for British International Pictures. 'I'm not sure why he took a fancy to me,' Nerina muses, reflecting on this odd alliance between a right-wing hunchback and a black-clad bisexual bohemian. 'I was always insulting his employees.'

Marie Ault, she wrote, had 'a face like an appetising loaf of bread'; Nelson Keys was 'a Baby Austin ladykiller'; Madeleine Carroll was 'a ruthless Madonna'. Not everybody took it quietly: Elinor Glyn wrote a five-page letter of complaint when Shute reported her attempts to hypnotise a parrot by declaring, 'You must be quiet. You must be a gentleman. This is Elinor Glyn speaking.'[9] E. A. Dupont so objected to Shute's writing that he barred her from the filming of *Two Worlds* (1930), obliging her to sneak on to the set disguised as a rabbi. Dupont's great discovery Lya de Putti took legal advice when Shute's column noted that the voice of the Hungarian vamp had been dubbed for her first sound picture, a part-talkie version of *The Informer* (1929), and concluded that her career was as good as over:

It must hurt her more than words can express to renounce her career; to descend, so suddenly, from a famous star to a mere private individual. But Lya de Putti is brave. She pretends that she doesn't care. She fights to keep smiling when she tells you that the decision is her own, she doesn't want to *make* pictures. It doesn't ring

'Still very sweet, but there is something mournful about her':
Chrissie White on the set of *The Call of the Sea* (1930)

true, I'm afraid. Talkies have ended her public life. And whatever she says, however she laughs, she can't quite disguise the tragedy of it.'[10]

Unfortunately, Shute was correct. De Putti never made another film, and died the following year, aged only thirty-four, from pneumonia following an operation to remove a chicken bone from her oesophagus. Reporting her death, the *New York Post* reflected that she was 'as unknown as a lost Chinese village'.[11] Nerina Shute was the last journalist to pay her any serious attention.

She was also present on set for the final film in which Chrissie White and Henry Edwards appeared together: a talkie at Twickenham Studios entitled *The Call of the Sea* (1930). Here, too, she saw melancholia and disappointment:

Because so many years have passed since she made her success, people imagine an old woman with greying hair and chilblains and babies and servants. Yet Chrissie White is young and lovely. I believe she is thirty-four – she looks about twenty-six. I found her in a gorgeous evening dress playing with Henry Edwards, a little part, I'm afraid, in *Call of the Sea*. It is her first talkie. All this time she has been touring with her husband, and making heaps of money, and saving it up, for the three-year-old baby who will need it some day. Chrissie White and Henry Edwards are one of the happiest couples I've ever met. They are not in the least like actors. They never pose. They never seem to quarrel. Chrissie is still very sweet, but there is something mournful about her face, as though she were almost in tears. It's strange – I don't understand it.[12]

'I think', Shute reflected, after three years of bouquets and assassinations, 'I must have been at one time the most unpopular young woman connected with British film stars and the British film world – and this was because I could not help writing my frank opinion of all the most famous people. Sad to relate, I have not yet learnt to be good.'[13] Nor had the stars about whom she wrote, and this ensured that their misdemeanours were reported in a mainstream press that was just waking up to the marketability of movie scandal. Some of her colleagues, however, were even less capable of polite behaviour.

The *News of the World* had been supplying breakfast-time impropriety, atrocity and glamour to British readers since the first decade of Queen Victoria's reign. In the 1930s, the newspaper and its Sunday rivals realised that running photographs of film stars could have a welcome effect upon circu-

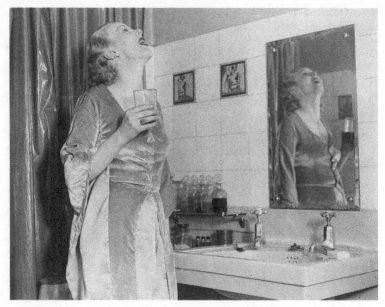

The movies as an aid to public health:
Anna Lee gargles with anti-flu mixture in 1937

lation. (During the flu epidemic of 1937, some even printed shots of British film stars swilling medicated mouthwash.) Their most lucrative realisation, however, was that the moral lapses of cinema personnel were just as attractive as those of vicars and guardsmen. When Edward Browne, the head of Steuart Films, locked the door of his room in a Great Ormond Street boarding house and blew his brains out with a revolver, the papers broke out the large type. (The story was given a further twist by the revelation that, on the day before his suicide, Browne had visited the secretary of British Equity to implore him to prevent the entry into the country of an unidentified American actress.) When the Finnish film star Ellen Sylvin was discovered working as a domestic servant in Belgravia, the paper tut-tutted over the fickleness of film fame. Imported scandals – tales involving Hollywood 'girl "extras" [who], in order to secure minor parts have been compelled to participate in orgies that beggar description' – were matched by British stories of major catastrophes in the lives of minor film players. Even the misfortunes of walk-ons could be used to colour the inside pages, as they adumbrated the possibility of more widespread corruption. An extra named Mary Bird had her name displayed more prominently than it had ever appeared on a cinema screen when George Vatine, a con-man posing as a French viscount, attempted to perform an illegal abortion upon her. George Dodds, an extra in a picture about the French Foreign Legion, received posthumous recognition when he became convinced that he was a deserter from the army, attacked his wife with a dogwhip and drank a fatal dose of disinfectant. Lionel Belcher had not made a film since 1919, but the papers described him as a 'cinema actor' when, in 1931, he clubbed a woman unconscious with a bottle during a gramophone party in Southend-on-Sea.

It was a visiting American actress, however, who provided journalists with the most consistently lip-smacking material. At the end of her life, Tallulah Bankhead was the opposite of lubricious, obliged to grease her dry gums with Vaseline to get her words out – most of which were 'daaarling!'[14] But during her eight-year sojourn in London, she was expected to misbehave. When Gaumont-British signed her for *His House in Order* (1928) on a salary of £5,000, they provided her with the means to live as ritzily as she pleased. Diners at the Savoy Grill averted their eyes when the wife of one of her boyfriends marched up to her table and slapped her in the face. Fifteen hundred fans turned up to cheer when she did the same to the critic Hannen Swaffer at the offices of the *Daily Express*. Hugh Williams – a slick-haired matinee idol who, by the early 1930s, would emerge as one of Britain's most significant film stars – fled to Australia to forget her. Gossip columnists and intelligence men loitered on the banks of the Thames in Berkshire, looking for evidence to substantiate the rumours that she had mauled a gang of Eton schoolboys in a suite at the Hotel de Paris, Bray. The school's headmaster, Cyril Alington, declined to co-operate with the authorities, and meted out his own discipline. Agent FHM of MI5 concluded that his quarry was 'both a Lesbian and immoral with men ... I hear from another master that one or both of Sir M[atthew] Wilson's older sons used to motor down to Eton with her to see the third son who was then smuggled away for the afternoon under a rug in the car.'[15] Tallulah read the newspaper reports, sunned herself in the publicity, and returned to America, considerably more bankable than when she had left. 'It doesn't matter what they say, darling,' she declared, 'as long as they talk!'

A number of British film stars were glad to see her go: Renée Gadd, for instance, an Elstree contract player of the early 1930s, and Tallulah's rival for the affections of Hugh Williams. She lived out her last years in a grandiose 1920s mansion block in Hove, on the East Sussex coast. It was an appropriate location for a retired film star. In the years around the turn of the nineteenth century, when Hollywood was still a tangle of cacti and orange trees, Hove had been a world centre of film production. In the park overlooked by Renée's flat, the pioneering film-maker George Albert Smith constructed a studio which could be piloted along rails, to follow the movement of the sun. His contribution to British cinema is commemorated in the local museum. Gadd's is long forgotten. Her face last appeared on a cigarette card in 1936; her name on a credit roll in 1950. When I visited her, a year before her death in July 2003, it was hard to guess what she had been doing since then. Even she seemed unable to say.

Renée Gadd, the 'stocky little dancer' whose money
Hugh Williams spent at the roulette tables of Le Touquet

I almost abandoned my visit to Renée before it began. After ten minutes of buzzing at the entryphone, one of her neighbours, surmising that housebreakers do not customarily arrive bearing bunches of hyacinths, took pity on me and let me into the block. I found her door ajar, and called out from the corridor. There was no answer, but I could hear the bop-pop-bop of Wimbledon coverage from the television. I called again, and this time a small figure wrapped in a pink towelling dressing-gown lumbered into the hallway, supported by a walking frame. Although she had clearly forgotten our appointment, forgotten who I was or why I had come to visit, she instructed me to come in, to find a vase for the flowers, to hunt around the dusty drinks trolley and the kitchen cupboards for a bottle of vermouth. I explained that I wanted to interview her about her film career. 'Why would you want to know about all that?' she asked, in a voice made flat and masculine by age. After a few moments of thought, she concurred that this would be the subject of our afternoon's conversation, and directed me to a painted trunk stowed under a table in the living room.

Renée Gadd was born in Bahia Blanca, a sea port four hundred miles south of Buenos Aires, in June 1906. The photograph albums in the trunk proved it. Here she was, three years old in a neat pinafore dress, a tiny figure leading a horse through an ocean of pampas grass. Here was her mother, Carlotta Le Bas, the daughter of colonists from Jersey, off to a fancy-dress party in habit and wimple, sharing a sly fag with her sister on the veranda. Here was her father, Talbot Gadd, an American railway manager, who abandoned his wife in 1914, shortly after the birth of their eighth child. 'He'd had enough of us, and I think my mother had had enough of him, too.' So the six surviving Gadd children decamped to England with their mother, where the boys were sent to public school and the girls lodged with a fierce maiden aunt and a series of strangers who took in other people's children as paying guests. 'It was a higgledy-piggledy childhood,' she told me. 'We had hardly any schooling, and we were all quick-tempered and rude.'

She was a chorus girl in Brighton from the age of fourteen, using her dancing to support her hard-up family and pay for her sisters to go to school. 'I had to work. Mother was left with these six children, all of various ages, and wasn't used to working. Somebody had to work.' Two years later, thanks to an audacious letter written to the powerful West End producer Basil Dean, she danced around Henry Ainley in James Elroy Flecker's Oriental fantasy *Hassan*. From this came more significant West End

parts and eventually, in 1931, a contract with British International Pictures.[16] 'Three pounds a day rather than three pounds a week,' she reflected, 'though they made you work like a black.'

Her two years at Elstree had left her with nothing but a vague distaste
for Walter Mycroft and his cohorts, and – like many performers absorbed
by the studio system – the conviction that she was wasted in unsuitable or
insignificant roles. She was probably right. In her two years at BIP, Gadd
was a foil to unremembered comedians, and a love interest for light-
romantic leading men. For *Letting in the Sunshine* (1933), possibly the first
British sex comedy about a window cleaner, she spent three days sitting in
a bathtub. Unimpressed by any of these experiences, she decided that the
surest way to escape from her contract was to be as unpleasant and uncooperative as she could be. 'I was pretty obnoxious in those days,' she
admitted. 'I could be a bitch.'

There were husbands during this period, some of them rich and good
looking, but she could not remember their names without referring to
the press reports of their register-office weddings. The lovers with whom
she betrayed them, however, were still lively in her mind. The first was
Fred Astaire, opposite whom she was cast in the 1926 London premiere of
Lady be Good, and again, two years later, in *Funny Face*. She described the
strength of her feelings for him, his debilitating shyness, and the advantage she enjoyed in her friendship with his notoriously possessive sister,
Adele. As she spoke, I turned over a still from *White Face* (1932), a film she
made on loan from BIP to British Lion. It showed Renée, in nurse's uniform, standing in the doctor's surgery with a pensive Hugh Williams.
Without a pause, her conversation skipped from one lover to the next.
'We had a great love affair for a long time,' she said, mournfully, gazing at
the photograph of the man for whom she left her first husband. 'It was
about the longest I ever had. I loved him terrifically. We should have got
married, but he went off with somebody else.'

Hugh Williams – known everywhere but on the posters as Tam – was a
leading man whose carefully cultivated nonchalance brought him from
the West End to films at roughly the same time as Renée Gadd. His
scrupulously scraped and parted hair was always raven black; particularly in later years, when its lustre was improved with Cherry Blossom shoe
polish. In the 1930s, when leading men and pansies shared the uniform of

Brilliantine and lounge suits, Williams made a show of stillness, confidence and certitude. He knew exactly how to lean at a cocktail bar, exactly how to angle to his fedora, exactly how to play a scene on the telephone while keeping a lit cigarette held firmly between the index and middle fingers of his left hand. Watch his films and you'll see that he rarely looks his fellow actors in the eye. The only exception he makes is for his leading ladies, with whom, customarily, he also slept – in order, he explained, 'to keep them happy'. His hands are rarely involved in his performances – when he plays policemen, they barely escape his coat pockets. He opens his mouth – a plump rose marooned in the massive flat bone of his chin – only when absolutely necessary. Films featuring an appearance by Hugh Williams's teeth are relatively rare. He is all poise, all assurance – the *ne plus ultra* of 1930s leading men.

It is the oddly corruptible character of this confidence, however, that makes him an interesting actor – and suggests why Renée, Tallulah and all those other actresses were willing to hop into bed with him. Even when Williams is playing a dime-straight heroic role, he seems on the point of being rumbled. When he confronts Bela Lugosi in Walter Summers's *Dark Eyes of London* (1939) – a horror flick in which the *Dracula* star plays a crooked insurance broker who uses a blind hunchback to kill his victims and dump their bodies in the Thames – you wonder if he's going to ask for a cut of the dough. He is a bigamist and a confidence trickster in Bernard Vorhaus's *The Last Journey* (1935), charming a moneyed Judy Gunn into marriage. In *Rome Express* (1932), he pairs up with Conrad Veidt to swipe a stolen Van Dyck concealed in the spine of Donald Calthrop's portmanteau. In this railway thriller, his con-man is swiftly reformed by love, in the form of Esther Ralston – a former shopgirl turned movie star, miserable under her peroxide wave, and desperate for Williams's brand of erotic escapism. The film opens with a delicious gag shot: a railway news-stand ranged with pornographic postcards, and beneath them a row of copies of *Film Weekly*, all bearing Ralston's face – and, on the inside pages, we presume, Nerina Shute's column.

Williams's relationship with Ralston may be a joke at his own expense, a crack about the Tallulah business that, in September 1927, sent him and his first wife, an actress named Gwynne Whitby, on a recuperative theatrical tour of Australia. The affair exerted a detrimental effect upon his health as well as his marriage: friends observed his sudden weight loss, and wondered whether Tallulah would kill him with sex. Williams attempted to recommit himself to Whitby, but just over a year later, after fathering two more children with her, elected to return, alone, to London. A tour of the United States, as Stanhope in *Journey's End*, R. C. Sheriff's drama of the First World War trenches, took him briefly to Hollywood, where he played one of the leads in the first talkie version of *Charley's Aunt* (1930). By November 1930, he was back in London. The British film business was ready for him, and so was Renée Gadd.

White Face, the picture on which their relationship began, is an Edgar Wallace story about a doctor who turns jewel thief and blackmailer in order to fund the construction of a hospital in the East End. The film is lost, but a copy of the script survives. Williams plays Michael Seeley, a sensation-hungry reporter wooing Gadd's Whitechapel Nightingale, Janice Harman. Hearing that she has accepted a date from another admirer, a lounge-lizardly South American named Barios, Seeley turns up at the same restaurant on the arm of Gloria Gaye, a glamorous film star, just to excite her jealousy. Gaye is an interviewee; Janice assumes that she is a lover. The ruse works.

BARIOS: I do not like that young man, I hope he is not a great friend of yours.
JANICE: I'm afraid I happen to like him very much.
BARIOS: Perhaps you are not a very good judge of character, my dear.
JANICE: (*looking at him steadily*) Perhaps you're right.

The affair between Hugh Williams and Renée Gadd was played out in extravagant terms, mainly at the latter's expense. After a day on set or a night in the theatre, the couple would charter a plane to Le Touquet, where they played the gaming tables – always with Renée's money – before returning the following day. The spree came to an end, however, in mid-1933, when Williams was offered a two-year contract with Fox. He departed for California, renting a bungalow in the Garden of Allah – that colony of stars and screenwriters and drunks at 8152 Sunset Boulevard, presided over by the actress–producer Alla Nazimova and occupied, from time to time, by Tallulah Bankhead.

Once Gadd had worked through her contract with BIP, she too went to Hollywood, where she found that producers at Universal and MGM were keen to see her. Williams was less forthcoming; another woman had already taken her place. The former lovers acted opposite each other in George Cukor's lavish adaptation of *David Copperfield* (1935): Williams played Steerforth, the hero's charismatic and utterly untrustworthy schoolmate; Gadd was Betsey Trotwood's long-suffering housekeeper, Janet. Hollywood, however, soon tired of both their talents. The following year found them both back in London.

Renée Gadd and Hugh Williams,
lovers on the set of *White Face* (1932)

Resigned to the loss of her lover, Gadd married a wealthy septuagenarian businessman, Harry Hardman, who, after the wedding ceremony, took her on a three-month holiday around Europe. The marriage did not last: when Gadd's sisters turned up at Victoria to meet her from the boat train, they found the honeymooners in separate compartments, and Renée on the arm of the actor Raymond Huntley.

Her long absence from British screens made it difficult for her to recuperate her career. She struggled on in low-budget quickies until the close of the thirties, slipping further down the cast list with each engagement.

After that, her film appearances were little more than cameos. She is the wife to whom Mervyn Johns awakes from the nightmare of *Dead of Night* (1945), Raymond Huntley's self-centred spouse in *They Came to a City* (1944), a stern probation officer in *Good-Time Girl* (1948). Her last day in front of the camera was spent playing a short scene in *The Blue Lamp* (1949), the Ealing crime drama in which Dirk Bogarde earned star status by sinking two bullets into Jack Warner outside the Coliseum Cinema. She is a motorist who is stopped by a policeman for failing to halt at a pedestrian crossing. She listens, sourly, to the reprimand, a cigarette burning in her gloved left hand. 'Haven't you anything better to do?' she asks, handing over her licence. 'One of your own men shot down in cold blood and all you do is waste your time pestering the lives out of innocent, respectable people. I'm not surprised all these murderers get away with it.'

Renée Gadd had no recollections about this period of her career. With no cuttings to prompt her, she was lost for words. Judging by her credits, she seems to have become dependent on the patronage of the Ealing director Basil Dearden. His name, however, meant nothing to her. I tried to ask more about Williams, but she would only repeat that she would have married him, if he had been able to obtain a divorce from his first wife. (Gwynne Whitby, by an odd coincidence, also has a brief role in *The Blue Lamp*.)

Hugh Williams remarried in 1940, and managed to sustain his film career until his death in 1969, despite being twice declared bankrupt. The war requisitioned his nonchalance and made it look like bravery: in the 1940s, his casual manner was more often used to outwit the Nazis than to deceive moneyed girls. In *One of Our Aircraft is Missing* (1942), Michael Powell cast him as a film actor on a mission for the RAF: once the crew has bailed out into enemy territory, Williams drags up as a Dutchwoman, with jangly earrings and a centre-parting under his headscarf. (Powell shows him enjoying the artifice, smoothing his eyebrows, coquetting for the mirror.) In *The Day Will Dawn* (1942), he is a pleasure-loving racing hack who first opposes the war on the grounds that it will mean the cultivation of potatoes at his favourite sports venues, but is soon ennobled by his involvement in the destruction of a secret U-boat base in a Norwegian fjord.

Once hostilities had ended, Williams grew a moustache and regained his amorality. In Roy Ward Baker's *Paper Orchid* (1949), he is a steel-hearted newspaper editor who betrays Hy Hazell's reporter for the sake of a fat front-page story. ('Have you had experience?' he asks, when she comes to his office to talk her way into a job. 'I mean, newspaper experience.') The poetry of his son, Hugo Williams, charts these later years and measures the increasing difficulty with which his father attempted to maintain the sleek perfection of his 1930s image:

> I knew it wasn't my father
> Who was bankrupt and poor.
> He had a war.
> He had a scar.
> He was on Famous Film Star
> Cigarette Cards
> with Janet Gaynor.
> It couldn't be my father
> who hit the registrar
> and had to be bound over for a year
> to keep the peace,
> so who were they talking about
> in the newspaper?[17]

Hugo and his brother Simon recall that, during their childhood, Renée Gadd was occasionally mentioned in the Williams household, as 'a stocky little dancer' who accompanied their father to casinos and race meetings.

A few weeks after my visit, Hugo, intrigued to learn that this fragment of his family history had outlived his parents and their contemporaries, took the train to Hove, and found his father's former lover full of recrimination. 'Tam was a devil,' she told him. 'He was very attractive. He went after anything. He used to introduce me to them sometimes.' Hugo explained who he was, but his hostess seemed unimpressed: 'You're Tam's son? You don't look like him.'

Let the relationship between Hugh Williams and Renée Gadd stand as an exemplum of the studio affair: one of the few that, after so many years, can be reconstructed in any detail. Contemporary magazines such as *Film Weekly* rarely noted such relationships, unless a divorce case moved them beyond the range of the libel laws. Nerina Shute knew such gossip, but did not share it with her readers. Although she could be savage, she was usually discreet. She related Tallulah's opinions on the state of the British film industry, but remained silent about her impact upon the marriages of some of its personnel. She described Henry Ainley taking a talkie test at Elstree, and noted that illness had forced him to spend two years in a convalescent home on the Isle of Wight, but declined to mention that chronic alcoholism had put him there.[18]

There was one British film scandal, however, that she could not afford to ignore. The Sunday papers christened it 'the Film Studio Horror', and, for once, they were not resorting to hyperbole. It snuffed out a life, ended a marriage, triggered debate in the House of Commons, and transformed the career of one of Britain's most highly regarded film actors.

'The Film Studio Horror' began with a commonplace scene of showbusiness adultery. On the evening of 31 March 1930, Donald Calthrop, driving from his home on Chandos Street to Twickenham Studios, took a detour to the stage door of the Piccadilly Theatre. The previous week, the cast and crew of the talkie in which he was appearing – a gypsy musical entitled *Spanish Eyes* – had commandeered the theatre, lining the street with electric generators, packing the seats of the art deco auditorium with evening-dressed extras, and filling the stage with ballerinas borrowed from the chorus. (The Piccadilly was accustomed to cinematic incursions: in September 1928, the British premiere of *The Jazz Singer* had taken place on its stage; Al Jolson turned up to duet with himself.) After the shoot, Calthrop had gone home without his dressing-gown, and it was this that he picked up from the stage door, just as the night's performance of Arthur Schwartz's musical comedy *Here Comes the Bride* was closing. He also picked up a gaggle of chorus girls. Among them was Anita Fay Tipping, a twenty-year-old dancer who worked under the stage name of Nita Foy and lived with elderly relatives in Maida Vale.

With only one stage, Twickenham Studios maximised its capacity with a twenty-four-hour shift system. The personnel of *Spanish Eyes* worked through the night, vacating the building each morning at seven-thirty to make way for their counterparts on Carlyle Blackwell's revenge drama, *Bedrock*. (According to John Mills, morning arrivals at Twickenham were met with an overpowering aroma of 'cigarette butts, orange peel, stale beer, make-up and several unmentionable gasses'.)[19] It was exhausting work.

Talking pictures relied upon moonlighters from the West End, who occasionally fell asleep during takes. 'You look tired,' Calthrop told Tipping, when they met in a studio corridor around midnight. 'Yes,' she replied. 'Bored.' She was already in costume – an elaborate crinoline frock – and he invited her into his dressing room for a brandy and soda. As she sat on the sofa, Calthrop noticed that her eyes were white with powder. 'Surely you cannot go on,' he said. 'It is bad for your eyes.' Calthrop's red tin of mascara was sitting on a shelf above an electric fire. 'She leaned forward to pick up a little brush which one uses,' Calthrop later recalled, 'and I remember turning to the door to call for a syphon of soda. Then there was a flash behind me, but no scream or anything like that as far as I can remember. It was almost an exclamation, and I turned round to see Miss Tipping a sheet of flame. I looked round the room to see what one could do. I think one's brain stops at moments like this.' He threw his dressing-gown around her, burning his hands and face in the process. The pair stumbled out into the corridor, where Tipping collapsed on the linoleum. Rosie Young, ballet mistress of the Piccadilly, managed to put out the flames. Bert Coote, the assistant producer, ran to fetch a doctor who, to Coote's frustration, refused to hurry to the scene of the accident and insisted on putting on a suit and cufflinks. Meanwhile, down on the studio floor, the director, George Samuelson, became aware of the sound of distant screams. 'But they were very, very faint,' he told the coroner, 'because the studio had been shut off to deaden the sounds from outside. It flashed through my mind – why, I do not know – that some white mice we had down there had got loose and that was why the girls were screaming.' At the inquest into the death, the coroner was unimpressed by his evidence. 'I have seen some of your pictures, Mr Samuelson, and I think this will be a lesson to you.' After an agonising ten hours in a bed at the Richmond Hospital, Anita Fay Tipping died. The dressing room in which she had been incinerated soon became a site of ghoulish pilgrimage.[20]

Once *Spanish Eyes* had wrapped, Nerina Shute swept west to interview the dressing room's next occupant, Richard Cooper, a farceur with a strong line in helium-voiced toffs.

The electric fire which set her on flames stands in the same spot, a sinister thing even though protected, now, by a wire guard. And the strange thing is that Richard Cooper, known to most of us as 'Charley's Aunt', inhabits the room, and tries to invest it with an air of cheery good humour. He flings his clothes and his make-up on the settee on which Nita Foy must have sat and talked and laughed in the moments before she died. He tries to ignore the tragedy which lurks there, haunting the room with memories. But a feeling of mystery hangs about the fatal dressing-room. Some pass it with a quickening of breath. Others, more curious, peep through the door. 'Look! That's the very stove that caused the accident!'[21]

The death of Nita Foy had a dramatic effect upon Donald Calthrop. He aged twenty years in the space of ten. His marriage collapsed in October 1931, and was quickly followed by his finances. He began to drink heavily. To save money, he moved into a cheap hotel in Charlotte Street, but was unable to pay his wife's maintenance – for which she sued him in February 1933. At the end of August 1934, he collapsed on set at Elstree while shooting the George Arliss costume drama *The Iron Duke* (1935). In 1936, he was fined for being drunk and disorderly on Regent Street, and the following year was in court again, charged with obtaining money under false pretences. 'My father's career is not finished,' declared his son John, speaking as a character witness. 'In two months' time I am confident that he will be fit to resume his stage and film work, and he is determined to make a success of it.'[22]

Contrary to the roster of court appearances, and the cursory accounts of his life that feature in film encyclopedias, however, the Twickenham scandal did not destroy his career. The inquest exonerated him, and he kept his contract at Elstree. Other producers – Julius Hagen, Basil Dean, Michael Balcon – were happy to employ him in their studios, even if the parts he was offered were sometimes little more than cameos. In the five years following Foy's death, he made thirty films. Calthrop had specialised in characters down on their luck, or in and out of the courts. As his life came into closer conjunction with those of the roles he played, his work gained a strange kind of purity. His final role, in *Major Barbara* (1941), as Peter Shirley, a shipyard fitter sacked for being too old to do his job, is the greatest of his numerous portraits of down-and-outs. In one scene, he describes his attempts to disguise his age; how hair dye worked for a while, until, at the inquest into the accidental death of his daughter, it began to dribble down his face. He has a chilling dignity. 'Teetotaller,' he protests. 'Never out of a job before.'

Donald Calthrop was a member of a theatrical dynasty. The nephew of

Dion Boucicault Jr, his first significant film was *Masks and Faces* (1917), a fundraiser for the Royal Academy of Dramatic Art which massed a generation of Edwardian theatrical heavyweights: H. B. Irving, Gerald du Maurier, Irene Vanbrugh. His rare qualities as a cinema actor, however, first emerged when he played Andy Wilks, a devious, selfish and highly successful film comedian in *Shooting Stars* (1928). It was an important film for Calthrop, and one of the richest of the period. A. V. Bramble and Anthony Asquith's satire on the British movie business describes the treacherous effects of scandal upon film celebrity. Calthrop's Wilks is a study in the actor's hollowness: a sly, sleazy man who hides behind the elaborate whiskers and chequered pants of a Chaplinesque screen persona. Wilks has been signed by a Hollywood studio, and is making one last picture on British soil: *Chased Lily*, in which he is pursued across beaches and through hotel bars by a gun-toting rival (played by the twenty-six-stone South African actor and former elephant hunter Tubby Phillips). Wilks's married lover and fellow film star Mae Feather (Annette Benson) has also signed a Hollywood contract – one with an ominous clause declaring the arrangement null and void if she is involved in any scandal. When her co-star and husband Julian Gordon (Brian Aherne) discovers the affair, Mae attempts to safeguard her future with murder, filling the gun by which he is to be shot on the set of their latest horse opera with live ammunition. With horrible inevitability, the gun finds its way on to the set of *Chased Lily*. We see Calthrop dangling from a chandelier, then Phillips aiming the gun at him and discharging its barrels. Wilks's body crashes to the studio floor; the chandelier swings more violently, the bullets having refreshed its momentum. (Tubby Phillips was also a member of the cast of *Spanish Eyes*. A month after the death of Nita Foy, he was killed when his car collided with a milk lorry on the Tottenham Court Road. He was buried within sight of Elstree Studios. 'Larks sang beautifully overhead,' trilled the *Bioscope*, 'and hearts chilled by regret were yet warmed by recollections of this big smiling man whose dust they were laying away.'[23])

Today, Donald Calthrop's reputation rests upon his work with Alfred Hitchcock. The director cast him as Tracy, the snake-eyed insinuator who commits the eponymous crime of *Blackmail*, and watched him walk away with the picture. Calthrop's performance, the first notable work by an

Donald Calthrop on the set of *Rome Express* (1931), months before
the immolation of Anita Fay Tipping

actor in a British talkie, remains confident and powerful. As he observes
Anny Ondra disappearing into the apartment of the artist whom she will
later stab to death in self-defence, his mouth is a thin, cruel streak. When
Calthrop rolls up at her father's tobacconist shop, to torture the guilty
woman and her policeman fiancé (John Longden) with his knowledge,
Hitchcock turns them into his dumb auditors. Calthrop sings to himself,
takes a cigar, snips the top fussily, lights it at the gas-jet on the counter,
puffs smoke with absurd ceremony. It is a fragile bravado. When Longden
decides to arrest him, Calthrop immediately caves in: 'I had some cash
from you,' he twitters, 'but I wasn't serious. I'm not bad really. Things
have gone wrong lately. And one's got to live, you know.' Which, of course,
he fails to do: after a chase across the dome of the British Library, he is
about to name Ondra as the killer when the glass beneath his feet splinters, sending him tumbling to his death. Walter Mycroft put him under
contract as soon as the reviews came in.

Calthrop was absorbed into Hitchcock's repertory company at BIP. In

Juno and the Paycock (1929), he was the tailor from whom Captain Boyle orders a suit on the strength of a legacy that fails to materialise. He was a ripe red herring in *Murder!* (1930), a stage actor questioned by the police during a performance in provincial theatre: as they quiz him, he exchanges a floral frock and bonnet for a set of manacles, and hops back on to the stage to continue his scene. In *Number Seventeen* (1932), he is a panicky jewel thief who causes disaster by killing the driver of the train on which he is attempting to escape.

Other directors, at Elstree and beyond, also called upon his talents, and admired the way that his mellifluous voice registered on their recording equipment. Calthrop was butler to Clifford Mollison in *Almost a Honeymoon* (1930), and hotel manager to Renée Gadd's maid in *Money for Nothing* (1932). He hobbled about with Hugh Williams in *Sorrell and Son* (1933), and the publicity manager at British and Dominions, in a small anticipation of Lee Strasberg's Method, boasted that Calthrop had retained his character's limp throughout the production. He is Bob Cratchit in Henry Edwards's version of *Scrooge* (1935), looking ossified and gnarled beyond his years, hugging himself to keep warm in the wintry atmosphere of his employer's office. In *Broken Blossoms* (1936), he is an impossibly wizened Limehouse antique dealer, peering up from his ledger with ironical amusement. In Alexander Korda's *Fire over England* (1937), he is Don Escobal, an emissary from the Spanish court, at his best during a drunken dinner scene, collapsed in his chair, giggling helplessly, and disappearing into a monstrous ruff.

Fan magazines celebrated him as a versatile character actor and an accomplished scene-stealer, and urged producers to give him bigger roles. 'It is one of the prime weaknesses of the British film industry that so fine an artiste as Donald Calthrop should be neglected and allowed to waste his talents upon the desert celluloid,' complained one. 'Time after time he is signed to make a short appearance in a picture. He never fails to contribute a work of character-acting which is a little masterpiece. And yet no-one has bothered to build him up into the stardom he deserves.'

Nerina Shute shared the opinion. 'If Donald Calthrop were advertised in the way that he deserves his name might carry the "drawing power" of an Emil Jannings or a Lon Chaney. His performance in *Blackmail* proved that. And then he would be helping British production (his only ambition) quite as much as himself. But he won't do it, of course.' Calthrop told her:

If I were a producer I'd spend thousands on a carefully thought-out campaign. I'd make my pictures as famous as Hollywood pictures. But British producers don't believe in it. They refuse to realise that publicity counts more than anything else. So why should I trouble? I'm only an actor now. So long as I have enough money to buy my friends a drink, I'm perfectly happy. Why should I change?[24]

Shute was fortunate to extract any kind of comment from him. Despite his enthusiasm for film publicity, Calthrop ran from interviews. 'Since I've known him,' wrote Shute, 'Donald has treated me like a dose of castor oil in case I should write about him in *Film Weekly*. He hates to talk about himself.'[25] He might have been afraid that she wanted to truffle for quotes regarding Nita Foy. He might even have recalled the scene in *Shooting Stars*, in which the banality of film journalism is satirised in the shape of Asphodel Smythe, a fur-wrapped, fuzzy-brained studio correspondent who records her interviewee's most anodyne observations. 'Beauty to her is the very Breath of Life,' she scribbles, as Andy Wilks's lover Mae Feather holds court in her dressing room. 'Adores all furry and feathery things.' But Nerina Shute wrote nothing so vapid. 'Oh Donald, Donald!' she mourned, when Calthrop used the poor publicity sense of British producers to excuse his own reticence. 'Was there ever such a stupid argument?' He was given no opportunity to reply.

Even before her death in October 2004, Nerina Shute had relinquished her memories of many of the figures with whom she was in daily contact. In her youth, she wooed and cornered and cajoled a generation of stars, bore witness to the transition from silence to sound, celebrated the triumphs of the winners and supplied the epitaphs of the losers. Reflecting upon these events, with seventy-five years of hindsight, she was only slightly repentant. 'I was always writing very rude things about very well-known people,' she concluded. 'I called it having the courage of my convictions. I would call it bloody rudeness now. But people were rather frightened of me. And I was glad about that.'

CHAPTER FOUR

A Short Chapter about Quick Films

Renée Gadd and Lesley Wareing attempt to gaze dreamily upon the sinister features of quota comedian Ernie Lotinga in a publicity shot for *Josser Joins the Navy* (1932)

Uniquely in critical discourse, with the possible exception of Bible study, British cinema history is dominated by a single work. Rachael Low's seven-volume *History of the British Film* is the founding text of the field. Before the first volume was published in 1948, anyone interested in the early years of moving picture production in these islands could only thumb through back issues of the *Kinematograph Weekly* or ferret out the address of a loquacious survivor and write to request an interview. A young Ph.D. student when she began her project, Low was the first person to write about the lives and careers of the pioneering British film-makers. Her study took nearly forty years to complete, during which time interest in her subject underwent a slow awakening. Film magazines began to survey the past with a more serious eye. Academic interest in British cinema began to stir. As each new volume appeared, the usefulness of her work grew – as did its tyrannous influence upon the writings of her successors. Over the years, Low's conclusions and prejudices were absorbed, reproduced and became critical orthodoxies. Today, bibliographies are naked without a reference to Low; journal articles redundant if they fail to offer her a nod. Has any work, in any other area of the humanities, wielded such a tremendous influence?

Low's story has a villain: the Cinematograph Film Act (1927), which aimed to stimulate British film production. Then, as now, the principal distribution companies were American owned, but the Act obliged them to fund the production of a rising percentage of British and Commonwealth movies before they would be allowed to continue to handle Hollywood pictures. They also had to abandon the sharp practice of blind booking, through which they muscled their customers into exhibiting bad American films as well as good ones. The cinemas, meanwhile, were forced to show ever more British pictures. The legislation, which was effective for ten years, until a further Act relaxed its terms, created a guaranteed market for home-grown productions. As a result, American distributors invited tenders from British producers willing to supply them with cheap films to meet their quota obligations; and investors opened their wallets to create new studio space to house these productions.

The Act, Low argues, was a disaster from which the British film business struggled to recover. 'The 1927 quota legislation had a profound and damaging effect upon the structure of the British film industry,' she writes. 'British production was swamped by the boring, badly made and routine work of the quota producers ... the flood of cheap pictures which was caused by the badly framed 1927 Act did, in fact, harm the reputation of the British film.'[1]

Although she was not the first to go into print with such an opinion, she was its most lucid and informed proponent. Others satisfied themselves with put-downs. Basil Wright, one of the principal figures of the British documentarist movement in the 1930s, uses his book *The Long View* (1974) to canonise his own work and establish quota production as its shoddy coeval: 'a great dreary mass of tasteless, ill-made films which debased the spectators if they didn't send them to sleep'.[2] Ernest Betts, a Fleet Street journalist who got his fingers burned dabbling in the film business, recalls 'the Bad Thirties' in his book *Inside Pictures* (1960): 'American companies made cheap quickies to fulfil the letter of the law,' he writes, 'and in many cases didn't even trouble to show them. British film producers also made quickies, but unfortunately showed them, thus throwing the industry into disrepute.'[3] William K. Everson, in the notes to accompany a Michael Powell and Emeric Pressburger retrospective, notes the pair's work in low-budget production in the 1930s, describing how they 'disregarded both the lack of money and the lack of interest in their finished films, and tried to make something out of nothing ... It takes a thorough knowledge of all the horrors of the "quota quickies" to realise the magnitude of some of their achievements – and if the films were watchable at all, it was an achievement.'[4]

Today, few possess such thorough knowledge. Many of these pictures have been lost: the process of re-evaluating the remains has barely begun.

It would be foolish to deny that there are quota quickies in the archive that offer perfect examples of the horrors to which Everson alluded. *The Woman from China* (1930), for instance, probably the last silent feature to be shot on British soil, is a cack-handed melodrama of the white slave trade, in which a father-and-daughter team of Oriental master criminals kidnap a typist and hold her hostage at their secret base in Brentford. It was commissioned by the American distribution company Jury-Metro-Goldwyn, when it found itself in need of an extra British picture to meet its obligations to the quota. The picture was directed by Edward Dry-hurst, a former cinema pianist who, at the age of seventeen, had forged his father's signature to enable him to set up offices for the Albanian Film Company on St Albans High Street and raise the cash to hire Flora Le Breton for a two-reel domestic comedy entitled *The Cause of All the Trouble* (1923). Julie Suedo, who had offered cocaine to Ivor Novello in *The Vortex*, filled the title role of *The Woman from China* – principally because she was the girlfriend of the producer. For the part of the villainous Chang-Li, Dryhurst engaged Gibb McLaughlin, a cadaverous character actor from Sunderland, known principally for his portrayals of effete butlers.[5] The hero was played by Tony Wylde, an actor of tedious good looks who supported himself in the long gaps between jobs by selling himself to middle-aged women at a Covent Garden night-club called Chez Henri. The heroine's part went to Frances Cuyler, a fragile young actress who became Dryhurst's lover and was reported as a missing person the following year.

The film is comprehensively hopeless. A romantic interlude on the deck of a P&O cruise liner is disrupted by high winds that cause the heroine's hat to flap like a deck-chair on a February beach. Scenes set in the villains' opulent dockside lair are marred by the streams of freezing air that issue from the actors' mouths: an unpaid bill had prompted the electricity company to cut off the studio's supply, forcing Dryhurst's crew to rely on power generated by an elderly traction engine which produced an ear-bashing din and filled the set with petrol fumes. The conclusion of the film, a rugby scrum of stabbing, poisoning and posturing, is largely incomprehensible.[6]

I feel qualified to pronounce upon the irremediable awfulness of *The Woman from China* as I am one of the half-dozen people who have watched the BFI's print of the film. Others, I suspect, have insisted upon the poverty of such pictures without going to comparable trouble. Despite the recent efforts of a small band of scholars, a rich mythology of shame and dreadfulness remains around the quota production – a mythology sustained by colleagues of those same scholars who have declared that 'most of the "quickies" were best forgotten'.[7] The most popular story in the litany claims that many films made purely to satisfy the quota were screened at breakfast-time to empty houses. It's an attractively absurd image: headscarved chars moving down the empty aisles, scooping ash from the filthy little pods between the seats, prizing wads of chewing gum from the upholstery, harvesting discarded coffee creams from the carpet; while on the screen, some minor stage actor hired for a ten-day shoot on a one-pound-a-foot quickie mouths silently above the rows of seats. Michael Balcon's autobiography contains the principal evidence for the existence of this practice. The culprits, he claims, were 'certain American-controlled cinemas in the West End of London'.[8] He seems to have been right: the 1938 *Kinematograph Year Book* reports a test case against two London cinemas for scheduling British quota pictures before midday.[9] The magistrate ruled against the practice, closing a loophole in the law. An earlier case, however, suggests that the practice cannot have been very widespread before the date of the prosecution. In 1932, the Alexandra Hall in Weymouth programmed an Australian picture entitled *Odds On* (1928) without advertising it in the local press. Although the management distributed a thousand handbills and screened the film at 6 p.m., the case went before the Weymouth magistrates.[10] If West End cinemas were making habitual and serious breaches of the quota regulations, this case would hardly have been considered newsworthy.

Many of the other charges routinely made against low-budget productions of the 1930s are equally dubious. 'As an act of kindness,' asserts David Puttnam, 'these "British" films were usually shown after the main Hollywood feature, when the vast majority of the audience had already left the cinema.'[11] Listings in the contemporary press, however, suggest that, beyond the super-cinemas of the West End, these pictures often formed the main attraction.

George Perry, in *The Great British Picture Show* (1985), argues that producers of the period, out of touch with popular taste, churned out drawing-room melodramas of limited interest to a general audience and transformed British cinema into a 'middle-class institution' characterised by 'the "cultured" West End accent' and 'the mores of the country drawing room'.[12] The list of titles released under the 1927 Act, however, suggests that the music hall was as powerful an influence as Shaftesbury Avenue. (Moreover, a survey conducted in 1934 for the Granada chain of cinemas indicated that the 'society drama' was the most popular film genre with all audiences over twenty-one.)

Charles Drazin, in his biography of Alexander Korda, suggests that 'ninth-rate' quota pictures were 'never seriously intended to make any money at the box office'.[13] But the trade papers reveal some dramatic exceptions: *This Man is News* (1938), a thriller produced under contract to Paramount on a bare-bones budget of £6,000, was among the highest-grossing films of its month. The very popularity of quickie programming caused annoyance to some in the British film business: the studio executive Bruce Woolfe railed against 'the half-wits who go to kinemas not to see a certain film or person, but in order to get three hours of pictures', principally because cheap second features had reduced the market for the non-fiction shorts produced by his own company.[14]

Korda's position in this landscape has also been distorted by myth – not least by the producer himself. He was a flamboyant Hungarian émigré with a talent for extracting money from credulous financial institutions. Investors were impressed by the presence of Winston Churchill's name on the company notepaper, and the Gauguins and Matisses on the walls of his penthouse apartment in Claridges Hotel. Those who worked alongside him viewed him with appalled admiration. ('He was a villain with the charm of the devil,' says the director Roy Ward Baker, whose opinion is a common one.[15]) Korda is remembered as a producer who disdained low-budget production to concentrate upon ambitious projects pitched at the international market – yet he arrived in London in 1931 to shoot a quota film for Paramount, and stayed precisely because he wanted to take advantage of the favourable conditions generated by the 1927 Act.

His pictures from this period remain highly regarded; rather too highly regarded, perhaps. Even the best owe their effectiveness more to the extravagance of their art direction than the coherence of their narratives:

Sanders of the River (1935) is an uneasy alliance of anthropological stock footage, studio-based melodrama and lectures on empire-building; *Things to Come* trusts in the gobsmacking scale of its vision to obscure the poverty of its script. At their worst, Korda's pictures were decorative transatlantic follies. *The Private Life of Don Juan* (1934), for example, evinces a lifelessness that only money can buy.

Quota quickies, though they struggled with truncated shooting schedules and skeletal budgets, were not subject to the indulgences that make some of the big-budget movies of the period seem so vulgar and flatulent. As the documentary film-maker John Grierson wrote in 1937,

The most curious result of the quota war has been the new orientation in British film values. Before it, our eyes were focused on Denham and the 'bigs'. Today the big pictures, like dinosaurs, appear to be too big to be economic and are heading for extinction. We are all interested now in what can be done with fifty thousand pounds . . . we are even interested in what can be done with twelve thousand pounds. The record of these cheaper pictures is a lot better than the more pretentious ones. I do not mean better in production values, I mean better in essence . . . without any pretension to those values, some of the cheaper pictures have a vitality which luxury ones lack.[16]

If you want to experience that vitality, look no further than the work of Tod Slaughter, a twitching, cackling actor–manager who spent most of his professional life touring the suburbs with self-consciously overpowered versions of Victorian melodramas. Slaughter was the unlikely star of a series of quota films produced at Shepperton by the parsimonious independent producer George King, and his cinema is one of unembarrassed theatricality. He leers, he cackles, he licks his lizardy lips, he rolls his eyes and 'R's with equal abandon. Watching his films – adaptations or pastiches of popular nineteenth-century barnstormers – you feel certain that the cinemas in which they played would have been filled with cheers, hisses, boos and whoops. *Maria Marten, or Murder in the Red Barn* (1935) begins with a prologue in which the proprietor of a rowdy Victorian playhouse stands before the cloth to introduce the characters of the drama. The audience shouts and applauds when Slaughter glides across the boards as 'that scoundrel Corder – a villain whose blood may be blue, but whose heart is black as night!' (The killer's punning name is a delicious historical accident.) 'That's Tod Slaughter himself,' notes the proprietor, adding

– rather unconvincingly – that the cast has been 'retained at enormous expense'. *The Crimes of Stephen Hawke* (1936), in which Slaughter plays a respectable money-lender who spends his evenings burgling houses and cracking the vertebrae of their occupants, offers a preamble in which Slaughter is interviewed in a BBC radio studio. 'Have you any favourite method of murder, Mr Slaughter?' asks the interviewer. 'I keep a perfectly open mind on the matter,' says the star, before turning to the camera and gloating over the horrors of his most recent 'new old melodrama'. Even when they appeared without such framing devices, these films encouraged their audiences to respond to them in a very different way from the internationalist spectacles of Korda's cinema. In *Sweeney Todd, the Demon Barber of Fleet Street* (1936), Slaughter's performance never loses its consciousness of the presence of the audience. 'Now see the welcome Sweeney Todd gives to gentlemen who return from foreign parts,' he declares, narrating his own actions and unleashing a protracted cackle that covers his progress from the barber's chair to the hidden lever on the other side of the shop. In *It's Never Too Late to Mend* (1937), he is a magistrate with a predilection for the cat-o'-nine-tails: 'I think a little discipline is called for,' he purrs. 'Just a little discipline.' Unless the mores of the country drawing room incorporate flogging, garrotting and spine-breaking, middle-class values are absent: Slaughter embodies a murderous form of bourgeois hypocrisy calculated to elicit the noisy opprobrium of a working-class audience.

The archive has been kind to Slaughter: his films remained popular in the 1940s, and they are occasionally programmed in the small hours of the television schedules. Other successful stars of the low-budget sector have not been so fortunate. Most of the films of Leslie Fuller, a knockabout comic who starred in nineteen productions in the first half of the 1930s, have been lost to neglect and fungus. Fuller's claim that the comedies he shot for BIP made a 300 per cent profit was a wild exaggeration – though the signatories of a subsequent contract believed it for a while.[17] Little remains of the work of Sydney Howard, a pudding-faced comic with the stately grace of a freshly decommissioned battleship and a style that depended upon the deadpan delivery of sexual innuendo. (In one of his surviving vehicles, *Splinters in the Navy* (1931), he plays Joe Crabbs, a sailor whose attempts to tell a concert-party gag are frustrated by the drumming of the band: all we hear is the punchline – 'and that's how the captain lost his telescope!') The surviving work of Ernest Lotinga – a jut-jawed, gap-toothed Tasmanian devil of seditious bad manners who got up the noses of judges, sergeant-majors and assorted toffs in a series of comedies for BIP – offers another taste of the vigorous, aggressively low-brow comedy favoured by the quickie producers. In *Josser in the Army* (1932), he is a factory foreman who steps into the breach when the best man goes missing at a genteel wedding. Before the reception is over he has gulped down the cake, shoved one guest into the pond and another through a cucumber frame, and chuntered through a dozen smutty quips. ('Can I have a look at the lady's trinkets?' asks the society reporter from the *Morning Star*. 'I don't know about that,' replies Lotinga. 'I'm only the best man.') Much of the humour is in this vein: films produced for domestic consumption had no need to worry about the terms of the Hays Code. In the mud of the Western Front, therefore, he reads a letter from home which could never have been broadcast in Hollywood: 'My sister had a lovely baby born yesterday . . . what a pity you can't come to the wedding.' In *Josser Joins the Navy* (1932) he is paired with Renée Gadd's Miss Beecham ('I've tried your powders!') in a plot about the recovery of a secret military formula. When I showed Renée Gadd a still from the picture, it stirred a long-forgotten feeling of contempt. 'Ernie Lotinga,' she mused. 'That ghastly, crude little man.'

The films of Arthur Lucan and Kitty McShane, two music-hall stars who transferred their talents to the screen at the end of the quota period and remained popular until the beginning of the 1950s, are better repre-sented, and offer the best illustration of the chaotic, anti-authoritarian flavour of low-budget 1930s comedy. Lucan's alter ego, Old Mother Riley, was a scrawny Irish washerwoman with a taste for uproar and violence. It was not quite a drag act: the bonnet and shawl signified femininity; the monstrously bony elbows, always kept bare, signified something else entirely. 'I'm a lady,' she shrieks, in the last of the series, *Mother Riley Meets the Vampire* (1952), 'and I defy you to prove it!'

A new Cinematograph Act was introduced in 1938, sharpening the origi-nal legislation with the addition of stipulations about minimum cost. The quota quickie was left wriggling on the spike. Production slumped so badly that in February 1938 voluntary organisations in Borehamwood opened a soup kitchen to feed the children of those who had lost their positions at Elstree.[18] British films would never again be made in such enormous volumes.

The few survivors of the quota quickie period wrinkle their noses at the memory of their involvement in these pictures. Ernest Dudley, contracted to Fox-British at Wembley in the mid-1930s, whoops with horror when he and I sit down to watch his pair of quickies, *Dial 999* (1938), a crime drama involving a diamond-smuggling cartel headed by a masked villain named 'the Badger', and *Concerning Mr Martin* (1937), the adventures of a gentleman crook and his wisecracking Chinese manservant. He recalls that the star of the latter, Wilson Barrett, the son of a celebrated Victorian actor, was foisted upon the picture by Ernest Gartside, the head of the company. 'We didn't want him for the part, you know,' he explains, as Barrett, his hairpiece visible under the unforgiving klieg lights, got to work on a night-club safe. 'It was supposed to be for somebody terribly virile, and look at him – he's about as virile as a rice pudding.'

Geoffrey Toone, a star of low-budget productions at Elstree, looked back on this period of his career with sceptical amusement. 'I was good looking,' he told me. 'That's all you had to be in those days.' (He was accustomed to being swooned over in certain London night-clubs, in which, 'sooner or later the ugliest boy in the place would come up to me and whisper, "You're the most beautiful man I've ever seen in my life".') He threw up his hands when he recalled his casting as a lorry driver in the quota quickie *Night Journey* (1938). He guffawed at the memory of the corny lines addressed to him at the climax of *Sword of Honour* (1939), in which he played a Sandhurst cadet who rides in the Grand National, despite suffering from a nasty case of equinophobia: 'You have won a much greater victory!' he declaimed, with preposterous exaggeration. 'Over your fear!'[19]

The most authoritative survivor of the period, however, took a very different view. Until his death in the summer of 2003, Sir Anthony Havelock-Allan was the most passionate defender of the quota quickie. His name is associated with prestige pictures of the 1940s – *Brief Encounter*, *In Which We Serve* (1942), *Great Expectations* (1946), *This Happy Breed* (1944) – but he spent the best part of the thirties as a producer of quota pictures. In 1933, he was headhunted from his job booking acts at Ciro's night-club to work in the casting office at the British and Dominion studios at Elstree. Death soon earned him a promotion: Robert Cullen, who was overseeing production of a slate of quickies under contract to the British arm of Paramount, was felled by a fatal coronary, and Havelock-Allan took his place. Under the slogan 'I only want you to be happy with the best of absolutely everything at the lowest possible cost,' he gathered a team of collaborators who were capable of turning out films on a ten-day schedule. Many of these names have been forgotten: Gerald Elliot, the defrocked clergyman who scripted *Blondes for Danger*; Donovan Pedelty, the Irish film journalist who had been PR man to Maria Corda, Alexander Korda's vengeful former wife. Others are remembered with more clarity. Robert Morley and Terence Rattigan worked on the script of *The Belles of St Clements* (1936). Vivien Leigh was given her first film role in *The Village Squire* (1935), though she denied it to her death. David Lean attacked the raw footage in the cutting rooms. Havelock-Allan never paid more than £150 to a screenwriter or £250 to a star. But his generation of film-makers, he maintained, would never have learned their craft without the training ground of low-budget studio production. Without the quota quickies, he argued, there would have been no *Brief Encounter*, no *In Which We Serve*, no *Great Expectations*, no *This Happy Breed*.

A few weeks before he died, I wrote to him to ask if I might visit him to discuss his first ten years in film production. He reminded me that he was ninety-eight, losing his sight, and keen that death should not prevent him from finishing his memoirs. He did, however, agree to answer a few queries over the telephone, on condition that I faxed them to him in a suitably enormous font. My first question was an obvious one: 'Did the 1927 Act do more harm than good to the British film business?'

'No,' came the reply. 'No, no, no, no.'

CHAPTER FIVE

Our Father, which Art in Ealing

Victoria Hopper, who owed her brief period of stardom to the tragic death
of her husband's lover

In a revue sketch popular in London just after the Second World War, two fading starlets drift through a dreary lunch at the Ivy. They pick at their food in silence until someone passes their table, whereupon they look up, and break into desperate smiles. 'Hello, Ivor! Still working?' they trill. He fails to reply. They deflate. Another long silence. One of the pair issues a long, languorous sigh. 'I wonder', she ventures, 'what became of Victoria Hopper?'

Even in 1945, it was a good question. Most film histories are vague on the question of whether Victoria Hopper is alive or dead – not surprising, perhaps, since her film career came to an abrupt conclusion in 1938. When I visit her, she is living alone in a remote cottage on Romney Marsh, and professes not to have been interviewed since the 1930s. She gives me a tour of her home, showing me the baby grand piano, the pottery that she brought back from Salzburg when she made the Mozart picture, and the window that the burglars jemmied open. As we speak, her pet sheep, an aged and bedraggled creature, razors the back lawn with quiet diligence, her cats pursue ping-pong balls across the tiled floor, and Victoria herself, a tiny figure with a tiny voice, reclines on a wicker daybed in the conservatory, nibbles chocolate biscuits, and expresses a mournful bewilderment at the brevity of her time in front of the cameras. 'I loved it,' she confesses. 'I'm sorry nobody knows me now.' She adored, she says, the trappings of the film star's life; delighted in the knowledge that she and her friends Peggy Blythe and Renee Clama were known in the Berkeley Grill as 'the three blondes'; and enjoyed her fame and status. She does not seem to mind that her husband, Basil Dean, the man who plucked her from drama school and turned her into a star, did so for a strange and morbid reason: in Dean, Hopper stirred memories of a talented actress for whose premature death he was held responsible. 'I used to go to the Ivy such a lot,' she says, plaintively, 'and do you know, if I rang them today, I wouldn't have a chance. They wouldn't have a clue now.'[1]

The last portrait of Meggie Albanesi, taken days before her death

Hopper was born in Vancouver in 1909, and schooled in Trail, a small town in the Canadian Rockies. The family moved to England when she was fourteen, with the intention of taking over her grandfather's ailing business in Newcastle. She regards the emigration as a mistake, not least because her younger brother died shortly after they arrived in Britain. 'He was given a fairy cycle,' she recalled, 'and he went to school one day and I don't know how it happened, but he wasn't picked up, and he was knocked down and killed by a lorry.' While at school, she skipped a drawing class and went to a cinema in Gateshead to see Ivor Novello in *The Constant Nymph*. It made a strong impression upon her: she and her school friend acted out scenes from the film, fantasised themselves as lovesick as Tessa Sanger, and wrote a feverish fan letter to Mabel Poulton. Hopper had intended to pursue a career in music, but in her final year at Webber-Douglas, her glossy fair hair won her the lead role in the college production of Jean-Jacques Bernard's *Martine*. The play was granted a West End run at the Ambassador's Theatre; one night, Ivor Novello was in the audience. When Basil Dean took him to lunch at the Ivy a few days later, hoping to persuade the actor to reprise the role of Lewis Dodd in a talkie remake of the *Nymph*, Novello sweetened his inevitable refusal with a tip: over the street at the Ambassador's was a young actress who would make a perfect Tessa. She was, said Novello, just like Meggie Albanesi.

Victoria Hopper knows the story, and knows she owes her first marriage and her career to it. Her biography has a strong flavour of *Trilby*; the Albanesi connection gives it a touch of *Vertigo*. Meggie Albanesi died in 1923, but exerted a posthumous influence upon the remainder of Basil Dean's personal and professional life. Dean commissioned Eric Gill to sculpt her memorial tablet. He kept a framed photograph of her in his study. He retained all the correspondence relating to her short life. He named his pet Alsatian – an unpredictable creature which once attacked the Bishop of Khartoum and ripped the seat from his trousers – after her. He mulled over her memory in his two-volume autobiography – a work that gives considerably less space to the three women to whom he was married. He spent much of his career in search of an actress who could take her place in his life and in his estimation, and exchanged wedding vows with the most promising candidate.

Hopper considers his fantasies to be misplaced. 'I was nothing like

Meggie Albanesi,' she protests. 'Basil and the coterie around him thought that she was a wonderful actress. I've read all I can about her because her reputation was so extraordinary.' The impulse is understandable. Hopper's career is the product of Albanesi's early death. To understand the rise and fall of Victoria Hopper, it is necessary to know the fate of the woman in whose image Dean attempted to mould her.

Meggie Albanesi could shed tears easily. Directors loved her for it. It wasn't, apparently, a trick of technique. Indeed, she was celebrated for her very lack of artifice, praised for her nervy sincerity, her low, tremulous voice, her expressive black eyes. It was said that she underwent an uncanny absorption in her roles; that her performances collapsed the distinction between the player and the part; that she broke down, exhausted, after every curtain call, and required an hour's recuperation before she felt able to emerge from her dressing room. Directors usually cast her as breakable, fingermarked waifs: a country girl seduced by a thoughtless town boy; a Chinese aristocrat carrying the child of an English visitor; a Polish refugee, suicidal after a traumatic miscarriage. 'She had a various and unique faculty of emotional truth,' wrote John Galsworthy, in the foreword to her biography. 'I never saw her fumble, blur or falsify an emotional effect. She struck instantaneously, and as if from her heart, the right note of feeling . . . Not often does Death so wastefully spill.'[2]

Her family occupied that stretch of social territory shared by the privileged and the gifted, the patrons and the patronised. Her mother, Effie Maria, was an author of middlebrow romantic fiction, now forgotten; her father, Carlo, was a violin instructor at the Royal Academy of Music. Before her teens she was paraded in her silks and bows before the plutocrats and minor poets who cluttered the Albanesi drawing room; before she was twenty she did the same at Sir Herbert Beerbohm Tree's Academy of Dramatic Art. For the former she was awarded peppermints; for the latter, the Bancroft Medal. By 1919, she had excited the admiration of Basil Dean, who quickly absorbed her into his repertory company. 'With each successive production,' he recalled, 'sympathy and understanding grew between us, until at last people behind the scenes used jokingly to talk of Trilby and Svengali.'[3]

Albanesi's first film appearance was the serendipitous product of a fellow actor's poor time-keeping. Taking a tour of Twickenham Studios, she found George Pearson bereft of a French waitress for a scene in *The Better 'Ole* (1918), and slipped on the apron.[4] As her stage reputation grew, production companies began to petition Dean for her release into daytime movie work. For *Mr Wu* (1919), Maurice Elvey cast her as Nang Ping, a mandarin's daughter who is ritually murdered by her father when he discovers that she is expecting the child of her English lover. (Matheson Lang played the Oriental patriarch and Albanesi became infatuated with him, despite his having partially shaved his head for the part.)

The following year she shot the film version of a stage success, Galsworthy's *The Skin Game*, for B. E. Doxatt-Pratt. In Hugh Ford's *The Great Day* (1920) – a Famous Players–Lasky picture on which Alfred Hitchcock received his first credit – she was cast as a vamp, and shimmied about the set with a Pekinese under her arm. In 1922, a Lasky director invited her back to Poole Street to cry for him on camera, but the money shot eluded her. 'She went through a veritable agony,' recalled her mother, 'for not one single tear would come! Over and over again she had to go forward for the "close up", only to be dismissed once more.' The director lost his temper: 'I only engaged you because you could shed real tears on stage, and now you can't shed a tear! You are no use to me!' It was an established trick of the silent cinema: yell at the girl until she wails, can it and print it. 'Strained to a nervous degree beyond description, the child began to cry, and she cried, and she cried, and she cried, and they could not stop her!'[5]

Her mother worried that Meggie was smoking too much, eating and sleeping too little, and reading too many pornographic books. She acquired a reputation for drug use, but this was hardly an uncommon vice, when half of theatrical London spent its weekends at Jack May's club under Maidenhead Bridge, snorting cocaine off the glass dance floor. It was her promiscuity that really set tongues wagging; her disinclination to use contraception; her consequent visits to the abortionist. Dean was fascinated by her appetite for pleasure and jealous of her lovers – who were jockeys, comedians, stage-hands. In the summer of 1923, however, he and Albanesi began a sexual relationship. Sharing a taxi from the Carlton Grill, the pair threw themselves upon each other so violently that they drew a complaint from the driver. 'Meggie was not offering herself for love,' wrote Dean, recalling these events forty-five years later, 'but out of the passion for artistic achievement that we shared; perhaps, also, because of a deeply felt need for her own sexual regulation.'[6]

That winter, those around Albanesi began to notice her increased pallor and listlessness. On 1 December, the actor Henry Kendall met her in the dining car of the midnight train to Birchington, and failed to cheer her up with his favourite theatrical anecdote – which involved Dean, Somerset Maugham, George Grossmith, and the punchline, 'I see Basil is burning the Kendall at both ends.'[7] A few days later, lunching at the Ivy with his set designer, Dean noticed Albanesi at another table, eating little, saying nothing, and looking decidedly sick. He instructed her to take a few days off, to go to bed and rest. She obeyed his orders, and booked herself into one of her customary bolt-holes, the Kingsgate Castle Hotel in Broadstairs. On the train down from Charing Cross, however, she suffered a severe internal haemorrhage. A fellow passenger found her slumped across a table in the Pullman car, groaning in pain, and took charge of her. A makeshift bed was set up and a hot-water bottle procured. On arrival in Broadstairs, a local doctor named Brightman transferred her to the South Court nursing home. It soon became clear that Albanesi's condition was more serious than Brightman's initial diagnosis of 'gastric chill'. Dean was telephoned with the news. A surgeon and the patient's mother were summoned from London, arriving on the same Saturday morning train. An exploratory laparotomy was performed: inside Meggie Albanesi's abdomen was a mess of abscesses. Further treatment was deemed pointless, the surgeon returned his patient to the care of Dr Brightman, and Effie Maria Albanesi instructed her husband to come to Broadstairs by the morning express. He arrived at 12.20; by 12.45 his daughter was dead. 'Intestinal perforation' was the vague term favoured by the official family memoir. The death certificate is similarly euphemistic. Dean and his circle, however, knew the truth of the matter: Meggie Albanesi had undergone one abortion too many. 'She had virtually no inside left,' the surgeon told Dean.

Effie Albanesi held Dean responsible for driving her daughter to the point of collapse, and said so in one of a series of articles in *Nash's Magazine*. Dean wrote to her and protested his innocence. He had never 'over-rehearsed her merely for the artistic pleasure I received in witnessing her perfections as an artist'. On the contrary, he argued, he had attempted to save her from her own excesses.[8] Little wonder that *The Constant Nymph* touched such a chord in Dean. For him, it seems, Tessa Sanger and Meggie Albanesi underwent a kind of elision: the frail and helpless girl who dies in the arms of her married lover – who also happens to be an artistic genius. It must have been irresistible.

Dean's film career is one of the most underestimated of the period, though he is one of its most significant figures. He emerged stung and humiliated from his decade as a movie mogul, having lost many of his friends and several hundred thousand pounds of other people's money. Between 1928 and 1938, however, Dean's contribution to the business of film-making was considerable. He founded his own movie company, brokered a generous co-production deal with a large American studio, and, on Ealing Green, established the world's first purpose-built complex of sound stages. He attempted to shape British talkies in the image of British theatre by taking its scripts and stars, then relocating them from the stage to dramatic outdoor locations. The notion might now seem wrong-headed, but it was a legitimate response to the coming of sound. West End actors already had voices that matched their faces; literary sources came with marketable names attached; audiences disliked airless studios as much as Dean disliked labouring in them. Hollywood involvement would ensure that the films received distribution in American markets – essential since the end of silent production had intensified competition for the attention of Anglophone audiences.

It was John Galsworthy who secured Dean his first megaphone and folding canvas chair. In September 1928, Walter Wanger, head of Paramount Studios on Long Island, offered Galsworthy $20,000 for the rights to make a talkie of his convict drama *Escape*. Galsworthy accepted, on condition that Dean was allowed to direct. Wanger concurred, on condition that Galsworthy let him put a girl in the picture. Then, quite unexpectedly, Dean received a call from a consortium of City speculators, who offered their services in the flotation of a new talking-picture company. The two deals proceeded simultaneously – Dean signed for a picture with Paramount, announced the formation of Associated Talking Pictures, and sailed on the *Olympic* for New York.

When he arrived on Long Island, however, he discovered that Wanger had cancelled production of *Escape* and reassigned him to a studio-bound Sherlock Holmes picture. Dean swallowed his pride, took the job, and used his time in New York to negotiate another deal with a shiny new outfit called Radio-Keith-Orpheum. When he returned to London, he was able to call an extraordinary general meeting of ATP shareholders and take the stage of the Vaudeville Theatre waving a piece of paper in his hand: a letter from the President of RKO, with whom ATP was going to build a new, prestigious, literary form of British cinema. Somerset Maugham declared: 'It would be grand if the pictures ceased to be an outrage to the intelligence of an educated person.'[9] Even Adrian Brunel, unemployed after an unsuccessful attempt to sue Michael Balcon, was ready to plead for a job with the Basilisk.[10] Shaftesbury Avenue was poised to colonise Wardour Street, and for this it needed a new base of operations.

There had been a film studio at Ealing since 1902, when Will Barker, a cinema pioneer who had made his name shooting Queen Victoria's diamond jubilee, decided that his film-making facilities at Stamford Bridge were no longer adequate for his needs, and migrated west. He bought two properties and a patch of land upon which, by 1907, he had built three glass-roofed film studios. Here, in 1912, Barker shot the first screen *Hamlet* (1913); Sir Herbert Beerbohm Tree played Cardinal Wolsey in *Henry VIII* (1911) and took home £1,000 a day for his trouble; thousands of extras dragged up in medieval dress for *Jane Shore* (1915); and in the 1920s, when Barker's fortunes dwindled, small independent companies rented the space to make shorts.

Dean and his financial chief Reginald Baker planned to build stages and workshops on the same site, and transform a large Regency villa facing the Green into the front office. As Dean had heard that the colour red made people feel cheerful, he decided that the doors, chairs and tables would all be painted crimson. The funding was provided by a cat's cradle of loans and insurance policies, and new investment from Stephen Courtauld, a member of a family of millionaire textile manufacturers, who, keen to dabble in the glamorous world of motion pictures, joined the board of ATP in 1931. Courtauld was a taciturn, serious-minded patron of the arts; he would save Dean from bankruptcy on several occasions, but eventually became the agent of his expulsion from the company.

ATP's relationship with RKO soured in its first year. Dean shot his cherished Galsworthy project, *Escape* (1930), under the terms of his agreement with the company. Days before the agreed US release date, however, RKO pulled the picture from 700 cinemas – in order, it claimed, to purge the soundtrack of English expressions considered incomprehensible to American ears. *Escape* was given a limited release, and made no impact. Unfortunately, it fared little better in its native land. Sound had increased class-consciousness in the cinema, and the vowels of the West End worthies who led the cast of *Escape* seemed preposterous to those who were not taking private lessons in how to emulate them. The film failed to recover its costs; RKO renegotiated its deal with ATP on considerably less favourable terms for the latter.

Some of ATP's setbacks were beyond Basil Dean's control. It would be difficult to blame him for the Gaumont cinema chain's decision to premiere the musical comedy *Looking on the Bright Side* (1932) at the Capitol, a primarily Jewish picture house, during Yom Kippur. It also wasn't his fault that, on the set of the thriller *Love on the Spot* (1932), a cast member lost a pair of false teeth in the swimming pool built for the picture: the water was coloured, and hours were squandered while technical staff swam around looking for the dentures. However, other difficulties were entirely his responsibility. Dean was an autocratic manager of people: he had a talent for wounding sarcasm, and a reputation for reducing his employees to tears. His son Winton recalls an altercation between his father and Carol Reed, who was employed at Ealing in the mid-1930s as an assistant director. 'He gave him a tremendous bollocking, over something extremely trivial. He was so upset that he had to leave the room. Basil could be very aggressive about rather unimportant things.'[11] More significantly for the health of the company, Dean's refusal to scale down his theatrical commitments allowed problems at the studio to multiply unchecked, and delays of days to grow into weeks. He was not above using Ealing's resources for private ends, chivvying the staff carpenters into supplying scenery for his plays. Associated Talking Pictures had a jolly slogan on its headed notepaper: 'Get Together and Save Time: Co-operation Means Better Pictures!' Dean, however, found his own advice difficult to follow, and the studio lurched from crisis to crisis. Then, a crashingly tactless telegram from the Vice-President of RKO let slip the company's true attitude to ATP: 'Our function in Great Britain is to distribute the quota pictures which you make for us.' RKO, it seemed, had no intention of giving ATP access to American markets: it was using Dean to make glorified quota films for them, on which their own imported product could ride into British cinemas. In September 1932, the two companies instituted divorce proceedings.

Some much-needed income was secured by renting out the studios to Gloria Swanson, who brought her circus to Ealing Green in the summer of 1932 for a vanity project entitled *Perfect Understanding*. The principal members of the troupe were her new baby, Michelle; her young husband, Michael Farmer (so jealous that he carried a revolver to dispose of possible rivals); Laurence Olivier, a firm-jawed, long-lashed British actor making his film debut; and an inexperienced American director named Cyril Gardner, who spent the shoot in a state of nervous anxiety because a fortune-teller had warned him that his parents were about to die, and that he would perish on the voyage home. Swanson gambled her stock in United Artists on the venture and increased the potential risk by casting Farmer, an Irish socialite who had never acted before, as one of the leads. The latter problem proved remediable: the film's editor, Thorold Dickinson, pared back Farmer's screen-time and, according to Dickinson's assistant Sid Cole, reconstructed the boat-race climax of the movie to allow Olivier to be first past the flag. Other handicaps proved more difficult to surmount: flu claimed half the cast; Olivier was involved in a car crash; a fire at the lab destroyed a portion of the negative; and news arrived from America that Cyril Gardner's parents had indeed died. To complete the picture, Swanson was forced to sell her interest in United Artists: the commercial failure of *Perfect Understanding* meant that she was unable to buy any of it back.[12]

It was during the production hiatus at Ealing that Dean accepted the offer from Gainsborough to direct a talkie version of *The Constant Nymph*. Unable to persuade Ivor Novello to repeat the role, he awarded the part of Lewis Dodd to the 'despairing final choice' of Brian Aherne.[13] However, taking up Novello's advice to visit the Ambassador's, he instantly realised he had found the perfect Tessa Sanger, his new Meggie Albanesi, and his new wife.

The Constant Nymph (1933): Brian Aherne and Victoria Hopper as Lewis Dodd
and Tessa Sanger, the Humbert and Lolita of the Austrian Tyrol

In her Romney Marsh retirement seventy years later, Victoria Hopper recalls the progress of their courtship. 'I was intrigued by him,' she says. 'I was a good twenty years younger than Basil, and he'd been taking me out to the opera and the ballet, and he was a very charming man, despite what people have said about him. He was much more sophisticated than the men I'd been used to, and, yes, I did fall in love with him.'

Having secured Hopper's services, Dean took a Gaumont-British crew back to the locations in which the silent *Nymph* had been filmed. He was more confident this time, taking problems in his stride. He shrugged when he was unable to convince the mother of Peggy Blythe, the actress playing Tessa's sister, that her daughter's bathing scene with Victoria Hopper should be conducted in the nude. When extras in a scene set at a Tyrolean country fair could not be discouraged from staring into the camera, he loosened them up with beer. He did not mind that his new star was nervous about her lack of experience, as this was partly what had drawn him to her: he admired her delicacy, her greenness, the softness of her voice. The film is full of adoring close-ups of Hopper, lying among banks of Alpine flowers, the sunlight catching her blonde hair as she whispers phrases such as 'growing up isn't very nice' into the mountain air. Dean shoots her scowling, or skipping upstairs with Brian Aherne, or lying on her belly in the meadow grass. He seems fascinated by her fragility: she clutches her heart and gazes imploringly into the camera when she hears that Lewis Dodd is to marry her aunt Florence; her death-mask fills the screen as she lies lifeless in Dodd's hotel room during the final frames. All of Dean's films with Hopper would contain shots of her asleep, unconscious or dead, the twin curves of her huge eyelids bisecting her face.

As Dean and Hopper dallied in the Alps, Reginald Baker was working to resuscitate the fortunes of ATP. He persuaded Major Jack Courtauld, a gregarious MP more at home on the turf than at the cinema, to join the board of Associated British Film Distributors, a new company formed to take over the role that RKO had relinquished. He tickled more money from Stephen Courtauld; quite a feat, as he and his wife Virginia were busy transforming the ramshackle remains of a medieval manor in south-east London into a grand art deco retreat.[14]

Others were also working on Dean's behalf. The young director Carol Reed was despatched to another Tyrolean location to take atmosphere

shots and stills for a new ATP production made possible by the Courtaulds' investment: Dodie Smith's *Autumn Crocus* (1934), the story of a
virginal thirty-five-year-old schoolteacher who falls in love with the married owner of a Medratz *gasthaus*. Doubles of the film's stars, Fay Compton and Ivor Novello, roamed the valleys under Reed's supervision, but as
soon as Dean was finished with the Gaumont *Nymph*, his diligent assistant was relieved of his duties. Under Dean's supervision, the ATP construction team worked through the night to plant 10,000 paper crocuses
in an artificial Alpine hillside, and Compton and Novello did their best to
trip delightedly through a back-projected Tyrolean dance festival.

Dean was a great advocate of using real locations, but *Autumn Crocus*
was not ruined by the decision to abandon them. It is a well-observed
social comedy that treats Dean's most urgent theme – the inadequacy of
bourgeois marriage – with wit and honesty. While Hollywood was in
retreat from grown-up or socially radical ideas, Dean was rushing forward
to meet them. The film's central debate is this: should the lovesick spinster,
Jenny Gray, initiate a semi-secret sexual relationship with her holiday host,
Andreas Steiner? Novello makes his offer with blithe cheerfulness and a
cute Teutonic accent. 'My wife,' he purrs, 'need she ever know?' (Austria
during this period, it seems, was considered a haven of free love by middle-
class Britons.) Unwilling to risk pregnancy, Gray returns to her post in
Manchester – where Dean has decided that it always rains – and contents
herself with giving yodelling lessons to her infants' class. She does not con-
cede that Steiner's offer is immoral, only that her English peers would consider it to be so. ('You've spoiled everything,' she tells her fusty travelling
companion, whose unsolicited advice has 'made it all ugly and sordid'.)
The secondary characters are engaged in the same debate: Audrey and
Alaric (Diana Beaumont and Jack Hawkins) are 'two conscientious young
people living in freedom for scientific reasons'. Alaric tells a fellow guest, a
wide-eyed vicar played by George Zucco, that he is the author of a book
entitled *A Remedy for Sex*. 'Isn't that a little drastic?' asks Zucco.

Autumn Crocus was completed quickly in order to capitalise on the
availability of its two stars, but the short schedule also allowed Dean to
boomerang back into the theatre for a Christmas production at Sadler's
Wells – a revival of Engelbert Humperdinck's *Hansel and Gretel*. In a fore-
shadowing of the plot of *Citizen Kane*, Dean put his wife in the opera,

despite her inadequacies. Basil's son, Winton, who would grow up to be an eminent Handel scholar, was not impressed by Hopper's vocal talents. 'She had a very thin soprano voice, and sang quite out of tune,' he recalls. 'But I don't think Basil would have even noticed that.'

Hopper, however, was not the passive figure that these events – and her film performances – might suggest. In August 1934, acting on the advice of her agent Sydney Carroll, she broke off her engagement with Dean, took a part in *Three Sisters*, the new Jerome Kern–Oscar Hammerstein musical at the Drury Lane Theatre, and moved into the Courtaulds' house in Grosvenor Square. Dean begged his friend and collaborator Dodie Smith to help persuade Hopper to return to him. They pushed their way past the doorkeeper at Drury Lane and appeared at Hopper's dressing room. Dean was distraught: Smith remembers seeing him crawling in supplication at Hopper's feet. 'Even my second wife', he sobbed, 'would get upset if she saw me in this state.' Smith was shocked by Hopper's behaviour – particularly as Dean had just procured his fiancée a lucrative film contract with ATP. 'Vickie merely put some more powder on her rigid little face and went back to play another scene,' she recalled. 'She behaved throughout with a courtesy and poise that were quite astounding in so young a woman.' As Dean hid from the gossip columnists in his office, sustained only by the take-out menu of the Ivy, Smith held a conference with Hopper in the former's top-floor flat in Dorset Square. 'All I managed to gather from her was that she did care for Basil, but had been persuaded that marrying him would damage her career.'[15] On the following Saturday, however, Smith received a phone call from Dean, inviting her to a post-nuptial party at the Courtaulds' house in Grosvenor Square. Victoria Hopper had married him that morning at the register office in Great Dunmow, with Peggy Blythe and Virginia Courtauld as witnesses. Dean's sons, Winton and Joe, learned of their father's third wedding in the morning newspapers.

Lying on her day bed, aged ninety-three, her Twix bar melting against the heat of her teacup, it's hard to imagine Victoria Hopper as the glassily ambitious toughnut described by Smith. When she relates events from her life, she constructs herself as a meek, acquiescent figure. She tells me how, after her divorce from Dean, her acting career slipped from her grasp; how a neighbour, John Trevelyan, then Secretary of the British

Board of Film Classification, had used his influence to secure her a job as an elocution teacher at Ashford Technical College; how she did a little work in schools until her second husband pressured her to give it up, on the pretext that she was catching too many coughs and colds from her pupils. Would she have spoken in the same fashion, I wonder, if I had interviewed her in 1934?

It's not hard to guess what promises Dean might have made to persuade his fiancée that marrying him would do her career no harm. 'After her considerable success in *The Constant Nymph*,' he wrote, 'and an appealing performance as Gretel, it was understandable that Vickie should long for further opportunities. As her husband I naturally wanted to make them for her. This was a mistake.'[16]

The first, but not the biggest, mistake was *Lorna Doone*. Against the wishes of Stephen and Jack Courtauld, the film went into production in the summer of 1934 without the necessary funding in place. Almost

Victoria Hopper, John Loder and Peggy Blythe on location
for *Lorna Doone* (1935)

immediately, ATP suffered one of its periodical brushes with financial collapse. The bank demanded repayment on its loans and Reginald Baker was forced to scurry about finding money to meet its request and to keep the cameras rolling. He and Dean agreed to conceal their anxieties from their backers: 'I shall have my headache entirely to myself,' grumbled Baker.[17] Dean, writing from a plush hotel in Lynton, where he and his crew were spending money that ATP did not possess, was blasé about these problems, exclaiming:

For heaven's sake, don't go into a flat spin every time I leave the studio and go on to location! It adds to my worries. I'm well aware of the general situation – indeed it was I who kept on warning you of what was going to happen. So you can't claim originality this time, you blighter. We've just got to push and scramble and bounce our way through the present situation. It is a better policy than the 'go-slow' of last year, from the ill effects of which we have not recovered. In our business we have to spend money to get money. And if I can get more money on to the screen, foot for foot, than other companies I feel justified and completely confident of the eventual outcome.

At which point, presumably, he ordered another pink gin from the bar and watched the sun set over Exmoor, refusing to acknowledge that the Courtaulds considered *Lorna Doone* to be another lavish waste of their money. 'I don't want it supposed that, in making "Lorna Doone" the company is conferring a favour upon me,' Dean declared. 'It is doing something in its own interests.'

When Dean and his seventy-strong crew had returned to Ealing, the ATP construction department assembled a Devonshire village in a meadow on the outskirts of Perivale, a west London suburb now sheathed in tarmac and semi-detached houses. It took ten days to create and two expensive all-night shoots to sack and incinerate, under the eyes of the local police and an increasingly depressed Stephen Courtauld. Shooting had dragged on from August to the end of November, and the village alone had cost £2,000 to build.

Courtauld became more despondent when the finished picture premiered at a charity gala at the Prince Edward Theatre in Soho. The script's archaisms, which seemed particularly odd in the mouths of those members of the cast who opted not to attempt the North Devon dialect, annoyed the audience. ('He be outside,' says Peggy Blythe's maidservant

Gwenny, in a voice somewhere between Totnes and the Berkeley Grill, 'guarding they ricks.') Dean's habit of using intertitles also inspired scep- tical sniggers – particularly one that described the chill winter of 1625 as 'The Great Cold'. The constant repetition of 'Lorna's Theme', however – a mournful little aria composed by Rutland Boughton, sung four times in the film by Hopper – produced the most cruel laughter, particularly when it made its final reappearance at the climax of the film, just after the hero- ine has been felled by the villain's bullet. 'Never', wrote Dean, 'shall I for- get my agonising sense of failure after the performance.'[18] When the film was put on general release, the final burst of 'Lorna's Theme' was excised from the soundtrack.

The film is no disaster, but its visual plenitude provides no compensa- tion for its narrative incoherence. The location work is impressive: dra- matic scenes transform Exmoor into an Arizona of hard crags and rocky promontories; pastoral scenes of haymaking and harvest festivals suggest that somebody in the crew might have found his way to a screening of Dovzhenko's *Earth* (1930). The final confrontation between the hero Jan Ridd (John Loder) and his nemesis Carver Doone (Roy Emerton) is shot from a very low angle, framing the actors against a vast canvas of grey sky, and lending them a gargantuan quality. (The performances here adhere closely to the practices of silent cinema: when Emerton sinks to his death in a moorland quagmire, Loder throws an arm across his eyes in a grand gesture of horror and pity.) The studio material, however, despite Dean's frequent use of energetic whip pans and stately travelling shots, is merely decorative. He crams the screen with artificial trees, light-relief yeomen in Puritan wigs and corn-decked extras swinging pewter tankards, giving the picture the same twee artificiality found in the comic operettas in which Laurel and Hardy were sometimes cast.

The critical and commercial failure of the picture stood in sharp con- trast to the enormous success of two stars whom Dean had signed to ATP in a spirit of financial pragmatism. Dean's personal projects lost money. Gracie Fields and George Formby, on the other hand, became the biggest box-office draws of the decade. They were not West End, not literary, and not suitable co-stars for Dean's wife, but without them Ealing Studios would have been bankrupted.

*

With her shrill, eardrum-bursting coloratura, unblinking cheerfulness and predilection for whoop-de-do slapstick, Gracie Fields was exactly the kind of screen personality that disinclined Somerset Maugham to spend his evenings in the dark with a carton of Kia-Ora. She was born Grace Stansfield over a Rochdale fish-and-chip shop in 1898, and never let any-body forget it. Dean was baffled by her popularity – in a confidential memo, he referred to her 'almost freakish drawing-power' – but knew that his movie career would not have lasted long without it.[19] At least the feeling was mutual. 'You can get good fish and chips at the Savoy,' Fields reflected in 1960, 'and you can put up with the fancy people once you understand that you don't have to be like them.'[20]

Dean had seen Fields on the stage of the St James's Theatre in 1928, act-ing opposite Gerald du Maurier in his play SOS. But it was Fields's hus-band–manager, Archie Pitt – a Cockney music-hall turn whose lack of comic talent was made irrelevant by his unerring entrepreneurial instincts – who first suggested to Dean that the Lancashire comedienne should be in pictures.

The story of Hopper and Dean has a shadow in the story of Fields and Pitt. The latter figures as a brutal, domineering presence in Fields's mem-oir, Sing as We Go (1960), and throughout her life she never lost an oppor-tunity to describe how aggressively she was dominated, and how much she had in common with the heroine of Trilby. Pitt, she wrote, 'was not Svengali, but he was a passable imitation'.[21] The truth seems to have been rather more prosaic, and Dean's view that Fields's husband was 'a sad, cautious little man with a commonplace mind' was probably nearer the mark.[22] The Pitts were a professional couple in a relationship of conve-nience. They had begun their association when Fields was in her teens, and married in 1923, after nearly a decade of touring the halls in musical revue. She was twenty-four and he was forty-three: they were not, and had never been, in love, and therefore felt unconstrained by their wed-ding vows. Pitt conducted a long-term affair with his personal assistant, Annie Lipman, who had her own bedroom at the couple's hideous Hampstead mansion. Fields, meanwhile, pursued her own extra-marital activities. In March 1928, her sister Betty introduced her to a soft-spoken Irish painter named John Flanagan. After a row with Archie in which her mink coat was hurled into the mud of Hampstead Heath, she moved into

Flanagan's studio in St John's Wood and filled it with expensive vulgarities. The Pitts gave up pretending to like each other shortly afterwards, but their professional relationship endured until 1933; their legal attachment until 1939.

Dean respected a music-hall success as much as a West End one; Fields mistrusted the cinema. Used to the immediacy of stage work, she was frustrated by the slow pace and the delays customary on film sets, mainly because it put her in the intolerable position of having to wait around for other people. Worse still, she was forced to shave her upper lip before her first appearance on camera. But, despite her squeamishness and dissatisfaction, cinema built Gracie Fields into a national icon. By the end of the thirties, she had been transformed from a popular stage act to a kind of clog-shod Britannia: a symbol of native optimism and self-reliance. She was loud, brassy, immodest and looked like a rugby forward in a dress, but no other performer commanded such loyalty from her audience. A generation of filmgoers knew her as 'Our Gracie', and, to Dean's growing pleasure, she was, contractually, his. When her first picture, *Sally in Our Alley*, opened in 1931, it took £100,000 at the box office.[23]

'We have always regarded Miss Fields's pictures', confessed Dean, 'as a matter of successful commerce and not of art.'[24] The company churned out as many films as her contract would allow, knowing that they would not enjoy her services for ever. Her final contract with ATP gave her £22,000 per picture. It was a price worth paying for the most bankable star in Britain, even if she became embarrassingly over-fond of quoting the calculation that the deal would bring her two pounds per working minute. Ironically, the best of her films kept her character close to the working-class background that Fields had long ago exchanged for affluence. J. B. Priestley scripted *Sing as We Go* (1934) and *Look up and Laugh* (1935), the two films that are the most intelligent responses made by British cinema to the economic depression of the 1930s. Fields's final pictures for ATP, *Queen of Hearts* (1936) and *The Show Goes On* (1937), were both backstage musicals which placed less emphasis on social commentary and shifted her status from a figure of working-class hope to lower-middle-class aspiration. *Queen of Hearts* was directed by a future Mr Fields, Monty Banks, a former Orient Express steward who had migrated from Italy to America in his teens, where he became one of the original

Keystone Kops. It was Banks who facilitated Fields's next step upwards: the pair spent Christmas 1937 in Hollywood with Darryl F. Zanuck, the head of Twentieth Century Fox. Zanuck offered her £200,000 for four films: the first, appropriately, was entitled *We're Going to Be Rich* (1938). Dean, however, was prepared for the defection, and had already taken out an insurance policy, in the person of George Formby.

Michael Balcon thought George Formby 'an odd and not particularly lovable character'.[25] Some of the women who were contractually obliged to stare adoringly at the comedian as he plucked his ukulele were less complimentary. Formby's father, also called George, was a music-hall entertainer celebrated for his feckless character John Willie and his catchphrase, 'coughing better tonight?', which disguised the tuberculosis that eventually killed him. George Snr had grown up in desperate poverty – his mother was a prostitute who clocked up 142 convictions for drunkenness – and knew enough about life in the halls to feel obliged to do all he could to insulate his son against its charms. George never saw his father's act, and, at the age of seven, was sent away to Dublin to train as a jockey. George Snr lifted his ban on George performing only once – in 1915, when he allowed Will Barker to pay his son the sum of one pound to appear in *By the Shortest of Heads* (1915), a five-reel racecourse picture starring Moore Marriot. After his father's death in 1921, George noticed that other comedians were billing themselves as 'the new George Formby'. With the help of his mother, Eliza Booth, he reconstructed his father's turn, and began to secure bookings on the circuit. The act was only moderately successful until he met and married Beryl Ingram, one half of a clog-dancing act called the Two Violets. At first, she resisted his advances, but acquiesced after he proposed to her by standing under her window and serenading her on the ukulele. It was an eccentric beginning to one of the most peculiar and profitable marriages in showbusiness.

Noting the success of Gracie Fields, Beryl Formby rang Dean to pitch him the idea of a similar comedy vehicle for her husband; Dean was dismissive. However, the Formbys then received an offer from John Blakeley of the Mancunian Film Corporation, a Manchester-based company that produced improbably cheap films using talent from the music-hall circuit, for distribution in the towns where their acts were popular. *Boots!*

Boots! (1934) was a poverty-row flick featuring Formby as a combative and conniving hotel attendant. It recycled more of George Snr's material, cost just £3,000, and was shot in fifteen days in a disused warehouse above the Albany garage on Regent Street. A teenage dancer named Betty Driver – who would later spend several decades on *Coronation Street*, preparing hotpot for the regulars of the Rovers Return – was also booked for the picture, and became the first casualty of Beryl Formby's jealousy. Her rapport with George was too convincing for Beryl's taste: she pressured Blakeley to cut Driver's scenes from the picture.[26] Not that *Boots! Boots!* was complex enough to be marred by such editorial meddling: it was a loose collection of sketches aimed at an audience who wanted to see a movie version of a music-hall bill, and it grossed so much in northern towns and cities that Blakeley immediately signed his star for a second picture, *Off the Dole* (1935). Ben Henry, Basil Dean's north of England representative, advised his employer to try to entice Formby away from Blakeley. That John Maxwell of BIP was also reported to be interested in the comedian added a sense of urgency to their deliberations. On a Saturday afternoon in spring 1935, Dean sat down to view a copy of *Boots! Boots!* at the ATP preview theatre. The following day he invited the Formbys to the studio to discuss terms. Having suffered more than enough unwelcome suggestions and ropy script ideas from Archie Pitt, he had no intention of allowing another pushy spouse to interfere with the production process. Formby was offered a five-year contract, and his wife was told that her presence would be tolerated on set only as a professional adviser to her husband. She would not be invited to appear alongside him, as she sometimes did on stage. Two days later, the contract was signed.

Formby's films have their admirers – most of them are to be found once a year at Blackpool Winter Gardens, sticking out their teeth and plucking their ukes in his memory. Beyond these hardcore retainers, however, the star and his pictures are generally regarded with contempt. This may be a consequence of his fans' nostalgic enthusiasm, which has obfuscated the programmatic oddness of his work. Watch his work in the way that you might watch a Harmony Korine or a Lars von Trier film, however, and something fascinating begins to emerge. Formby would not have been out of place in Chloë Sevigny's swimming pool in

Gummo (1997) or in the Copenhagen commune of *The Idiots* (1998). (He takes a comparable dip with Googie Withers in *Trouble Brewing* (1939); even his acolytes customarily describe his screen persona as 'semi-imbecile'.) Formby's act isn't cute; it is deeply peculiar. He might be the progeny of the Depression-era underclass – some malnourished unfortunate who learned to play the ukulele for coppers. He might equally be like one of von Trier's characters, 'spassing' to amuse, repel and confuse his audience.

Southern England's first view of George Formby: a gormless, shambling figure with a flat cap slapped backwards on his head, emerging from his mother's chicken coop in a blizzard of feathers. He is like a human being reflected in a tap: the receding chin, the huge mouth full of monstrous clothes-peg teeth, the jug ears, the disproportionately strong nose sloping back to tiny eyes and a slick of Brylcreemed hair. But the weirdest aspect of Formby – both the actor and the characters he plays – is that he never acknowledges how strange he is. In the first five minutes of his ATP debut *No Limit* (1936), we see him in his mother's back yard, dry-humping a tethered motorbike: the engine roars, the exhaust fumes billow, and the local children cackle and jeer at his absurdity, but George just keeps slamming his body up and down in the saddle. The scene isn't funny in any obvious way until the jack slips down, the wheels of the bike hit the ground, and George is sent crashing through the garden fence. Until this point, his actions are simply bizarre – and the rest of the film acquaints us further with this quality. He is a helpless boy–man with a slow, squeaky voice and a dopey, stooping posture. He drinks lemonade when his girlfriend orders port, calls upon his absent mother for help in moments of panic, and – despite the smutty songs and suggestive winks – seems terrified by the prospect of sex.

This oddness has a secret, and it is one inherited from the music hall. Halfway through *No Limit*, Formby's leading lady, Florence Desmond, bullies him into doing his act on a beach on the Isle of Man. Unable to pay the exorbitant three-pound bill at his boarding house, she has convinced him that he must busk for the cash. He emerges from a beach hut clutching his ukulele, his face smeared with boot polish, a white border around his mouth exaggerating the size of his lips. As he croons his song, 'In a Little Wigan Garden', the landlady to whom he is indebted strolls up the beach with a male friend. 'Isn't that one of your boarders?' asks the friend. 'A black man?' she retorts. 'The idea!' Seconds later, however, she has recognised him. And of course she has, as Formby behaves just like a blackface character even when he is unbesmirched by Cherry Blossom: the slack vertebrae, the sleepy expression, the shyness and passivity, the waddling walk, the state of toothy happiness that comes over him when he has his little ukulele in his hand. Formby was a black-and-white minstrel who realised that the act worked just as well without the make-up. He is as much Louisiana as Lancashire.

Dean signed Walter Greenwood, the author of *Love on the Dole*, to provide the script for *No Limit*, and he happily turned in a story about a feckless chimney sweep's assistant who wins the TT motorbike race. For those members of the cast and crew who had to spend time in the company of the Formbys, however, *No Limit* was a battleground. Monty Banks, assigned to direct, petitioned Dean to bar Beryl Formby from the set. Florence Desmond took the female lead only after Dean had promised her pay and billing equal with Formby – though he made her sign a separate document agreeing to keep the financial part of this deal to herself. Beryl took exception to Desmond's casting, and fearing, as she always did, that the actress might make sexual advances towards her husband, demanded full access to the set. If her stipulations were not met, she would make arrangements with a rival studio to buy her husband out of his contract. Dean, it seems, agreed to everybody's conflicting conditions, and then retired to a safe distance.

Perhaps he was wise to do so. On all of Formby's pictures, Beryl kept vigil on set, supervising George's business, preventing him from spending money or accepting social invitations, and acting as a kind of sexual policewoman. Her presence warned that harsh retribution would fall upon any leading lady who dared make a pass at the comic. By 1937, she was even employing spies to keep watch on him when he went to the canteen. There were few signs that George resented this interference: it screened his own misanthropy and meanness. Some of Beryl's actions, however, beg for a psychoanalytic appraisal. In June 1937, she checked into a private nursing home for a hysterectomy. There was nothing wrong with her: the operation was a perversely drastic measure to dissuade her husband from infidelity. (She reasoned that if she was unable to conceive,

George would never have to seek consequence-free sex elsewhere.) The press were told that she was having her appendix removed, following a fall from a horse. By this time, the bizarre nature of the Formby marriage was the subject of newspaper gossip. When the critic Hannen Swaffer spotted Beryl at the 1938 Royal Variety Performance, timing George's act with a stopwatch, he noted: 'Not content with keeping her husband on a leash like a pet monkey, Mrs Formby has now taken to *clocking* his every movement.'[27]

Alert audience members might also have detected evidence for this tension in the films themselves. They were formulaic romantic comedies, in which George, customarily a shy and lowly barber, photographer's assistant or concert party musician, would triumph over humiliation, foil a bunch of villains, and overcome a more attractive rival to secure the affections of the leading lady. The element of romance, however, usually betrays signs of compromise with Beryl. In *No Limit*, Formby and Florence Desmond enjoy an intimate evening on a hillside overlooking the sea: there is a strange jump cut as Desmond plants a chaste kiss on George's cheek, as if someone had taken a pair of scissors to the footage. The obligatory embrace that takes place between Formby and his leading lady in the final moments of each film is an index upon the jealousy that structured the Formby marriage. In *No Limit*, it happens on the finishing line of the TT race: Desmond plants her lips on her co-star's cheek as he turns his face to the camera and grimaces in what could be pleasure, but might just as easily be fear or nausea. The final kiss in *Keep Fit* (1937) follows the same pattern, and as Formby is sitting behind Kay Walsh on a stretcher, it takes some struggling for them both to crane their necks into the correct position. In *Come On, George* (1939), Pat Kirkwood announces, 'I'm going to kiss you!' and Formby looks into the camera in panic as the actress lands a kiss half on his cheek, half on the side of his mouth. In *Feather Your Nest* (1937), George drops Polly Ward in a muddy puddle as he carries her over the threshold of their new home. In *Trouble Brewing* (1939), George and Googie Withers tumble backwards into a vat of beer, locking their mouths together as they surface. Withers remembers that when the scene was shot, Formby whispered to her, 'Give us a kiss when we go under, love; Beryl can't see us there,' and then struggled to keep her under the surface for as long as possible.[28] Beryl is known to have been horrified by this scene, but her method of ameliorating the damage was counter-productive: twenty-three takes were shot until she decreed that something sufficiently innocent was in the can.

For Formby's screen character, the prospect of physical contact with a woman produces scenes of pantomime terror. He doesn't seem to mind other people doing it – he delights in photographing a pair of kissing honeymooners in *I See Ice!* (1938), for example; and his most celebrated song, 'The Window Cleaner', is a cheerful celebration of sexual voyeurism. But when he believes that women are attempting to seduce him, he whimpers his plaintive catchphrase, 'Oh mother!' True, he will make the exhortation in any stressful situation – hanging from a Manx cliff in *No Limit*, riding a runaway pram in *Keep Fit*, assaulted by masseurs in *Feather Your Nest* (1937), dressed as a Cossack and careering around on skates in a hockey game in *I See Ice!*, flying over the handlebars of his bike in *Come On, George* – but the plea becomes particularly insistent when he believes that he has become an object of lust. In *Keep Your Seats, Please* (1936), he undergoes a medical examination, for reasons that are too ludicrous to enumerate. When the nurse attempts to remove his shirt and vest, he says, bashfully, 'I like a bit of fun, but . . .' And when she makes a grab for his belt buckle, he screams and jumps on top of the wardrobe, slapping her hands as she reaches up to coax him down. A few moments later, the nurse has manoeuvred him on to the examination table, and is yanking off his pants. 'Oh mother!' he howls, as she makes good progress. Although George's mother rarely arrives – she is seen in the flesh only in *No Limit* and *Turned Out Nice Again* (1941) – her substitute is present in the form of a female co-star who will mend his clothes, straighten him out, and save him from the consequences of his fecklessness. On the other side of the camera, Beryl was determined to do the same.

As *No Limit* went into production, *Lorna Doone* went on general release, and Dean made plans for a new prestige costume project which, he hoped, would correct the failures of his Blackmore adaptation. *Whom the Gods Love* (1936) was to be a lavish life of Mozart, shot on location in Salzburg and Vienna, with Sir Thomas Beecham and the London Philharmonic Orchestra providing the music, and Stephen Haggard – a stage actor and protégé of Edward Marsh who specialised in portrayals of frag-

Basil Dean (in shorts) directs Mozart and his circle (in wigs) on location
for *Whom the Gods Love* (1935)

ile, highly strung adolescents – at the harpsichord. Like many of the
actors Dean admired – Meggie Albanesi, Ivor Novello, Owen Nares –
Haggard's talent was for romantic hysteria. His Mozart is a jittery,
excitable figure, one moment sunk in angry despair, the next belting out
a bawdy song to offend an ignorant aristocrat, fainting on the dance floor,
or slapping his thigh like a pantomime principal boy and declaring, 'Ooh,
I shall like that!' (This is Mozart as extrovert, volatile star: a prototype for
the Milös Forman model.) Haggard, in contrast, was a quiet, studious figure who told his colleagues little about his private life. When he married
his fiancée, a stage manager named Morna Gillespie, he was doorstepped
by the *Daily Mail*, to whom he admitted: 'We kept the ceremony secret, as
we believe that if you wear your heart on your sleeve other people cut it
off.'[29] Dean signed Haggard to a three-picture deal in April 1935, and
immediately sent out press releases forecasting a stellar future for the
actor. He also announced that the part of Constance Mozart would be
played by Victoria Hopper. This decision was the beginning of the end of
his relationship with the Courtaulds.

During the preproduction period for *Whom the Gods Love*, Dean received a hastily jotted pencil note from Virginia Courtauld. 'Don't put Vicky in the new film,' she urged.

After thinking most of the night my opinion is this, which I frankly give you. After two failures ... it is not in the Company's interest, not in Vicky's, to force her again on to the public in [a film made by] the same organization. Vicky needs learning and experience; be wise Basil, and lend her out to get it. Take this in the spirit it is meant – for *you* know, no one better, that it is dictated by loyalty & reason.[30]

Dean filed the letter carefully in his archive, and ignored Virginia's advice. 'It was like a wonderful holiday,' recalls Victoria Hopper, remembering the months she spent in Vienna. 'It was the most exciting time of my life.'

When *Whom the Gods Love* opened the following year, it proved another critical and commercial disaster. It is a fussy, decorative thing, upon which Dean's instinct for self-aggrandisement is clearly legible. An opening caption announces that the film will show its hero experiencing 'an alternate of gaiety and despair, of success and splendid failure, as seen through the eyes of his loving wife'. And his wife – Mozart's, played by Dean's – is the dutiful helpmeet of a misunderstood genius. 'A man doesn't lose faith in himself just because a few people have been unkind,' she insists, her mouth a thin line of urgency. 'Some day, years after we're both dead, they'll discover that you were a great man. And they'll say about me, "His wife was a stupid little thing."'

The Courtaulds were not amused. Over the summer, the relationship between Dean and his backers suffered a total collapse. At the end of July 1936, Virginia wrote Dean a letter in angry green ink: 'My hurt is a very deep one, Basil,' she thundered. 'The more so, as the process has been gradual. Stephen has been let down – this to me is the unforgivable thing – and the responsibility is – must be – yours. Morally he has been disillusioned, materially saddled with heavy financial liabilities.' She left Dean in no doubt as to whom she blamed for ATP's problems. 'I have been forced to the conclusion that your ambition (coupled with two dangerous traits, autocracy and infallibility) has been the cause of much that has taken place, because it has always come first with you. I believed in you, and hoped – now I do neither, so what have you left me, Basil?'[31]

From this point, Dean became increasingly marginalised in his own studio. He kept an eye on the Formby unit, and continued to search for suitable replacements for Gracie Fields. One promising signing was that early target of Beryl Formby's jealousy, Betty Driver, who subsequently replaced Fields in Archie Pitt's revival of *Mr Tower of London*. Driver's first picture for Dean, *Penny Paradise* (1938), was one of the last films he produced at Ealing. Two planned vehicles for Victoria Hopper – *Grace Darling* and *Come Live with Me* – were abandoned. Dean retreated back to the theatre, and immersed himself in government committee work on the White Paper which formed the basis of the 1938 Cinematograph Act. During these meetings he encountered Alexander Korda. Dean admired Korda, but he was envious of his ability to see grand projects through to completion. Winton Dean recalls going to see Korda's *Things to Come* (1936) with his father and stepmother: 'When we got back to their flat in St John's Wood, he was in a terrible temper. He went straight to bed with a plate of oranges.'[32]

Korda, however, was prepared to offer what the Courtaulds would not: a choice of directorial assignment. And for this, the last film Dean would ever make, he decided to raise the ghost of Meggie Albanesi. Galsworthy's play *The First and the Last* had fascinated him since the early 1920s, when he produced it with Albanesi and Owen Nares in the principal roles. He commissioned Graham Greene to produce the script: the plot's double suicide was removed on grounds of taste and plausibility, and the title altered to *Twenty-one Days* (1937). Dean lobbied Korda to secure Laurence Olivier for the picture, and got him – but the head of London Films vetoed his choice of the Norwegian ballerina Vera Zorina for what Dean referred to steadfastly as 'the Albanesi part'. Galsworthy's widow, Ada, expressed herself delighted when Vivien Leigh was awarded the role, but Dean was less sure of the appointment, and his misgivings are visible on the screen. Leigh's hardness is inimical to the part. Olivier, twittering, wringing his hands and pawing at his temples, seems inexpressibly more fragile. The finale of the film sees Olivier staggering towards a Soho police station to turn himself in for the accidental killing of Leigh's husband. Leigh, who has just heard that the suicidal down-and-out wrongly convicted of the crime has died on his way to prison, storms through the streets to prevent her lover from confessing. She succeeds, of course, and Olivier stumbles down the stairs of the police station and into her arms. Delicate, doomed Meggie Albanesi would have done nothing so forceful.

Dean suspected that acting as host to Leigh and Olivier's real-life affair would disrupt the production process, and he was right. Stuart Freeborn, the film's make-up artist, banned Olivier from his room: once Freeborn had finished his work on Leigh, Olivier would bustle in and kiss her until her face was a mess of powder and lipstick.[33] The couple refused to take the film seriously, and photographs taken on location – Olivier and Leigh perched on a Southend whelk stall, or sitting in the carriage of a roller-coaster – conjure the larky atmosphere in which its director refused to participate.

Dean's sons might have derived some comfort from this teasing. A letter from Joe to his brother Winton, written from Harrow in June 1937, offers a portrait of the director's careless attitudes towards his children. 'Thursday is speech day. Our Father, which art in Ealing, was going to come down cum wife, but he never answered the invitation.' Then, a week

Laurence Olivier and Vivien Leigh on location in Southend for *Twenty-one Days* (1939). They insisted on addressing Basil Dean as 'sugar' throughout the shoot.

later: 'Speech day on Thursday went off excellently, though the Holy
Ghost was engaged in a Korda film, or rather the Father was, and Vicky
turned up alone. She was very nice indeed.' The Dean boys always liked
Hopper. 'We got on very well with all his wives,' recalls Winton. 'Better
than he did, probably.'

Even on this relatively simple picture, Dean was incapable of sticking
to his budget. He halted filming for a day because a scene at a café table
featured what he considered to be the wrong kind of sugar. (Olivier and
Leigh addressed him as 'sugar' for the rest of the shoot.) His profligacy
soon began to antagonise Korda. The mogul scribbled a note to his director in perfect Hungarian: 'I have forgot to tell you: You have shot so far
176,000 feet of film. This is about 50,000 feet more, than for instance I
have ever shot in my life. This sort of things of course cost money, and my
only anxiety is *money*. That's why I have to insist that the ship-scenes must
not take more than *one* day. I hope you understand this.'[34] Dean, it seems,
didn't. Eventually, Korda told him that the sound stage on which he was
working was urgently required for another production. Assuring Dean
that he could have the space back very shortly, he then gave the film's two
stars leave to go to Elsinore to play Hamlet and Ophelia in a Shakespeare
production sponsored by the Danish tourist board. Korda's gentle act of
sabotage was reflected in his negative response to the finished film. It sat
on the shelf for two years, and was released only when the worldwide success of *Gone with the Wind* (1939) had increased the likelihood of its generating some profit. Dean, affronted that Korda had interfered with his
work, never saw the film.

Stephen Courtauld moved in for the kill in April 1938. In a confidential
letter written from Eltham Palace, he told Dean that he believed it to be
undesirable for a member of ATP's board to produce films for the company. The doubling of roles, he asserted, made the control of budgets
impossible, as board members could block decisions to curb their own
spending. 'There are two other reasons against your acting as our Producer in the future,' he went on. 'Your resumed theatrical work interferes
with your work on the films; and George Formby, who is our principal
asset in production, has taken an unreasonable dislike to you.'[35]

Dean went without a struggle, and agreed to offer his resignation to the
board at a meeting on 4 July. 'When I reflect upon the eight or nine years'

toil to create the organisation I have a natural desire to make the "extraction" as brief and painless as possible,' he told Courtauld. 'No doubt you will feel the same.'[36] In solidarity with her husband, Victoria Hopper also volunteered to rescind her contract. And once Dean had agreed to withdraw from the studio, Courtauld, rather tactlessly, continued to give him further reasons for going. 'Yours is the name most prominently identified with the companies,' he argued, 'and although we have had some successes, it is well known that the enterprise as a whole has been a failure, and rightly or wrongly you are generally held responsible for this.'[37] Dean kept his dignity, and at least his children derived some benefit from his absence from Ealing. 'I am sorry I shall not be at the Studio to receive you this morning,' he informed Stephen Courtauld at the end of June. 'It is my youngest boy's speech day, and I have long promised to go.'[38]

When the date of Dean's departure had been determined, he and Courtauld considered how the news should be broken to shareholders and the press. 'I suggest', wrote Dean, 'reference should be made to my stage activities in the event of pressmen questioning me. I do not think it advisable to have it mentioned in the form that you have sent me, in case at any future date I decided to re-embark upon film production.'[39] A draft of the minutes of the 4 July meeting recorded that 'Mr Dean advised the Board that his increased activities in his stage production business would prevent him from carrying out in the future the functions of the appointments which he had held in the past on behalf of the Company,' and added that his resignation was accepted 'with regret'. The final draft, however, was much vaguer, and referred only to 'a private understanding with Mr Courtauld'. When Dean's departure was made public in the middle of September, Reginald Baker dutifully told the press that his former colleague wished 'to devote himself more fully to the theatre side of his activities' – still the explanation offered in most film histories.[40]

At the same time, the studios were retitled: ATP was thrown in the scrag bin of history, and a new name, Ealing Studios Ltd, was declared. Michael Balcon was installed on the board, and, almost immediately, began working at Ealing in the very double capacity – producer and chairman – from which Courtauld had barred his predecessor. Under his stewardship, it would become Britain's most celebrated film company.

*

Dean's ATP stars stepped forward into difficult futures. Peggy Blythe gave up her film career and emigrated to Malta, where she still resides. Stephen Haggard continued to act, wrote a well-regarded novel, and in March 1943 was killed in the Middle East on active service for British Intelligence. George Formby worked out the rest of his contract at Ealing, and then cut a better deal with Columbia, who squeezed out a further seven films until the public lost their taste for his gormless style of humour. In 1944, he was hauled up before the Dance Music Policy Committee, who rather strangely suspected that the songs from *Bell-Bottom George* (1944) contained 'enemy-friendly' lyrics. He and Beryl remained together until her death from cancer on Christmas Eve 1960, but a few weeks after the funeral, Formby announced his engagement to Pat Howson, a thirty-six-year-old schoolteacher. The wedding did not take place: Formby suffered a fatal heart-attack in March 1961. To the disgust of his mother, Eliza Booth, the entire estate was willed to Howson, who sold Beryldene – the Formbys' home in Lytham St Annes – and disposed of its contents at public auction. A marquee was erected in the back garden, and over a thousand lots went under the gavel: Formby's cars, his trouser press, his electric razor, his presentation cigarette box from the National Cancer Fund, even his soiled underwear. The legal wrangling over the proceeds continued for decades. Neither Howson, who died in 1971 aged 46, nor Booth, who died in 1981 aged 102, lived to spend the money.

Gracie Fields was saved from misery only by sheer effort of ego. The zenith of her public adoration came in the middle of 1939, when she underwent treatment for cervical cancer. Outside the hospital, fans prayed for her recovery and straw was spread on the pavement to deaden the sound of their footsteps. Inside, Monty Banks, soon to become the second Mr Fields, minced the best raw steak he could find and induced her to drink the blood. Her recuperation was a cause for national celebration – 250,000 get-well cards were sent – but it did not last long. When war broke out, she left for California with Banks and a Treasury-sanctioned nest-egg of £28,000, and the British press rounded on her. No matter how much she protested that she had gone for the sake of her parents' health, or to save her husband from being imprisoned under the terms of the wartime Aliens Act, no matter how many times she sang for the troops, the loss of prestige was never quite reversed. She made several

Hollywood pictures during the war, then retreated to Capri, the Italian island which she had first explored with her lover John Flanagan. She lived there as quietly as her *soprano profundo* voice would allow, until her death in 1979. In the intervening years, the vague sense that Fields was a wronged woman of some sort effected her rehabilitation in her homeland. Her autobiography, *Sing as We Go* (1960), a comeback concert at the Palladium and a series of self-justifying newspaper interviews produced a sentimental response in the British public, who took holidays on Capri and considered her one of the principal tourist attractions.

Basil Dean's departure from Ealing had grave consequences for Victoria Hopper's career. 'It all went to pieces,' she recalls, 'which was very unfortunate for me. And there was a certain amount of jealousy.' There was very little sympathy for her among British film personnel. 'As you see from *Citizen Kane*,' reflects Roy Ward Baker, who in 1938 was working as an assistant director at Gainsborough Studios, 'this is what happens when suddenly some man gets hold of a gorgeous woman who can't act for toffee and has no personality whatsoever. Victoria Hopper was utterly condemned by everyone. She couldn't do it, poor girl.' The judgement is harsh, but accurate: Victoria Hopper owed her career to a delusion. On screen, she is a faint, forceless presence – and nothing, one presumes, like Meggie Albanesi.

After her expulsion from Ealing, Hopper spent some time without a manager, until an agent named Eric Glass offered his services. 'Everybody knew that things had gone wrong with Ealing, and Eric Glass was the one person in all of London who came to offer me a job,' she recalls. She played Tessa Sanger on television, and continued to appear in Dean's stage productions, notably in the first run of J. B. Priestley's *Johnson over Jordan* (1939) opposite Edna Best and Ralph Richardson. Her husband's reputation was saved by the outbreak of war: the government handed him the job of heading the Entertainments National Service Association (ENSA), the body responsible for sending out plays and concert parties to entertain the troops. Gracie Fields and George Formby were among his first recruits.

During this time, Dean began a long-term affair with a married woman. 'I had the worst time of my life during that time,' admits Victoria Hopper, 'because everybody knew that this was going on. In the end I

Basil Dean's holiday snaps: Gracie Fields and Victoria Hopper on Capri, 1946.
The Deans' marriage had collapsed, as had Fields's film career.

could see that she was always going to be in the picture, so I got a solicitor and divorced him. Neither of them wanted one.' Dean also fell out with Winton when he refused to accept his son's argument that Basil's brother, Vernon, was suffering from a serious mental illness – even after Vernon had been caught vandalising sea defences on the south coast. Dean also accused his son of shirking his responsibilities during the war. Winton suffered from gastric trouble which ensured that he was rejected for service, and eventually secured a job in Oxford with the Admiralty, interpreting and editing reports from enemy territory, but his father did not seem satisfied by this. 'He was very quick to condemn people on moral grounds,' reflects Winton, 'when his own morals weren't very good.'

In his final years, Basil Dean lived with Winton in a grand Edwin Lutyens-designed house outside Godalming. The house is still occupied by Winton and his son Stephen. Basil's picture gazes down from the drawing-room wall. Here, the former chairman of ATP wrote his memoirs and ordered his archive, sorting and stowing scrapbooks, letters and photographs. Among them was a large portrait of Meggie Albanesi – a murky soft-focus picture taken days before her death – and a number of snapshots from a holiday at Gracie Fields's villa on Capri, just after the war. Dean took the pictures himself, and they are among the most potent images he ever created. Gracie Fields perched on the back of a donkey cart, moving slowly through the heat. Gracie Fields posing glumly in a floral-patterned swimming costume, her legs resting awkwardly on the cement wall of her villa, her hand sunk into the folds of a matching towel. Victoria Hopper, sitting forlornly by an Adriatic as flat as the untouched cup of tea by her side, the brim of her hat shadowing her eyes like a veil. A picnic by the rocks, Fields sinking her teeth into a piece of fruit and scowling into the lens; Hopper, by her side, hiding under another hat, picking despondently at her nails. They are women at the end of an event, unsure how success slipped through their fingers, knowing that the man behind the camera could take some of the credit, some of the blame.

CHAPTER SIX

Balconisation

Research scientist Sidney Stratton (Alec Guinness) tampers with forces best left alone in *The Man in the White Suit* (1951)

Had Russia and America unleashed nuclear holocaust upon the world, the preceding days of panic would have triggered the mobilisation of the BBC's wartime broadcasting service. As the world's TV sets would have been swiftly destroyed by the electromagnetic pulse that accompanies any nuclear explosion, no television service was planned to meet the entertainment needs of those who crawled, unincinerated, from the rubble of Britain. The BBC, however, did identify a number of programmes suitable for broadcast in the last hours of high alert, before the majority of licence-fee payers were blinded by the nuclear flash.

The final transmission of BBC Television would have comprised a pulsing light, the strains of so-called 'Dalek music', and the pre-recorded voice of the newsreader Peter Donaldson, announcing the end of civilisation. According to recently declassified government documents, the penultimate broadcast might well have been an Ealing comedy. Not a Formby or Fields vehicle made under Basil Dean, but one of that select sub-group of eight or nine pictures produced at the studio by Michael Balcon: *Kind Hearts and Coronets* (1949), perhaps, or *The Man in the White Suit* (1951). Imagine it: the citizens of Britain packing their last tins of Spam into their shelters and leafing through *Protect and Survive* one final, desperate time, as the familiar features of Alec Guinness loomed on the television – the last human face to be projected on a British screen.[1]

Even if you've never watched the conspirators of *The Lavender Hill Mob* (1951) melting down gold bullion into Eiffel Tower souvenirs, never observed the islanders of *Whisky Galore!* (1949) concealing their salvaged liquor inside cash-registers, under pie-crusts and beneath the covers of their babies' cots, never seen Professor Marcus and his gang of crooks in

The Ladykillers (1955) as they are despatched by a sweet old dear with a parrot named General Gordon, you'll probably still have some idea what the phrase 'Ealing comedy' means. You'll probably understand why one of these movies might have been chosen to usher us into oblivion, and why some might consider them the cinematic equivalent of a paper bag over the head. Of all British films, these are the most involved in the smoke of sentimentality and nostalgia, the most subject to academic reading and re-reading. To many of their advocates, they are the repository of a lost England in which bowler-hatted men from the ministry were routed by resourceful urchins and eccentric spinsters in floral hats, where small private concerns always won the day over multinational or bureaucratic interests, where cranky individualism triumphed over corporate will. To others, they are cosy, whimsical and genteel productions which encouraged British citizens, dazed by the loss of their empire, to retreat into a world of woolly fantasy. For the film critic Alexander Walker, they were 'comfort food for middle England that sat well with the national stomach'.[2] For Ken Russell, they were 'weak situation comedies in search of an identity'.[3] For the film-struck novelist Jonathan Coe, they are works that divide conservative and progressive opinion. 'You can still find diehard nostalgics who will swear that no British films were ever more delightful,' he noted in 1997. 'Mention the Ealing comedies to any cineaste under about forty on the other hand, and you can brace yourself for a torrent of invective about provincial narrow-mindedness, snobbery, sexual repression, verbosity, archness and sentimental nationalism.'[4]

The name of Ealing now has several resonances. It is always invoked when an unambitious British comedy totters into our multiplexes: the makers and publicists of *The Englishman Who Went up a Hill but Came down a Mountain* (1995), *House!* (2000), *Saving Grace* (2001) and, most forgettably, *Mrs Caldicott's Cabbage War* (2002) all dropped the name of the studio in their press packs. Less visibly, perhaps, it is an official commercial banner under which pictures are still being shot: the studios in W5 are now a mixed-use production facility owned by a consortium of movie-makers and property developers that has managed, in a modest way, to bring feature-film production back to Ealing Green. The first of these, Oliver Parker's fey adaptation of *The Importance of Being Earnest* (2002), blew desperate kisses to *Kind Hearts and Coronets* from every frame, but its poverty of ambition was neatly illustrated by the goodie bag of famous 'British brands' with which film hacks were sent home from the press launch: the sachet of Bird's instant custard seemed excessively appropriate.

Outside the cinema, the phrase has colonised a certain kind of altercation between the individual and the state. When bureaucrats are bested by small bands of middle-class protesters, or a loophole in the law reaps some bounteous reward, 'Ealing' appears in the newspaper reports. More contentiously, it has also found its way into liberal critiques of establishment incompetence, narrow-mindedness or xenophobia, particularly when judges, civil servants or members of the Tory Party are involved. When the Conservative Prime Minister John Major characterised Britain as 'the country of long shadows on county grounds, warm beer, invincible green suburbs, dog lovers and old maids bicycling to Holy Communion through the morning mist', he was ridiculed in the *Guardian*: 'The images are those of some dowdy Ealing comedy from the fifties, all lovable coppers and middle-class English actors putting on funny voices to play working class.'[5] (Most commentators failed to spot that the last and dowdiest of these images was a direct lift from George Orwell's *England, Your England* (1941).) When the Scottish Labour MP Tom Harris attacked a proposed Conservative addition to the government's 2003 Extradition Bill as 'imperialist nonsense', he declared, 'I hope that the Opposition will force that amendment to a vote, as it defines the philosophy of the modern Conservative party far more than many other things. It is the Ealing comedy amendment.'[6] A profile of the Tory MP Teddy Taylor published in *The Almanac of British Politics* (2002) described him as 'a character from an Ealing comedy' who accompanied his 'Europhobia with across-the-board rightwing sentiments on hanging, homosexuality, abortion and immigration.'[7] Ealing, in these terms, denotes a particular state of mind: backward-looking, insular, snobbish, nostalgic for empire, mistrustful of foreigners, suspicious of the welfare state. It is the state of mind of right-wing grotesques such as David Irving, who celebrated the studio's films for their images of 'how Britain used to be before the foreigners came flooding in'.[8]

This is a gross and depressing distortion. If you want this kind of reassurance, if you want to lose yourself in a mythical realm in which

Britain did not give up its colonies or limp humiliated from the banks of Suez, then sit down with a James Bond film. Watch *Goldfinger* (1964), for instance – a film whose title demonises a celebrated architect of modernist social housing – and listen to 007 bore for England on the subject of brandy and vintage champagne, or express fogeyish distaste for youth culture. 'My dear girl,' patronises Sean Connery, 'there are some things that just aren't done, such as drinking Dom Perignon '53 above the temperature of thirty-eight degrees Fahrenheit. That's just as bad as listening to the Beatles without earmuffs.'[9] Might such sentiments have any place in an Ealing picture? Only, perhaps, in the mouth of a bumptious patriarch played by Basil Radford or Cecil Parker. (It's not so far from Parker's assertion in the sub-Ealing *It's Great to Be Young* (1956) that jazz 'ruins character', a remark calculated to elicit a storm of raspberries from the cheap seats.) In Ealing's *Barnacle Bill* (1957), Alec Guinness's Captain Ambrose encourages a gang of teenagers to slash the seats and smash the fittings in the auditorium of a run-down seaside pier, and jives onstage with their skiffle band until he is dragged away by the police, accused of attempting to 'subvert the morals of our young people'. This disapproval is expressed by the villains – Maurice Denham and his cabal of civic fat cats. In *Goldfinger*, such views are the credo of the hero.

The fantasies of Ealing were much less flattering to their audiences, and usually shattered by the movements of the plot: the dream of a free-market free-for-all briefly entertained by the protagonists of *Passport to Pimlico* (1949), before the incursion of spivs and impending social chaos forces them to reaffirm the communitarianism of the war; the sleepy complacency of the citizens depicted in *Next of Kin* and *Went the Day Well?* (both 1942), from which they are awoken by Nazi brutality; the scientific aspirations of Alec Guinness in *The Man in the White Suit*, squashed by the pressure of vested interests in which most audience members would have had a stake. It would be hard to deny that, towards the end of Balcon's two decades at the head of the company, his productions seemed less and less inclined to emerge from their own illusions: in *The Titfield Thunderbolt* (1953), the steam locomotive and its cargo of provincial comic stereotypes is permitted to chug cheerfully up and down its branch line in defiance of any economic logic; in *Barnacle Bill*, Captain Ambrose's pier is reclassified as a ship, detached from its moorings and

and transformed into a rest home for loveable eccentrics. As Charles Barr observes in his definitive study of the studio's output, 'it's as if the tide of inevitable change – made more inevitable by the soft, innocent philosophy of those resisting change – surrounded Pimlico, which had decided change *wouldn't* happen, and floated it off into the sea. It still, just, remains attached: a part of England.'[10] Before this break with reality occurred, however, Balcon's studio was responsible for some of the most politically astute films in the language.

Although Ealing is now synonymous with comedy, the movies for which the studio tends to be remembered formed less than a tenth of its output. Unless you count *The Man in the White Suit*, science fiction was the only genre upon which the famous cartouche-like logo failed to appear. *Dead of Night* (1945) was the template for the portmanteau horror films produced by Amicus in the 1960s and 1970s: a compendium of Freudian terrors featuring a sentient ventriloquist's dummy, a mirror that reflects the undercurrent of murderous sexuality in the marriage of its owners, and a country cottage whose occupants are imprisoned in a mysterious time-loop. *Mandy* (1952) was an irresistibly lachrymose medical drama with a preternaturally fine performance from its young star, Mandy Miller. *Scott of the Antarctic* (1948) was a lavish exercise in nationalist mythography which celebrated British victory in Europe with a story of British failure at the South Pole. *Saraband for Dead Lovers* (1948) was an attempt to elevate the bodice-ripper popularised by Gainsborough Studios with Technicolor and a high-minded script; *Nicholas Nickleby* (1947) was an experiment in literary adaptation; *The Overlanders* (1946) was a Western transplanted to the Australian bush. Comedy did not emerge from the studio in any distinct form until halfway through Balcon's tenure. Indeed, in 1949, the head of Ealing published an essay entitled 'Film Comedy', in which he reassured the public that the studio's new interest in humorous subjects would not undermine its commitment to realism or 'social content'.[11]

Now, that body of nine irresistible movies, from *Hue and Cry* (1947) to *The Ladykillers* (1955), has so eclipsed Balcon's other achievements that it seems bizarre he felt obliged to issue this printed alert. But if the studio had ceased operations, say, in 1951, the year that the British electorate returned Winston Churchill to power, Ealing would have entered the twenty-first century with a very different reputation. It would be noted for having reoriented British pictures towards the concerns of working-class audiences, quietly killing the upper-class gentleman heroes of the 1930s in the process. It would be recognised for having envisioned the future of Britain as a Keynesian democracy, cleansed of patronage and privilege. It would be remembered as the studio that was more willing than the government to subject the realities of war to public examination, warning its audiences that postmistresses and vicars' daughters might be forced to kill and be killed for their country. Such a reputation would not account for all the complexities and contradictions in the Ealing project, but it would express more of its nature than the miasma of cheerful complacency that currently surrounds its name. Balcon's Ealing was forged by war. War determined the concerns of its films, and facilitated its dialogue with the fears and aspirations of its audiences. War settled who was allowed to remain working and who was sent off elsewhere. It put propaganda at the core of the studios' activities and made the Ministry of Information a partner in production. War kicked Basil Dean's aspiration to literary film-making into touch, and replaced it with a new interest in documentary realism. And Michael Balcon and his team of collaborators made the potential destruction of England their most urgent theme.

Whenever he watches *The Ladykillers*, Jonathan Balcon is reminded of the day that war broke out. The smartly upholstered Packard motor car used as a getaway vehicle by Alec Guinness and his gang of thieves was the property of Jonathan's father. It was a remnant of Michael Balcon's short and unhappy attachment to Metro-Goldwyn-Mayer – a honeymoon gift from an organisation whose British operations he oversaw until Louis B. Mayer stormed into his office one morning in 1938, and, standing as near to the open window as possible, yelled, 'I'll ruin you, Balcon, if it costs me a million dollars.'[12] (Balcon's observation that he would settle for much less went unheard by passers-by.) On 3 September 1939, Jonathan, then seven years old, and his sister Jill, fourteen, were sitting in the car with their parents, parked on the gravel drive of their home at Upper Parrock, Sussex. Through its top-of-the-range radio set, they listened to Neville Chamberlain's declaration of war.

That's how Jonathan remembers it. His sister, however, recalls that it was the Bush radio set in the dining room around which the family gathered to hear the speech. It's one of the many points upon which they differ. Michael Balcon's children have been locked in a kind of cold war since the mid-1990s. When Jill's son, the actor Daniel Day-Lewis, was asked to unveil a commemorative plaque at a former Balcon residence, Jonathan gave an interview to the *Daily Mail* in which he expressed the opinion that his father would been appalled by his grandson's 'lax moral character'. The breach has never been healed.

Jonathan is the living image of his father – whom he always refers to by his Christian name. He is also the embodiment of good-natured middle-class belligerence. One of his email tags is 'Disgusted of Tunbridge Wells'. He loves a spat with the district council, a ding-dong on the letters page of his local paper, a curt exchange of letters with an official body. (He was appalled by BAFTA's sneaky decision in 2002 to alter the name of the 'Michael Balcon Award for an Outstanding Contribution to British Cinema' to the 'Michael Balcon Award for an Outstanding British Contribution to Cinema' – which is not the same thing at all.) His most irresistible anecdote involves the presentation of a BAFTA fellowship to the impresario Lew Grade. Jonathan was sitting in the audience between his mother, Aileen (then in the first stages of Alzheimer's), and the actor Christopher Reeve. As the winner accepted his gong, Aileen exclaimed, 'There's that awful shit Lew Grade! Your father hated him!' His second most irresistible anecdote concerns Basil Dean pushing Michael Balcon down the steps of the Garrick Club, but this, by his own admission, is probably apocryphal. Jonathan spent his career in the City, his father having forbidden him to enter the cinema industry, but maintained his connection with that world by working in film insurance: his proudest achievements are having secured policies to cover the ancient Katie Johnson on *The Ladykillers*, and the distinctly delicate Edward G. Robinson on *Sammy Going South* (1963).

Jill Balcon also bears a strong resemblance to her father: she could be nobody else's daughter. In her long career as an actress, she has been most consistently celebrated for her finely modulated voice – even when on the phone to the council to complain about its inability to collect her rubbish, she sounds like a solo on the cor anglais. In the studio, she modelled for Jacob Epstein, who importuned her in the Caprice and asked if he might immortalise her head. On the stage, she survived the experience of playing

The Balcon family – Michael, Jonathan, Aileen and Jill – on a visit to Eton,
June 1945

Zenocrate to Donald Wolfit's Tamburlaine – despite his habit of bashing
her head about during the death scene. On the screen, she gave fierce life
to Madeleine Bray in *Nicholas Nickleby*, a young woman determined to
save her ailing father by consenting to be married to a monstrous patriarch; relished a vicious dormitory scrap with Jean Kent in *Good-Time Girl*
(1949); and brought dignity to the honorific roles that Derek Jarman
bestowed upon her in *Edward II* (1991) and *Wittgenstein* (1993).

Her relationship with her father was frequently explosive. 'I was very
frightened of him at times,' she says. 'I wasn't beaten or anything, but I
was frightened of his wrath. He was a formidable figure in the home.'
Their points of difference were legion. He was dismayed by her choice of
career, and though he paid her drama-school fees, she has no recollection
of him ever praising any of her performances. ('I remember when I went

The Balcons attend a family wedding at the Liberal London Synagogue,
St John's Wood, late 1940s

to work at the Bristol Old Vic, he said, "Couldn't you find a job in London?"") He was particularly horrified when, during a spell working for
the BBC as a radio announcer, she changed her professional name, briefly,
to Jill Barclay. He disapproved most deeply, however, of her choice of a
husband – Cecil Day-Lewis, Oxford Professor of Poetry, a married man,
and the lover of the novelist Rosamond Lehmann – though his disapproval was not, perhaps, as deep as that of Day-Lewis's then wife. ('Jill
Balcon comes into the picture,' wrote Mary Day-Lewis in her diary.
'Everything has the feeling of a nightmare.')[13] Michael Balcon refused to
attend the wedding and made the briefest possible appearance at the
reception. Charles Tennyson, the grandson of the Victorian Poet Laure-
ate, gave away the bride, whose cleaning lady, Mrs Pizzey, was a witness.

Jill Balcon managed to resurrect her relationship with her father before his death in 1977, partly through the agency of her son, Daniel, whom he adored. (It is her greatest regret that neither her husband nor her father lived to see Daniel Day-Lewis's phenomenal success as an actor.) Her relationship with her brother, however, seems to have deteriorated beyond repair. It is hard to talk about one in the presence of the other without feeling that you are betraying both. For the purposes of this chapter, however, let us imagine these siblings returned to the condition of childhood, reunited under their parents' roof by the radio and the guilty men of Munich, and also, perhaps, by the Packard and Professor Marcus's gang of St Pancras cash-grabbers.

On the outbreak of war, the Balcons decided instantly that Jonathan would be safer at a nearby prep school, Ashdown House, which was so close to Upper Parrock that he was able to stoke his misery by watching its lights twinkle from the wrong side of the River Medway. Ironically, some of the first bombs of the war were dropped on the school grounds. He still owns a souvenir chunk of the parachute mine which blew every pane from the back of the building, but left the impressive glass portico at the front utterly untouched. 'I remember in our dormitory there was the son of Air Vice Marshal Evill who, in a small voice in the middle of the night said, "Please sir, may I get out of my bed? It's full of glass."'[14]

Jill was despatched to the Lake District when her school, Roedean, relocated to the Station Hotel, Keswick. On one of her journeys north, she exchanged a few hot words with a captured German airman, Franz von Werra, whose cross-country escape became the subject of Roy Baker's *The One that Got Away* (1957). (Her father expended a great deal of energy in ensuring that this detail of the fugitive's story failed to appear in the press reports of his apprehension.) She also spent many nights in the basement of her parents' apartment block in London, trying to sleep under a blue light bulb, with the bombs exploding overhead. 'I can remember going out to the Hungaria restaurant, and spending the night under a table in one of the worst air-raids of the war. We came out alive. But where Swan and Edgar's was, where Tower Records is now in Piccadilly Circus, there were sheets of glass covering the pavement, and water mains bursting everywhere.'

Jonathan remembers that in June 1940, the Balcon family and their handful of staff were summoned to the dining room at Upper Parrock, where the head of the household announced that he had turned down several offers to send the children to safety in the United States. 'I am quite convinced that we will come through this war victorious. If we don't, it will be disastrous for this family. But if we go down, we all go down together.' (Jill, conversely, recalls making a similar speech to her father.)

Accounts of Ealing Studios often allow the perceived cosiness of the films to colour their assessments of the man who ran them. Michael Balcon is customarily represented as an avuncular, prudish, unworldly figure: an indulgent headmaster who presided over a class of talented but unruly students. There is an element of truth in the caricature. Although he tolerated an extraordinary amount of drunkenness among his staff, Balcon was, in many respects, enormously straitlaced.[15] On Charles Frend's *The Loves of Joanna Godden* (1947), he refused to allow Googie Withers to slap Jean Kent across the face. *It Always Rains on Sunday* (1947) lost a sequence in which a killer on the run (John McCallum) interrupts his flight from the police to relieve himself in a *pissoir*.

Balcon's indulgence had strict limits. He cultivated an atmosphere of co-operation and collaboration at the studio, listening to suggestions from anyone who cared to make them, and allowing directors to comment upon and occasionally reshape one another's work.[16] But he also demanded absolute loyalty from his colleagues, resenting their attempts to strike out on their own and responding with fury if he believed them to have betrayed his trust. To keep his employees within the organisation, he would often insinuate that they were not equipped to survive on the other side of its walls. He was upset and appalled when the director Henry Cornelius went moonlighting to make *The Galloping Major* (1951) as an independent production. When a resident producer, Alberto Cavalcanti, asked to renegotiate his contract on a non-exclusive basis, Balcon fired back a letter headed with a bitter allusion to Orwell's *Animal Farm*: 'I know somebody made the comment about Soviet Russia that "all men are equal but some are more equal than others". I am afraid that this cannot apply to Ealing studios because . . . it could only result in complete chaos and the undermining of everything we have built up for years.'[17] The cinematographer Douglas Slocombe recalls that when John Grierson of

Group Three Films rang Balcon to ask whether he might use his services on a one-off basis, the telephone receiver was thrown down in disgust. (Hal Mason, the studio's general manager, chose the secrecy of the gents' to report the news to Slocombe.) '[Balcon] was a very insecure man,' reflects Slocombe. 'He was afraid of saying too much in case he was mis-interpreted, or someone thought that his remarks were shallow. At pro-duction meetings, he was very rarely able to make artistic comment. He took refuge in making comments about mechanical problems like scratches or a hair in the gate, which nobody else had noticed. His behaviour was governed by a very strict set of rules.'[18]

Balcon's children can add new details to this picture of their father's personality. His love-letters to Aileen were signally passionless. He was cautious with money, and, towards the end of his life, was convinced that he was on the point of financial ruin. (When, in the early 1960s, black-mailers threatened to kidnap his grandchildren if he did not hand over £10,000, his response was disbelief that anyone might think he had access to such a sum.) His attitude to his Judaism was paradoxical: he was happy

Ealing director Henry Cornelius (left) and his camera operator
Cecil Cooney at work on *The Galloping Major* (1951) – made against
the wishes of Michael Balcon

for his children to be married in the Church of England, but took great exception when Jonathan's daughter Deborah visited Upper Parrock wearing a gold crucifix, and declined to attend the christenings of Daniel and his sister Tamasin. He avoided pork scrupulously, but loved bacon, lobster and oysters, and raised pigs whose hams, hung in the chimney, were an obligatory part of every visitor's tour. When the nephew of the playwright Warren Chetham-Strode came angling for work at the studio, and told Balcon that he was soon 'off to Palestine to beat up those bloody Jews', it was his secretary, Miss Slater, who took offence. He had a horror of scandal, and wept when he saw the story in the London *Evening Standard* that named his daughter as co-respondent in the divorce of Cecil Day-Lewis, but was always ready to help out friends and acquaintances who were being hounded by the press. After Captain Peter Baker MP, the son of Ealing's financial chief Reginald Baker, was arrested on fraud charges, Balcon stood him bail, and did his best to ensure that the newspapers did not discover that the member for South Norfolk was in hiding at the Priory clinic. At the height of the affair, a reporter from the *Sunday*

A production meeting around Ealing's round table: left to right, Michael Balcon (chewing glasses), an American distributor, Reg Baker, Kenneth Winkels of the Rank Organisation

Express rang Upper Parrock and was told by Aileen that her husband refused to comment on the case. 'To whom am I speaking?' asked the hack. 'Diana Dors!' replied Aileen, and slammed down the phone.[19]

Balcon's political interests, which inform so much of Ealing's output, have also been downplayed – not least by Balcon himself, who, late in life, chose to ignore his early radicalism. 'By and large,' he said, in an interview conducted two years before his death, 'we were a group of liberal-minded, like-minded people. I don't know if anyone was terribly politically involved . . . we were middle-class people brought up with middle-class backgrounds and rather conventional educations . . . We voted Labour for the first time after the war; this was our mild revolution.'[20] The summary suggests that Balcon and his colleagues were a bunch of nice bourgeois boys who, at the end of the war, made a tentative experiment with a ballot paper and a pencil, and dared one another to plant a cross next to their local Labour candidate's name.

The truth was rather different, biographically and politically. There was nothing conventional about Robert Hamer, the director of *Kind Hearts and Coronets*. He was a brilliant young Cambridge intellectual whose university career was interrupted by rustication for his involvement in a homosexual scandal, and whose working life was cut short by his destructive devotion to alcohol. (Hamer's volatile relationship with Herbert Wilcox's daughter Pamela, which ended with Hamer dead and his lover living rough on the streets of London, is movingly described in her memoir, *Between Hell and Charing Cross*.[21]) 'Middle-class' hardly describes Ealing's Director of Publicity, Monja Danischewsky, a rubicund refugee of the Russian Revolution, whose dinner-party trick was to persuade his pet bantam cock into parading around the table perched on the back of the family dog. The category 'ordinary' seems ill-suited to Commander Charles Lamb, the studio's naval adviser, whose career as a ladies' man was mysteriously unimpeded by his emasculation by the propeller of a Swordfish bomber.

Balcon's statement about the apolitical nature of his employees is particularly hard to digest. Years before the 1945 election was called, Ealing had a thick streak of red in its make-up. The film editor Sidney Cole was a militant union activist and committed socialist who, with fellow Ealing employees Thorold Dickinson and Norman McLaren, went to Spain during the Civil War to make short films financed by the British Communist Party (of which the studio's chief art director Michael Relph was also a member). Cole's editing-room colleague Mary Kessel sold the *Daily Worker* outside Ealing's gates. Ivor Montagu, a Balcon collaborator since the 1920s, was a staunch communist from a clan of plutocrats, and was estranged from his relations after he abandoned his wife for his secretary. Queen Mary disapproved of his action, sending the bereft Gladys Montagu a telegram of commiseration – 'feeling for you, Mary' – but Aileen Balcon adored him, and was even able to forgive his habit of eating her Camembert with dirty fingernails.[22] 'Michael Balcon', recalls one old comrade, the former Labour leader Michael Foot, 'was a great friend of the Labour Party, and more sympathetic to its aims than any other member of his profession.'[23]

Balcon's political awakening came late, but forcefully. 'I was, myself, brought up in the Gladstonian school of Liberalism,' he confessed, in a lecture to the Workers Film Association in 1943, 'and like many people of my generation and upbringing, I began to feel, in the years that immediately preceded the war, first that there was no longer a place in the world for us old-fashioned Liberals, and that something more progressive must replace it; and, second, that all of us should contribute in our own capacity towards solving the problems which were menacing the world with another war.'[24] As early as 1938, he had been lobbying the government to engage with him in the production of films that 'could serve to fight against Fascism both in this country and elsewhere'.[25] He was fiercely critical of British cinema personnel who fled to America during the war, his old friend Alfred Hitchcock included. He was sufficiently hungry for a Labour post-war electoral victory to involve himself with an informal offshoot of the 1941 Committee, established by Lord Sainsbury to mobilise post-war opinion against Churchill and in favour of Clement Attlee. He had many other friends in the Labour movement in addition to Michael Foot: Jill Craigie and Hugh and Dora Gaitskell were frequent visitors to Upper Parrock. Foot was employed to script the commentary for *Yellow Caesar* (1941), a documentary exposing Mussolini's part in the Spanish Civil War. In 1940, Balcon exhorted the Ministry of Information – with whom he had been co-producing propaganda films – to strengthen their output through the study of Soviet examples.

This aspect of his sensibility has been forgotten in the memoirs of most of his colleagues, who preferred to dwell on his propensity for comic vagueness. His children, however, agree on the political atmosphere of the Balcon household. Jill professes that she was 'weaned on the Left Book Club'; Jonathan recalls that his masters at Eton wrote worried notes on his school reports about his addiction to the works of the leader of the British Communist Party, Harry Pollitt. Only Peter Ustinov – another left-wing intellectual recruited from a government film outfit – has written of Balcon as a sharp political operator. 'There was something about his authority,' he reflected, 'as secret, as exclusive, as that of a chief of MI5, or of a Minister of Intelligence.'[26]

Balcon had one young left-leaning protégé who meant much more to him than all the others, and did most to awaken his interest in the social and political possibilities of film-making. Penrose Tennyson was a good-looking, restless, steely young man whose death in a plane crash at the age of twenty-eight robbed Ealing of one of its most promising and political-ly committed talents, and Balcon of one of the most intense relationships of his life. 'Let me put it to you this way,' says Jonathan, attempting to describe his father's bond with the director. 'I never doubted my father's sexuality, except he did have this extraordinary thing about Pen. He was part of our family. Mick absolutely doted on him.' His sister concurs: 'Pen was glamorous, brilliantly talented. My father regarded him as a son.'

Accounts of the brief life of Pen Tennyson glow with that burnished, Homeric quality common to all stories of privileged young men felled in battle. His father, Charles Tennyson, commemorated him in a short memoir, in which he recalled that from the age of five the boy had exhib-ited a passion for stories of the Trojan Wars. 'I can see him now in the lit-tle nursery at Cheyne Row, in the character of Ajax, attacking the brass knob of the door with a sword of rolled up newspaper and an expression of noble and concentrated fury.'[27] Tennyson's teenage years were less heroic, and made miserable by fainting fits, stomach aches, haemorrhoids and Eton – where he spent several unhappy years cheeking his masters and writing sarcastic essays on 'the Value of Lent'. This combination of lit-eral and metaphorical dyspepsia remained with him through his life: a letter home from a convalescent holiday in Lausanne contains the confes-sion that he has bought a copy of James Joyce's *Ulysses* – 'Don't write and tell me that I ought not have done it because I know that perfectly well.'[28]

His entrance into British film was procured through the purest nepotism: his mother took C. M. Woolf to tea, who, thrilled to have a great-grandson of Alfred Lord Tennyson dangled before him, found the boy a place as a camera assistant under Michael Balcon. 'When he entered the Gaumont British studio at Shepherd's Bush early in May of 1932,' recalled Charles Tennyson, 'a rather frail, sensitive-looking boy of nineteen, the studio, which had some experience of failures from the universities, were not convinced that he would last more than two months.'[29] He stayed with Balcon for the rest of his career, following him from Gaumont to MGM to Ealing.

At Gaumont he was assigned to assist Alfred Hitchcock. On *The Man who Knew Too Much* (1934), he became acquainted with the fifteen-year-old star, Nova Pilbeam – a wholesome blonde with dark, accusing eyebrows like Tenniel's Alice – who, during the war years, would marry him and bury him in quick succession. On *The 39 Steps* (1935), he was subjected to an indignity of which, according to Jonathan Balcon, he never learned to see the funny side. Hitchcock told him that Madeleine Carroll had refused to be hoicked across the film's set of the Scottish marshes, obliging the assistant director to drag up in a blond wig, skirt and heels, and submit to a manhandling from Robert Donat. It seems that Hitchcock invented this actressy squeamishness: even when her character is being pulled by Donat through the bars of a fence, it is clearly Carroll in every frame. (She might have had good reason to be difficult: when Hitchcock was dissatisfied with a shot in which she was required to react in horror to the appearance of a pair of sinister pursuers, the director provoked a more extravagant reaction by whipping his penis from his trousers.)[30]

Working with Hitchcock provided Tennyson with a rich and strange education in the movies. It also convinced him that to take on the responsibility of directing a feature film was a certain path to madness. He wrote:

Many lunatics are credited with the belief that the rest of the world is insane and that they alone are supremely sensible. In the entertainment business we see about as much of the outside world as the small boy sees of sex who peers at it through the slot-machines on Brighton Pier. I think in some mysterious way that a film director's complete isolation from the world proper and his inevitable, if partial, isolation from even his own world of moviedom are the principal causes for the collapse of his reason.[31]

When he came to tackle his own first feature, he ensured that its subject was as close as possible to the movements of everyday life.

There Ain't No Justice (1939) is one of the first British films of the sound era to make a serious attempt to represent the lives of working-class Londoners. It stars Jimmy Hanley, a good-natured juvenile lead with cow eyes and colourless lashes, as Tommy Mutch, a boy recruited into the boxing ring from the audition of a bloody street brawl. It is lush with documentary detail: the Notting Hill café proprietor who fries rancid sausages below a sign reading, 'Eat Here and Keep Your Wife as a Pet'; the school-age wide boys in hats and sharp jackets, lolling at the pinball machine; the teenage waitress sitting in her mother's kitchen, applying lipstick between mouthfuls of fried kipper.[32] Its technical flair betrays the influence of Tennyson's master: the climax of the picture combines the thrill of a two-minute countdown with an exhilaratingly violent riot; a scene in which Tommy attempts to prevent his sister cutting her throat with their father's razor leaves you amazed that both have survived with their fingers intact. Hitchcock would also have appreciated his apprentice's pitiless sketch of female sexuality: Nan Hopkins, in what seems to have been her only film role, is gloriously graceless as Dot Ducrow, a posh-Cockney *vagina dentata* in a fox-fur wrap. She licks residual smears of chocolate from the wrapper ('Don't do that,' chides her lover, 'you'll spoil yer face'); her tongue plays over her lips as she watches Tommy pulverising his sparring partner; she spices her conversations with smutty aphorisms, of the Mae West school – 'Me and the mounties', she smirks, 'always get our man.' But the picture is informed by a social awareness that is found nowhere in Hitchcock, not even in the latter's boxing picture, *The Ring. There Ain't no Justice* boasts a spiv villain whose predilection for American gangster slang embodies the same anxieties about Hollywood's impact upon British criminality expressed in Orwell's *Decline of the English Murder*; the scarred, sightless fighter who appeals for charitable donations before Tommy's big match suggests that the cheery working-class sport contains a world of exploitation and misery; the homoerotic interest shown in Tommy by his trainer – a broken-down old boxer with the figure of a pugilist tattooed on his right cheek – gestures forward to the passion that William Hartnell feels for Richard Harris in *This Sporting Life* (1963).[33] A film as rich as this does not deserve to be lost in obscurity.

Tennyson's follow-up picture is also rarely seen, despite the magnitude of its star, Paul Robeson. By 1939, Robeson had already shot four films in Britain, where he enjoyed greater popularity than in his homeland. He took pride in one: *Song of Freedom* (1936), a sophisticated comedy which contains the world's first screen kiss between two black actors, and on which Robeson had final cut approval. He expressed gentle indifference towards *Big Fella* (1937), a comic thriller set on the Marseille docks, and *Jericho* (1937), in which he plays a fugitive American soldier who reinvents himself as a North African chieftain. (The latter film suffers from the unedifying sight of John Laurie, the beetle-browed Scot made famous by *Dad's Army*, declaiming, 'You speak with the will of Allah!' from under his kaffiyeh; but it also features a lovely moment in which Robeson's character demonstrates his cultured intelligence by giving the name of Anatole France to the military thugs on his tail.)

His first British movie, however, became a matter of bitter regret. For Korda's *Sanders of the River*, Robeson had been persuaded into earrings and leopardskin, to boom his submission to Leslie Banks's colonial governor. ('Sandi the strong! Sandi the wise! Righter of wrongs, hater of lies!' he sings, in his seismic bass, from the prow of a dugout canoe coasting down the Thames at Shepperton.) Robeson disowned the picture, telling journalists that it was the only one of his films that had been screened in Italy and Germany, 'for it shows the Negro as Fascist States desire him – savage and childish', but his later claim to have walked out of the premiere in disgust was a reinvention of history.[34]

In 1938, depressed by the quality of the roles he was being offered by British and American producers, Robeson renounced the commercial cinema. Tennyson's *The Proud Valley* (1940) brought him back to the medium. It is the story of David Goliath, an unemployed American sailor who rolls up in a Welsh pit village and is given a job in the mine principally because the choirmaster (Edward Chapman) wants him to compete in the Eisteddfod. Its plot was formulated by Herbert Marshall, a director of the socialist Unity Theatre, and the picture went into production at Ealing days before war was declared. The timing was unfortunate. If it

had been completed in peacetime, it would have been the most uncompromisingly Marxist picture ever produced in Anglophone cinema: a
British film with an African-American star, about a group of Welsh miners who band together to turn their pit – closed by its owners after a cave-
in – into a syndicalist co-operative. But the outbreak of hostilities obliged
Balcon and Tennyson to bring their story to a more conciliatory conclusion. The finished movie retained its admiration for its band of South
Wales Stakhanovites; it continued to preach its message that class solidarity was a great weapon against bigotry ('Why', says the choirmaster, 'damn
and blast it, aren't we all black down that pit?'); it declined to soften its
images of Valleys poverty (shots of its cast sifting through the slag heaps
for chunks of good coal recall Orwell's accounts of this activity in *The
Road to Wigan Pier*). Instead of taking control of the means of production, however, the miners meet with the management, which, shamed by
the foreman's eloquent speech about the necessity of coal production in
wartime, allows the men to clear the sealed section: 'You know the risks
that will have to be faced in the trenches, in the sky, on the sea, aye, and by
our women and children in their homes. Coal in wartime is as much a
part of our national defence as guns or anything else. So why not let us
take our chance down the pit?'

Filming began on 23 August 1939 (the day that the Nazi–Soviet Pact was
signed) and concluded one month later. On 28 September, Robeson and
Tennyson sat down to watch a rough cut of the picture, and the star pronounced himself delighted. Robeson and his family then boarded the
USS *Washington* for the voyage back to New York. When they walked into
the ship's restaurant, the head waiter informed them that black passen-
gers were obliged to take their meals in their cabins. They refused to com-
ply.[35] When the liner docked in New York, Robeson made a statement to
the press which was to have grave consequences for *The Proud Valley*. 'The
gentlemen of Munich', he told waiting reporters, 'are seeking to preserve
. . . a Nazi Germany with one exception – without Hitler.' The pact
between Stalin and the German Chancellor, he argued, was a consequence of British and French disinclination 'to collaborate with the Soviet Union in a real policy of collective security'. The war, he reasoned, was
an imperialist campaign in which Russia would be the next target.[36]

Just before the grand Leicester Square premiere of *The Proud Valley*,

Balcon and Tennyson learned that the press magnate Lord Beaverbrook, owner of the *Daily Express*, *Sunday Express* and London *Evening Standard*, was intending to launch a campaign against Robeson from the pages of his newspapers, with the intention of sabotaging the prospects of the film. Balcon demanded an interview with Arthur Christansen, Editor of the *Daily Express*, but instead received a savage phone call from Beaverbrook, in which he denounced Robeson and declared that his titles would simply ignore *The Proud Valley*, denying the film publicity. The story did not emerge until 1947, when a Royal Commission was established, with the object of 'furthering free expression of opinion through the press'. One of the witnesses called was Michael Foot, Editor of the *Evening Standard* between 1941 and 1943. Foot told the committee that a blacklist existed at Beaverbrook's newspapers, and that Robeson's name had been added after a personal quarrel with the proprietor. 'Names were put there', said Foot, 'in order that the person concerned should not get any publicity.'[37] E. J. Robertson, General Manager of Express Newspapers, denied that Robeson's name had been banned from the paper, though he did confess that Noël Coward was subject to a boycott after his decision to follow the sinking of a British destroyer in *In Which we Serve* with a shot of a copy of the *Express* floating in the water, its headline reading, 'No War This Year'.[38] When Beaverbrook appeared before the committee, however, he denied everything. 'I have seen Robeson twice,' he said, 'once when he came down to my place in the country and once when he dined with me in town, and we have never had the slightest quarrel. I should say that there are names on the list sometimes for the protections of persons and not for the protection of the newspaper, but never political.'[39] Nearly fifty years later, Michael Foot is adamant that Beaverbrook was lying. 'There was certainly a blacklist at the *Evening Standard*. Mountbatten was on it, for something that he'd said at Beaverbrook's house. Robeson was on it for political reasons, because of his views on Russia and on the British Empire. But his being black had nothing to do with it.' He illustrates his point by describing his first interview with Beaverbrook for a job on the *Standard*: he walked into the proprietor's office to find him putting an Ella Fitzgerald record on the gramophone. Their mutual enthusiasm for her recording of 'A-Tisket-a-Tasket', he suspects, secured him employment on the paper.[40]

Edward Chapman and Judy Campbell brave the Atlantic crossing
in *Convoy* (1940)

For his final film, Pen Tennyson was briefed to produce a script about
the Atlantic convoys, and, in the company of his cameraman Roy Kellino,
boarded the HMS *Valorous* to conduct research and take footage under
attack conditions. He returned to Ealing to find that his instructions had
been revised: the naval drama now required the addition of some female
love-interest, in the form of Judy Campbell, a new signing to the studio,
and the actress for whom Maschwitz and Manning had written 'A
Nightingale Sang in Berkeley Square'. Before her death in June 2004,
Campbell was the only surviving cast member of a Pen Tennyson film.
She had no fond memories of the experience.

Her first film appearance was in *Saloon Bar* (1940), Ealing's adaptation
of a popular stage whodunnit, in which she pulled pints as a hard-as-
nails barmaid called Doris. 'That was easy,' she reflected, 'because we
were just photographing the play. I wore a shiny satin dress, lots of lipstick, and had good melodramatic Cockney lines to say, like "I've seen a

broken bottle pushed in a man's face and I've laughed, see?"[41] *Convoy*
(also 1940), however, robbed her of one of her best features and a sizeable chunk of her self-esteem. 'I lost my eyebrows thanks to that movie,'
she said. 'As you can see, they go up separately, and this so enraged the
make-up man at Ealing that he sat me down, took a cut-throat razor and
shaved them off. I was paralysed in the chair. I had lovely eyebrows, like
Audrey Hepburn, but in those days they didn't like that kind of thing, so
new ones were pencilled in.' The indignity did not end there. The make-
up artist told her that her lower lip was too thin and would need building up with thick black make-up. Then he picked a quarrel with her
nose. He would have to draw a line down the middle of it to give it more
shape. Had she, he asked, considered plastic surgery? And then there was
the gap in her teeth – plugged first with candle wax, and later with a den-
tal bridge. The public-address system at Ealing carried regular bulletins
announcing that Miss Campbell's teeth had been found at the bottom of
a soup-plate in the studio canteen. That Tennyson resented her presence
on the set did not help. Nor did the fact that he made her play her scenes
in carpet slippers, in order to reduce her height relative to that of the
male lead, Clive Brook. 'I had the feeling that the cinema world wanted
to keep its secrets, like cooks who don't pass on their recipes,' she told
me. 'There was a complicity between people involved in film, and somehow, I was outside it. I felt that they all thought I was a stage actress and
was going to overdo it, so I tried frightfully hard to keep a stiff upper lip,
literally. The relief of leaving that film studio, driving to the Comedy
Theatre where *New Faces* was playing amid falling bombs, and getting
out on that stage to sing "A Nightingale Sang in Berkeley Square" was
immense.'

As Campbell discovered, Ealing was a relentlessly male institution.
(One of its few female members of staff, Diana Morgan, was customarily
referred to as 'the Welsh bitch'.) But Campbell's unhappiness and Tennyson's ambivalence about her place in *Convoy* are appropriate to a film
that is so transitional in nature, so caught between two styles of cinema,
two ways of regarding the war. *Convoy* is a propaganda piece, a morale-
booster. Its object is to slice the sides from the HMS *Apollo* and the ships
it protects, to show us the brave crews putting personal differences aside
and standing firm against the enemy. George Orwell, anatomising the

English character the year after *Convoy* was produced, described how 'in moments of supreme crisis the whole nation can suddenly draw together and act upon a species of instinct, really a code of conduct which is understood by almost everyone, though never formulated'.[42]

Tennyson, it seems, could not quite obey this instinct. Even during the chaos of the attack, the ranks do not wander from their separate orbits. On the bridge, Captain Armitage (Clive Brook) and Lieutenant Cranford (John Clements) conduct a gentlemanly fight over Judy Campbell – resolved by that old standby, the act of self-sacrifice in the blazing pump-room. The men below, however (represented by, among others, Edward Chapman and Edward Rigby, former residents of *The Proud Valley*), are only prepared to offer limited allegiance to their superiors. They mutter sarcastic comments during Brook's speeches; they break regulations by offering rum to the Nazi POWs brought aboard for transfer; they complain about the injustice that one of their comrades who married two hours before they left port 'hadn't the time nor the opportunity to consummate the union'. Only the Captain's batman – who brings him cocoa as Nazi torpedoes pummel the ship – seems able to move between these spheres. All the warmth, however, is reserved for the men below decks. You can sense Tennyson's discomfort with his obligation to make heroes of officers who can only smile out of one side of their mouth and address junior colleagues as 'young fellow m'lad'.

In June 1940, once *Convoy* was completed, Tennyson took up a long-deferred commission in the Royal Navy. He attended several months of lectures, during which he scribbled ideas for films in his notebook. By the end of the year, he had been recruited into the Admiralty's instructional film unit. During his periods of leave, he and Nova Pilbeam stayed at Upper Parrock. At the end of June 1941, Tennyson spent a few days at the Balcons' London flat before departing for a shoot at Scapa Flow. 'I was sleeping in a camp bed at the foot of my parents' bed,' recalls Jonathan Balcon, 'and Pen came in one evening, and said, "Johnny, I've got this for you." It was a very battered old watch, and he said, "There's a twelve-bore shotgun at the gunsmith's in Charing Cross, which is being done up, and I want you to have it when you're old enough to learn to shoot." I think he must have had some kind of premonition.' On 7 July, the work at Scapa completed, he jotted a telegram to his wife – 'Will be with you tomorrow

Nova Pilbeam and Pen Tennyson honeymooning in Southend

evening – cheers' – and hopped on a plane to Rosyth. An hour later, in fine weather, the plane smashed into a Scottish hillside. Charles Tennyson was staying at Upper Parrock when the news of his son's death came through. A fortnight later, Pen's brother Julian was killed in action in Burma.

Balcon paid tribute to his lost colleague in the letters pages of the newspapers, praising his lyricism and his social conscience.[43] He charged Monja Danischewsky with the organisation of a memorial service at St Martin's in the Fields, at which the actor John Clements read William Cory's translation of a poem by Callimachus – 'They told me, Heraclitus, they told me you were dead' – despite the objections of Ealing's resident composer, Ernest Irving, who dismissed the verse as 'just an old pederast's lament for his boy friend'.[44] Years after the tragedy, Balcon continued to place a notice in the 'In Memoriam' column of *The Times*, marking the occasion more publicly than the Tennyson family. He founded a library in Pen's name at Eton, and throughout his lifetime paid to have new books on cinema bound in vellum and filed on its shelves. When he came to write his autobiography, Balcon placed Tennyson's photograph on the same page as those of his children. 'A brilliant talent,' reads the caption, 'tragically cut off by the war.'[45]

Balcon gave Pen Tennyson the credit for determining Ealing's wartime aesthetic. The young director 'was socially conscious and it seemed to him the most natural thing in the world that this consciousness should be reflected in his work'. *There Ain't no Justice* had given Balcon 'food for thought'. *The Proud Valley* was 'a step in the right direction'. *Convoy* achieved a new synthesis of 'the strictly documentary and the story elements', even if, with hindsight, its producer believed that 'the balance went a little too much in favour of the story at the expense of realism'.[46]

It took several months, however, for Balcon to mould the studio's war pictures around these new principles. Ealing's next treatment of the conflict, *Ships with Wings* (1941), was a retrograde step in every respect: despite the critic Alexander Walker's bizarre description of it as a 'docudrama', the film is an encomium to nonsensical derring-do, in which acts of extravagant self-sacrifice by yah-yah Fleet Air Arm officers are represented by yards of substandard model work.[47] Balcon was furious with his son for suggesting that the special-effects shots were achieved with the use of Dinky toys: perhaps this small remark also helped to enshrine documentary realism as the studio's guiding principle.

A more obvious impetus for this change came from Balcon's shifting relationship with the Ministry of Information. In 1940, he had made a bid to take over the running of the GPO Film Unit, the outfit responsible for landmark documentaries such as *Coal Face* (1935) and *Night Mail* (1936). When this plan was blocked by the Ministry, Balcon retaliated by encouraging the unit's most gifted staff to defect to Ealing. Alberto Cavalcanti, the Brazilian film producer who headed the unit, and the cinematographer Douglas Slocombe, who had risked his life filming Nazi atrocities in Danzig, were among the new recruits.

Like Pen Tennyson, Slocombe had Homeric tales read to him as a small boy. He can recall sitting on the knee of a visitor to his family's Paris flat, a short-sighted young man who loved to bash out old Irish songs on the piano. He can recall listening, or trying to listen, as the same myopic Dubliner read aloud from the manuscript of his unpublished novel – a modernist epic that squeezed an immense tract of human history into the actions of a single day. A similar act of compression would be required to do justice to Slocombe's life. He was a newspaper columnist and a photo-journalist. He was imprisoned by the Gestapo, bombed by the Luftwaffe and torpedoed by the German navy. As a cinematographer, he photo-graphed Burton, Taylor, Bogarde, Guinness, Coward, Olivier, Katharine Hepburn and the more significant Redgraves. He received three Oscar nominations, a clutch of BAFTAs and a lifetime achievement award from the American Society of Cinematographers. His CV is a list of everyone's favourite films: *Kind Hearts and Coronets*, *The Lavender Hill Mob*, *The Man in the White Suit*, *The Servant* (1963), *The Italian Job* (1969), *The Great Gatsby* (1974), *Close Encounters of the Third Kind* (1977), *Raiders of the Lost Ark* (1981) and its sequels. Listing all of his credits would entail something like that inventory of warships at the beginning of the *Iliad*. Spending time with him also has its Homeric aspects. A botched course of laser treatment deprived him of the use of his right eye – the one which once gazed through camera viewfinders – and the vision in his left has been deterio-rating since being injured in a jeep crash during a location recce. 'Until this happened I never worried about that,' he tells me, brightly, on my first visit. 'So long as you've got one good eye, the other one is just back-up.'

His father, George Slocombe, was Paris correspondent of the London *Evening Standard*. He counted Hitler and Mussolini among his interview subjects, and was instrumental in securing Gandhi's release from jail. Douglas was schooled in France but returned to England in 1933, where – after a stint writing a column on Parisian life from the London offices of British Universal Press – he began working as a freelance photojournalist. A series of pictures shot in Danzig in 1938 – images of Hitler Youth marches, goose-stepping troopers and attacks on Jewish businesses – altered the course of his career. 'It was the first time in my life that I had become aware of the political situation, and what the Nazi regime meant, what war meant. It made one wonder what the future would bring, what the impact would be on the world.' The American documentary-maker Herbert Kline asked him to return to the city armed with a movie cam-era, and Slocombe's life through a lens began. He stole a press pass from a British journalist, took shots of Goebbels addressing a rally, and escaped from an auditorium packed with aggressive Brownshirts by scurrying under their outstretched arms as they *sieg heiled*. He filmed the burning of a synagogue, for which he was imprisoned in a Gestapo cell, but talked himself out of his predicament so eloquently that the officers sent him on his way with a cup of tea. He was in Warsaw when hostilities began, and witnessed Polish recruits discarding their newly issued boots and fleeing, barefoot but uniformed, across the muddy countryside. He attempted to escape from Poland by rail, but the train was attacked from the air. Once the machine-guns were silent, he emerged from beneath the carriage, camera in hand. 'I filmed a shot of a young girl who had been hit. She died within minutes. It was the first time I'd filmed anything like that. She was so young and pretty.' After many weeks travelling cross-country on foot and horseback, he reached the Latvian border hours before it was closed by the Russians – and returned to London via Stockholm.

Much of Slocombe's war was spent at sea, filming material for the Ministry of Information, with his salary paid by Ealing Studios on condition that they could also make use of his footage in their own productions. Supplying material for Charles Crichton's *For Those in Peril* (1944), he persuaded naval commanders to sink depth charges and heave their destroyers around for the benefit of his camera. He retained a civilian rank: 'It enabled me to blackmail the senior officers by saying that the Ministry would frown if they weren't able to get the footage they wanted. And when the war was over, the documentary background enabled me to think in terms of quality of lighting, which stood me in good stead. A journalistic background enabled me to pinpoint the central feature of a situation, so that I didn't just make pretty pictures or compositions; I could go to the heart of the story.'

With the arrival of Slocombe and like-minded talents, the character of Ealing's war pictures underwent a shift: they re-engaged with the social themes favoured by Tennyson's pre-war work, and gained something of the newsreel's hard urgency. *Next of Kin* (1942) was a warning to the garrulous which featured a cocaine-addicted stripper used by a Nazi agent to extract information from servicemen, a domestic murder scene as beautifully choreographed as anything by Hitchcock, and a stark and violent reportage-style portrait of a disastrous raid on a German submarine base. *The Foreman Went to France* (also 1942) railed against the complacency of British business, sending Clifford Evans's resourceful engineer into enemy territory to prevent valuable machinery falling into German hands. *The Bells Go Down* (1943) depicted a disparate group of men – a small-time crook, a greyhound racer and a veteran of the International Brigade – finding a meaningful role (and, in one instance, a horrific and unexpected death) fighting the effects of Nazi fire-bombs. 'Our cities are still behind the lines,' declares their senior member (William Hartnell), who has seen comparable horrors on the streets of Madrid. 'When someone starts to pin medals on us, it'll mean they've moved right up to the front. It'll mean another Rotterdam, another Warsaw, right here in England. They'll call us heroes if it comes to that. I'd rather they went on laughing.' Hartnell's words summon up a vision of England as an inferno in which firemen are honoured over soldiers because they are the last line of defence against the incineration of its people.

Of this group of films, *Went the Day Well?* (1942) – on which Douglas Slocombe received his first screen credit – deserves the closest attention. The title of the picture was borrowed from a book to which Balcon had contributed a eulogy for Pen Tennyson; the source for the plot was a short story by Graham Greene. Cavalcanti's picture looses a Nazi platoon upon Bramley End, the kind of English village customarily represented on the lids of biscuit tins. Nazis in British films from this year tend to be shrill, corpulent caricatures: Peter Ustinov's fascist Billy Bunter in Ealing's *The Goose Steps Out* (1942); Francis L. Sullivan in *The Day Will Dawn* (1942), a monstrous sea-cow in black leather; Robert Morley in *The Big Blockade* (1942), a pouting, posturing, heel-clicking bureaucrat. Cavalcanti's Nazis arrive with khaki uniforms and perfect English accents, and the spare rooms and sofas of Bramley End are put instantly at their disposal. The audience knows from the outset that the platoon's machine-gun posts and rolls of barbed wire are to be used to aid, rather than resist, an invasion, and that a tweedy, soft-spoken villager named Wilsford (Leslie Banks) is a fifth columnist who has been promised power in exchange for his collaboration.[48] The villagers are offered clues to the true nature of their guests: when writing, one man puts a continental dash through his '7's; another carries a Viennese chocolate bar in a kit bag; an officer eats an éclair in two fascistic gulps; one of his men professes to come from Manchester but knows only London's Piccadilly. The inhabitants of Bramley End pay a cruel price for failing to act swiftly upon their suspicions: the vicar is shot dead as he attempts to summon help with the church bell; the Home Guard, returning home on their bicycles, are mown down in a machine-gun ambush. Their counter-attack, however, is brutal and efficient, and all the more shocking because it is executed by stock comic figures of English rural life. Nora (Valerie Taylor), the vicar's unmarried daughter, shoots Wilsford in the act of unbolting the doors of the manor house, inside which the village's defenders have barricaded themselves: the shot rings out, he tumbles to the carpet in slow motion, and his executioner empties two more cartridges into his body. Mrs Fraser (Marie Lohr), a matronly parish-council type, saves the village's children by picking up a grenade that has been hurled through the window of the besieged nursery, but fails to prevent her own death in the explosion. Mrs Collins (Muriel George), the scatterbrained village postmistress and shopkeeper, is forced to the most brutal deed. Held hostage in her own home, she cooks breakfast for her captor, telling him that her encounter with the Germans has been a very pleasant surprise, as the papers are always describing them as 'fiends in human form . . . sticking babies on the ends of bayonets'. The soldier is baffled by the remark. 'Babies on bayonets? What would be the advantage of that?' Mrs Collins responds cheerfully: 'That's just what I say.' Her guest finds that the pepper-pot is clogged: Mrs Collins pops open the lid to clear the obstruction, and her next words betray her mortal thoughts. 'I never had any children myself. Mr Collins blamed me for it, and I blamed him, so we never found out.' And with this wistful remark, she sends pepper streaming into the soldier's eyes. As he falls from his chair, tipping over the tea table, Mrs Collins reaches for the axe beside the kitchen stove and swings the blade down upon her guest. We see his lifeless hand splayed amid the broken china, and Mrs Collins, weeping with horror, trying to tidy her hair. She runs to the switchboard and buzzes the exchange in the next village, but the two young telephonists who should take her call are in the middle of an energetic gossip. ('That's old mother Collins,' sneers one. 'She can wait.') But she can't. A trooper is at the post office door. Mrs Collins crouches on the floor in a futile attempt to avoid his gaze. His bayonet plunges into her body just as the telephonist answers her call. The line is as dead as Mrs Collins.[49] It is Ealing's greatest contribution to the cinema of civil defence, and a gesture towards its films to come. As government documents indicate, the publicans, postmen, vicars and nannies who populate Ealing's post-war world are the very people who would have formed the core of the British resistance if the swastika had ever flown over Buckingham Palace.

What kind of peace did Ealing's film-makers envisage for Britain, in the event of its survival? *They Came to a City* (1944) – adapted from the play by J. B. Priestley – predicted a socialist Utopia to which the greedy and the venal would not be admitted. (Renée Gadd plays one of those too selfish to remain within its walls.) *The Halfway House* (also 1944) suggested that the fire of war might be used to burn away the corruption, superstition and discord of the past. In Cavalcanti's film, the ghosts of a Welsh innkeeper and his daughter (played by Mervyn and Glynis Johns) nudge a rag-bag group of malcontents and sinners towards moral recuperation: a black marketeer renounces his trade; a pair of divorcees repair their relationship; a married couple driven apart by the death of their son resolve their differences in a cathartic endgame (she holds a séance to contact the boy's spirit, during which her husband switches on the radio, allowing the voice of a young serviceman to ring out, as if in answer to her invocations). At the conclusion of the film, the inn is destroyed by German bombs, the guests troop from the rubble to new lives, and their host and his daughter are consumed by the flames.

In the first month of 1945, Balcon declared that he was confident that Ealing's work could project a new image of Britain to the rest of the world: 'Britain as a leader in Social Reform . . . in the defeat of social injustices and a champion of civil liberties; Britain as a parent of great writing, painting and music; Britain as a questing explorer, adventurer and trader; Britain as the home of great industry and craftsmanship; Britain as a mighty military power standing alone against terrifying aggression.'[50] Six months later, Labour achieved the election victory for which he had been working for the previous four years: Attlee's administration came to power just days before Hiroshima and Nagasaki, conflagrations more terrible than anything William Hartnell's firefighter could have envisaged, marking the world's passage from hot war to cold war. The new government implemented the Beveridge Report, initiated a programme of nationalisation, and – without a word to Parliament or public – spent £100 million on the development of a British nuclear bomb.

With Labour in power, Balcon was no longer in opposition. He no longer had to wrangle with Churchill or the Ministry of Information. His friends were cabinet ministers. As if in reflection of this new status, he commissioned *Scott of the Antarctic*, and saw it through to completion, despite being forced to secure the co-operation of one of the survivors, Teddy Mount Evans, with a £2,000 bribe, and beg Scott's widow for her consent as she lay on her sickbed at the Marylebone Hospital. Balcon received a knighthood for his trouble.

But his patrons did not stay in power for long. The election of 1950 slashed Labour's majority to five seats. The following May brought the defections to the USSR of the diplomats Guy Burgess and Donald Maclean. In June, communist North Korea marched south: Attlee made desperate telephone calls to Washington, and persuaded them not to inundate Pyongyang with mushroom clouds. Britain was back at war, but it was a conflict guided by a new set of political polarities. By the end of October, despite securing a larger share of the vote than the Conservative Party, Labour found itself back in opposition.

What would be the reputation of Ealing Studios, if it had been wound up at the same time as Britain's first experiment in socialist government? Its final year of production would have comprised Basil Dearden's *Cage of Gold* (1950), about a young doctor who chooses service in the NHS over the material rewards of private practice; Charles Frend's *The Magnet* (also 1950), a picaresque comedy starring the young James Fox as a psychiatrist's son; Dearden's *The Pool of London* (1951), a fine documentarist melodrama starring Earl Cameron as a Jamaican sailor on leave in the capital; Charles Crichton's *The Lavender Hill Mob*, centred upon an unlikely plot to rob the Bank of England; and Mackendrick's *The Man in the White Suit*, released in August 1951, and the last Ealing film to enter cinemas under a Labour administration.

Before he discovered the unperformed stage play from which *The Man in the White Suit* was freely adapted, Alexander Mackendrick had been 'trying to think of a comic way to deal with the moral issue of the invention of nuclear weapons'.[51] It wasn't a cranky aspiration. *Seven Days to Noon* (1950) was a rare attempt to deploy the atomic bomb for dramatic purposes. More common was the approach of *Mr Drake's Duck* (1951), in which the army besieges a farm on which one of the birds has taken to laying uranium eggs. (Their unusual quality is detected when Yolande

Donlan boils one for breakfast and finds that it repels the spoon with a harsh electric twang.) *The Man in the White Suit* is the story of a research chemist whose formulation of an indestructible artificial fibre triggers a painful crisis in a large industrial town. But the nuclear issue is visible through its clothes – not least because Sidney Stratton blows up several laboratories in the course of his work.

In 1945, when Clement Attlee returned from Washington after a summit on the use of atomic weapons, his lecture to the Royal Society offered a perfect adumbration of the thematic concerns of Mackendrick's picture:

The scientist and the poet have to live in the world with other citizens and have their civic responsibilities. If, as I believe, it is right that in all departments of our national life, and particularly in those of government, we should seek the advice of scientists and should understand as far as we can the problems in which they deal, it is equally important that scientists should understand the problem of those engaged in government and the difficulties with which they are confronted. I believe that the ideal of scientists for free interchange of knowledge can only be realized in a world from which war has been banished. It is not merely the dangers to which, through scientific achievements, the human race is exposed that should be in our minds, but we must realize the beneficent advantages which science can give us and which can only be fully utilized in a world of peace where free peoples freely cooperate to their common ends.[52]

As Attlee had just been informed by the Americans that, contrary to their wartime treaty, the launch of further nuclear attacks would not require British consent, he must have known that such a world was as far away as it had ever been.

'Each character in the story', Mackendrick told his biographer, 'was intended as a caricature of a separate political attitude, covering the entire range from Communist, through official Trades Unionism, Romantic Individualism, Liberalism, Enlightened and Unenlightened Capitalism to Strong-Arm Reaction. Even the central character was intended as a comic picture of Disinterested Science.'[53] Nobody escapes criticism, but this is not satire in the manner of the sour, plaguey comedies of the Boulting brothers, which encouraged their audiences to feel an unearned superiority towards any ideological position. *The Man in the White Suit* has genuine agony twisting inside its narrative. Sidney's invention is a scientific

triumph. It is also an economic disaster for a Britain struggling to remedy the physical and fiscal destruction of the war. ('Why can't you scientists leave things alone?' rages Sidney's former landlady. 'What's to
become of my bit of washing when there's no washing to do?') Capital
and labour, it seems, prefer their traditional armed neutrality, and Sidney
is left, sprawling and trouserless, on the cobbled streets. Should we lament
or applaud his (temporary) defeat? And how could we possibly know,
when he is played by an actor like Alec Guinness?

Let Guinness, the actor most identified with Ealing, accompany this
chapter to its conclusion. In the following few paragraphs, which appropriately take about four minutes to read, I'd like to suggest why *The Man
in the White Suit* would have offered no reassurance at all to anybody facing nuclear obliteration.

Alec Guinness's memoirs offer their subject in the persona of the
Knightsbridge curmudgeon, grumbling about the regional accents of
radio announcers, shopping for Issey Miyake shirts, swapping pleas-
antries with Dirk Bogarde at the veg counter. Sometimes this voice seems
nothing more than an amusing noise, like the brilliant impersonation of
a London tram that he performs in *Malta Story* (1953) – 'mmmmm-
mmmmm-ynggggggg-yaaaaang', near enough. His literary tastes may offer
a better map of his true nature. Guinness was fond of quoting T. S. Eliot,
another artist who sought sanctuary from the bleak conclusions of his
work in the rose garden of Catholicism. Nobody has bettered Guinness's
readings of Eliot's poetry: that ruminative, resonant, gurgling voice
cleanses every 'weialala leia wallala leialala' of the stain of the ludicrous.
When he appeared as the Unidentified Guest in the original production
of *The Cocktail Party* (1949), Guinness became the mouthpiece for the
poet's meditations upon the malleable nature of identity:

> And nobody likes to be left with a mystery.
> But there's more to it than that. There's a loss of personality;
> Or rather, you've lost touch with the person
> You thought you were. You no longer feel quite human.[54]

And yet, Guinness was no blank space, no man who wasn't there. He
wasn't like Peter Sellers, whose disguises – in *Dr Strangelove* (1963), *I'm All*

Right Jack (1959) and everywhere else – concealed nothing but panic at his own emptiness. Guinness was born with a capacity for anonymity. The illegitimate son of a barmaid named Agnes de Cuffe – from whom he dissociated himself at the age of eighteen – his birth certificate bore a white space where the name of his father should have been. (With characteristic drollery, he called his first autobiography *My Name Escapes Me*.) He was fond of relating how he had once handed in his coat at a hotel cloakroom, been told that it was unnecessary to give his name, and discovered at the evening's end that his ticket bore the inscription 'Bald with glasses'. He was delighted when he managed to attend a screening at the National Film Theatre of Ronald Neame's *The Card* (1952) without being recognised by anyone in the audience. 'Alec as a person was almost invisible,' recalls Neame, who produced the film. 'He was like one of those dolls which I remember from when I was a kid, on which you would hang different things to make them a soldier or a pilot.' Knowing his predilection for disguise, directors dressed him up in wigs, skins, epaulettes, corsets, cassocks or turbans: he was haunted by six ancestral versions of himself in *Barnacle Bill*, slaughtered several times over in *Kind Hearts and Coronets*, attempted to murder himself in Hamer's *The Scapegoat* (1959) and everybody else in *Murder by Death* (1976). He frequently played across racial boundaries: he is quietly imperious as Prince Feisal in *Lawrence of Arabia* (1962), preposterous as Professor Godbole in *A Passage to India* (1985), and knowingly foolish in *The Comedians* (1967), as a bogus major who drags up as a Haitian washerwoman in order to escape the rifle butts of the Tonton Macoute. (The sequence in which Elizabeth Taylor happens upon Peter Ustinov, Richard Burton and a floral-frocked, boot-polish-smeared Guinness standing in her hallway is the most peculiar moment in the careers of all four.) But for all the variety of these roles, these characters share something. They are men at one remove from the people who surround them; men suspended in a private dream; men who know something we don't, and would never blab. Little wonder that John Le Carré was so satisfied when he heard whom the BBC had cast as his inscrutable cold warrior George Smiley. Look into the eyes of Sidney Stratton, and you see a man who might blow up the world to satisfy his scientific curiosity.

'Most people', said Mackendrick, 'think of Sidney as an entirely idealis-

Alec Guinness emphasises the sinister side of Sidney Stratton in a publicity shot
for *The Man in the White Suit* (1951)

tic and sympathetic young man. He's nothing of the sort. If you look at it
closely, you'll see that he's just as selfish and self-interested as any of
them.'⁵⁵ Had history played out differently, *The Man in the White Suit* may
well have been the Ealing comedy which counted down the last hours
before Britain's obliteration. How many of us would have been calm
enough to gaze upon the face of Alec Guinness, and wonder what
thoughts were moving behind those feline eyes, or guessed at the knowledge that he nursed, but never yielded?

CHAPTER SEVEN

They Were Sisters

The Gainsborough girls: Jean, Pat and Phyllis

Patricia Roc, Phyllis Calvert and Jean Kent: three women in the back of an army truck; three prisoners of Vichy France in transit to a Nazi detention centre. A spy, a reporter and a bubble dancer. The audience, of course, having seen them a dozen times before, are on first-name terms: Pat, Phyl and Jean; one in a military greatcoat, one with her hair tied up in a Rosie the Riveter headscarf, one slouching in her slatternly fur wrap. All have perfect hair and immaculate make-up. 'My name's Thompson,' breezes Phyl. 'Freda Thompson. What's yours?' Pat turns her eyes to the canvas wall. 'Rosemary Brown,' she says, her voice dull with reluctance. 'We haven't run across each other before, have we?' asks Phyl. 'Your face strikes a chord, somehow.' Pat says that she doesn't think so, although it's clear that she does. This interrogation is cut short by Jean, who, in her mildly transatlantic bar-room drawl, breaks in on their conversation. 'Do I exist?' she demands, with a sullen stare. 'You do,' bristles Phyl, 'but I feel it's a mistake.' She makes the introduction anyway. 'This is Bridie Johnson, known to half of Paris – the male half – as Bubbles Kelly. Married, divorced, married again, divorced again – stop me if I've missed one.' Jean fixes her with a murderous stare. 'I'd like to strangle you,' she snarls. They have been sharing a cell for the past six months. 'Just imagine', chatters Phyl, 'listening for six months to the unexpurgated version of her love life. The only way she could get to sleep was to count men jumping over a stile.'

The picture is *Two Thousand Women* (1944). The studio is Gainsborough. And from its opening moment, when the Regency lady on the title card inclined the brim of her flower-decked hat, the audience would have known what to expect: a drama of passion and restraint, love and brutality, played out in the bedrooms and hallways of the eighteenth, nineteenth or twentieth century by a cast of familiar faces. They would see Pat, Phyl and Jean, in crinolines or jodhpurs or twin-sets; Margaret Lockwood emoting in the back kitchen, her bosoms trussed in frills, her beauty spot black as a punctuation mark; Stewart Granger, with skin-tight trousers and a grin like Flynn, flaunting his reckless charm; James Mason, in business suit or breeches, basking in the heat of his own sadism; Dulcie Gray, all cried out in a comfortless armchair, her hand reaching towards the whisky decanter. Bad marriages, emotional pragmatism, physical violence: these were the themes of Gainsborough's dramas. In *Two Thousand Women*, the detention-centre inmates delight at the sight of a pair of genteel ladies beating each other up for first dibs from the camp dustbins. In *Love Story* (1944), Margaret Lockwood slaps Pat, and Pat slaps her back – hard and several times. In *Fanny by Gaslight* (also 1944), a servant feels the back of Phyl's hand. In *They Were Sisters* (1945), James Mason cuffs Dulcie Gray across the face, sending her skittering from the house and into the path of an oncoming car. *Jassy* (1947) offers a cavalcade of household savagery: in the first twenty minutes, Dennis Price has lost his family seat in a game of dice and put a bullet through his skull; Pat Roc has witnessed her father thrashing his wife's lover in the rose garden; and Margaret Lockwood – a gypsy girl with telepathic powers – has been rescued from being ducked as a witch, learned of her father's brutal murder and undergone incorporation into a household in which the maid has received the blacksmith's horsewhip across her face and lost the power of speech.

Like the Hepworth Company before it and Hammer after, Gainsborough articulated the individuality of its productions with a repertory company of contract stars. The names on the posters were paramount. Nobody would emerge from a Gainsborough picture and discuss the fortunes of Lord Manderstoke, Angela Labardi or Fanny Rose Flower; the talk would be of the performers who filled their costumes. Unlike Hepworth's stock company, however, these actors lived to see their work repeated on television, revived at the National Film Theatre and anatomised in academic studies.

In the course of researching this book, I was able to conduct interviews with four of these stars: Phyllis Calvert, Patricia Roc, Jean Kent and Dulcie Gray. I was struck by their no-nonsense attitudes, their polite refusal

to be intoxicated by the sentimental enthusiasms of others, or be persuaded of the cultural value of their film work. 'If anybody asks me why I
did them,' declared Phyl Calvert, on one of my visits to her London flat
before her death in the winter of 2002, 'I don't mind saying that it was
entirely for the money. I can be absolutely frank about that.'

For much of its life, Gainsborough was a family business. Its owners, the
five Ostrer brothers, were the sons of Jewish refugees from the Ukraine,
and survivors of a childhood of textbook East End poverty: they compet-
ed for the use of the family's two shirts; they lived on a diet of scraps and
broken biscuits; they left home and used their entrepreneurial skills to
amass a great deal of money. James Mason regarded them as a kind of
gestalt entity: 'Isidore had the brain, Mark was comfortable in white tie
and tails. There was David, the oldest, who was married to a mid-Euro-
pean wife and was allowed to look after foreign sales. He looked like an
unsuccessful Ruritanian Pretender in a UFA film. Then came Maurice,
who was Isidore's shadow, and lastly, you got Harry, who, having been a
school teacher, became the literary department of the studios. The five of
them had one opinion and one brain.'[1]

Their rise from the poverty line to the pink of the plutocracy was
breathtaking. Isidore was virtually penniless when he persuaded a dancing teacher named Helene Spear-Morgan to jilt her well-connected fiancé
and join him in a life of penury in Southend. In the first years of their
marriage, he paid the rent by playing dominoes for cash on the trains
between the Essex coast and Liverpool Street, while his wife produced
three children, drifted out of love with her husband, and consoled herself
with an Aberdeen Scottish terrier. As her affections waned, however,
Isidore's fortunes rose – with astonishing celerity. The brothers obtained
the dominant shareholding in Illingworth Moss, a textiles business that
machined glad-rags for popes and presidents and supplied the cloth for
Dunlop tennis balls. They added the *Sunday Referee* to their portfolio.
They founded a merchant bank. In 1926, they acquired a controlling
interest in the Gaumont-British Picture Corporation, its production
facilities at Shepherd's Bush and its chain of nearly 300 cinemas. Two
years later, they absorbed Michael Balcon's Gainsborough outfit: its studios on Poole Street, Islington, became a production base for both com-

panies while the Ostrers rebuilt the Shepherd's Bush stage as a sleek white block crammed between the terraced houses of Lime Grove. *Rome Express*, with Hugh Williams and Esther Ralston, was the inaugural production on these premises.

The transformation of Isidore Ostrer from small-time hustler to big-shot movie mogul was not sufficient to save his marriage. In the same year that the Ostrer Brothers Merchant Bank was founded, Helene Ostr-

A Gainsborough Picture

Pamela Kellino (née Ostrer, later Mason), the apex
of a Baker Street love triangle

er announced that she had fallen in love with an Italian count whom she had met on holiday in France. Her husband did not permit her a dignified exit. He cited her adultery in the divorce case and was awarded custody of their children, who, in compensation for the loss of their mother, were indulged in every whim. His eldest daughter, Pamela, a clever young woman with dark good looks and a sure sense of what she wanted, was particularly brazen in her exploitation of parental guilt. Well into her twenties, she was not ashamed to sit flirtatiously on her father's knee and sweet-talk him into acquiescence. At the age of nine, she persuaded him to liberate her from the bothersome duties of full-time education. At sixteen, she was granted permission to set up home with her fourteen-year-old sister in an apartment on New Cavendish Square. At eighteen, she decided, with extravagant inevitability, that she wanted to be a cinema actress, and was supplied with a part in Balcon's production of *Jew Suss* (1934). The cameraman, Roy Kellino, an attractive young man from a family of circus acrobats, gazed at her with hungry eyes and conveyed his passion to the finished print. When Pamela Ostrer determined to marry the man for his trouble, Isidore Ostrer was powerless to resist.

Pamela's appetites were responsible for the recruitment of her father's most celebrated star. On the set of *Troubled Waters* (1936) – a quota quickie made for Fox-British at Wembley – Roy Kellino found himself peering through his viewfinder at a taciturn young actor named James Mason. When a day of filming overran into the evening, Pamela, with a confidence rare among cameramen's wives, marched into the studio to retrieve her husband. Kellino introduced his wife to the cast of the picture – whereupon Mason decided to put his energies into cuckolding his colleague. Destroying the marriage of the boss's daughter is an unusual way to build a career, but it worked for Mason. He would turn up every day on the doorstep of the Kellinos' flat in Dorset House, a smart mansion block on Baker Street, occupy their sitting room and engage the couple in long and passionate discussions about film-making. The trio built cardboard maquettes of movie sets, discussed ideas for scripts, argued over the niceties of lighting and camerawork. They rented a summer home in Kingsgate, next door to Helene Spear-Morgan's seaside retreat, and scandalised the latter's friends by traipsing up and down the promenade in a manner that caused people to question who was married to whom. They holidayed together in Switzerland and worked on the first draft of a script entitled *Deadwater*, which, in March 1938, went into production as an independent feature funded by their pooled savings. Pamela expected her family to help out, but in a rare show of steel, Isidore and her uncle Maurice declined to back or distribute the picture – though Uncle Mark did hold a country-house party to raise funds for its completion, at which *I Met a Murderer* was adopted as a more suitably commercial title.

Perhaps the family's dissociation from the film was on moral rather than financial grounds. By the time that the director, his wife and her lover had decamped to Cookham to begin work on their joint venture, Roy Kellino had resigned himself to sharing his spouse with Mason. *I Met a Murderer* provides the evidence for his surrender. Mason plays a farmer who has killed his wife in retribution for her destruction of his favourite dog. He flees to the woods, where he meets a young writer (Ostrer) on retreat. He moves into her caravan; romantic sparks begin to fly. Kellino, in the director's chair, might have made monsters of them. Instead, his vision is benign, sympathetic.

When filming was over, the Baker Street *ménage* underwent a reconfiguration. Mason moved in with Pamela; her husband took up the unoccupied bed of Mason's new flat in Bickenhall Mansions, a redbrick block on Marylebone High Street. An intercom was installed at Dorset House, in order that messages might be taken for both men without exposing Kellino's departure from the household. Announcement of the couple's separation was delayed until after the premiere of *I Met a Murderer*, but their worries about adverse publicity were unnecessary: the release date coincided with the outbreak of war, and the picture sank without trace.

During the divorce proceedings, Kellino awoke suddenly from his passive state. Just as his father-in-law had done with the Italian count, he named Mason as co-respondent – much to the horror of their families and the delight of the Sunday papers. Amazingly, however, he maintained friendly relations with his former wife and her new husband. Years later, he directed them together on their American television show. Perhaps he guessed that Mason would eventually grow to loathe Pamela's pushy garrulousness. (One Hollywood wit suggested that Mrs Mason had been 'vaccinated with a phonograph needle'.[2]) Perhaps there was more to the relationship than the transfer of Pamela's affections from one man to another. 'I uncovered no evidence that he was gay,' conceded Mason's biographer Sheridan Morley, 'but there was a strong element of bisexuality in Mason's performances . . . what's so interesting is that it's a secret. He left you guessing.'[3]

Whatever the case, Mason emerged from this marriage enriched by a cosy five-picture deal with the family firm – in spite of his undisguised contempt for the pictures he made for his father-in-law's studio, his undiplomatic attitude towards producers in general, and the bad publicity he generated when he registered as a conscientious objector. He was forgiven when, on the first day of filming for *The Man in Grey* (1943), he floored the director, Leslie Arliss, with an enthusiastic punch in the face. Nobody raised a complaint when he decided that drinking on the set was the best way to persuade Gainsborough directors to shoot his scenes first and send him home.

Such behaviour must have appeared to be an extension of his screen persona. Gainsborough cast him as a series of smouldering sadists: he attacked Phyllis Calvert with a poker in *The Man in Grey*, administered a thrashing to Margaret Lockwood in *The Wicked Lady* (1945) and gave Dulcie Gray that furious slap in *They Were Sisters*. He professed that these roles were a trial and a bore, but the films he shot in addition to his contracted work at Shepherd's Bush suggest that he was fascinated by the bloody borderline shared by sexuality and violence. His participation in *The Seventh Veil* (1945), a cheap independent film shot at the tiny Riverside Studios, was not the result of obligation, yet it shared many of the themes of his Gainsborough pictures. It detailed the plainly Sadean relationship between a music teacher and his schoolgirl ward (Ann Todd), whom Mason's character improves to concert standard through cruel sneers and an attempt to smash her fingers with his walking stick. Despite her signs of resistance – 'Why don't you kill me properly?' she demands, in the film's most chilling exchange – Todd is persuaded by a psychiatrist that she and Mason are helplessly in love, and the film closes as she embraces her tormentor. By the time the film had won an Oscar for Sydney and Muriel Box, its husband-and-wife screenwriters, half the women of England were eager to feel the back of James Mason's hand against

their cheeks – or at least, that was what the letters pages of the fan magazines suggested.

Dulcie Gray, one of his most anguished victims, lives in a vast Palladian
mansion overlooking the Buckinghamshire town of Amersham. In 1970,
she and her late husband, the actor Michael Denison, bought the place for
a million pounds and converted it into apartments – occupying the
grandest one themselves. For decades, the couple were a West End and
touring romance, the sort of autumnal double act which, in a play by
Wilde or Ayckbourn or Agatha Christie, could pack a matinee house to
capacity with candy-floss perms. Their film careers, healthy in the 1940s,
did not survive the following decade – but the stage and TV kept them
busy until Denison's death in 1998. (Gray spent the 1980s as a sweet-tem-
pered matriarch in *Howard's Way*, a BBC soap opera about adultery
among the catamaran-owning classes.) When I visit her in the spring of
2002, she is recovering from a leg injury which, to her frustration, has
forced her to withdraw from a touring adaptation of *The Lady Vanishes* in
which she had filled the Dame May Whitty role. She is wearing a tasteful
wig and a neat little dress, upon which is pinned a jewelled butterfly
brooch. She is dwarfed by the immensity of her Regency drawing room: a
mile of thick carpet seems to separate her armchair from the focal point
of the room, a table decorated with photographs and mementoes of her
long marriage. I admire the pictures: a lunch-party group in which the
Denisons share the frame with Frankie Howerd, Dick Francis, Rebecca
West and the Queen Mother; the couple's wartime wedding photographs;
a recent publicity shot of Denison, smiling his mandarin smile. 'He was
wonderfully good looking, wasn't he?' she enthuses. And then, quite suddenly: 'People think I'm twee. Perhaps I am.' Her early life and her Gainsborough pictures, however, argue against this dismissal.

Dulcie Gray was born in a police officers' mess in Kuala Lumpur, to a
pair of British expatriates who were bounced out of their fortune by some
dodgy rubber shares and took out their unhappiness on their daughter.
She escaped them at the age of sixteen, climbing from the window of her
locked bedroom and rattling off into the night in a rickshaw. While still in
her teens – and still in Malaya – she ran a girls' boarding school, ate
opium, crushed monstrous black scorpions by the brace and wrote a pop-

ular song entitled 'You Tickle Me Spitless Baby', which, if pressed, she can still perform. In 1936, she relocated to London, where she studied painting under the surrealist Amédée Ozenfant, worked as an artist's nude model and met the head girl of her old school, touting for business on the pavement opposite the Ritz and trailing a black poodle behind her. ('A lot of tarts had them in those days,' she reflects. 'What the poodle was supposed to do when the main business got going I've no idea.') On the suggestion of a friend, she applied for a scholarship to attend the Webber-Douglas drama school, from which she emerged three years later, married to her classmate Michael Denison, and trying to choose between several offers of work. (One of these, made by a man in an upper-storey office in Soho, included a one-way ticket to Buenos Aires: when he asked her to remove her sweater, she knew it wasn't her sort of gig.)

Her first film experience was a screen test for an Associated British picture at Welwyn Garden City entitled *Banana Ridge* (1941), during which a technician let slip that the part for which she was auditioning had already been allocated to Nova Pilbeam – and that there wasn't actually any film in the camera. Gray was so furious that she stormed up to Walter Mycroft's office and told him that he was beneath contempt. Mycroft was so surprised by her outburst that he awarded her the role of Malayan Technical Adviser.

It was her role in the stage production of *Brighton Rock* that brought Gray to the attention of the Ostrers. (It also brought her to the attention of Aleisteir Crowley, who wrote to her to express his desire to sacrifice her at Stonehenge during the summer solstice.) Thereafter, Gray became Gainsborough's fall girl: the one who got kicked and slapped, and withered away. In *Two Thousand Women*, she is the comic skivvy, scuttling around the detention centre with a bucket of hot water in each hand; a faint-hearted girl who has a strip torn off her by Phyl Calvert when she dares to suggest that Pat Roc has betrayed them to their German captors. 'I was always playing very dreary women,' Gray confesses. True, her nickname in the studio was Gracie Dull, but there was a strong neurotic element to her passivity that elevated her performances beyond dreariness. In *They Were Sisters*, she is a wide-eyed ingénue who offers herself as substitute when James Mason's county-ball chancer fails in his half-hearted attempt to seduce her elder sibling (Anne Crawford). 'She's the kind that likes a man to wipe the floor with her,' scoffs Crawford, as Mason initiates a courtship that will result in him marrying Dulcie and killing her by degrees. The rest of the film illustrates how Mason sates his wife's sado-masochistic appetites until they yield to a thirst for alcohol. A chilling little scene depicts their maidservant on her way to bed as Dulcie's sobs thrum around the house: instead of running to her aid, she snaps off the light with a look of glum resignation. At the climax of the picture, when Dulcie is mown down by the passing motorist, one can't help thinking that she stood in his path deliberately.

Gray received enthusiastic notices for her performance. When she was summoned for a meeting with Maurice and Isidore Ostrer, she assumed that they intended to congratulate her and improve the terms of her contract. She remembers going to the appointment by bus and coming face to face with a photographic poster of herself on the lower deck. ('Dulcie Gray – Rising Dramatic Actress,' ran the strapline.) 'And when I got there,' she recalls. 'I got the sack. They told me I hadn't been run over glamorously enough.' Perhaps, she concedes, she didn't play the game as smartly as some of her contemporaries: Pat Roc, for instance, who – no matter what agonies and humiliations her characters were dealt – always remembered not to wrinkle her forehead. 'Pat Roc couldn't act for toffee apples,' Dulcie asserts, 'but she was beautiful. She was a very clever girl who knew her limitations exactly and didn't give a damn about them. She was no fool.'

Pat Roc's only foolish act occurred at the beginning of February 1975, when she was fined twenty-five pounds for stealing a bottle of bubble-bath and three boxes of tissues from the Oxford Street branch of Marks and Spencer. ('Have I? I'm sorry,' she is reported to have said to the store detective, when challenged about the items secreted in her bag.[4]) Soon after this moment of humiliation, she and her third husband took up permanent residence in a comfortable villa on the banks of Lake Maggiore, a few miles' drive from the Swiss resort of Locarno. Her last film work was in 1959 – three days' shooting on *Bluebeard's Ten Honeymoons* (1960), in which George Sanders shoved her from a railway bridge and into the path of an oncoming train. In later years, she jogged memories of career by consulting the autograph book that she kept throughout the 1930s and 1940s.

She was looking through it when we spoke in 2002, flipping it open on a run of pages compiled during the shoot of *Two Thousand Women*. 'From your friend,' she read, 'the one with a face like a chewed string, Thora Hird.' A few pages later, there was an inscription from Will Fyffe, the Glaswegian actor who played her father in *The Brothers* (1947). 'He was a character,' she mused. 'He committed suicide, didn't he? Threw himself through a window . . .' Looking back on her Shepherd's Bush years with five decades of hindsight, she professed to remember nothing but pleasure: 'It was as smooth as silk,' she said. 'We were the Gainsborough girls. There was never any vanity or rivalry.'

Roc was born Felicia Reise, but that soon changed when she was spotted in a West End revue by a pair of Alexander Korda's talent scouts, who rechristened her over supper at the Berkeley Grill. ('Anne Kent', she recalled, was a near miss.) It took Gainsborough, however, to realise her potential: in Frank Launder and Sydney Gilliat's *Millions Like Us* (1943), she was cast as a shy young working-class woman awoken from her daydreams by some nail-breaking work in a munitions factory and a cruel lesson in wartime love and loss. No totalitarian state ever produced such a finely nuanced propaganda picture: the stoical optimism that occupies her eyes in the closing shots of the film bears comparison with the expression employed by John Hurt when standing before the telescreens of Michael Radford's *1984* (1984).

The film won Roc a contract with the Ostrers, and established her as a symbol of war's transformative effect upon the status of women. Her characters, whether they wore whalebone or dungarees, were unpretentious, self-sufficient and pragmatic in sexual matters – which may explain how she came to be known around the studio as 'Bed Roc'. In *When the Bough Breaks* (1947), she plays a lone mother who gives up her baby to a childless middle-class couple, and learns a tough lesson when she capitalises upon the unofficial nature of the adoption to reclaim the boy. In *Love Story* (1944) – one of Gainsborough's most bizarre romantic dramas – she is an ENSA theatre director who tussles with a terminally ill concert pianist (Margaret Lockwood) for the attentions of Stewart Granger's rakish molybdenum prospector. (Granger, the narrative reveals, is in danger of losing his sight after an aerial accident, and is contemplating suicide between his Braille lessons.) The corners of this triangle find accommodation: although Granger proposes to Roc – ripping the fag from her mouth as she saws at a loaf of bread – she relinquishes him to Lockwood on a temporary basis. 'We're all living dangerously,' argues Granger. 'There isn't any certainty any more . . . Let's take the happiness we can, while we can.'

Roc lived by this sentiment. Just before the outbreak of war, she married a successful Harley Street osteopath twelve years her senior, but this did not prevent her pursuing affairs with Michael Wilding and David Niven. Her assignations with the latter took place in a room in a smart apartment block on Hallam Street which she shared with a prosperous prostitute. (Two long-time residents can attest to a compromising encounter with the pair during an air-raid.) The war had a profound impact on the day-to-day business of Roc's career. The Gainsborough stars often slept in their dressing rooms at Shepherd's Bush, while fire wardens kept constant watch on the roof. Roc recalls the spontaneous chorus of the 'Marseillaise' that broke out on the set of *Johnny Frenchman* (1945) when the liberation of Paris was announced; the moment when the cast of *Madonna of the Seven Moons* (1944) gathered around the radio to listen to the news of the D-Day landings; the afternoon when the Battle of Britain interrupted the shooting schedule of *The Farmer's Wife* (1941) ('We saw the bullets and shells shooting across the sky, and to protect ourselves we went under the hedgerows'). A Spitfire pilot, she remembered, performed a victory roll over the field in which they were sheltering. 'The war was a great time for camaraderie,' she told me. 'One hasn't got it today at all. Everybody was your friend. You talked to people, no matter who they were.'

That idea found expression in many of Gainsborough's pictures. In *Fanny by Gaslight* (1944) Stewart Granger lays out James Mason on a dance floor, assuring him that, in the twentieth century, 'class distinction . . . will be done away with'. Some hierarchies within the studio, however, remained unchallenged. Even the seating arrangements in the canteen reflected the status of stars and satellite actors. 'There was a pecking order at Gainsborough,' recalls Jean Kent, in a cheerfully brutal assessment of her contribution to the work of the studio. 'First Margaret, then Pat and Phyllis, then me. I was the odds-and-sods girl. I used to mop up the parts that other people didn't want.'

If Roc's heroines were forced into moral compromise by circumstance, Kent's embraced it with a flick of a fur stole. In *Good-Time Girl* (1947), she plays a venal young woman invigorated by a hair-yanking bitch-fight with Jill Balcon in a reform-school dormitory, and exhilarated by the murderous amorality of her GI boyfriend. Her job in *Fanny by Gaslight* is to provide a tart, tarty contrast to Phyllis Calvert's besieged heroine. 'It's not nice for a young lady to parade herself before an audience,' warns her father, but as he's the front man for a brothel patronised by gangs of champagne-swashed toffs, she declines to take him seriously and has soon emigrated to Paris to splash around in a mermaid costume on the stage of the Moulin Rouge. In *Two Thousand Women*, she tells the desk sergeant at the Nazi detention centre that her habit of talking in her sleep will necessitate her being billeted in a room of her own. 'Lots of people talk in their sleep,' he retorts, watching her stir the dust on his mahogany. 'But not quite the way I do, Sergeant,' she purrs. 'I'm not thinking of myself – it's the girl I'd have to share with.' Phyllis, watching from the other side of the room, recognises the shtick: 'The rat', she informs Pat Roc, 'is about to enter the trap after the oldest cheese in the world.' He does. And when all three women have been processed, they find the other inmates preparing a hot bath. Jean argues that the first to undress should be first in the water. 'Oh no,' protests Phyllis. 'We're not competing with pros.'

When she was thirteen, Jean Kent took her cousin's birth certificate to an audition at the Windmill Theatre, the notorious West End house which provided non-stop variety sketches, production numbers and nude tableaux to a shifting clientele of sailors on shore leave and pin-striped masturbators. The manager, Vivian Van Damm, an avuncular figure in rubber-soled shoes, known universally as 'VD', put her to work in the chorus. Trolling about the stage in a pair of net knickers – embroidered with a telephone number which, fortunately, was not her own – led to cabaret work at the Kit-Kat Club on Regent Street, live television musical comedies from Alexandra Palace, and her first film role: a tiny part for Henry Edwards in a swimming-party scene for *The Rocks of Valpre* (1935).

Jean Kent and Stewart Granger do Romany romance in a publicity still
from *Caravan* (1946)

('Would you like some cake?' was her only line.) Stooging for Max Miller
in a stage revue titled *Apple Sauce* earned her a screen test for Gainsborough. 'They dressed me up, did my hair and make-up, took me out to one

of the sound stages, and filmed me climbing on and off a bar stool and smiling at the camera,' she recalls. 'For all they knew, I had a voice like a Christmas cracker.' She didn't complain: although she spent her first year at Gainsborough delivering feed lines to Arthur Askey and Tommy Handley, she was earning five pounds a day, and was allocated dressing room 47 at Shepherd's Bush: the only one in the studio with its own lavatory.

With the exception of Pat Roc, all the Gainsborough stars I interviewed expressed irritation with nearly every aspect of the studio's operations: the quality of the scripts (particularly those of the sanguine melodramas favoured by Maurice Ostrer); the ability of the directors (Leslie Arliss in particular); casting decisions that they perceived to be unimaginative and arbitrary; the insistence upon glamour at the expense of realism. 'I think we were all victims of the Jeanette MacDonald tendency,' reflects Kent. 'Taking a bath in your jewels with perfectly tidy hair.'

Nobody could accuse these women of taking an indulgent view of their film careers. Phyl Calvert was particularly withering about this part of her curriculum vitae. 'It was all done rather frivolously,' she said, with the blithe honesty common in actresses old enough to have earned the right to say exactly what they think. 'For instance, Granger and I were about to play a scene in *The Magic Bow*, and waiting for the director, Leslie Arliss, to come back from breakfast. We got fed up waiting, so we shut the door, put the red light on and shot the scene ourselves.' Eventually, 'Arlissing about' became a Gainsborough phrase for slackness. (Listen carefully to the scene in *They Were Sisters* in which James Mason is carried down a staircase by his drunken friends, and you can hear him use the expression on camera.)

Phyl had no time for sentimentalising upon the magic of the movies, and appeared slightly baffled by my interest in this part of her career. She greeted compliments for these performances with sympathetic indulgence, or deflected them with a bathetic anecdote. 'Did you know that my love scene with Granger in *Madonna of the Seven Moons* was one of the first in which both actors took both feet off the floor?' I didn't. What did she remember about the scene? 'We shot it just after lunch, and his breath smelled terribly of sardines.'

Despite her protests to the contrary, there *was* a kind of magic at work.

The films transformed Phyllis Bickle, the penniless daughter of a drunken London blacksmith, into Phyllis Calvert, a symbol of female integrity besieged by sadism and war: a Clarissa Harlowe for the 1940s. Phyl's stories of her childhood were bloody vignettes involving her father's violent rages and injured tram-horses being shot as they flailed on the cobbles. She spoke of her discovery of the Margaret Morris Dance School on the King's Road – where she was taken on as a free pupil – like an escape through an enchanted wardrobe. (Not everything in this world was benign: her professional surname was inherited from a photographer who took some shots of her in her ballet gear, and whose interest in her, she intimated, was not entirely professional.) The stage was the object of her ambitions: film became a means of providing financial security for herself and her family. She remained as sceptical about the medium as the producers who controlled it. 'Even great stars made an awful lot of rubbish,' she said. 'The other day I watched *Mrs Miniver* for the first time, and I couldn't believe it. Greer Garson hardly moved a muscle in her face, except for one shot where she had a tiny little frown, and they cut away pretty quickly. That's what we had to do in those days. It wasn't until I did *Mandy* that I was allowed to crumple my face when I cried.'

Ted Black was the Gainsborough production chief responsible for recruiting Calvert to the company; Carol Reed, poached from Ealing with the offer of a salary of £100 a week, was the director who put her to best use. Calvert was the Cockney maid in *Kipps* (1941), returning as a stranger to the phonetics that Margaret Morris had drilled out of her. She struggled to secure her role in *The Young Mr Pitt* (1942), as its star, Robert Donat, wanted the role for Rosamund John, a young actress with whom he was having an affair. (Calvert was forced to endure forty-six make-up tests before Donat gave his consent to her casting in the picture.) In *Madonna of the Seven Moons*, she played a rape victim who develops a split personality and runs off with the gypsies. (Although the plot is pure railway-bookstand Freudianism, she manages to invest the transformation with a fierce, neurotic energy.) In *They Were Sisters*, when James Mason attempts to bribe her into covering up Dulcie Gray's suicide by promising her custody of his daughter, it's impossible to tell whether her sudden acquiescence is genuine. Could Calvert's heroine be so chillingly expedient? Would she betray her dead sister to remedy her own childlessness? The dreamy hunger in her eyes suggests that she might – and it's impossible to be sure until the film's courtroom finale. Phyl Calvert thought that it was ridiculous to take these films so seriously. 'It was like being on a conveyor belt,' she insisted. 'I had children to bring up – on my own after 1957, when my husband died. Sometimes I wish I hadn't made so many tatty films. They were just jobs, really.'

And they were jobs that entailed a large amount of unpaid overtime. The duties of the Gainsborough girls and their male equivalents did not end with the wrap: they were contracted to promote their pictures on evangelical tours of the country. Dulcie Gray and Michael Denison spent two chilly winter days being driven around London in an open-top carriage, waving awkwardly at passers-by. Dennis Price made numerous personal appearances, at which, to his bemusement, he was often introduced to the audience as Michael Denison. ('What do you think your dear little wife is doing tonight?' asked one enthusiastic cinema manager. 'She's probably in bed with Dennis Price,' he replied.) Jean Kent, with her background in revue, needed no encouragement to trot around Britain, belting out a number to the circle in every cinema she visited. ('I always took my own bouquet,' she recalls, 'in case they didn't have one.') Phyllis Calvert and her husband Peter Murray-Hill were sent out as a pair: their surviving itineraries adumbrate a world of municipal boredom and provincial toadying. On 15 June 1946, for instance, their visit to Norwich incorporated a ceremony of welcome at the railway station, lunch with the Lord Mayor and Lady Mayoress, tea with the Lord Lieutenant of the County, visits to an industrial exhibition and Everard's shoe factory, a personal appearance at the Haymarket cinema, the coronation of the Ipswich Queen of Industry, a prize-giving and a charity ball. 'Was all this as dull as it sounds?' I asked Calvert. 'Oh no,' she replied. 'Much worse.'

These practices succeeded, however, in generating a somewhat hysterical relationship between the public and the Gainsborough regulars. Dulcie Gray remembers walking into a haberdasher's in Birmingham and watching the assistant collapse in a faint as she went to fetch her a reel of black cotton. Jean Kent recalls, with genuine horror, running from a Liverpool branch of Boots in which all the staff and customers had converged upon her. She also notes that the Sunday newspapers checked constantly for cracks in her marriage to Jusuf Ramart, a film stuntman who had been part of King Zog's entourage when he absconded from Albania in 1939. When Kent took a holiday with the German actor Anton Diffring and his sisters, newspaper reports insinuated that she was having an affair with him. ('He was as queer as a three-dollar bill,' she remembers, 'but nobody seemed to notice that.')

Phyl Calvert's most informative experience with the press came in 1946, when the *Daily Mail* instituted its annual film awards, voted for by its readers. The most hotly contested category was Best Actress. 'I was taken out to dinner with the Duke of Norfolk and Lord Rothermere,' she says, 'and told that I'd won it. Then I started talking about how I didn't want a contract any more and wanted to go to America and be independent. The next day I was told that there'd been a re-count and that my chum Maggie Lockwood had won by fifteen votes. Which I couldn't care less about. But it showed you couldn't take film too seriously.'

By this time, the Gainsborough repertory company had already begun to dissolve. James Mason emigrated to Hollywood in 1947 – despite being prevented from working by a bitter legal tussle with an independent producer who took him to tea at Claridges and bamboozled him into signing a man-trap of a contract. He was never as big a box-office certainty in the States as he had been in his homeland, but that ineluctably Masonic quality – a kind of amoral authority, perhaps – lent logic to the plot of *North by Northwest* (1959) and brought a melancholy warmth to *Lolita* (1962) which was surely beyond the comprehension of its director. The limit on his magnitude, however, gave him the autonomy to pursue more obscure projects. If he had been the kind of actor whose name was always billed above the title, he would have been asked to play the Nazi in more boring war films (as it stands, two outings as Rommel is one too many on any actor's CV). He would also have been less free to make intelligent diversions such as *Autobiography of a Princess* (1975), a witty Merchant–Ivory two-hander in which he and Madhur Jaffrey conjure the ghosts of the Raj simply by drawing the curtains, running a few old newsreels and chatting together on the sofa. He died respected, rich and in Switzerland.

Stewart Granger, a significantly less sophisticated talent, made the move across the Atlantic in 1950. His good timing allowed him to become a beneficiary of Errol Flynn's appetite for self-destruction. By this time, late nights of drink, drugs and over-elaborate sex were doing to Flynn's body what two charges of statutory rape had failed to do to his reputation. As casting directors increasingly summoned Flynn from his yacht only to play alcoholics and broken-down movie stars, Granger, four years younger than the idol he had spent much of his career attempting to mimic, took their calls instead. He smiled his insouciant smile in a variety of doublets, ruffs and safari suits, and massaged more henna into his hair to conceal the evidence of age. For *Bhowani Junction* (1959) he allowed us to see that the tips of his sideburns had turned a snowy white, like the first trickle of an avalanche hitting the lower slopes. By the time he was cast as the Duke of Edinburgh in *The Royal Romance of Charles and Diana* (1982), he had evolved, quite naturally, into something more staid and soppy-stern than the Romanies and rakes he impersonated at Gainsborough. To Olivia de Havilland, playing his regal mother-in-law (despite being three years his junior) in the same film, he was a vision of how Flynn might have turned out, had she been able to save him from the consequences of his own excesses. To Granger, who confessed that Ealing's *Saraband for Dead Lovers* was his only noteworthy film, inheriting the position of his idol soon became burdensome. If Flynn had lived, he too may have ended his career comfortably bored in Eurothrillers and TV movies. Watch Granger in his last theatrically released film, and you can see that his eyes have lost their twinkle. In *Hell Hunters* (1986), he stars alongside George Lazenby as a Nazi war criminal who uses tropical spider venom to create an army of fascist zombies. Flynn, looking upon him from a more literal form of Hell, would not have been too jealous.

The Gainsborough girls had briefer and more compromising encounters with Hollywood and the American showbiz hacks who loved to bait British actresses for their hoity-toity naïveties. Lockwood took her skimmity-ride early: in 1939, she stepped from the New York quayside to a press conference and was asked if she had modelled her hairstyle on Brenda Frazier, a prominent Manhattan socialite of the period. (Frazier is memorialised in a portrait by Diane Arbus, taken when she had long exchanged nights at the Ritz-Carlton nibbling canapés and vomiting bulimically into her evening bag for nights in her apartment popping pills and rearranging the contents of her dresser drawers.) Lockwood, of course, had never heard of her, and said so. The assembled reporters could not construe this as anything but a deliberate act of nose-thumb-ing. The New York *World Telegram* headlined their Lockwood story, 'Study of a British Glamour Gal in a Fit of Loffter, Learning About Amer-icker and Its Red Indians'.

Patricia Roc received similar treatment during her six months in the States shooting *Canyon Passage* (1946) with Dana Andrews and Susan Hayward. Her problems were more semantic than social. A journalist asked her if she liked cheesecake. Roc innocently took the question to refer to baked confectionery, not soft pornography. ('And I said: "I love it. Where is it? How about it?"') She made another *faux-pas* when she instructed one of the studio managers to come to her dressing room at four in the afternoon to 'knock her up'. 'In Hollywood they couldn't wait for you to have a scandal,' she recalled, 'and they made it up if you didn't have it, and put it in the *Hollywood Reporter*. In Britain they had a certain amount of respect for you. They didn't have any in Hollywood.'

Phyllis Calvert had the most combative and character-building experi-ence. In 1947, she signed a contract with Universal-International on the understanding that her first film would be directed by Robert Siodmak, whose work on *The Killers* (1946) had convinced her that he would be able to make something of the ropey script she had received. 'They gave a big party in the studio when I arrived, and as I was leaving, the producer came to me and said he was terribly sorry, but Siodmak wasn't going to be available.' Her subsequent protest won her no friends. The following day's *Variety* stated that the new British recruit was raising a fuss about her leading man: a false story planted by the studio in order to put Calvert in her place. Over fifty years later, she could still quote the article: 'But let us tell Miss Calvert that beauty and talent are just a drug on the market here, so she'd better go straight back home.' It became a war of attrition. Calvert won the first battle: Siodmak was recalled from Europe and reas-signed to her film, *Time out of Mind* (1947), though he made it clear that he was only following orders. But Universal was now growing dissatisfied with Calvert's inability to generate publicity stories for the gossip colum-nists. When the studio manufactured a fictional pregnancy for its star, the first she knew about it was reading the story in the Hollywood press. News of her tragic miscarriage, several months later, was relayed in the same way.

Phyllis Calvert, Peter Murray-Hill and their daughter Auriol pose for press
photographers on the deck of the *Queen Mary*, 1947

Universal subcontracted its new star to Paramount, but Calvert was no
happier under new management. In an attempt, she believed, to manoeu-
vre her into breaking her contract, Paramount presented her with what
she regarded as a series of increasingly unsuitable scripts – including one
which would have had her running about in a pair of cami-knickers, pursued by Bing Crosby. If she rejected three in a row, the studio was within
its rights to tear up her final pay cheque and paint out the letters on her
dressing-room door. Her employers offered her the part of a nun in an
Alan Ladd thriller, *Appointment with Danger* (1950), knowing that this
was exactly the kind of wholesome, virtuous role from which she had
been trying to dissociate herself at Gainsborough. (Universal's executives
may even have known that she had turned down the wimpled character
in *Two Thousand Women*.) Certainly, she wrongfooted them by accepting
the part: they did not have a script to show her, and were obliged to send
her off on a six-week holiday while they hacked one out. Apart from taking a few javelin lessons for a part in Cecil B. De Mille's *Samson and
Delilah* (1949) that was eventually reallocated to Angela Lansbury, it was

Calvert's last film work in the United States. 'I hated America,' she stated unequivocally, 'and they hated me.'

Despite the vampiric influence of Hollywood, the closure of Gainsborough Pictures occurred as a result of domestic forces. In October 1941, Isidore Ostrer sold his controlling share in the company to the burgeoning film empire of J. Arthur Rank, the owner of Pinewood Studios, and, in the following decade, the single most powerful figure in the British film business. It took until 1944 for the transfer of ownership to be finalised, during which time a power struggle was played out between Gainsborough's two production chiefs, Maurice Ostrer and Ted Black. The latter had a taste for social realism; Ostrer's instinct was for melodrama. But there must have been more to their rivalry than aesthetics: after Black defected to Denham in 1944, he spent his time piloting projects that were just as fanciful as any produced by Ostrer. When he took control of the production of Alexander Korda's shapeless and profligate costume epic *Bonnie Prince Charlie* (1948), his first act was to instruct the designers to abandon their attempts at historical verisimilitude and model the production on 'a tin of McVitie's shortcake'.[5] By 1946, Maurice Ostrer had resigned from the studio to make a brief foray into independent production, and Sydney Box, the man responsible for the S&M psychodrama of *The Seventh Veil*, had been installed in the studio's biggest office.

Rank demanded output at a rate and volume that recalled the days of the quota quickies, but Box responded to the challenge by commissioning pictures that addressed post-war social issues in explicit terms. *The Years Between* (1946) cast Michael Redgrave as a prisoner of war who returns home to find that his wife (Valerie Hobson) is in possession of a seat in Parliament, and unwilling to return to pre-war domesticity. ('How long has it been going on?' he demands, as if her political career were a species of infidelity.) In *My Brother's Keeper* (1948), Jack Warner is a convict with an impressive war record who goes on the run with a young rapist (George Cole). Warner wishes that his life were 'untrodden like a field of snow', but, knowing that his escape has doomed him to die in prison, walks away from his pursuers across a patch of ground seeded with landmines. (Once he has become a dot on the horizon, an explosion wipes him from the screen.) *Lost People* (1949) offers an interesting picture of

Europe in the aftermath of war, putting Dennis Price in charge of a dispersal centre for refugees. (Its attempt at realism, however, is significantly undermined by the ludicrous miscasting of Richard Attenborough as an anguished Magyar in a goatskin jerkin.)

New faces also appeared to replace the stars lost to California. Dennis Price added arch, sexual sophistication to *The Bad Lord Byron* (1949), and must have sent audiences home with a few suspicions about exactly what forms his badness took. Eric Portman – a fastidious actor with a rich, burbling voice and a morbid horror of watching women eat – brought a new, Iago-like form of villainy to the studio's pictures. In *Daybreak* (1946) he is a hangman who has little trouble in keeping his line of work secret from his new wife; not just because she's played by the lucent, sexless Ann Todd – as incapable of a suspicious question as a plaster virgin – but because his vitreous eyes seem made for lying. In *Dear Murderer* (1947), he is a waspish cuckold who kills his wife's lover (Dennis Price) with an ingenious fake suicide involving a half-finished letter, a gas fire and a length of rubber tubing. (Seven years later, Price chose a similar method in an unsuccessful attempt to end his own life. It's claimed that his first words after regaining consciousness were 'What glory, Price?')[6]

In 1950, Gainsborough lost its identity as a separate production outfit and was absorbed in the belly of the Rank Organisation. Two of its final films, however, allocated roles to a young actor who would help to define the character of British cinema in the decade to come. In *The Boys in Brown* (1949), Dirk Bogarde is a leering Borstal inmate keen to exploit new arrivals. He manages to suggest barrack-room bullying and buggery just by the way he leans on his mop. In *So Long at the Fair* (1950), Bogarde is a delicate young man at the centre of a bizarre mystery during the Paris Exposition of 1900: not only has he disappeared, but the hotel room in which he was staying also appears to have vanished. (The riddle, we learn, has a pathological solution.) Bogarde was recruited by Rank, not Gainsborough, but, as we shall see in the next chapter, Phyl Calvert, Jean Kent and their contemporaries would have recognised the dilemma by which he was tortured. For some actors, the love of an audience is easily won. Professional satisfaction, however, is much more elusive – even if you are only in it for the money.

CHAPTER EIGHT

Breaking Rank

'Anacleto likes cats, but not from kindness': Dirk Bogarde as a Mexican bandit in *The Singer Not the Song* (1961)

In February 1961, as an extravagant enterprise entitled *The Singer Not the Song* was dying at the box office, the principal players of the Rank Organisation met to plan the funeral of British cinema. It would be a quiet affair. Contracts would be allowed to expire. The company's production activities would be wound down; the majority of its cinemas closed or converted into casinos, bingo halls and bowling alleys. Instead of films, reprographic equipment would be enshrined at the heart of the company's operations; the mass production of moving pictures abandoned for the mass duplication of memos, application forms and the bare bottoms of office-party drunks. The rights to screen the hundreds of titles in its back catalogue, representing the majority of British movies shot between the end of the Second World War and the beginning of the 1960s, would be leased to television. With these decisions, the Rank Organisation closed down the British studio system, and ensured that its work would shape Britain's sense of its native cinema for decades to come.

No British movie mogul, before or since, has exercised the power of J. Arthur Rank. He owned studios, cinemas and stars. He controlled production, distribution and exhibition. He employed 34,000 people. His corporate ident – 'Bombardier' Billy Wells, greased and semi-naked, whacking a great plaster gong – was so familiar to British cinemagoers that its sight must have induced a Pavlovian hunger for choc-ices and Kia-Ora. And even in death, the life of the organisation that bears his name has been tenacious. The contract artists of its heyday – Norman Wisdom, Kenneth More, John Mills, Dirk Bogarde – have remained the mainstays of matinee programming. How many times have you spent a rainy Sunday watching More loosing the *Titanic* lifeboats as the band strikes up 'Nearer My God to Thee'; Wisdom being dragged through a pond by a runaway lawnmower; or James Robertson Justice, ruddy and bewhiskered, demanding, 'What's the bleeding time?' of Bogarde's callow medical student? Thanks to television, these films remain as familiar today as they were to their paying audiences.

That familiarity has bred love and contempt in equal measure. For many viewers, they comfort like hot-water bottles or mashed potato. For most writers on cinema – a few crusading revisionists aside – they are regarded with disdain and suspicion.[1] Lovers of nostalgia celebrate the Rank era as a golden age; detractors deride it as a period during which social and aesthetic conservatives betrayed the radicalism of the 1940s. Neither view illuminates much save for the prejudices of its proponents. It is time to look at the Rank Organisation with a fresh eye.

The man behind the gong, J. Arthur Rank, was not obvious movie-mogul material. He was a millionaire flour-miller who went into film to spread the word of God, and ended up funding the production of the *Carry On* films. He was a Methodist Sunday-school teacher whose name became rhyming slang for masturbation. He was a teetotaller whose naïve inability to judge a measure of alcohol led directly to his guests' involvement in several drink-driving incidents. He was a tall, bulky man whose crumpled face and pendulous nose gave him the appearance of a proboscis monkey emerging from an old paper bag. A staunch conservative, he disapproved of the welfare state and refused a knighthood from the Attlee government, gambling – correctly – that a future Tory administration would repeat the offer. He kept a box of chocolates in his desk drawer, into which he dipped throughout his working day. He loved cigarettes, golf, hare-coursing and grouse-shooting, but rarely went to the cinema. His entry in the *Dictionary of National Biography*, drafted by his despised henchman John Davis, made little mention of his film activities. Even today, Rank's family tend to issue stiff letters to those who write about his life without keeping his charitable work with the Methodist Church at the centre of the story.

In common with many saints and serial killers, Rank embarked upon the most celebrated part of his career believing that he was acting on instructions from God. In 1933, he identified cinema as a medium through which his brand of evangelical Methodism might be disseminated, and joined the Guilds of Light, an organisation founded to distribute movie projectors and Christian-themed shorts to churches and Sunday schools. Its members were hardly cinephiles: the board included R. J. Bennett, editor of the *Methodist Times* and co-author of *The Devil's Camera: Menace of a Film-Ridden World* (1932), a toxic concoction of moral panic and anti-Semitism which appealed to 'the ultimate sanity of the white races' in the hope that they might dismantle 'the greatest crime-producing agency of this generation'.[2] Under Rank's influence, the organisation was renamed the Religious Film Society and became, in effect, a modest film production company. Its first project was a biopic of an East End minister named W. H. Lax, in which the clergyman agreed to star as himself – after Rank had greeted his initial refusal with an instruction to go home and pray. ('Mr Rank,' he had protested, 'what you have proposed to me I could not possibly tell my wife.'[3]) *Mastership* (1934) occupied space at the tiny Merton Park Studios for a week, and although Rank pronounced the result 'lousy', he consoled himself with the report that a screening of the film had instantly gathered six Chinese communist sailors to the bosom of Jesus.

From this peculiar beginning, an empire grew. Rank gained a controlling interest in General Film Distributors, founded Pinewood Studios with the help of Charles Boot and Lady Yule, and bought Denham Studios from Alexander Korda and his creditors. He outbid John Maxwell, the head of BIP, for the Amalgamated Studios at Elstree, simply to prevent him expanding his operations. (To Maxwell's disgust, Rank immediately leased the buildings for the storage of government records.) Gaumont-British cinemas fell under Rank's control in 1941, and in the same year the sudden death of the exhibition magnate Oscar Deutsch allowed him to add an enormous chain of well-upholstered art deco picture palaces to his portfolio. The Odeons – the name is an acronym of the phrase 'Oscar Deutsch Entertains Our Nation' – became the organisation's greatest asset. And throughout this period of ruthless acquisition, Rank professed that the greater glory of Christ was his principal motivation. To prove it, he opened cinemas on Sundays and introduced *Thought for the Week*, a series of three-minute religious homilies delivered by Stewart Rome over a mocked-up garden gate. Audiences tended to talk, boo or kiss through these items, but it was only when a screen in Edgware was pelted with tomatoes that Rank was persuaded to abandon their production.

For a man whose idea of fun was watching a pack of dogs disembowel a flop-eared animal, Rank proved surprisingly sensitive to the artistic designs of the film-makers allied to his organisation. He is customarily caricatured as the enemy of creativity; he deserves to be recognised as one of its most unquestioning allies. That his munificence was eventually succeeded by austerity was partly a product of external economic factors and partly due to policies pursued by his unimaginative lieutenants, but it was also the fault of extravagant directors and producers who exploited his wide-eyed faith in their aesthetic judgement.

Even the most hostile commentators on British cinema are prepared to admit that the late 1940s was a time of rich productivity. Rank was the man who picked up the tab for this work. He underwrote the activities of Ealing Studios from 1944 onwards, and can therefore take some credit for the existence of *Kind Hearts and Coronets, Passport to Pimlico* and *The Lavender Hill Mob.* He bankrolled Michael Powell and Emeric Pressburger, allowing them to construct a Tibetan nunnery, a celestial escalator, Canterbury Cathedral and a Hebridean whirlpool on the sound stages and backlot of Pinewood and Denham. (Without Rank, there would have been no *Black Narcissus*, no *A Matter of Life and Death*, no *A Canterbury Tale* and no *I Know Where I'm Going!*) He footed the bill for David Lean's and Ronald Neame's work with Dickens and Coward, enabling them to make a star of Alec Guinness and redefine romantic self-sacrifice on Platform 2 of Carnforth railway station: thank Rank for *Oliver Twist, Great Expectations* and *Brief Encounter.* He funded Frank Launder and Sidney Gilliat's Individual Pictures, facilitating the production of *Green for Danger* (1946), perhaps the most perfect comic thriller in the language. He opened his chequebook for Filippo Del Giudice's company, Two Cities, ensuring that Olivier's *Henry V* (1945) and *Hamlet* (1948) made it to the screen. Less wisely, he did the same for Gabriel Pascal, a well-connected fraud who made a film career by schmoozing George Bernard Shaw for the rights to his plays and taking the credit for the work of a number of talented assistant directors. The director sated his profligate appetites on *Caesar and Cleopatra* (1946), a historical epic that staggered close to a million pounds over its budget. 'There was a time at Rank', recalls Ronald

Neame, 'when the creative people were entirely in control. We could do whatever we liked, and we did. And we narrowly avoided destroying the Rank Organisation in the process.'[4]

By the end of the 1940s, the relationships between Rank and these producers had deteriorated beyond remedy. Most took refuge with Korda, resurrected in new premises at Shepperton. Others were not so lucky. Del Giudice, perhaps, was the most unfortunate casualty. A fast-talking Italian lawyer who had come to England in the 1930s as a refugee from Fascism, he had acquired a career in pictures by persuading Noël Coward to write *In Which We Serve* and Major Arthur Sassoon to stump up £250,000 to produce it. He entertained lavishly at Sheepcote, a Buckinghamshire manor house which boasted a private cinema in which establishment worthies such as Ernest Bevin and Stafford Cripps came to drink good sherry and wake from their slumbers in time to applaud the credit roll. 'The breach with Rank came', recalled Del Giudice's friend and collaborator Peter Ustinov, 'when they were peeing side by side in the gents, in a break from a long meeting. Del Giudice turned to Arthur Rank and went on talking, and peed all over his feet. As an intelligent Italian, what he was saying took precedence over what he was doing. And Rank never forgave him.'[5] A decade later, after forming and losing another film company, Pilgrim Pictures, Del Giudice returned, penniless, to his native Italy, where he died in a Florentine monastery on the last day of 1962.

Del Giudice's expulsion from the Rank Organisation signalled its shift away from the production of big-budget prestige pictures to the mass marketing of smaller, cheaper films featuring contract stars. From 1952 onwards, Rank relinquished the running of his movie empire and submerged himself in the business of flour. John Davis – accountant, downsizer, wife-beater, sadist and unquestionably the most hated man in the history of British cinema – was the man he entrusted with salvaging the business. (Earl St John, a square-jawed Louisiana showman with a booming voice and a taste for big cigars, assisted Davis as Head of Production.) Davis saved the Rank Organisation from collapse, but he made many enemies in the process – quite cheerfully and deliberately, according to his former colleagues. 'He was the hate figure,' recalls Roy Ward Baker, one of the period's principal directors. 'Nobody liked him. I didn't like him but I got on with him. And that excited a certain amount of envy. People said I was up his arse. Not true. It's very rare that you'll come across somebody who is universally despised, but he was one. And he couldn't help it. He enjoyed being disliked.'[6] Anecdotes about Davis's steeliness are legion, but the progress of his divorce from the actress Dinah Sheridan gives the sharpest assessment of his character. It took the judge fifteen minutes to release her from the marriage on grounds of cruelty. *The Times* report of the case refers to 'grave allegations, some of a very unpleasant nature [which] showed the husband in a very bad light'.[7] (The judge considered the details of Davis's sexual cruelty too repulsive for the ears of the court.) In May 1993, when Sheridan's son Jeremy Hanley opened the papers to see Davis's obituary, he picked up the phone to his mother and serenaded her with a chorus of 'Happy Days Are Here Again'.[8]

It is the work of Norman Wisdom, perhaps, which best represents Davis's break with the Rank Organisation of Lean, Powell and Del Giudice. A little man who dressed like the guest of honour at a chimps' tea-party, Wisdom broke records at Gaumont cinemas with his debut picture, *Trouble in Store* (1953), and maintained a commanding position for a decade. (Somewhat improbably, one of his formulaic little comedies pitched *Dr No* from the top position at the box office.) Nowadays, his films are frequently screened on daytime television. His catchphrase – 'Mr Grimsdale!', delivered in shrill, panicky vibrato – is known to most of the population of Britain. And yet he enjoys surprisingly little public affection. His contemporaries – Sid James, Peter Sellers, Kenneth Williams – have been thoroughly canonised by biographies, letters, stage and television tributes. Outside Albania, where he still commands universal admiration, it is hard to find anybody over the age of twelve who has a good word for Norman Wisdom.

Children, however, love him. They see nothing inappropriate in his predilection for behaving just like them: sticking out his lower lip when he's upset; crying to get his own way; wailing for adult help at the slightest problem. I loved him myself, once; adored that grand stunt sequence in *A Stitch in Time* (1963), in which his plaster-encased body is hurled down a flight of stairs, through a brick wall, on to the roof of a speeding ambulance and through the window of a hospital ward; delighted in the riot that

Norman Wisdom (right) tries it on with Mr Grimsdale (Edward Chapman)
in a scene from *The Square Peg* (1958)

he unleashed into the world with soda siphons and fire engines; approved
when his underdog yapped back at the forces of petty authority.

Thirty years later, all grown up and watching his entire back catalogue
on DVD, I could still appreciate his talent for physical comedy: his grace-
ful progress as he scoots along on a set of library steps in *The Man of the
Moment* (1955); his inventive use of stilt-walking during a police medical
in *On the Beat* (1962). Most of the time, however, I found myself siding
with the diplomats and dowagers and managing directors whom he
molested with ladders and hosepipes and vulgar nudges. His little man,
crammed into that tight porridge-tweed suit and cloth cap, seemed less a
good-hearted incompetent who caused inadvertent chaos and more a
Rumplestiltskin-like imp who indulged in fits of destructive passion.
Most bothersome, perhaps, was the way in which his appeals to pathos
were interspersed with moments of sly carnality. Wisdom asks his audience to pity him, like a shoeless orphan boy in a Victorian engraving ('Just

give me one more chance!' he snivels, in nearly every picture), yet he also requires us to cheer him in his sexual pursuits. In *Trouble in Store*, he flips ice-cream down a diner's décolletage, scoops it from her breasts, then licks the spoon. In *Follow a Star* (1959), he offers to light Fenella Fielding's cigarette with a flaming piece of paper – which he then places at an awkward angle, obliging her to bend forward and give him a more comprehensive view of her cleavage. In *The Bulldog Breed* (1960), he joins the navy to meet women in grass skirts, and nuzzles up to one in the final frames of the picture. His carnal 'cooorrrr' – only slightly less filthy than the one issued by Sid James in the *Carry On* films – hardly seems appropriate to a character whom we are encouraged to regard as a lost and pitiable child. (His dirtiest exclamation is in *The Man of the Moment*, when he discovers a bell-pull over his bed that summons a doe-eyed chambermaid to his hotel room.) How, I found myself wondering, did the poor actresses cast as his girlfriends gaze adoringly into his eyes when he serenaded them with a self-deprecating romantic ballad? How did they overcome the urge to jump on a chair and scream?

Visiting Norman Wisdom is an overpowering experience: my five hours with him feel as much like a hostage crisis as an interview. He lives on the quiet side of the Isle of Man, in a bungalow christened 'Ballalaugh'. Although his live-in PA, Sylvia, answers the door, there is no possibility that I've come to the wrong house. In the garage, the BMW and the Rolls-Royce bear the registration plates NMN 16 and NMN 17. In the hallway, a bust of Norman Wisdom gazes towards the downstairs lavatory. The legend 'Sir Norman Wisdom', in jigsawed wooden letters, is perched on the architrave of the kitchen door. In the rococo-cum-ranch-style lounge, a corner cabinet houses the Norman Wisdom VHS Collection. A porcelain figurine of a cloth-capped Norman Wisdom is lodged by the bookshelf, on which sits *Don't Laugh at Me* (1992), the autobiography of Norman Wisdom. When the original of all these graven images appears, he walks towards me, proffering a hand – and performs a comedy stumble on the shag pile.

Although Wisdom's last starring role was in 1969, thoughts of a comeback are lively in his mind. He gives me the pitch for the script on which he's been working for the past thirty years. 'It's the story of a lonely old bloke who's getting on in years who'd like to have a lady friend before he kicks the bucket,' he explains. 'So he finds a way of using Chinese mythology to make a woman, which he does. She moves into his flat, and she begins to nag him. Then she wants to try and kill someone and take over their identity so that she can become real. It's got comedy and pathos, and songs.' To prove it, he sings one of them, in a tiny, faltering, emotional voice. Bo Derek, he says, has been pencilled in as the evil Oriental succubus. 'Though she might be a bit old for it by now.'

Adam and Evil, I learn, is derived from a J. B. Priestley story entitled *Tober and the Tulpa*. The script has existed since the late sixties, when William Friedkin – who directed Wisdom in *The Night they Raided Minsky's* (1968) – declared an interest in putting it into production.[9] Wisdom first attempted to option the story in 1962, but its author, on finding out who was asking, declined to release the rights. Wisdom, however, tends not to be discouraged by the scepticism of others. 'I found out where J. B. Priestley lived and went round there,' he recalls. 'After about three-quarters of an hour he looked at me – and this is honestly true – and apologised and said, "I've made a terrible mistake. If there's anyone who can do this, you can."'

This is a common element in Wisdom's accounts of himself. Just as in his films, the sceptics are usually won over by his shambling charm. His anecdotes about working with directors – Friedkin, John Paddy Carstairs, Robert Asher – are invariably ones in which a conflict is settled by their admission that he was right all along. Throughout his career, Wisdom has craved affirmation, demanded indulgence, required love. (Why else would he have chosen five of his own records on *Desert Island Discs*?) The reasons for this are vividly discernible in the story of his childhood: 'I was born in very sorry circumstances,' he says. 'Both of my parents were very sorry. My father was a chauffeur and used to be away for months at a time, and he'd never leave any money for food, so my brother and I had to go out and nick it. That's really true. We would go to Harrow Road and steal groceries from the displays.' When Norman was nine, his mother moved out of their home in Marylebone, and found a more satisfactory situation with a lover eight stops further down the Bakerloo Line. Frederick Wisdom, unwilling to take on the role of single parent, despatched Norman and his older brother to live with a series of foster-families. 'We ended up at Deal in Kent,' he remembers, 'where they kept my brother, and chucked me out.'

From this point in his narrative, rejection is the principal theme. He found work in a hotel, but got the sack after dropping a breakfast tray down a lift shaft. He threw himself in front of cars and bicycles on the Bayswater Road, in the hope of being offered a few compensatory shillings. A friend suggested that he accompany him to Cardiff and find work in the mines. At the end of the two-week trek, the boy's family refused to let Norman stay in their house. He went down to the docks and was engaged as a cabin boy: the sailors gave him a basic training in pugilism, forced him to enter a prize-fight, and spent all his winnings, abandoning him in a bloodied heap in a bar in Buenos Aires. When he returned to England, he implored his grandparents to give him shelter, but they declined, telling him to seek his father's charity. His father – who had since remarried – threw him back out on to the street. He then spent three years sleeping rough in London, until – so his tale goes – a coffee stallholder took pity on him, fed him Bovril and pies, and advised him to join the army as a musician. This was a major turning point in his life, not simply because he was accepted by the 10th Royal Hussars and rescued from a life of poverty, but because it proved a dramatic demonstration of how he could use pathos to achieve what he wanted – an idea at the core of his act.

At the job interview, the officer asked Norman, then fourteen, if he knew what A flat was. Norman didn't. A sharp? No, he didn't know that either. 'And he looked at me and said – it's really true, this – "You don't know anything at all about music, do you?" So I did the best acting I've ever done, be it at the Palladium or in films or anywhere else.' As he tells the story, his eyes fill with tears. 'I'd like a chance to learn,' he mumbles, mangling his voice to a tremulous, childlike whimper. 'Please, sir, then I can earn a living . . . be in the band, and people will think I'm someone . . . *normal.*' A tear meanders down his cheek. He wipes it away with the back of his hand. He apologises for his emotion, and I wonder whether to put an arm around his shoulder. Only a peculiar sense of *déjà vu* stops me: just before leaving for the Isle of Man, I had watched a television interview with Wisdom in which he told the same story in the same words, crying in all the same places, and offering an identical apology for breaking down.

Once you've seen him turn this on, it's instructive to go back to his films and watch him employing the same strategies on camera. Adult viewers tend to despise Norman Wisdom for this mawkishness, and it's true that there is something repulsive in the quick recourse he makes to playing the maimed innocent, and of these films' canny deployment of orphans and sick children and girlfriends in wheelchairs. Sentimentality, however, is how Wisdom's characters get what they want; how they absolve themselves of responsibility for the disasters they have caused. In *A Stitch in Time*, Norman launches an impassioned attack on the hypocrisy of attendees at a charity ball held to raise money for 'children's sunshine homes'. ('I improvised all that,' he insists. 'Not bad, eh?') In *Follow a Star*, he allows a hypnotherapist (played by Richard Wattis) to regress him to childhood, whereupon he sings a plaintive song about his dead father, 'I Want to Go to Heaven for the Weekend'. (According to Norman, this would regularly reduce audiences to floods of tears.) The script of *Adam and Evil* also contains such a scene, set in a dating agency to which its hero applies. Sitting in his favourite armchair at Ballalaugh, he performs the speech for me in its entirety – a soliloquy on loneliness and wasted opportunities. 'That'll get 'em, won't it?' he exclaims, wiping more tears from his eyes.

It was the Texas-born Rank executive Earl St John who, in 1952, signed Norman Wisdom to a seven-year contract with the Rank Organisation. Five months after the deal was done, Ronald Neame took a few test shots of the comedian playing a scene with Petula Clark – a Rank employee since the age of eleven – in which, according to Wisdom, he was obliged to make love to her with the meaningless line, 'Your eyes are as light as gossamer.' The results could not have been particularly edifying. Neame declined to direct the picture. The producer, John Bryan, got cold feet. Clark refused to co-star with Wisdom – a decision which effected her separation from her overbearing father–manager, who had kept close control of her career for the previous fifteen years. The film was cancelled, and Wisdom paid off. In August 1952, *Picturegoer* reported, 'It has been three months since the perky little clown with the clever line in poignant comedy signed his first film contract. Now decision time is at hand. After months of worrying about Norman Wisdom's debut, the Rank studio chiefs have reduced the field to three or four possible scripts. But let's be blunt, the odds are dead against him in this new venture.'[10] A year passed without progress, and just as Wisdom was beginning to suspect that he would be bought out of the entire contract, Earl St John assigned him to the mid-budget comedy *Trouble in Store*. Jill Craigie, a documentary-maker then married to Jeffrey Dell, author of a satire on Korda, *Nobody Ordered Wolves* (1939), wrote the first draft of the script. (Although her name does not appear on the final credits, this was not, as has often been reported, a consequence of her objection to Wisdom's involvement.[11]) Few within the organisation expected the film to make a profit. However, when it opened in thirty Gaumont cinemas in suburban London, it took £9,000 more in its first week than any of their previous presentations.[12] (Wisdom adores telling the story of the preview, at which the Rank top brass offered him cool nods on their way into the cinema and effusive handshakes on the way out.)

Once the figures for *Trouble in Store* had been digested, John Davis instituted the regular production of Wisdom pictures. Their star put in so many hours – shuttling between Pinewood and the Palladium – that by the time of his third picture, *The Man of the Moment*, his health had begun to suffer. He lost weight, and his skin sprouted a layer of carbuncles. 'When I fell over on stage or on the film set,' he recalls, 'I could hear the soft sound of boils bursting.' As soon as *The Man of the Moment* was in the can, he admitted himself to St Stephen's Hospital, Barnet, where he was diagnosed with malnutrition. When he was a homeless teenager, he had used a well-timed sob or tremble of the lip to escape hunger. At the zenith of his success, starvation had sneaked up on him quietly.

Wisdom is a little cagey about the end of his relationship with the Rank Organisation. His autobiographies, *Don't Laugh at Me* and *My Turn* (2002), are vague on the subject. The cuttings suggest that he was looking for a deal with an American studio from the mid-1950s. In April 1956, a production company allied to Columbia Pictures signed him to star with Anita Ekberg in a comedy about an Englishman's misadventures in Las Vegas. One year later, however, a spokesperson for Warwick Films announced that the deal was dead: 'We have abandoned the picture. We are also cancelling our contract plans for Norman Wisdom. The decision was reached mutually after disagreement over the script. He did not think it was funny enough. We agreed with him.'[13] Two independent features in the early sixties – *There Was a Crooked Man* (1960) and *The Girl on the Boat* (1962) – were relative failures. Wisdom claims that around this time,

Paramount attempted to put him under contract, but that the deal collapsed under the weight of the greed of his agent, Bernard Delfont, who demanded a £10,000 cut. It's natural, I think, that he should decline to examine his fall from public taste. This is the one failure for which he will take no commiseration.

Five hours after my arrival at Ballalaugh, an obscure psychological effect – Stockholm syndrome, possibly – has cured me of some of my unease about Norman. As he gives me an exhaustive guided tour of his awards – from his BAFTA to a step-dancing cup won during his army days – I ask him what he considers to be his proudest achievement. His answer wanders from his success as Willie Mossop in *Walking Happy*, a Broadway musical version of *Hobson's Choice*, to the collapse of his marriage. 'I was getting offers from Hollywood. And then my wife left me – she'd found someone taller than me – so I came back to England to look after the kids. I'm very pleased I did. I was determined that my kids wouldn't have to grow up like I did. I think any decent person would have done the same thing.' A well-rehearsed routine, I feel sure – particularly the self-deprecating crack about his height – but in it I think I can detect the ring of sincerity. It reminds me of one of the few moments in his film career when, to my mind, he managed to sound a genuine note of pathos. The scene is from *A Stitch in Time*. Norman has been doing his best to cheer up a little orphan girl on a hospital ward, and manages, finally, to coax a smile from her. A nurse, who has noticed this, thanks him for his efforts. 'You must have a gift,' she says. 'Oh no,' counters Norman, 'I don't want anything.'

I am about to ring for a cab when Norman offers to drive me back to the airport. I climb into the passenger seat of his BMW; Sylvia settles in at the back. We spin down narrow, hedgerowed lanes, Norman saluting each driver as we pass. Some of them look blank; others wave back cheerfully. 'Do you like this car?' he asks. Before I can answer, he stamps on the accelerator, and the G-force pins me to the upholstery. 'Can't do that too much,' he giggles. 'It frightens Sylvia.' We climb higher up the side of the Manx hills. A thick fog descends, reducing visibility to almost nothing. Norman, sitting low in the seat, his face a mask of concentration, keeps on driving.

*

Wisdom's unhappy first year with the Rank Organisation illustrates one of its principal problems: the difficulty of finding stars and suitable vehicles in which to showcase them. At the height of the contract system, ninety actors were signed to the organisation, many of whom were employed only grudgingly – or not at all – by its directors and producers. Most actors felt badly served by the arrangement, and inconvenienced by the tough schedule of publicity work to which they were held. (Spending a run of evenings being presented with the same bouquet three times a night in three different cinemas was, it seems, only Jean Kent's idea of fun.) Rank's most prominent and systematic exercise in star-formation was the Company of Youth – a talent-spotting and -shaping unit quickly nicknamed the 'Rank Charm School' by a sceptical press. David Henley – a former associate of the legendary theatrical agent Binkie Beaumont – was nominally in charge, but Olive Dodds, Rank's Head of Contract Artists, did most of the work. Under her eye, young recruits were corralled in a church hall in Highbury, taught elocution, deportment, and how to be at ease in front of a camera. The school produced squads of presentable young people who knew how to suck an olive from a cocktail stick and smile without showing their gums, and who – in the absence of any offers of employment from Rank directors – were despatched around the country to open fêtes and judge glamorous-grandmother competitions. Nobody seemed to mind that they weren't famous: their association with the organisation was sufficient to satisfy the crowds.

The Charm School has often been dismissed as a joke – principally by its graduates. More disconcertingly, it has also been characterised as a sexual sweetie-jar into which Rank executives liked to sink their fists. (Sidney Box was forced to issue a verbal warning to the men in suits who wanted a piece of one fifteen-year-old starlet.) It would be a mistake, however, to dismiss the venture completely. Many of its discoveries demonstrated that they could do more than walk in a straight line and turn a doorknob correctly, even if some proved ill-equipped to handle the fame for which they had been groomed. Those with genuine acting talent were, at the very least, undamaged by the experience. Christopher Lee – an actor blessed with volcanic black eyes, a towering frame and a voice like a bassoon – emerged from the school to be typecast by Rank directors as Nazis, pashas and Uruguayan night-club owners, until Ham-

mer Films typecast him, much more fruitfully, as an aristocratic vampire. Those whose talents were more a matter of carriage or glamour
made less certain progress – particularly when, in the 1960s, such accom-
plishments lost their value. The well-turned mannequin Anthony Steel
provided a popular filling to a number of naval and RAF uniforms in
1950s British war pictures, but when he went to Hollywood with his wife
Anita Ekberg, his career evaporated. (Being introduced to everyone as
'Mr Ekberg' humiliated him almost as much as the roles he was later
forced to take in softcore sex flicks.) Diana Fluck was a teenager from
Swindon who, at fourteen, pouted in her swimsuit to win *Soldier* magazine's Modern Venus competition. Olive Dodds recruited her a year later,
and promptly reprimanded her for trolling through Highbury in hot
pants, eating cherries from a brown paper bag and gobbing the stones
into the gutter. She also exchanged her Fluck for Dors. (There is a story,
doubtless apocryphal, about a nervous vicar, eager not to mispronounce
her name, who introduced her to fête-goers as 'Diana Clunt'.) Patsy
Sloots was a clerical trainee at the Ministry of Information who, under
the name Susan Shaw, enjoyed a substantial career playing compromised
working-class beauties and – on one occasion – the Queen of Jupiter.[14]
(After her husband, Bonar Colleano, was killed in 1958, she sank into
drink and poverty: at the time of her death in 1978, she was barred even
from the seedier London drinking clubs.) Belinda Lee was a hotelier's
daughter from Budleigh Salterton who lent a disproportionately Amazo-
nian presence to a number of middling Rank comedies, before becoming
a heroine of European pulp cinema, signing a suicide pact with an Italian prince, and dying in a car crash in 1961. The Charm School may have
inculcated skills which the next generation would reject as affectations,
but it did more than produce genteel nobodies.

The career of Kenneth More demonstrates how precarious life under
John Davis could be, even for an established star. More's first job was at
the Windmill Theatre, where he monitored the audience for telescopes,
binoculars, opera glasses and unauthorised masturbation. The better
class of patron, he maintained, used a bowler hat to conceal his activities;
the rest employed a folded newspaper. 'I would pick up the house telephone and say: "A14 Wanker, *Times*. C17, *Daily Mail*." The commissionaire

would then stride down the aisle to seat A14, and then to seat C17, tap the man on the shoulder, and say, "The manager wishes to see you in his office".[15] From these duties, Vivian Van Damm promoted him to playing in the comedy sketches which gave the showgirls time to change between tableaux. The pay was meagre, so More supplemented his income by supplying interested punters with besmirched underwear from the backstage washing basket. His progress into films was slow, not least because some of his first appearances in front of the camera – in Peter Ustinov's *School for Secrets* (1946) and Charles Frend's *Scott of the Antarctic* – were obscured by a stout pair of goggles. The following decade, however, saw him emerge as one of the principal stars of British cinema.

By the beginning of the 1950s, the Rank Organisation had fallen out of love with Powell, Pressburger, Lean and Neame, and reoriented its desires towards middlebrow material that would please the punters in the well-upholstered suburban Odeons. More, with his steak-and-potatoes figure and air of hectoring confidence, was perfectly attuned to their sensibilities. He was heroic in a cocky, big-brotherly way – like a public-school prefect who might have saved a new boy from a beating, but expected three terms of shoe-polishing and crumpet-toasting in return.

Sometimes this attitude brings out the worst in a picture. More is gross and bullying in *Genevieve* (1953) – again under a pair of goggles – and insufferably smug in the first colour remake of *The 39 Steps* (1958): the vulgar facetiousness of both films only encourages him. He is so sweetly insolent in the first few reels of *The Admirable Crichton* (1957) that his destiny as master of Cecil Parker's brood of shipwrecked toffs is a certainty before they have even set sail. (Once the island has become his private fiefdom, and he has taken to wearing skins and feathers, and washing in a Fred Flintstone mechanical shower, he seems signally less authoritative.) In *A Night to Remember* (1958), however, the grandest celebration of British failure ever staged, the *Titanic* seems to sink merely in order to wipe the cherubic self-assurance from his face. The plutocracy goes dinner-dressed to the frozen deep (unlike the protagonists of *Carry On Up the Khyber* (1968), stoicism does not save them from death), and Second Officer Lightoller, the Kenny More-ishness sluiced from him, is left to deliver the epitaph. 'Because we were so sure,' he murmurs, as the ship is swallowed by the waves of the Pinewood water-tank, 'I don't think I'll ever feel sure again. About anything.' Wendy Toye's *Raising a Riot* (1955) achieved the same humbling effect with less extravagant props, by putting his chauvinist into the kitchen to prepare nursery tea from a string of sausages. (His decision to snip them with a pair of rusty garden shears indicates that his moment of recantation is not far away.)

It was Daniel M. Angel – the son-in-law of More's former employer Vivian Van Damm – who best understood how to exploit the star's boorish energy. On war service in India, polio had robbed Angel of the use of his legs, which is perhaps why *Reach for the Sky* (1956), the biopic of Douglas Bader, offers More's bloody-mindedness as such a transcendental phenomenon. For the underrated comic Western *The Sheriff of Fractured Jaw* (1958), Angel persuaded Raoul Walsh to cast More as the son of a gunsmith who decides that the Wild West is the perfect market for his father's merchandise. All steam-ironed cuffs and hail-fellow-well-met bravado, More breezes into the shack of a family of squatter farmers. The weather-beaten patriarch hunkers down at the table, shovelling food silently into his mouth; his scrawny wife, sitting beside him, explains that her husband will not speak and eat at the same time; their filthy child, smeared in the remains of its dinner, wriggles in a high chair. Undaunted by this scene, More assembles the hunting piece on the kitchen table and brays its efficiency to his audience. The baby reaches into the gun case, plucks out a shiny new revolver, pulls the trigger and sends a bullet zinging across the shack. The parents are not remotely fazed by this precocity, and More, as if demonstrating a vacuum cleaner to an unimpressed Pimlico housewife, makes a polite, brisk exit from the homestead.

In 1959, John Davis agreed to release More to Carl Foreman, who was keen to lure him to Shepperton for *The Guns of Navarone* (1961). Then, at a BAFTA dinner at the Dorchester, More made the mistake of heckling Davis during his speech, and found that the decision had instantly been reversed. 'I should have controlled myself,' recalled More, 'but I was now beyond control. So in front of all John Davis's fellow directors, all his lieutenants, all his rivals in the industry, I called him every name to which I could lay my tongue.'[16] The following morning, sober and terrified, he rang to apologise, but found Davis impassive. Meetings between their respective lawyers failed to remedy the problem. More's career as a studio

star was over. The Rank Organisation paid him off for his contract, and
he spent a year unemployed. 'I lived on my past successes,' he recalled in
1978, 'and pretended that I had no need or wish to make more films.'[17] He
played his next role for expenses.

Dirk Bogarde was not so guileless. A newsreel celebrating twenty-one
years of Pinewood Studios shows him proposing a toast to Davis, his face
a mask of obsequious fervour. Perhaps it's unfair to judge him on such
evidence. Bogarde may have sold his body to the Rank Organisation, but
his soul – a sullen, savage, unpredictable entity – always remained his
own. When he signed his contract, Bogarde was a morbidly nervy
ingénue with a lanky body, narrow shoulders, indifferent posture and
huge Egon Schiele eyes. He escaped the purge of 1952 – when knives glint-
ed in the eyes of Jean Kent, Googie Withers, John McCallum and a gaggle
of contract artists – only because Olive Dodds persuaded him to nod,
smile, take a cut in salary and accept any role that the front office chose to
throw his way. They rejected his petition for a role in *The Cruel Sea* (1953)
on the grounds that he was not officer material. He was cast so frequently as a pretty-boy convict on the run that *The Times* suggested he would
be odds-on favourite in any film-actors' cross-country event. However,
gradually, Rank conceded him parts for which daily shaving was necessary. In *Appointment in London* (1953), he played a wing commander trying to keep his mind on bombing and off Dinah Sheridan. The previous
year, in *Penny Princess*, he had played a charming British tourist who
helps Yolande Donlan use a recipe for alcoholic cheese to revive the economy of a bankrupt European principality. In *Doctor in the House* (1954),
he played straight man to Donald Sinden's and Kenneth More's demoni-
cally hearty medical students.

Seventeen million tickets were sold for *Doctor in the House*. The smell
of money transformed Rank's tolerance for Bogarde into ardour. The
organisation put all its energies into enshrining him as the 'Idol of the
Odeons', the epitome of tennis-club charm, the sort of boy whom suburban parents prayed would be forced to marry their daughter. Pinewood's
design department constructed sets to the advantage of his left profile –
his right ear, almost lobeless, ruined the romance of the other side of his
face. Pinewood's publicity department ensured that the real Dirk Bogarde

– a hot-tempered, rather helpless ex-serviceman whose heart had been chilled by his wartime experiences – was obscured by a thick layer of PR gloss. His fans were supplied with fey and mimsy details about his private life: they learned that he made his own lampshades, bred tropical fish, and was descended on his father's side from Anne of Cleves. They were not told that his first sexual experience had been furnished by a man who picked him up in a Glasgow fleapit and took him home to demonstrate how the ancient Egyptians bandaged their mummies, or that he had stolen the actor Tony Forwood from his wife, Glynis Johns – the pouting, husky, scaly heroine of *Miranda* (1948) – and set up home with him in a farm on the Sussex Downs.

Though Bogarde grew to hate the persona Rank had created for him, he enjoyed its protection all his life. Even in his last years, he declined to make an unambiguous statement about his sexuality. ('I'm still in the shell and you haven't cracked it yet, honey,' he told a TV interviewer in 1986.) In seven volumes of autobiography, Tony Forwood remained unacknowledged as anything other than a business manager. (Bogarde, perversely, delighted in telling interviewers that his partner couldn't bear homosexuals.)[18] In the early days, both his diffidence and his homosexuality suited the Rank Organisation. Nothing would have poisoned his name at the box office more effectively than a wedding, and in the absence of female lovers, press and publicists were free to concoct imaginary girlfriends who were never a serious threat to the illusions of his fans. Throughout the 1950s, legions of teenage girls pinned up his portrait from the *Picturegoer*, slipped his ludicrous talky-talky records on to their Dansettes, listened to him intone romantic nothings to light classical background music, and sighed. Sometimes they did more than sigh: sufficient numbers of his admirers were so demonstrative that he was forced to sew up the flies of the trousers he wore to public appearances.

They stopped grabbing after *Victim* (1961), Basil Dearden's social-problem thriller, in which Bogarde played a lawyer blackmailed over his clandestine sexual relationship with a young man with the suggestive nickname of 'Boy Barrett'. The scene in which he confesses his desires to his wife is one of the most electrifying moments in 1960s cinema – 'I wanted him! I wanted him!' he rages, his back pressed against the mantelpiece, the light blazing in his eyes. The actor, however, never conceded that his engagement with the subject of homosexuality was anything more than imaginative and political.

Bogarde was born in Hampstead in March 1921 with several more vowels in his name (the happy event took place in a nursing home, not a taxi, as he sometimes claimed). His autobiographies supply ample information about his childhood in a verdant swathe of the Thames Valley, and still more about his belief in it as a Shangri-La – presided over by his adoring nanny, Lally – that was smashed up by adulthood and the Second World War. The war, he insisted, exerted a profound influence upon his character. The metaphor he preferred was one of tattooing: war's needles had marked him with images he could not erase. Paradoxically, however, these images shifted and mutated every time he committed them to paper. He claimed on several occasions to have visited Belsen concentration camp in the middle of April 1945, but his various accounts contain many puzzling inconsistencies, and his letters home betray no hint of atrocity: 'We have been having the most beautiful weather here,' he informed his sister on 21 April. 'I've actually been sunbathing, and got quite brown.'[19] After reading these cheery lines, it's hard to know how to assess the litany of wartime horrors enumerated in his memoirs. Did he really witness hellish scenes on the road from Falaise to Turin – or was this a way of expressing a more generalised sense of terror and disgust? ('Dead horses indescribably chunked by flying shrapnel . . . charred corpses huddled in the burned grass . . . crisped faces with startling white teeth, fists clenched in charcoaled agony.'[20]) Did he really carry out a mercy-killing after the army convoy in which he was travelling drove over a landmine – or was this a useful fiction that aided his campaigning work for the Voluntary Euthanasia Society? ('During the war I saw more wounded men being "taken care of" than I saw being rescued,' he claimed. 'Because sometimes you were too far from a dressing station, sometimes you couldn't get them out. That hardens you.'[21]) One constant in Bogarde's screen career from Rank to Visconti: he always maintained a detachment from everybody's feelings but his own.

It is often claimed that Bogarde's escape from Pinewood propelled him in a totally new and unexpected direction; allowed him to discover capacities within himself that the padded prison of the Rank Organisation had done its best to suppress. Bogarde himself is the source of this notion:

British critics, seduced by the actor's sardonic contempt for the first fifteen years of his career, have tended to reproduce his prejudices. This view overestimates the complexity of his post-Rank performances: *Hot Enough for June* (1963) or *A Bridge Too Far* (1977) hardly invite close study. More unjustly, it underestimates the unsettling and frequently perverse qualities to which Bogarde exposed the patrons of the Uxbridge Odeon during his indenture to Rank. The roles from the 1960s and 1970s which made his reputation in Europe are clearly rooted in his work at Pinewood. The title role in *The Servant* (1963), a sweaty bruiser from the back pages of the *News of the World*; the academic in *Accident* (1967), corroded by jealousy and impotent lust; the composer in *Death in Venice* (1971), killed by a surfeit of inarticulate desire: rather than representing an escape from the past, these characters are like relics of his youth – those men on the run made deeper and more complex by age and disappointment.

It was not Joseph Losey who allowed Bogarde to discover his true nature. The edge of erotic sadism so visible in *The Servant* and *The Night Porter* (1974) is present right from the outset of his career. His maleficent Borstal inmate in *Boys in Brown* (1949) is a piece of rough trade with whom Reggie Kray might have slicklegged. The relationship between the doppelgänger characters he plays in *Libel* (1959) makes material the audience's suspicion that the person most fascinated by Dirk Bogarde is himself. His character in *The Spanish Gardener* (1956) offers a preliminary essay in the kind of boy-love by which *Death in Venice*'s von Aschenbach is tortured. (José squeezes little Nicholas's biceps to assess his strength; when his father forbids them to speak to each other, they communicate by passing secret notes.) In Charles Crichton's *Hunted* (1952), Bogarde's anti-hero abducts a six-year-old boy who has witnessed him commit murder in the cellar of a bombed-out house. The relationship develops from one founded upon coercion and violence to something more tender and outré. The boy has lacerations on his back where his foster-father has beaten him, and is surprised when Bogarde fails to punish his clumsiness in the same fashion. Instead, Bogarde parts his hair, pets him, cheers him up, and, in a scene of almost paedophilic intensity, holds him close and rubs his face in the boy's hair as they attempt to sleep on a rain-lashed cliffside.

The Blue Lamp (1950) supplies us with the young Bogarde at his most transgressive. Watch that remarkable scene in which he shows off his revolver to his girlfriend (a jittery teenage runaway played by a pale, fragile Peggy Evans), and see how aroused he becomes by his power to terrorise her. 'If you got one of these in your hand, people listen to you,' he argues, proving his point by levelling the gun at her chest. She begs him to put down the weapon; then attempts to defuse the situation by throwing her arms around him. Bogarde's mouth is buried in her blond hair; his eyes stare over the curve of her shoulder. 'Scare easy, doncha?' he observes, with some satisfaction. She moves away from him; he strokes the barrel of the gun, a filthy smile forming on his lips, his eyes flickering up and down her body. 'You thought I was going to do you in just now, didn't you?' he leers, taking a seat opposite her, the better to enjoy her tears. 'I reckon a bit of a scare's good for your insides. Makes you think quicker. You're all keyed up and then, afterwards, you feel terrific, like . . .' He stops, seeing that she is also excited by his words. Her mouth is pushing towards his. They kiss, as a train clatters past the window of their mean little bedsit.

Even in the most highly processed Rank material, Bogarde could suggest that there was something dreadful burning under his skin. For all his easy confidence, there's a vein of dissatisfaction and contempt detectable in Simon Sparrow, the clear-eyed, sports-jacketed hero of the *Doctor* comedies. Watch him patronising Muriel Pavlow in *Doctor in the House* (1954) or trying to conceal his disgust when Dilys Laye attempts to seduce him in *Doctor at Large* (1957) and you'll see the faintest beginnings of the storm of rage which broke in that climactic scene in *Victim*. By the time of his final film under the Rank contract, he was confident enough to play his character as a sleazy, leather-clad, nancy-boy sadist – whether his director liked it or not.

Roy Ward Baker was the man entrusted with the direction of *The Singer Not the Song*. Mention the title to him today, and he makes an expression like an old Labrador which would like to be left to sleep by the Aga. 'That dreadful picture,' he mutters, 'which put paid to my career.' Baker regards the end of the Rank Organisation as British cinema's greatest wasted opportunity, and *The Singer Not the Song* as the longest, shiniest nail in its coffin. 'Rank excited a great deal of envy and jealousy,' he recalls. 'He was never forgiven for being a monopolist. He was grinding the faces of the

Roy Ward Baker, finding himself in charge of a gay western he never
wanted to direct, shares his sorrows with Mylene Demongeot on the set
of *The Singer Not the Song* (1961)

poor in the dirt, and people in his own studios, if, say, some arc lamps
went wrong or there was a half-hour hold up, would all shrug their shoulders and say, "Oh well, it's only another few bags of flour." It was a cynical
and ungrateful way of thinking but a popular way of thinking. But those
people who were so keen to dance on Rank's grave were soon laughing on
the other side of their faces.'

Baker's career divides roughly into five phases. In 1934, he joined the
staff of Gainsborough Studios, where he was promoted from tea boy to
Hitchcock's assistant director on *The Lady Vanishes* (1938). After the war,
he worked as a freelance director of realist thrillers: *The October Man*
(1947); the submarine drama *Morning Departure* (1950); and *Highly Dangerous* (1950), a Cold War oddity in which Margaret Lockwood foils a plan
to use bees as agents of biological warfare. A Hollywood contract followed, under which he spent three years working for Fox on vehicles for

Tyrone Power, Marilyn Monroe and Robert Ryan, and experimenting with 3-D. The Rank Organisation claimed Baker for the rest of the 1950s: the director shot a drunken Peter Finch conducting a burial at sea in *Passage Home* (1955), sent Hardy Kruger fleeing across wartime England in *The One That Got Away*, and choreographed icebergs on the Pinewood backlot in *A Night to Remember*. Then, in 1959, he found himself under pressure from John Davis to accept a project which, with hindsight, he wishes he had managed to avoid.

The Singer Not the Song is a Mexico-set Western based on a grotesquely successful book by Audrey Erskine Lindop – an English novelist who had never been further south than Torquay – and concerns a triangle of intense relationships between a sardonic bandit, an Irish priest and a fifteen-year-old girl. Davis considered the bandit, Anacleto, an ideal role for Dirk Bogarde, and the best chance of persuading him to renew his contract with Rank. Baker was assigned to the film in spite of his reluctance to shoot it. In December 1958, he had proposed three alternative subjects to the Pinewood production committee, which, he hoped, would take the Rank Organisation in a fresh direction: *The Grass is Greener*, a sex comedy by Hugh and Margaret Williams, which he envisaged as a vehicle for Kenneth More; Willis Hall's jungle drama *The Long and the Short and the Tall*, then playing at the Royal Court with Peter O'Toole in the lead; and an adaptation of Alan Sillitoe's novel *Saturday Night and Sunday Morning*. The first was rejected as immoral (Columbia, with no such qualms, turned it into a vehicle for Cary Grant); the second as obscene (Associated British, after a few flourishes of the blue pencil, assigned it to Leslie Norman); and the third as 'common' (Bryanston Films inherited that option, and, with Karel Reisz and Albert Finney, inaugurated the British New Wave).

Although Baker did not know it, *Saturday Night and Sunday Morning* had a history with the organisation. Some months before, Dirk Bogarde had suggested it as a vehicle for himself. ('Earl St John', he recalled 'gave me a splendid lunch in his private, pine-panelled office, and, after he had lighted his cigar, asked me, gently, how I imagined that anyone could consider a film which began with a forty-year-old woman inducing an abortion in a hot bath?')[22] For reasons that are difficult to determine, however, the rights department had already optioned the novel. Rank, on reading the book, interceded personally, ringing Sillitoe's publisher to tell him that he was waiving his entitlements and inviting the author to keep the cash. 'There was too much sex and drinking in it for him,' mutters Baker.

With all three proposals rejected, Baker was forced to accept Davis's invitation to revive *The Singer Not the Song*. His suggestion that the whole project be handed over to Luis Buñuel fell on deaf ears. 'I resisted for fifteen months,' he remembers.

The policy was entirely based on the idea that Dirk Bogarde, who was the only star they had left, was about to come to the end of his contract. And we had to throw everything we could at him. It didn't matter what he wanted, he got it. Kenny [More] had gone, the Charm School had been shut down, and there were no women at all – so Dirk was it. That's the origin of it and the only reason I can give you for the bloody thing being made in the first place: to get him to sign another piece of paper to commit himself to making more films for Rank – which he had no intention of doing. He couldn't wait to get out of it. He thought he could become a world star. He thought he was one already. But John Wayne he wasn't.

In 1959, Bogarde, anxious about his age, concerned that his decade above the title had produced no work of any value, was spoiling for a fight with the Rank Organisation.[23] He had lost *Saturday Night and Sunday Morning*. He had lost *Lawrence of Arabia*, a cherished collaboration with Anthony Asquith and Terence Rattigan, cancelled by Earl St John five weeks before shooting was due to begin in the Middle East. He had spent several months in Hollywood struggling under Liszt's candyfloss wig in *Song without End* (1960), delivering lines for which he had nothing but contempt, bashing the dummy piano until the keys were slippery with blood, and lying in the Lana Turner Suite of the Bel Air Hotel, 'full of misery and Hennessey and self-pity'.[24] Determined to reset the course of his career, he spent Christmas 1959 in Rome with his family and Tony Forwood, and announced that he considered his thirty films were junk, and, moreover, the sort of junk that was going rapidly out of fashion. 'I think my days of success', he told his father, 'are numbered. It's been a good innings, but if I don't catch the trolley, I'm for it.'[25] *The Singer Not the Song*, he determined, would be his farewell to Rank – or a parting shot, depending on how you see it.

Baker's files relating to the picture allow for a minute reconstruction of its production. They reveal that Graham Greene turned down the job of writing the screenplay on the grounds that Lindop's book was 'a poor imitation of *The Power and the Glory*'. (The job went to Nigel Balchin, lauded as the author of *The Small Back Room* and less celebrated as the inventor of the Aero chocolate bar.) They detail Baker's attempts to persuade Malcolm Arnold to score the film. ('I don't think this is the kind of picture that I can do well,' the composer concluded, 'and I think it would be safer for us both if I didn't take it on.'[26]) They reveal that the part of the heroine, Locha, was offered to Audrey Hepburn before it was accepted by the French actress Mylene Demongeot. Reams of correspondence with various Catholic bodies demonstrate how Baker became mired in local and religious details.

The casting of the priest, Father Keogh, proved the most insurmountable problem. The correspondence relating to this issue illuminates the tensions between reform and conservatism that, in the late 1950s, were paralysing the Rank Organisation. Baker's first choice was Richard Widmark – with whom he had worked at Fox – but this decision was blocked by Davis, who insisted on the casting of a British actor. Widmark was philosophical when Baker wrote to him to withdraw the offer, in December 1959.[27] A fortnight later Baker was certain that Peter Finch would be playing the part.[28] By the first week of the new year, however, Finch was getting cold feet. 'I can assure you,' Earl St John told him, 'I am putting everything I know behind this to make it a really outstanding picture as I have a great belief in it and I think you will agree that it could be perhaps the greatest part that you have had to date.'[29] Finch wasn't persuaded. On 3 February, Bogarde cabled Davis to ask if the rumours of Richard Burton's casting were true.[30] They would have been, if Burton had said yes. In March, it was James Mason's turn to refuse the role, declining to be billed below Bogarde.[31] Audrey Erskine Lindop was bitterly disappointed, but a memo from the Rank Organisation's Publicity Controller, John Behr, suggests that her views were not shared by everyone: 'I hear a rumour that James Mason is playing the priest. You will, of course, decide what is best for the picture. From my point of view it would be disastrous. He will not give any press interviews and is bloody awkward. He hates the R.O. As regards age, Trevor Howard is equal.'[32] Other candidates for the part included Paul Newman, Harry Belafonte, Anthony Perkins and John Cassavetes. Scripts – but not offers – were posted to Richard Todd, Michael Craig and Tony Britton. The part, however, went to an actor whose name appears nowhere on any of Baker's lists of candidates. His first appearance in the files comes in a draft contract, dated 23 March 1960, engaging him for a fee of £25,000 and an assurance that he will receive 'screen credit and billing immediately after the name of Dirk Bogarde and in size of type or lettering equal in every respect to the name of Dirk Bogarde'. John Mills's memoirs insist that he took the part only because he had been told that Marlon Brando had been signed to play the bandit.[33] This, it seems, is a fantasy.

John Mills occupies an exalted position in British culture. Oddly, however, some of the performances for which he is most celebrated are among his most phoney and ingratiating. His Oscar-winning turn as the mute village idiot in *Ryan's Daughter* (1970) is offensively ludicrous; his Willie Mossop in *Hobson's Choice* (1954) is a cringing gimp who begs us to love him for his humiliations. From the 1980s, Mills pursued that gentle whoring for which elderly knighted actors assume they will be forgiven – those easy afternoons of cheque-collecting in tails or plumed pith helmets, somnambulating through half a dozen lines. In that time – and through no fault of his own – Mills has come to personify an inaccurate, but widely held, view of British cinema as decent, doughty, conservative and modest. More than this, perhaps, his last years cast him as Britain's universal grandfather: tiny, gracious, blind, a little saucy, and utterly above criticism – an alternative Queen Mother, once the genuine article went to take eternal tea with Noël Coward and Cecil Beaton. Mills was one of the Queen Mother's most passionate admirers, provided the star turn at her centenary celebrations, recorded an advance contribution to the radio programme broadcast at her death, just in case he made it to the wings before she did. And through some strange process – perhaps because Mills, like Elizabeth Bowes-Lyon, is a locus of sentimentality about the Second World War – he has acquired a comparable status. The Queen Mother risked her heels in the rubble of Whitechapel to be filmed shaking hands with Blitzed East Enders. Mills kept his nerve in *The Colditz Story* (1955), sank a brace of U-boats in *Above Us the Waves* (1955), crossed a desert full of Jerries for a pint of Carlsberg in *Ice Cold in Alex* (1958).

Watch his pre-war films, and you'll be struck by a salient aspect of his performances: he can't act. Listen to the uncertain transatlantic twang with which he delivers Graham Greene's dime-novel dialogue in *Four Dark Hours* (1937) – 'Say, you've got nice eyes, kid ... You're a swell dame, you are' – and you'll understand that everything he knew about his chosen profession he learned on the job. His hoofing, conversely, has unquestionable grace and energy. (In the same film, he performs a sublime bar-room tap routine in which his shoes slap at the lino with the force and velocity of Mr Bojangles.) When he's speaking, however, he leads with his chin, with the tight little tendons in his neck, as if he believes that demonstrating his willingness to dislocate a vertebra will make us like him more. It was only when war came, and the tall, good-looking actors were all sent off to the front, that he was given the opportunity to discover his forte: the fatigued, the self-disgusted, the men who stayed behind, or ran away, or hit the bottle after losing theirs. Watch him as the sweaty, beetroot-red, stout-bibbing domestic tyrant of *The Family Way* (1966), challenging his son to an arm-wrestling match at the wedding reception, too thick to appreciate the viciousness of his beery bonhomie. Observe his shabby, sour detective in *Town on Trial* (1957), patronised by the RAF types at the tennis club where a brutal strangling has taken place, embarrassed by having spent the war years in the police force, rather than in the air. See him as the bitter fall guy in *The Long Memory* (1953), seeking vengeance on the false witnesses who sent him to jail. There's a scene in which he quizzes a waitress on the whereabouts of one of his victims: as she struggles, with imbecilic slowness, to remember the name of the man's employer, he glares at her as though he'd cheerfully strangle her with her own apron-strings. Best of all, perhaps, is the unreliable Captain Anson in *Ice Cold in Alex* (1958), his face lined by booze and disgrace. Everyone knows the famous scene in the bar, where, having redeemed himself by finding the strength to ferry his comrades safely across the desert, he comes begrimed and grizzled to down a draught of chilled lager. It's one of the most uncompromisingly erotic moments in British cinema: the silence of the bar-room; the lambent face of Sylvia Syms, gazing upon his pleasure in admiration; Mills, sunburnt and filthy, relaxing his throat muscles like Linda Lovelace, to allow the beer to cascade down his neck. It's so seductive that you forget you are watching him fall back into the arms of the addiction that brought about his disgrace. Fortunately, Father Keogh in *The Singer Not the Song* is also full of confusion and self-loathing.

Roy Baker made the best of Mills's casting. When, at a pre-production meeting, concern was voiced about whether the actor was sufficiently attractive for the part, Baker told the chair 'that it was fashionable nowadays for young girls to fall in love with older men'.[34] Bogarde, however, was not so easily convinced. 'I promise you,' he told Baker, 'if Johnny plays the priest, I will make life unbearable for everyone concerned.' He was, apparently, as good as his word. 'Dirk Bogarde's behaviour was absolutely disgraceful,' recalls Baker. 'Disgraceful. He had all the spite . . .' He trails off, biting his tongue. 'He was very nasty. Very nasty. Johnny didn't know what the hell was going on. He said, "What's the matter with this fellow?" I said, "He doesn't like you; that's the trouble." He was determined to rough the whole thing up. And I had to do my best to restrain him.' I try to draw him on the subject, and receive a warning shot:

I've always lacked one of the qualities that a film director should have, and that's the sense of intense curiosity in other people's business. If you invited Fellini to a party, he'd get a drink and sit in the corner watching everybody else and making

Roy Ward Baker and John Mills on the set of *The Singer Not the Song* (1961), possibly wishing they weren't

notes. Not participating at all, but taking it all in. I've always had this frightfully British attitude that people's private business is their own private business. It's not right. It's probably why I've made realist pictures.[35]

In recent years, claims have been made for Baker as an auteur. In the case of *The Singer Not the Song*, he seems strangely detached from the content of his own film. 'There's a lot of homosexuality in it and all that stuff,' he muses, as if his name were not on the credits. 'You don't really know who's in love with who.' The original reviewers agreed, thinking they had detected Baker's authorial intentions: 'What I think the director is trying to suggest is a Spiritual Relationship with Homosexual Undertones,' wrote the film critic of *Time and Tide* magazine.[36] The *Observer* sniffed out 'strong . . . hints of homosexual attraction'.[37] The *Evening Standard* was less certain: 'If you can discover what the film thinks this love between two men really is, you will be much cleverer than I,' conceded Alexander Walker. 'It might be Christian love. It might be a very unholy kind of love. The film hedges and dodges and ducks identifying it.'[38]

This aspect of the film is partly the responsibility of Nigel Balchin, who regarded the heroine of Lindop's novel as 'rather a nasty little bitch who wants her bottom smacked, and with whom no one is likely to have much sympathy', and consequently resisted Baker's instructions to develop her part.[39] ('The story is basically about the two men,' Balchin argued, 'and unless we abandon it and tell a completely different one, then Locha inevitably is mainly an instrument by which the plot is triggered.'[40]) Baker, in the editing process, then excised two of Locha's biggest scenes, amplifying the effect. It is Bogarde's performance and Bogarde's costume, however, which give the film its intensely fruity flavour.

'Don't go on about the leather pants,' pleads Baker, when I raise the subject. 'I remember him coming to me and saying he'd found the most wonderful tailor in Rome, who made the most wonderful leather trousers. Then, when we were in the middle of shooting in Spain, Ralph Thomas and Betty Box turned up, spying for Davis. I told them that Dirk was being very difficult. Ralph said, "Oh no, the only thing he worries about is the fit of his bloody trousers."' John Mills's performance also registers the importance of his co-star's clothes. In their first scene together, in which priest and bandit confront each other on the dusty streets of the town that Anacleto has been terrorising, you can distinctly see Mills run his eyes up and down Bogarde's body. There's plenty to look at: the braided bolero jacket, the pencil tie, the black leather boots and gloves, the arse-hugging fetish pants. Bogarde is like some quiffed eel: long and lithe and shiny and difficult to handle.

And the clothes are only the most obvious signs of Bogarde's homosexualisation of the character. His mannerisms are louche and effeminate. He rubs the handle of his silver duck-headed cane over his lips. He twitches an eyebrow imperiously. He leans, one arm akimbo, a yellow scarf on his neck, his crop swinging at his side. He's clearly somewhat older than the twenty-nine years mentioned in the script. His desires are obscure. We are told that he 'likes cats, but not from kindness'. (He pours milk into a saucer for his own fluffy white pet, and strokes it on the belly with a leather-sheathed hand.) He is prepared to murder the inhabitants of the town – in alphabetical order – to force Father Keogh to leave, but it's hard to see what he gains from his rule over the place. And despite Bogarde's disappointment that he didn't get to smoulder opposite Peter Finch or Richard Widmark, he manages to express a deal of agonised passion for Mills. ('It must be heartbreaking to fall in love with a man you can never have,' he tells Locha. 'I understand this.') The final scene, in which Anacleto and Keogh, both fatally wounded, die in each other's arms, has a fiercely homoerotic tone. As both men expire from their bullet wounds, Keogh exhorts the bandit to accept God in his final moments, begging him to squeeze his hand as a signal of contrition. The concluding shot is of Mills's hand gripping Bogarde's leather-clad thigh. Whether Baker likes it or not, those trousers are important.

The Rank Organisation promoted the film with great energy and a £23,000 advertising budget. They placed Mylene Demongeot on *Juke Box Jury* and *What's My Line*, and in the pages of *Tit Bits* and *Woman and Beauty*. *The Sunday Times* was offered access to the Mills family. Dirk Bogarde co-operated with *Woman* magazine on a seven-part serialisation of his life story, consented to a cardboard cut-out of himself being given away with *Roxy* magazine, and was doubtless bemused by the 'Dirk Bogarde Exhibition' that toured between branches of Lewis's department stores.

In Britain, however, the film was a notable flop. Just before its opening, Baker wrote to Demongeot, putting a brave face on his anxieties. 'The only showing we have had so far was to a group of about eighty critics and feature writers for magazines and periodicals,' he wrote. 'It is always extremely difficult to tell what these people really feel about a picture and it is certainly impossible to tell what they are going to write about it. Still they didn't actually throw anything at me and I feel they will treat the picture very seriously, which, of course, means that the standard of criticism will be higher.'[41] It wasn't. 'I'll never forget when we showed it to the critics and gave them their lunch afterwards,' he recalls. 'Not one of them could speak to me. Then they all went home and wrote about his trousers.'

Baker's files contain a clutch of photographs of the director on location, and a still of the cast and crew. Bogarde is conspicuous by his absence; Baker has a hangdog, despairing expression in all of them. There is also a small handwritten card from the star, penned some five years later. 'I have *always* thought [of] "Singer" as one of my preferred movies – it was ahead of its Time, and the unforgivable casting of JM all but ruined it – but it holds up remarkably well – and, as you know, is "tres snob" in France and Germany! – Funny after all that time.'[42] I look for a trace of amusement in Baker's face, and see nothing. 'Looking back,' he says by way of an answer, 'the problem was that Rank wanted to make pre-war films. And that's what we were doing. But the public didn't want them. They just didn't want them.'

The Singer Not the Song is a film caught somewhere between the past and the future. It is a gay Western struggling to emerge from a conventional studio picture. But there were others, beyond the boundaries of the Rank Organisation, who were more willing to go all the way.

CHAPTER NINE

No Future

Richard Todd demonstrates the aptness of Peter O'Toole's description
of him as one of the 'smallies'

For the new generation of actors and directors who came to prominence at the beginning of the 1960s, the studio system was a corrupt empire which deserved to collapse. If Peter O'Toole, Siân Phillips, Richard Harris and their coterie found themselves at a pub or a party with a performer who had been part of the system – John Mills, for example, or Richard Attenborough, or Richard Todd – they would loose a mutter into their glasses: 'Thy offence is Rank. It smells to heaven.'[1] They had a nickname for these company men: they were the 'smallies' – a bitchy allusion to the modest dimensions of their bodies and the modest ambitions of their films.

This animosity was even played out on screen, notably in Leslie Norman's *The Long and the Short and the Tall* (1961). The film is adapted from Willis Hall's landmark Royal Court play about a unit of British soldiers who are too busy raging against one another to notice that they have wandered into hostile territory – first they lose their bearings, then they lose their lives. The play brought Peter O'Toole, a long, lean Irishman with sapphire-blue eyes, to the attention of London theatregoers (and to David Lean, who immediately imagined those eyes glittering under a snow-white djellaba). It also imported a new kind of class antagonism to British drama: open hostility between officers and men. Military deference, the film argued, was dead; the military establishment could no longer rely upon its subordinates to charge cheerfully into the cannon's mouth. Norman's film is generally considered to be a cop-out, a bowdlerisation of its source. Certainly, the barrack-room language was disinfected; the references to homosexuality nipped and tucked; the original star jettisoned in favour of Laurence Harvey, bankable after his surly star turn in *Room at the Top* (1959). Perversely, however, these compromises serve only to increase the sickly, fractious nature of the piece; to gift it with several more layers of conflict.

The film was produced by Associated-British, the company into which British International Pictures had mutated in the mid-1930s, and which, two decades later, was providing the Rank Organisation with its only serious domestic competition. *The Long and the Short and the Tall* formed part of the company's attempts to pursue a policy similar to that advocated by Roy Ward Baker at Rank – to stay in business by diversifying into a tougher, more socially cognisant form of cinema. The film depicted British servicemen as a rag-tag bunch of decadent commanders, terrified innocents and parade-ground roaring boys. It stuck two fingers up at the officers and gentlemen of 1950s British cinema: those uniformed stoics, romantics and moral watchmen played by Donald Sinden, Kenneth More and Jack Hawkins. The film's casting pits these generations against each other. Richard Harris – with the scowl and dark complexion of a Navajo on the warpath – plays Johnstone, a tough, sardonic and foul-mouthed Welsh sergeant. Richard Todd plays Captain Mitchem – a member of the class that the coming generation seem destined to displace and destroy. The script suggests that Mitchem is sexually aroused by the insolent dynamism of his subordinate. You'll look in vain for an acknowledgement of these suggestions in Todd's performance. It's as if he is doing his best to suppress the plot's anarchic possibilities, its ungentlemanly desires.[2]

Richard Todd was one of the last British studio stars, possibly the last romantic leading man to appear on the pages of *Picturegoer* in tweeds, smoking a pipe. He was also a self-confessed smallie: Elstree press releases insisted he was five feet eleven inches tall, but he never tried to maintain the pretence in person. In 1953, he told a correspondent from the London *Evening Standard* that his lack of stature might deny him the lead role in *The Dam Busters* (1954): 'As I'm a little chap,' he remarked, 'they are probably afraid that the subject – and the part – are too big for me.' ('He seems unduly conscious of his height,' noted the interviewer, 'which is no less than that of James Mason or Dirk Bogarde.'[3]) Other British journalists were less polite. 'I looked down at him,' reported the man from the

Daily Graphic. 'He looked up at me. And for the hundredth time I wondered why Richard Todd has the sort of appeal that sets women scrambling for the box-office.'[4]

Meeting him is not like meeting an actor, and he knows it. Todd is a military man in bearing, language and sensibility. I had made an appointment to see him at his home in Leicestershire on 9 April 2002, a date which was subsequently announced as that of the state funeral of Queen Elizabeth the Queen Mother, the colonel of his regiment. As I roll up in a taxi, the television coverage is just finishing, and I reproach myself for not having given him the opportunity to reschedule our meeting. He says nothing, but as friends call him throughout the afternoon to offer their condolences, I realise I have made a crashing faux-pas. 'Remarkable woman,' he says, with an enthusiasm like that of Sherlock Holmes for Irene Adler, as he reminisces about half a century of officers' lunches at Claridges. As he speaks, though, it becomes clear that his admiration for this realm of bright brass buttons and gracious manners does not extend to the film world. 'I never got terribly celluloid in my attitude to things,' he confesses. 'I was a bit khaki-minded. I didn't ever let myself be pushed around, and I wasn't in awe of film moguls. As far as I was concerned, they were rather ordinary civvies.'

Todd has maintained these views for half a century, and is quite happy to confess his suspicion that he has spent a lifetime in pursuit of the wrong career. He called his autobiography *Caught in the Act* (1986), as if it were the story of an ensnarement. During his war service in the Parachute Regiment, he kept his theatrical experience a secret, not breathing a word of it to his comrades, fearing the nancy-boy indignities of a transfer to Basil Dean's ENSA. After his demob, he returned to his old repertory theatre in Dundee, simply because he couldn't think of any better way to occupy his time. In his absence, one of the company's founders, Robert Lennard, had become the chief casting director at Associated British. In 1948, Lennard invited Todd to screen test at Elstree. In the course of a year, the accidental actor was signed by Associated British at twenty-five pounds a week, cast opposite Ronald Reagan in *The Hasty Heart*, and nominated for an Oscar. By 1950 he was in Hollywood, dodging the leg-men employed by Hedda Hopper and Louella Parsons to loiter in hotel and restaurant lobbies, and reading stories in the gossip columns about his imagined marital crises. 'Hollywood', he says, 'was a dangerous place.'

Although he was happiest working for American companies on British soil – in Disney's *The Story of Robin Hood and his Merrie Men* (1952), *The Sword and the Rose* (also 1952) and *Rob Roy the Highland Rogue* (1953) – fame was hazardous in England, too. In one protracted and peculiar business, Todd was stalked by Norma Vorster, a South African beauty queen who accosted him while he was eating sandwiches in the Dorchester and inveigled her way into the Belgravia mews house he shared with two ex-servicemen. (When she presumed upon him for the money for an air ticket to Canada, he was only too happy to oblige.) By the end of the 1950s, however, Todd's contracts with Associated British and Disney had run their courses, and he was devoting most of his energies to managing a farm he had purchased in Oxfordshire. 'And then,' he recalls, 'suddenly films were not coming along. Associated British became extinct. The Rank Organisation broke up. The whole system changed. It was all independents. It changed my way of life enormously.' The content of the few scripts being sent his way became, he admits, 'a bit disgusting. I was doing some pretty awful low-budget pictures that I wouldn't have dreamed of doing a few years before.'

There are five principal candidates for inclusion in that category. In *The Very Edge* (1963), Todd plays an architect failing to cope with the consequences of his pregnant wife's sexual assault and resultant miscarriage. ('The only real cure for frigidity', a nurse tells him, scant days after the ordeal, 'is the right kind of love.') In *The Love-ins* (1967), he is cast as a lightly fictionalised version of Dr Timothy Leary, a university professor who fights for the rights of his students to conduct orgies and pop tabs of LSD. In *Asylum* (1972), he plays a brandy-sloshing, silk-scarf-wearing adulterer who takes an axe to his wife, packages up her remains with brown paper and string, and stows them in their new chest freezer. ('Rest in pieces,' he spits, as he slams down the lid.) In Pete Walker's *Home before Midnight* (1979), he is a lawyer arguing that a relationship between a twentysomething songwriter and a fourteen-year-old girl does not necessarily constitute a case of statutory rape. ('Innocence or guilt', he warns his client, 'is purely academic in a court of law until there's a verdict.') In a picture for the same director, *House of the Long Shadows* (1983), he is a publisher of pulpy horror fiction. I attempt to coax him into talking about these films, but it is clear that he would prefer to forget them. 'It was desperation,' he says, bluntly. 'I had to do something. I was well aware of the fact that it was a terrible come-down; that things weren't as they had been once upon a time. But I'd been neglecting my job and I deserved it. My film career was going down the pan.'

British cinema tends to be characterised through its most decorous traditions. What could be more British than a Merchant–Ivory picture? Certainly not Ishmael Merchant (who was Indian), James Ivory (who is American), or their regular screenwriter, Ruth Prawer Jhabvala (who is German). Our native cinema might be as easily characterised by its savagery, its enduring and energetic commitment to violence, sadism, nihilism and despair. The evidence, however, has been expunged from our cultural history. 'The more aggressive and excessive forms of British exploitation', concedes Ian Conrich, 'still await serious examination.'[5] These pictures have slipped from our grasp. The kind of cinema they represent, which once made up a large portion of British production, had all but vanished by the early 1980s, a victim of home video and an unfriendly taxation regime.[6] These films have suffered from long-term academic and journalistic hostility: look up the reviews in *Films and Filming*, and you will find only a drone of negative comments.[7] Most interestingly, perhaps, many of their participants share Richard Todd's sentiments, and look back on their involvement with unease.

Richard Attenborough, for instance, the most powerful of all the smallies, insists that he accepted the role of the serial killer John Reginald Christie in *10 Rillington Place* (1970) because he wanted to make a statement against the death penalty. 'I felt that steeping myself in this particular character,' he wrote, 'however unpleasant, would be worthwhile if, as a result, people were persuaded that hanging was not only barbaric, but could also cause irretrievable miscarriages of justice.'[8] The movie, unfortunately, has only the most obvious observations to make on the issue. It is, however, a first-class exploitation picture. In Christie, Attenborough found his final and greatest horror role: his eyes shine like malignant hard-boiled eggs; he suffocates his victims with as much care as malice, with nothing but his hot little breaths on the soundtrack. It is the culmination of years of work in the field, and the peak of his acting career.

Attenborough was born for sleaze and terror. Observe him as Pinkie Brown in *Brighton Rock* (1947), elucidating his contempt for Carol Marsh into the microphone of a make-your-own-record booth, thrilled by the cleverness of this act of deferred cruelty. See him as a sweaty teenage mechanic in *London Belongs to Me* (1948), running from the scene of his crimes and whimpering, 'Oh, Mum, I never meant to do it.' Study his mock-heroic abduction of a little girl in *Séance on a Wet Afternoon* (1964); the mildewed tenderness he employs in an attempt to assure her that she will come to no harm. ('Don't be afraid,' he breathes, dousing his hand-kerchief with chloroform. 'It's only a game.') Then compare the veracity and the energy of these performances with the pomposity of his directo-rial work: *Oh! What a Lovely War* (1969), an all-star travesty of Joan Lit-tlewood's East End agitprop satire, staffed by actors who were, in the main, all happy to go off and take the cheques for blood-and-bullets epics which idolised the succeeding generation of military leaders; *Gandhi* (1982), a lavish biopic of an ascetic life, which encouraged its audience to boo a chorus of Edwardian pantomime villains and congratulate them-selves for their own liberalism; *Cry Freedom* (1987), a film whose argu-ments against racist oppression in South Africa were not amplified when Attenborough was caught on camera, closeted with Nelson Mandela, pleading the case of Nestlé – a Swiss multinational whose marketing of powdered milk has been accused of causing the deaths of thousands of young Africans. To my mind, the cardigan-wearing murderers and fish-eyed razor boys of his acting work are more plausible and seductive cre-ations than, say, the figure depicted in the two-hour BBC *Arena* documentary which will doubtless form his principal television obituary: the director of films with easy-to-swallow progressive messages; the tire-less flesh-presser, committee member and owner of a chauffeur-driven Rolls-Royce (number plate RA III); the man of conscience sitting in his own private screening room, weeping at his own movies. How much bet-ter it would be if he were remembered as British cinema's most accom-plished player of panic, selfishness and malice; its gentlest and most comprehensible monster.

Attenborough is not customarily considered to be an exploitation actor. No doubt he would shrink from such a label. Even the most iconic stars of horror films seem to have evolved difficult relationships with their work. The career of Christopher Lee, for instance, incorporates the most canonical and literary permutations of British Gothic cinema and the most gleefully tasteless extremes of Poverty Row. Few horror actors can have exerted more influence upon the genre. His highly eroticised version of Count Dracula flavoured the work of an entire generation of Freudian Stoker scholarship.[9] And surely it was Lee's body into which Philip Larkin imagined himself when, in 1960, he wrote:

> Me and my cloak and fangs
> Had ripping times in the dark.
> The women I clubbed with sex!
> I broke them up like meringues.

When I interview Lee, however, he seems irritated by my interest in this part of his career. He tells me that he had only continued to accept roles in Hammer's Dracula pictures because the company's chiefs pestered him with 'hysterical phone calls' in which they confessed that they had used his name to pre-sell the productions to America. If he declined to don the fangs and blood-red contact lenses, they argued, significant numbers of British actors and technicians would lose their jobs. 'And that's how they got me back,' he insists. 'It's the only reason. It was a form of blackmail, really.'[10]

Things like this just seemed to keep happening to him. In 1969, he accepted a script entitled *The Bloody Judge*, a biopic of George Jeffreys, the noose-happy seventeenth-century Lord Chancellor, and was dismayed when it reached cinemas as *Night of the Blood Monster* (1970). Maybe he didn't detect the hint of profanity in the name of its director, Jesus Franco, or notice that the latter's CV included films such as *Miss Death and Dr Z in the Grip of the Maniac* (1966) and *Prostitutes in Prison* (1969). Perhaps he had no way of knowing that Franco would cut from a shot of him gazing fixedly into the camera to a close-up of his female co-star's pneumatic décolletage, or that his speeches would be dubbed over an image of the bloodied buttocks of a naked actress. When the picture went on release, however, he must have become sensitive to the irony of his position. Jeffreys, the film asks us to believe, consigns his victims to the torture chamber and the execution yard with very little understanding of what this actually involves. ('Oh, would that but once you had seen one of your own sentences carried out,' opines Leo Genn's Earl of Wessex, as the screen is deluged with more images of lacerated flesh.) In the closing moments of the film, Jeffreys stares through a window at a hanging being carried out at his behest. Horrified by the sight, he suffers a fatal heart-attack, crumpling to the floor with the words 'I never knew' curling from his lips.[11]

During my conversation with Lee, I keep thinking of this scene from Franco's film. 'Do you realise how long it is since I've done a horror movie?' he demands, not intending to wait for an answer.

The last one I did was *To the Devil a Daughter* in 1975. So why does the press refer to me as a horror actor? It's sloppy journalism. If you ask the press, or any casting directors, what Christopher Lee did when he was in America for ten years, they haven't a clue. I hosted *Saturday Night Live*. It was their third-biggest audience of all time. Fact. Fact. You can't fiddle those figures. And I did a hell of a lot of comedy in America. Fact. It's right there on the screen. Now, are you prepared to accept the evidence of your own eyes, or are you going to deny it? And they deny it.

Their denials – and mine – are explained by the presence of *The House of Long Shadows*, *Stirba the Werewolf Bitch* (1985), *Curse III: Blood Sacrifice* (1991) and *Talos the Mummy* (1998) on his filmography, and by the commonly held opinion that his involvement with the horror genre is infinitely more significant than his work on *Police Academy 7: Mission to Moscow* (1994).

The British exploitation film has its supporters, but, like those people who attempt to keep the memory of George Formby alive by goofing about on the stage of the Blackpool Tower Ballroom, the intensity of their interest is largely a measure of the indifference of everybody else.

Some American practitioners in this genre have gained a certain amount of critical respectability. Herschell Gordon Lewis, the eccentric talent behind *Blood Feast* (1963) and *10,000 Maniacs* (1964), has seen his work reissued on DVD by the arthouse label Metro-Tartan, and was saluted by the French film journal *Son et image* as 'le Douanier Rousseau de l'hémoglobine'.[12] Lewis abandoned film production in the 1970s, when he discovered that there was more cash to be made from the manufacture of porcelain souvenir plates – the kind of thing that you see on the back of downmarket colour supplements, usually bearing painted images of sad clowns or mischievous kittens. ('They are my natural bastard children,' he tells me. 'First we did a twelve-plate series based on the Book of Genesis. It was so successful that in six months we were on to Exodus.')[13] Despite this cheerful cynicism, there are a number of reasons why Lewis should attract the attention of the *Cahiers du cinema* crowd.. Exploitation cinema and avant-garde cinema both owed their existence to a series of legal challenges to the Hollywood system that were made in the 1940s and 1950s. In 1949, the Supreme Court forced the big studios to surrender control of their chains of cinemas, breaking their monopoly on distribution and allowing exhibitors to screen whatever they liked. Three years later, a second court decision ruled that the movies were a medium of free speech and should therefore enjoy protection from prosecution under the First Amendment. Independent cinema – of both the arthouse and drive-in varieties – was born. British cinema, which had been forced to accommodate the pruderies of the Hays Code and the American studio system in any domestic picture it hoped to export across the Atlantic, was an equal beneficiary.

During the 1950s, the conditions were created in Britain for the emergence of a new form of cinema. In January 1951, the 'X' certificate was introduced by the British Board of Film Classification. In 1957, a new Cinematograph Films Act made permanent an experimental tax scheme known as the Eady Levy, which paid back a percentage of a film's box-office receipts to its producers, on condition that they ploughed the funds into future productions. The following year, a former schoolteacher named John Trevelyan was appointed Secretary of the BBFC, and became the first British censor with a genuine interest in film and a relatively liberal attitude to what it might be permitted to depict.

These developments took place against a background of falling cinema attendance and widespread doubt about the future of studio production in the UK. As the decade turned, the Rank Organisation and Associated British embarked upon ruthless downsizing operations, cutting back their production activities and darkening hundreds of Odeons and ABCs. American companies with interests in Britain began to do the same. Pessimists declared that by the end of the 1960s, the cinema would be as dead as the stereopticon and the variety theatre. Optimists saw the possibility that a fresh, less bourgeois form of film-making might emerge from the ashes of these old empires. Entrepreneurs and opportunists made colder calculations, noted that the remaining cinemas had been starved of titles by the production slowdown, and perceived that although the market for Rank's kind of cinema had been eroded by the recent surge of free light entertainment from ITV, there was still a strong audience for more baldly transgressive material: films that would shock, appall or titillate. The desires and aspirations of a curious coalition of randy teenagers, Windmill Theatre knuckle-shufflers and culture vultures in cable-knit sweaters were ready to be exploited.

One of the most delicious realisations to be had from studying the evolution of exploitation cinema is that, as far as producers and exhibitors were concerned, no market boundaries existed between productions that would now be considered the preserves of totally different audiences. Films that today would be streamed into segregated spheres – the city-centre arthouse screen, the adults-only section of HMV, the wire basket outside the petrol station – all shared the same cinemas, the same producers, the same fan magazines, the same constituency of viewers. In March 1958, *Isle of Levant* (1957), a Swiss–Danish nudie flick about a trio of teenage backpackers splashing about naked on the Côte d'Azur, received its London premiere at the Oxford Street Cinephone on a double bill with *Street of Shame* (1956), the swansong of the Japanese director Kenzu Mizoguchi. The same month's issue of *Continental Film Review* featured articles on Czech animation, post-war Chinese film-making and Louis Malle, alongside a pull-out calendar pin-up of Marion Michael from *Jungle Girl and the Slaver* (1957), propping herself against a palm tree and shuddering in bare-breasted ecstasy. In 1962, the same distribution company was handling *Last Year at Marienbad* and *Call Girls of London*; their Christmas calendar, decorated with a shot of the popular model Pamela Green, plugged both titles.

Two scenes from two films by the same director illustrate the unpartitioned nature of this territory. In *Towers Open Fire* (1963), a soldier, his face veiled by a gas mask, bursts through the window of a spacious apartment, sweeping his rifle from side to side. He levels his gun at a cabinet of family photographs, and blasts away. Ping-pong balls rico-chet around the room, sending the photographs flying. Out on the street, people are evaporating inside their clothes. A man standing by a tree is reduced to an empty shirt and slacks. A pair of lovers standing in an alleyway become twin piles of crumpled clothes. A soldier seated at a desk picks up an R/T unit, and barks an order into the microphone. The screen becomes a cascade of frames, which flash by with near-sublimi-nal rapidity: chickens milling around their coop; a bullfighter sticking home his swords; a line of cars; a couple necking on the grass; a figure dancing under a bridge; a serious young man in a sinister pair of spec-tacles.

Towers Open Fire, officially identified as an experimental art film and screened several times at Tate Britain, was the fruit of collaboration between Antony Balch and William Burroughs. Everyone knows Bur-roughs; few know the name of Balch. A fellow denizen of the Beat Hotel, Balch made three films with Burroughs, the most important of which, *The Cut-Ups* (1967), so disorientated audiences at the Oxford Street Cinephone that the lost-property room was soon filled with abandoned umbrellas and coats. (It delighted a young director named Nicolas Roeg, however, who adapted its collage techniques in *Performance* (1969) and *Don't Look Now* (1972).) Balch, however, was not one of the self-important ascetics of the London Film-Makers Co-op, who pro-duced a type of avant-garde cinema that spoke only to their own acolytes. He was an enterprising distributor – an 'abominable show-man', according to his obituaries – who imported foreign pictures and marketed them under lurid titles such as *Don't Deliver Us from Evil* and *Weirdo Weekend*.

Six years after screening *The Cut Ups*, Balch shot *Horror Hospital* (1973), a commercial exploitation picture in which a not conspicuously sane scientist (Michael Gough) attempts to persuade a long-haired mal-content (Robin Askwith) to join his army of lobotomised supermen. A scene from the first half-hour of the film illustrates its kinship with the avant-garde. It opens with a shot of an immense dining table, at which two ranks of ashen-faced, red-eyed young men and women are sitting in silence, staring into space. At each place-setting we see an empty white plate and a wineglass of green liquid. The meal is presided over by a make-up-caked middle-aged woman in huge false eyelashes and a scarlet turban. Suddenly one of the diners begins to scream, clapping her hands over her ears. Two helmeted, leather-clad bikers rush upon her and drag her away – and the dinnerless dinner resumes, in silence.

Trevelyan's relaxation of the rules of censorship was not a gentle, even process. Conservative campaigners kept him within their sights. Alarmed by the success of Hammer's *Dracula* (1958), the novelist R. F. Delderfield attempted to rally opinion against the British horror film: 'There can be no doubt', he affirmed, 'that this steady tide of sadism presented on our screens and the equally repulsive cataract of violence and brutality flowing through our social life are intermingled.'[14] Other correspondents concurred: 'the cancerous growth of the horror film', argued a fellow novelist, Frank Baker, was 'capable of plunging a young mind into necrophilious swamps . . . Profit is the master who lurks behind these cynical excursions into the lowest depths of the human mind; and sadistic violence is the logical answer to these invitations to the morgue.'[15] According to Alexander Walker, Trevelyan's liberal treatment of Michael Powell's serial-killer thriller *Peeping Tom* (1960) almost cost the BBFC Secretary his job.[16] The critics – Walker included – railed against the film: something that an enterprising distributor might have turned into an advantage. Unfortunately, Nat Cohen, the chair of Anglo-Amalgamated, the company handling *Peeping Tom*, pulled the movie from the Plaza Cinema, fearing that it would spike his chances of a knighthood.

Guy Hamilton and Anthony Perry, two survivors from the studio system, were the film-makers fated to absorb the backlash. Perry, a graduate of the Rank Organisation script unit who had written *Simba* (1955) as a vehicle for Dirk Bogarde, went freelance in 1959 to reinvent himself as an independent producer. He recruited Charles Frend to direct *Girl on Approval* (1962), an intelligent realist drama about a middle-class couple who adopt a volatile teenage orphan. The following year, he secured the services of Guy Hamilton, a protégé of Carol Reed, to direct *The Party's Over* (1962), a piece about the beatnik life in Bayswater. Jack Hawkins put up the money, Oliver Reed was the star, and the Rank Organisation agreed to distribute the picture. Hamilton told *Films and Filming* that he was 'tired of studio work now'; the magazine's report from the set described a young team attacking a fresh, new subject with vigour and zeal.[17] In July 1963, however, John Trevelyan refused to grant the film a certificate, objecting to a scene in which Reed's duffel-coated hero has sex with a woman whom he fails to realise has died of a drug overdose. After Trevelyan's ruling, the Rank Organisation reneged on their distribution deal: the film made it into cinemas with heavy cuts, and Perry and Hamilton's names absent from the credits. 'I always thought', confesses Hamilton, 'that Trevelyan was the sort of censor who went around sniffing bicycle saddles.'[18]

It was unfortunate that Hamilton and Perry were dissuaded from making another picture of this type. Compared with many of their peers, they were imaginative and idealistic. Others were rather less scrupulous. Edwin J. Fancey, a penny-pinching producer who launched the career of Michael Winner, was said by his employees to have fraud and murder on his CV. Harry Alan Towers, a legendary wheeler-dealer, had several tussles with the law, but proved as indestructible as the villain of the *Fu Manchu* films with which he made his name. In 1961, Towers was arrested in New York and charged with operating a call-girl ring for the benefit of UN diplomats. (Maria Novotny, a future bit-player in the Profumo affair, was alleged to be his principal asset.) The accused skipped bail and fled to Moscow, but two decades on the run from the New York authorities did not prevent him making imaginative use of the tax laws to finance the production of some fifty feature films, some of which were never screened in the UK because his creditors would have been within their rights to impound the negatives.[19] Towers shot a remake of *Sanders of the River* (1963) in South Africa with Richard Todd, hoodwinked Klaus Kinski into playing Renfield in *Count Dracula* (1970) by giving him a script with a fake title, and took Christopher Lee to Spain for *Night of the Blood Monster* and *Eugenie . . . The Story of her Journey into Perversion* (1969). (Naturally, the star insists that he had no idea he was appearing in a porn film.[20]) Towers was cleared of the charges against him in 1980, and is still in business today. In 2002, he attempted to persuade Monica Lewinsky to take the lead in a Viennese costume romance set during the premiere of *The Merry Widow*. Go to the website of his company, Towers of London, and you will be greeted by an invitation to invest in such productions. 'I can't believe he's still alive!' whooped one of his former associates, when I informed him of the producer's recent activities. 'Only the good die young, don't they?'

Of all these wild men of Wardour Street, it was Tony Tenser, the London-born son of Lithuanian immigrants, who wielded the most influence and exhibited the most brazen ingenuity. 'The British film industry is gasping its last because there is no one like Tony Tenser to kick it back to life,' wrote the historian and screenwriter David McGillivray in 1992. 'He was the Irving Thalberg of the exploitation movie, and like the boy wonder of MGM, his career was too short.'[19] In 1972, Tenser resigned from his own company, took a wife twenty-seven years his junior, and moved to the Lancashire seaside resort of Southport to start a business trading in wicker chairs. He still lives in the town, though he and his wife have separated. She remains in the modern townhouse they shared for thirty years; he has moved into the rest home across the road – an experimental shift that slowly hardened into a permanent arrangement.

It is here that I meet Tenser in a tiny room as hot as a gecko's vivarium. A handsome, square-jawed octogenarian with a neat white moustache, he reclines on the quilt of his single bed and produces a boxed set of DVDs containing three films by Roman Polanski. The rest home has no DVD player, so we slip the disc into my laptop and watch some interview footage of Tenser talking about his work on *Repulsion* (1966) and *Cul-de-Sac* (1967). He seems pleased at his own reflection, but asks me to shut off the machine when one of the carers brings tea in a battered stainless-steel pot. 'Like the furniture?' he asks, waving a hand in the direction of his white-and-gold wardrobe. 'Jewish renaissance.'

Tenser grew up with his parents and six siblings in a two-room tenement flat on Christian Street, Shoreditch. ('The name was a paradox,' he says. 'It had no Christians living in it.') The family scraped a living by sewing piecework for local tailors, but Tenser worked hard at school, was awarded a scholarship, officially declared the second-cleverest boy in the East End and despatched to grammar school, where the teachers and the fee-paying boys did not allow him to forget his charitable status. After the war, he joined the ABC cinema chain as a trainee manager, and earned a promotion when he reported his boss for claiming wages for non-existent staff. At the Central Cinema, Cambridge, he developed his genius for the

PR stunt. When his employers forced him to screen a hopeless Jerry Lewis vehicle, he put up posters outside the building, begging patrons to stay away, and broke box-office records. For *Challenge to Lassie* (1949), he held a sheepdog trial, though he had to import the animals from Newcastle to sheepless Cambridgeshire. When a second run of the Margaret Rutherford comedy *The Happiest Days of Your Life* (1950) was scheduled for the cinema, he pretended that ABC was trying to prevent him from screening the picture, and invited his audience to sign a petition in protest. Naturally, the campaign succeeded.

He continued to deploy this talent for ballyhoo when he moved to London to work as publicity manager for a small distribution outfit called Miracle Films. ('We tried to avoid the obvious catchphrase,' he remembers. '"If it's a good film, it's a Miracle."') He repackaged European horror pictures for double-feature programmes, rechristening them with sensational new titles. He brought Brigitte Bardot to London and coined the term 'sex kitten'. He commissioned a naked waxwork of the actress to go on display outside the Cameo Cinema on Tottenham Court Road, told a journalist on the *Daily Mirror* that it was going to be stolen the next day, and arranged for it to disappear. (It was recovered after a few days and Tenser was rewarded with his photograph in the newspaper, standing at a bus-stop, arm-in-arm with the mannequin.) He imported Pierre Foucaund's comedy *En Effeuillant la marguerite* (1956), retitled the film *Madame Strip Tease*, and persuaded a girlie-show impresario named Michael Klinger to send his employees to picket the cinema in their tittie-tassles.

From this stunt, a partnership was forged. Klinger was a former hotdog salesman and disc jockey, whose parents, like Tenser's, were Jewish refugees from Eastern Europe. His clubs, the Nell Gwyn and the Gargoyle (the latter an old haunt of Lady Diana Manners), were lucrative businesses, but Klinger hankered after legitimacy and asked Tenser to help him transform himself into a movie mogul. Tenser cautioned against entering production, and argued instead that the pair should exploit a loophole in the law which allowed for the exhibition of uncertificated films at private members' clubs. In 1960, they leased the basement of a Soho office block, refitted the space with 170 seats and a projector, declared the Compton Cinema Club open, and persuaded John Trevelyan to become a founder member. With the censor on their books, they were virtually immune from prosecution. The pair formed their own distribution company, importing foreign pictures, screening them uncut at the club, and offering expurgated versions for wider presentation.

Encouraged by the success of this venture, Tenser acceded to Klinger's desires to go into production. In partnership with the owners of the Cameo chain of independent cinemas, they formed Compton Cameo Films. The firm's flagship house, the Cameo Poly on Regent Street, had screened the first X-rated feature in 1951. In 1896, when it was the London Polytechnic Institute, the building had hosted Britain's first public kinematograph show. In 1961, another landmark event took place in its auditorium: the premiere of the first collaboration between Tenser and Klinger: *Naked – as Nature Intended*, a cheap nudie flick starring Pamela Green.

A British sex comedy of the following decade offers a mischievous caricature of Tenser's professional practices. In *Eskimo Nell* (1975), Roy Kinnear plays Benny U. Murdoch, a Wardour Street warhorse whose enthusiasm for his films is matched only by the unseemly lengths to which he is prepared to go to promote them. In one scene from the picture, a young screenwriter–director (Michael Armstrong, one of Tenser's discoveries) sits with Murdoch in the crummy sixth-floor office of BUM Films Ltd, listening to the producer brag about his success with a film called *Midnight Forever*. Armstrong's character thinks he knows the movie. 'That wasn't that Philip Marsaud picture about the Spanish Civil War, was it?' 'No,' retorts Benny. 'It was about lesbianism in a convent. Didn't do a thing. So what did I do? Changed the title to *Dirty Knickers* and I cleaned up.' Murdoch is prone to moments of visionary inspiration – 'We have big close-ups of her tits in the metal trap!' – but demonstrates his greatest ingenuity when he decides to make three versions of the film, each in accordance with the differing wishes of three eccentric backers: Lady Longhorn of the Moral Reform Society, an elderly snob named Ambrose Cream and an extravagant old queen named Vernon Peabody, who insists that BUM productions turn out a gay musical Western: 'I think the film should be very violent, with lots of pretty boys in it, all having their bottoms smacked.' The footage that we see offers an interesting echo of *The Singer Not the Song*.

Eskimo Nell parodies Tenser's appetite for the grisly processes of exploitation deal-making, but it also offers an illustration of his most cherishable quality: his willingness to take a chance on untested talents. With the exception of Vernon Sewell – whom he assigned to *The Blood Beast Terror* (1968), a costume horror about an entomologist's daughter who transmogrifies into a vampire moth – Tenser rarely employed refugees from the studio system; nor did he allow himself to be bamboozled by big names. (When Orson Welles hoved into the office and invited him to invest in a production of *Treasure Island*, Tenser pretended that he was busy for the next two years, and allowed the honour of squandering money on the project to go to Harry Alan Towers.) Instead, Tenser favoured a series of keen young directors and screenwriters, some of whom were barely out of their teens. He provided Roman Polanski with the cash to make his first English-language picture, *Repulsion* – a hothouse psychodrama in which a young Belgian manicurist sinks into a murderous, delusional state – and *Cul-de-Sac* – an intoxicatingly bizarre comedy-thriller which looked back to the director's surrealist student shorts.[22] Tenser wrote the cheques which allowed a brilliant, neurotic director named Michael Reeves to shoot *The Sorcerers* (1967) and *Witchfinder General* (1968), before an accidental overdose of sleeping pills dealt British cinema its most vicious blow since the death of Pen Tennyson. Tenser gave Michael Armstrong his first scripting assignment on *The Haunted House of Horror* (1969), aiding his promotion to the director's chair on *Mark of the Devil* (1970) – a notoriously gruesome picture for which promotional sick-bags were distributed to patrons. Piers Haggard, the son of Stephen Haggard, Victoria Hopper's co-star in *Whom the Gods Love*, was another beneficiary of this trust: before the BBC gave him the job of directing Dennis Potter's *Pennies from Heaven*, he turned in *Blood on Satan's Claw* (1970) for Tenser.

Let us not sentimentalise Tenser's motives. For him, all these pictures were properties to be sold as aggressively as was possible. 'An exploitation film is a film with a gimmick,' he says. 'Something to get an audience in. Even *Repulsion* is a film with a gimmick. It's about a girl who's not getting any; she going mad and she's starting to hallucinate. That's a gimmick; that's something you can use to sell a film.' He liked Polanski and his peers for their cheapness, as well as their zealotry. Filming on the street was customarily carried out guerrilla-style, without permission from local coun-

Catherine Deneuve and her putrefying lunch in Roman Polanski's
Repulsion (1966)

cils. (After blowing up a car in the last scene of *The Sorcerers*, Michael
Reeves and his crew were forced to scatter to avoid being collared by the
police.) Small extravagances were discouraged. When Polanski was setting up the famous sequence in which Catherine Deneuve is pawed by a
series of disembodied hands that push their way through the mortar of
her hallway walls, Tenser haggled him down from twenty-four to sixteen.
The actor Roy Hudd recalls that when he played the part of a pickle-guz-
zling mortuary assistant in *The Blood Beast Terror*, he was told, 'Try to
look bigger as you come towards the camera,' to compensate for the inadequacies of the tiny forced-perspective set.[23]

Tenser's business interests went beyond the production of bleak, exis-
tential horror pictures. In partnership with Michael Klinger – and under
the aegis of his own companies, Tony Tenser Productions and Tigon
Films – he also invested heavily in softcore sex flicks. *Naked – as Nature
Intended* is a textbook example of the nudist-camp travelogue (a genre

discussed in the next chapter). John Bown's *Monique* (1970) is a creditably bittersweet sexual drama in which a married couple's suburban alienation is remedied by the arrival of a bisexual French au pair. (The final scene, as they all sit in bed, smoking fags, passing the wine and discussing abstract art – with somebody's knickers draped over the bedside lamp – is a sleazy genre's most winsome moment.) *What's Good for the Goose* (1969) is notable as Norman Wisdom's disastrous attempt to reinvent himself as a sex-comedy star. Watching him standing in his tight little white Y-fronts in a comfortless hotel bathroom, psyching himself to have sex with Sally Geeson, is like attending the funeral of his career.

Exploitation cinema was pragmatic, commercial and randy for profit – but its acute interest in anticipating the desires of its audience gave it a hotly intimate relationship with popular mores and anxieties. These films depict a society riven by intergenerational conflict. They argue that Britain's institutions – the Church, the state, the army, the medical, legal and educational professions – are corrupt, discredited and heading for a bloody collapse. They contend that the old are envious of the appetites and energies of the young; and the young, tired of being exploited by their elders, are responding with nihilistic rage.

Tenser's work with Michael Reeves exemplifies these themes. In *The Sorcerers*, the decrepit Professor Montserrat (Boris Karloff) visits a Wimpy bar and picks up a polo-necked malcontent, Mike Roscoe (Ian Ogilvy), with the promise of the thrill of a lifetime. Roscoe submits to a psychedelic light-show in Montserrat's seedy flat, unaware that the experiment has enabled the hypnotist and his wife Estelle (Catherine Lacey) to gain vicarious access to his physical and mental sensations. When Roscoe goes for a swim, the old couple sense the coolness of the water on their skins. When he goes to a night-club, they hear the music and feel the heat of the room. Estelle, hungry for second-hand thrills, manipulates Mike into beating up his best friend, taking a pair of scissors to his girlfriend (a fifteen-year-old Susan George) and fleeing the police in a breakneck car chase.[24] The crash kills Roscoe and the old woman who has been sharing his mind: age's jealous regard for youth has brought about the annihilation of both.

In *Witchfinder General*, Reeves cast Ogilvy as Richard Marshall, a young soldier in the English Civil War who deserts a Parliamentarian regiment to take revenge upon Matthew Hopkins (Vincent Price), a sadistic fraud who is enriching himself by torturing false confessions of witchcraft from the citizens of East Anglia – one of whom, Sara (Hilary Dwyer), is Marshall's fiancée. Reeves's film brings a new realism to the depiction of screen violence: when a man is shot, he doesn't simply crumple to the ground; he is smacked against the wall like a wet fish, leaving a thick smear of blood on the plasterwork. The film also offers new thoughts on the effect of violence upon its spectators. When Hopkins announces 'a new method of execution' that will furnish 'a fitting end for the foul ungodliness in womankind', the people of a Suffolk town gather to watch a suspected witch tied to a ladder and lowered, face down, into a blazing pyre. The crowd responds not with whoops and cheers, but with a strange, distracted blankness. They might be modern Britons watching the Vietnam War on TV.

Witchfinder General concludes with a great blossoming of brutality: Marshall rains a hail of axe-blows down upon Hopkins, but the villain's ordeal is cut short by a bullet from a fellow soldier. 'You took him from me! You took him from me!' yells Marshall, robbed of his moment of revenge, while, tied to the rack in the torture chamber, his fiancée unleashes a series of convulsive screams. The effect upon audiences was visceral: Tony Tenser recalls a screening of the film at which a young man jumped to his feet at this climactic point, screaming, 'Smash him! Kill the bastard!' John Russell Taylor in *The Times* argued that 'there is much in *Witchfinder General* which would win Michael Reeves an important reputation if he were dealing with some more pretentious, but fundamentally no more serious subject'. Alan Bennett, appalled by Taylor's enthusiasm, attacked the picture from his column in the *Listener*: 'It is the most persistently sadistic and morally rotten film I have seen. It was a degrading experience, by which I mean it made me feel dirty.'[25] Tenser was delighted with the picture, and more delighted by the controversy it aroused. He persuaded Reeves to sign a five-picture contract.

With genial enthusiasm, Tenser remembers their plans at that time. The next film was to be a drama of the Irish Civil War, entitled *O'Hooligan's Mob*. They had decided on an opening scene in which the hero, a young IRA recruit sleeping rough in a pile of straw, wakes to find that he has narrowly missed being doused in a vigorous stream of horse-piss. They had worked out a concluding scene in which the hero escaped the firing squad by grabbing a machine-gun and turning on his would-be executioners and on the watching crowd. Their plans evaporated on 11 February 1969. 'His girlfriend phoned me up to tell me that he'd died,' recalls Tenser. 'His housekeeper found him. Most people think he committed suicide, but I don't think that's true. He was getting on all right with his girlfriend. He was getting on all right with me. He'd just signed a contract to direct five more films. He was completely immersed in his work. He used to take tablets to help him sleep and my thoughts were that he'd taken these, and had woken up in the middle of the night, forgotten he'd taken them, and took some more. He just died in his sleep.'

Not all of Tenser's directors were so energised by despair and brutality. 'We are mostly all chest-deep in blood,' wrote Piers Haggard, reflecting on the work of British directors in an article for *Screen International*. 'I think our society is probably about to shatter. The whole structure is under threat for the first time. As working artists, our responsibility is to offer solutions which are strongly progressive, instead of merely offering confirmations of failed systems – which is what we do too often.'[26] His self-doubt only amplifies the odd power of his own contribution to the field, *Blood on Satan's Claw* (1974). The whoop-de-doo title is Tenser's. The unsettling atmosphere is all Haggard's work. The film describes a rural revolution in seventeenth-century England, in which the children of a West Country village turn on their elders and embark upon a spree of murder and rape. The film, like *Witchfinder General* and other close relations, reversed the customary reassurances of the traditional Gothic melodrama. In Hammer pictures, Jesus came to the rescue in the final reel, through the agencies of holy water sizzling on vampire skin, the cruciform shadow of a windmill's sails or the uttering of the correct biblical incantation. In the rural witchcraft genre, moral oppositions were less clear cut. In *Cry of the Banshee* (1970), for instance, Vincent Price's attempts to suppress the naked rituals of a local pagan sect are like the heavy-handed efforts of a landowner to break up a rock festival on his property. In *The Wicker Man* (1974), paganism and Christianity are offered as ideological equivalents, but the islanders' interest in folk songs and nudie maypole dancing is significantly more attuned to the sensibility of its audience than the prissy piety of Edward Woodward's virgin policeman. In *Blood on Satan's Claw*, the old remedies against witchcraft no longer seem effective, principally because the savagery unleashed upon the village does not seem wholly attributable to supernatural forces – despite the presence of a horned beast and patches of fuzzily demonic hair on the bodies of its teenage acolytes. The leader of the gang, Angel Blake (played with precocious force by seventeen-year-old Linda Hayden), might be disrupting her Sunday-school lessons for pure badness. She might be offering herself to the parson simply because she wants to see him cast from the village in disgrace. She might encourage the boys in her class to abduct and rape a maidservant simply to satisfy her own perverse desires.[27] Perhaps, suggests *Blood on Satan's Claw*, this is just what kids are like, or what their elders have made them.

Stanley Kubrick's *A Clockwork Orange* (1972), elevated from the category of exploitation by studio backing and an illustrious director, is one of the few explorations of this theme to have been admitted to the canon. Its vision of a concrete Britain stalked by gangs of drugged-up boys in bizarre clothes confirmed the doomy prognostications of newspaper columnists and put intoxicating images into the minds of the listless youths kicking about at the dowdy end of the King's Road. Kubrick, horrified by the monster he had created, suppressed the picture. It was a pointless exercise. For some years, and with comparably minuscule resources, British exploitation cinema had been depicting worlds in which the old were at war with the young; in which adults and children recoiled from each other in horror. Joseph Losey's *The Damned* (1961) told the story of a gang of children, maimed by radioactive experiments and sealed by the military into a cave near Weymouth. *Death Line* (1972) suggested that a lost race of cannibal troglodytes – the descendants of construction workers abandoned after a tunnel collapse – were living in squalid passageways under the tube system and subsisting by butchering ticketholders on the last train home. *Tower of Evil* (1972) sacrificed a gang of switched-on kids to the bloodlust of an insane lighthouse-keeper. ('We have sounds, food and some great grass,' announces Robin Askwith, in a voice too chirpy to go unsilenced by the old man's spear.) In Don Sharp's *Psychomania* (1973) George Sanders uses toad-related voodoo to bring Nicky Henson's snarling leatherboy roaring from the grave on a Harley-

Davidson, ready to destroy the British establishment – or at least crash through the window of the local supermarket, upsetting pyramids of marrowfat peas and Carnation milk. ('Do you know how many police-men there are?' asks the resurrected biker, helping himself to the contents of his mother's fruit bowl. 'And teachers? Preachers? Do-gooders? There's lots to be done.') In Alan Birkinshaw's *Killer's Moon* (1978), a gang of psy-chiatric patients, under the impression that their experiences are some kind of chemically induced collective hallucination, massacre a busload of schoolgirls stranded in the Lake District. The film is almost certainly the most tasteless in British cinema history. 'Look, you were only raped,' says one victimised girl to another, in a scene from the typewriter of the director's sister, Fay Weldon. 'As long as you don't tell anyone about it you'll be all right. You pretend it never happened. I'll pretend I never saw it, and if we ever get out of this alive, maybe we'll both live to be wives and mothers.'[28]

The family was the institution attacked most aggressively by the British exploitation picture. In *The Corpse* (1970), a minor but intoxicatingly poetic horror film, a mother and daughter conspire to murder the domestic tyrant who has turned their home into a well-upholstered prison. (The awfulness of the man is demonstrated in the opening scene, in which he runs his fingers over the still-warm saddle of his daughter's bicycle, before retiring inside to lather his hands with carbolic.) The Boulting brothers' *Twisted Nerve* (1968) offers a portrait of Martin Durn-ley (Hywel Bennett), a young psychopath whom the film suggests is an aberration allowed into the world only through his mother's selfish desire to produce a second child – the first having been diagnosed 'mongoloid' and packed off to an institution. Some of Martin's crimes comprise little more than regular teenage dissent: he won't get a job, he listens to loud music, he owns a secret stash of muscle mags. Others are more serious: he impersonates the childlike innocence of his Down's syndrome brother to infiltrate the household of a librarian whom he plans to rape – but not before he has taken an axe to her mother and terrorised the boorish lodger, a salesman of exploitation pictures given to boasting about the profitable nature of screen sex and violence: 'Cartoon, ice-cream, bit of the old S'n'V, and they're happy.'

*

At the beginning of the 1960s, a kind of détente seemed negotiable between the adults and troubled young people depicted in British films. The heroine of *Girl on Approval* for instance, after raging against her foster-parents – 'bloody bastard' is her insult of choice – is reconciled to them in the final reel. As the years moved on, though, this dialogue broke down: British cinema detected only abuse and mistrust in the relationships between the young and the old. In the broader culture, this attitude had been focused into a distinct movement: punk, identified with the Sex Pistols, a riotous gang of teens with a talent for chaos, and their manager, Malcolm McLaren, a shock-haired impresario with a head full of Guy Debord.

Punk produced only a dribble of cinematic texts: a couple of concert films, Derek Jarman's *Jubilee* (1977) and *The Great Rock 'n' Roll Swindle* (1980) – a history of the Sex Pistols retold by McLaren with Barnum-like veracity. Yet cinema – particularly British exploitation cinema – had been one of punk's formative influences. Siouxsie and the Banshees took their name from the Vincent Price flick; the Damned from Joseph Losey's tale of a lost generation of children. (McLaren and Vivienne Westwood kept a copy of the poster pinned to the wall of their King's Road boutique.) Pinkie Brown, the vicious young hero of *Brighton Rock*, was idolised by McLaren and the Sex Pistols' vocalist Johnny Rotten. ('Like Pinkie,' notes the band's biographer, Jon Savage, Johnny Rotten 'was ready to murder the world.'[29]) One British horror director of the period made pictures that coincided so perfectly with punk's view of the world that McLaren commissioned him to put the Sex Pistols on the big screen. Like the punk movement itself, the film was doomed to failure, but the story of its progress illustrates the strength of the relationship between these two areas of British cultural life, and might suggest a way of rewriting exploitation cinema back into the narrative of twentieth-century cultural history.

It's easy to see why Malcolm McLaren possessed such enthusiasm for the films of Pete Walker. In the mid-1970s, Walker shot a trilogy of ferocious, nihilistic horror pictures which attacked the Church, the law and the psychiatric profession. *The House of Whipcord* (1974) is set in a private detention centre devoted to the murderous suppression of the young. *Frightmare* (1975), on which Tony Tenser acted as executive producer, is

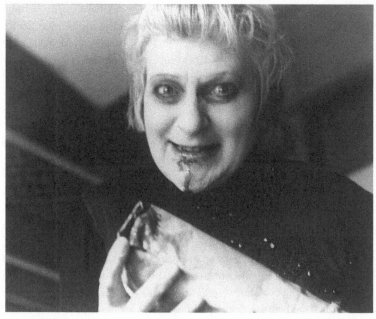

Sheila Keith proffers a parcel of human flesh in the dream sequence from
Frightmare (1974)

the story of a cannibalistic old lady with an affinity for power tools, who
is released into the community to lunch again. *House of Mortal Sin* (1976)
centres upon a murderous Catholic priest who uses a tape-recorder in the
confessional box to blackmail his parishioners – and strangles uncooperative victims with his rosary beads. Walker's cinema was one of cynicism,
brutality and black humour; a cinema that suspected it would all soon be
over for British films, and possibly for Britain itself. His pictures offered a
vision of the country as a dark, grubby, sordid place inhabited by sadistic
matriarchs and vengeful old men. All were subject to a fusillade of critical
objections. *The Times* thought *Frightmare* 'nasty, foolish and morally
repellent'.[30] 'Anyone attracted to it should head for the nearest psychiatrist,' agreed Ian Christie in the *Daily Express*.[31] 'My movies deliberately
deal with distasteful subjects,' Walker told *Photoplay* magazine in 1975.
'They are out to shock people.'[32]

Walker, however, was no art-school anarchist or Chelsea bruiser, but a lifelong Tory voter with a private plane and a passion for antique clocks. Today, you'd observe his easy manner, his air-conditioned Mercedes, the large, comfortable house in the stockbroker belt, and take him for a successful property developer – which is exactly what he has been since he bailed out of the film industry in 1983. It is a comfortable existence, punctuated by the hourly symphony of chimes, trills and toots produced by his collection of clockwork curiosities.

This was not, however, the life into which he was born. The illegitimate son of a chorus girl and a married stage comedian, he spent much of his childhood in Catholic boarding schools. His father, Syd Walker, was a music-hall turn whose fame was amplified when he joined the line-up on the radio variety show *Monday Night at Eight* in a regular spot entitled *Mr Walker Wants to Know*. This material was written by Ernest Dudley, who also coined the comic's popular catchphrase, 'What would you do, chums?' Writer and performer were not particularly chummy – Ernest made an unsuccessful attempt to sue Syd when he used the catchphrase for the title of a 1939 film.[33] (In Pete Walker's hallway, a variety bill commemorates their association, crediting Ernest for his contribution to the act.)

Syd Walker died in 1945, whereupon his wife inherited the estate. Pete's mother, Aymer Jesse, received a few pounds and the lease on their flat in Brighton. Unable to support her two young children, she deposited them in an orphanage and returned to the stage. By the time he was fifteen, Pete had decamped to London, and was working as a stand-up comedian in Michael Klinger's strip club, the Gargoyle. At the end of 1959, Sydney Newman, a maverick Canadian TV producer who would go on to create both *The Avengers* and *Doctor Who*, and Roger Proudlock, an old-school independent producer–director at the end of his career, hired the venue to make a documentary short, *Soho Striptease* (1960). 'I remember Michael watching all this shooting going on,' Walker recalls, 'and saying, "Pete, I'm being taken for a sucker. I have to pay wages to you people every week. He puts it on film and he's got it for ever."'

Walker agreed with Klinger's conclusions. He took an eighteen-month trip to America, working as a runner on low-budget movies. On his return in 1961, he used money garnered from gag-writing and small-part acting in films and television to establish a small production outfit named Heritage Films. Under the Heritage banner, Walker became a prolific producer of 8mm striptease shorts. He introduced his specialist clientele to Britt Hampshire ('the new 17 year old glamour starlet,' cooed the copy on the box) and June Grayson (in a fifty-foot epic entitled *Little Miss Muff-it*), but missed the chance of making his first million with a reel starring Mandy Rice-Davies, alumna of the Profumo scandal.[34] Walker remembers having lunch with Rice-Davies at the Fountain Café at Fortnum & Mason, while the other patrons peeked at her over their menus. She agreed to strip for a £3,000 fee, but for reasons that Walker cannot quite reconstruct, he never held her to the deal. 'You had to be careful about what you were doing then,' he reflects. 'One was very afraid that if you did that kind of thing and you attracted too much attention, it would do your business more harm than good. But it would have made an absolute fortune.'

The trials of the British and American studios, however, soon gave him an opportunity to transfer his talents to a larger film format. His first effort, *I Like Birds* (1967), was financed for £7,000 and bought by the Rank Organisation for release as the bottom of a double bill with the Hayley Mills vehicle *Pretty Polly* (1967). Although the film is only a flimsy farce with some short sequences of nudity, the character of Miles Fanthorpe, an anti-vice campaigner with the private life of a Home Counties Hugh Hefner, adumbrates one of Walker's key themes: 'Nothing makes my blood boil', Fanthorpe declares, 'more than to read in our national dailies flagrant evidence of a sharp decline in moral attitudes – divorce rate rising, obscene fashions, the miniskirt, abuse of the Queen's uniform and venereal disease.' It still bewilders Walker that the films he made in this vein – *Strip Poker* (1968), *School for Sex* (1969), *Four Dimensions of Greta* (1972) – were booked successfully into large theatres. *School for Sex*, which garnered a worldwide box-office gross of some £1.5 million, ran for seven weeks at the Jacey Tatler, a central London cinema, apparently to packed houses of pinstriped men. 'It was a clip-joint effect,' he reasons. 'Nobody could have possibly derived any satisfaction from it. For one thing, the standard of the girls wasn't that great. It was hard to find girls who would take their clothes off and who were also members of Equity.' He recalls looking in on a screening of the film at his local 2,600-seater ABC cinema. 'The manager was on the front of house in his dress suit. The place was about twenty-five per cent full, and they were all yobs, shouting and screaming and throwing things at each other. I thanked the manager and told him I was terribly sorry that business was so bad. "Bad?" he said. "This is the best Sunday night I've had for two years."'

Walker was frustrated by the limitations imposed upon him by the distributors, the budget and the censor. 'We had to make these films to a formula, otherwise we couldn't sell them. Tits in the first reel. A killing in the first five minutes, if it was a horror picture, and preferably before the credits.' These sensational demands then had to be squared with Trevelyan's proscriptions. ('Indoor nudity', apparently, was strictly prohibited.) 'I used to sit in his office and he'd bore me about how important he was,' says Walker. 'It was all bullshit. Token cuts. Sometimes you resubmitted a film to him and hadn't done anything, and he still passed it.'

Walker's difficult relationship with establishment figures such as Trevelyan helped clarify the themes of his films. In *The Flesh and Blood Show* (1972), the twentysomething members of an experimental drama group are terrorised by an elderly Shakespearean performer (Patrick Barr) with a psychotic grudge against the young. ('They're all the same, young actors,' he rages. 'Filthy and degraded lechers. All of them! And the females! Flaunting their bodies, offering their thighs and breasts. Scum! Ex-cre-ment!') In *The House of Whipcord*, a blind and senile former judge (Barr again) passes death sentences upon young women who have been abducted by his sister and her son in a bizarre attempt to eradicate permissive mores from British society. ('We do not countenance here reformers, prison welfare visitors or chaplains,' he warns. 'We do not provide comfortable rooms with chintz curtains, television. This, young woman, is a real prison.')

Walker – who resists political interpretations of his work with a smile and a roll of the eyes – concedes that intergenerational conflict is a central concern of his work. 'There was a yawning gap between the old and the young. Young people didn't have the confidence that they've got now, and consequently they *expected* to be second-class people. I was in my twenties, and I felt exactly the same way as these characters. I was being put down by the elders of the film industry.' To illustrate his point, he tells me how, one spring day in 1975, he received a phone call from the

BBC, requesting a colour transparency of his face. The photograph was required for the corporation's coverage of the BAFTAs. *The House of Whipcord*, the caller informed him, had been nominated for a technical prize. An hour later, Walker was on the phone to BAFTA, asking if he might attend the ceremony. An official assured him that he hadn't won and, Walker claims, informed him, 'We don't have space for people like yourself.' He can recall watching the ceremony on television, his face flashing up on the screen with the other nominees, and the presenter, Michael Aspel, exclaiming, 'I bet their palms are sweating now!' He gives a rueful laugh at the absurdity of the situation. 'It was that kind of business. I was one of the few people making films, but I was *persona non grata*. Totally *persona non grata*.'

Actors, however, showed few qualms about appearing in Walker's productions – despite occasionally being attacked in the tabloid press for doing so.[35] Leo Genn, a stalwart of the Rank Organisation, relished the melodramatic opportunities of exploitation cinema: 'We'll never get away with it,' was Walker's customary response to the actor's suggestions for how they might intensify a scene. Richard Todd, with rather less enthusiasm, signed up for *House of the Long Shadows* and *Home before Midnight*. ('Actors like to work,' says the director, with a shrug.) *The House of Whipcord*, it seems, might have formed a last reunion for the Gainsborough girls: Margaret Lockwood's agent proposed her for the part of the vicious prison warder. Jean Kent came into Walker's office to discuss the film. Peggy Cummins read the script and urged him to cast her, making the suggestion, 'I could scrape back my hair and play her as a lesbian.' Walker insists that they were all too good looking for the part – though they may also have been too expensive – and cast two relative unknowns in the lead roles: Barbara Markham, principally known as a dialogue coach, and Sheila Keith, a 'nice little Scottish lady' who stooged for comedians such as Arthur Lowe and Ronnie Barker.[36] Keith was a genuine discovery: a performer wholly attuned to the Guignol excesses of exploitation cinema, without any qualms about the nature of the material – whether she was thrashing the life out of permissive young women, devouring parcelled cuts of human meat, or cajoling a priest into committing matricide with a poisoned communion wafer.

I visited Keith in the spring of 2004, a year before her death. 'Some of my friends', she noted, reflecting on her career in exploitation cinema from the comfort of an armchair in Brinsworth House, a retirement home for variety artistes, 'were rather disapproving' – particularly, she recalled, when the façade of the London Pavilion Cinema was hung with a giant banner picture of the actress wielding a fearsome whip. 'I used to go and see the films in disguise, wearing a pair of dark glasses.' I showed her some stills from these pictures: there she was, tyrannising a topless teenage girl; there, sliding a pitchfork into a victim's belly; and there, grinning through a slick of gore. 'Which was the one where I drilled people's heads and ate their brains?' she asked, settling her teacup in her lap. I reminded her of the title. 'Ah yes, *Frightmare*. That was tremendous fun.'

Frightmare presents Sheila Keith at her unfettered best. She looms from the darkness of an ill-lit train compartment, a cadaverous spectre proffering a bloody paper package. She issues an asthmatic wheeze with each murderous swing of her axe. She lures victims to her house by offering tarot readings through the small ads in *Time Out*: 'It's all strife, isn't it?' she purrs, to a young woman upon whom she intends to dine. 'Strife and heartache and loneliness.' In the film's final scene, she is discovered hunched over the body of her daughter's boyfriend, a shrieking electric drill in her hand. It is a typically bleak Walker finale: the man who seemed to be the story's hero is reduced to a bloody mess, while the monsters are triumphant. It was a vision of anarchy for which Malcolm McLaren expressed his particular admiration.

The Sex Pistols' *annus mirabilis* was 1977. 'God Save the Queen' sold 150,000 copies in three days, in spite of being banned by the BBC, which caused several editions of *Top of the Pops* to end with an embarrassing harrumph. The *Sun* encouraged its readers to 'punish the punks'. The band was dropped by two record companies (they didn't feel obliged to return their advances) before being signed to Richard Branson's Virgin label. Throughout this frenzied period, McLaren was hustling to put together a film deal. He recruited the American exploitation director Russ Meyer to direct a script entitled *Who Killed Bambi?*, but the picture collapsed when Twentieth Century Fox withdrew their financial support. (Princess Grace of Monaco, it was reported, had led a shareholders' revolt, objecting to a scene depicting sex between Sid Vicious and his mother.) A replacement director, Jonathan Kaplan, was enrolled by McLaren's co-producer Michael White, and accepted by the band – but not by McLaren, who had a different candidate in mind.

McLaren's choice, Pete Walker, understood little about punk, but was enthused because the contract, brokered with new money from Warner Brothers, would have allowed him to put £250,000 in his bank account – and McLaren, of course, to do the same. The two men, united by their mutual love of a sweet deal and their mutual talent for exploitation, took to each other immediately. Even now, Walker cannot suppress a smile of admiration for McLaren's spivvy genius.

Walker enlisted Michael Armstrong to write the script – now entitled *A Star is Dead* – and the pair accompanied McLaren to the opening date of the Sex Pistols' Jubilee tour, in a gymnasium in the middle of a muddy field in Uxbridge. It was one of the band's filthiest and most furious gigs. Even the musicians were appalled by the behaviour of the audience. Walker, standing in his suit and tie on a raised gallery above the main auditorium, surveyed the scene, wide-eyed. ('They weren't human beings,' he reflects. 'They were a crowd of animals.') Backstage, however, he found that the men who inspired this chaos were rather less dangerous. 'Malcom McLaren was in it for the money,' says Walker. 'The whole anarchy thing was a fake. Johnny Rotten understood this, and played the game. He just wanted to be Rod Stewart. He wanted to be a star, and have the birds and the money and the cars. The others were a bunch of idiots.' Idiots to whom McLaren was doling a salary of eight pounds a week.[35]

Together with Michael Armstrong, Walker began work on the picture. 'We constructed this script in which all of the Sex Pistols were featured all the way through, but the only time they were together – which was when they could be trouble – was when they were doing their numbers. When you got them on their own they were just frightened little boys. So we gave everyone else the proper lines and laughs, and all they had to do was stand there and just say "cunt" or "fuck".' The plot of *A Star Is Dead* follows the film-within-a-film pattern of Armstrong's *Eskimo Nell*, and tells of a celebrated 1960s playwright who is recruited to write a script for a Sex Pistols movie. His first draft is a diatribe against the same regime mentioned in 'God Save the Queen'. The version that goes before the cameras, however, is a musical remake of *The Three Musketeers*, in which the band co-stars with a venerable old actor-knight, Sir Arthur Gates – a near-namesake of the psychotic thespian of *The Flesh and Blood Show*. In the role of Johnny Rotten's mother – a dominatrix who shares a council flat with her flatulent daughter – Walker had determined to engage Diana Dors. The casting of Sir Arthur, he anticipated, would be slightly more difficult. 'I imagine we would have had to ask a lot of people, but someone would have been persuaded to do it for a laugh. Richard Todd might have done it.'

Filming was scheduled to begin at Bray Studios, the home of Hammer,

Sid Vicious concludes his Frank Sinatra tribute by opening fire into the audience in *The Great Rock'n'Roll Swindle* (1980)

once the Sex Pistols had completed a tour of America. The band, however, did not return intact from the trip. They were picketed in Tulsa, caused a riot in Memphis and were pelted with beer cans and hot dogs in San Antonio. On 14 January 1978 they played the Winter Ballroom in San Francisco. At the end of the gig, Johnny Rotten left the stage with the words which proved to be the band's epitaph: 'Ever get the feeling you've been cheated?' In the following forty-eight hours, Sid Vicious was hospitalised by an accidental heroin overdose and John Lydon told the *New York Post* that the Sex Pistols had dissolved. With that announcement, *A Star Is Dead* was undone and Pete Walker's chance of a quarter of a million pounds evaporated. McLaren, undaunted by Lydon's desertion or Vicious's final heroin overdose in February 1979 – gathered up all the extant footage of the Sex Pistols and, with a young film-school graduate, Julien Temple, crafted *The Great Rock'n'Roll Swindle*, a gleefully mendacious exercise in which McLaren affected to have used a ten-point plan to engineer the rise and fall of the band he managed.

My first exposure to this film came in December 1996, when I attended a screening organised by the fashion magazine *Dazed and Confused*. Like many of the Sex Pistols' gigs, it almost failed to happen. Learning that the screening would be introduced by Malcolm McLaren, the surviving members of the band withdrew their permission to project the 35mm print. When the organisers discovered that Polygram owned sole rights to the video release, this was secured as a bleary substitute. McLaren, in tasteful suit and tie, took the microphone and described how the film was taken out of his hands and recut. He claimed to be in particular mourning for the loss of a cartoon sequence that depicted anal sex between Richard Branson and 'a young man by the name of Sting'. (The released version retains a line describing Branson living in a mansion that 'overlooked the tomb of Karl Marx and the bedroom of Lynsey de Paul'.) On the screen, McLaren sloshed about, bollock-naked, in a bath of snot-green liquid. In the auditorium, his older self quietly sipped the sponsor's gin – with tonic, ice and plastic stirrer – and stowed the empties under his seat. Sitting next to him, the editor of *Dazed and Confused*, Jefferson Hack, came closest to an act of anarchy when he lit up in the no-smoking cinema. After the screening, I spoke to McLaren in the foyer and discovered a man still amused by his own cinematic debut, created, he insisted, 'to make a statement that would keep the Sex Pistols as an idea intact; to prevent it from sitting in one of those well-anointed rock almanacs. The jury shall forever remain out. I love that. That's really rock'n'roll.'

It's just as difficult to reach a conclusion about Walker's work. *The House of Whipcord*, for instance, begins with a caption: 'This film is dedicated to those who are disturbed by today's lax moral codes and who eagerly await the return of corporal and capital punishment.' Did he mean it? 'You're asking me a question I really can't answer. I was then, and still am, concerned about today's lack of moral codes. Do I believe in corporal and capital punishment? I suppose I do. I'm old enough to have lived in a time when there was so much less violence and crime, much more honour. And it was fear that made that possible. You didn't kill because you'd swing for it.' Was he on the side of the monsters? 'I was just being mischievous. There could be something in capital punishment. When you see monsters like Shipman . . .' The clocks begin to chime midday. Walker's collection comes to life. Tiny hammers beat out 'The March of the Toreadors'. Air streams through organ pipes. A phalanx of automata judders into action. 'I'm a very conservative person,' he insists, raising his voice against the clamour.

Pete Walker made two more films after the collapse of *A Star Is Dead*. *Home before Midnight* was a return to the straight-faced sexploitation drama of the kind that Tony Tenser and Michael Klinger were producing in the early 1960s: a social problem film with a dash of *Lolita*. *House of the Long Shadows* was a horror spoof that assembled Peter Cushing, Christopher Lee, Vincent Price, John Carradine and Sheila Keith to send themselves up in a movie full of self-reflexive gags and gory special effects.

Richard Todd appears in both of these films, each time playing a minor but important role. In Walker's camped-up, all-star swansong, Todd's publisher tricks a cocky young writer (Desi Arnez Jr) into enduring a weekend of throat-cutting, eye-gouging and acid-throwing in a Welsh country mansion, culminating in a scene in which Christopher Lee staggers to the floor with an axe buried in his chest and blood spilling from the corner of his mouth. Before the carnage begins, however, publisher and writer go out for lunch to a smart restaurant. 'I just feel that you should be developing your talent more,' Todd's character urges. 'Not restricting yourself to the same type of subject all the time.' He suggests a change of direction: 'It's certainly the right time to do it as far as your career is concerned.' He notices his client's eye wandering to an attractive young woman sitting at another table. 'Love at first sight?' he asks. 'No,' drawls the writer, 'just feeling horny.' Todd attempts an indulgent laugh, but his discomfort is palpable. 'It's a cynical age we live in,' says Arnez with a grin. 'Don't I know it,' mutters Todd.

CHAPTER TEN

The Oldest Living Sexploitation
Star Tells All

Naked – as Nature Intended: (left to right) Bridget Leonard, Pamela Green, Jackie Salt, Petrina Forsyth

I am in a very peculiar position: kneeling on the bedroom carpet of a seventy-five-year-old woman as she shows me a poster-size monochrome close-up of her torso. Only one response comes to mind: 'Oh, *hello*,' in a feeble imitation of Leslie Phillips in *Carry on Teacher* (1959). Pamela Green, however, isn't batting a false eyelash. Here she is in her portfolio, naked except for an embroidered sun hat, leaning on a pillar pox, squeezing her thighs together. And here, splashing about in a rock pool with her head thrown back, the water spuming over her prodigious curves. And here again, spilling out of a scarlet corset, arms akimbo, fringe lolling over her left eye.

Not all of her reliquary is photographic. Rising from the floor, she disgorges the contents of her underwear drawer, inviting me to admire the paraphernalia of her film career: a green nylon negligée, spattered with tiny pink flowers; a ruby-red wig, rather faded with the passage of time; a brace of beady-eyed fox furs, dyed a lurid cobalt blue. 'And this', she declares, waving a wispy little thing in front of my face, 'is the negligee that I wore for Michael Powell.'

In the summer of 1959, the director of *Black Narcissus* paid a visit to number 4 Gerrard Street, Soho. It was a property full of dramatic possibilities. The basement housed an after-hours drinking club, the ground floor a pornographic bookshop, and the attic a veteran prostitute. The floors between were the studios of George Harrison Marks, a photographer and film-maker who supplied the grubby-raincoat market with pocket-sized jazz-mags and 8mm glamour shorts for home projection. Powell was searching for an actress to play a nude model in *Peeping Tom*, a study in psychosis, sadism and the dynamics of cinema that would, six months later, encourage reviewers to plunge a large spike into his reputation. He had fixed upon a model named on the pages of Marks's *Kamera* magazine as Rita Landré, a statuesque figure with marmalade curls and a wardrobe of tight-laced waspies. He was not the first reader who had to be told that Rita was Pamela Green in disguise. Green, who was Marks's lover, business partner and chief model, was delighted by Powell's interest. The director examined the Parisian street scene that she had designed and constructed on the studio floor, surveyed her racks of chiffon shorties, and invited her down to Pinewood to be gored to death. 'There's only one word for the way that he treated me,' she reflects. 'Sadistic.'

Peeping Tom is one of cinema's most brutal acts of self-exposure. Mark (Carl Boehm), the film's protagonist, is a quiet type who gets his kicks by impaling young women with the spear-sharp leg of his modified camera tripod, taking a close-up of his victims' faces as he slams the point home. With Freudian certitude, the film identifies the source of his disorder: home movies demonstrate how the boy spent his formative years being brutalised and humiliated by his father, a balding bully with a toothbrush moustache who shone a torch beam into the boy's face as he slept, tossed a lizard into his bed, and recorded his distress on Super-8. Powell cast himself as the parent, and his own son, Columba, as Mark's younger self. Stories from the set of the picture only intensify the elision between its director and its anti-hero. Powell wanted a shot of Pamela Green reflected, upside-down, in the back of Mark's camera. Five Brute arc lamps were placed around Green as she lolled against the plaster brickwork of a replica of her own Parisian street set, but the light was not sufficient to achieve the effect. Powell removed the glass safety covers. The heat from five naked filaments burned Green's skin and caused her eyes and eyelids to become red and swollen. ('The next day, he just told the make-up people to cover it up,' she recalls.) When it came to the filming of her nude scene, she surprised Powell by demanding that the set be cleared of unnecessary personnel – several members of the *Carry On* team and half the cast of Charles Crichton's *The League of Gentlemen*, Green notes, had wandered on to Stage F for a gawk. Powell agreed, reluctantly, but placed his two young sons, aged seven and eight, by the side of the camera. Tired of arguing, Green said nothing but her line: 'What have you got under there, a girlfriend?'

Peeping Tom is a film that plays games with the geography of London. The street names that are legible in the location scenes are Fitzrovian: Rathbone Place, Newman Passage, the thoroughfares of the more respectable north side of Oxford Street. Powell, however, does not intend us to register this deception: when Mark shuffles a stack of tabloid newspapers which depict the face of one of his victims, mimicking an unspooled strip of celluloid, their headlines declare, 'Murder in Soho' – the shared territory of the film business and the skin game.

These two industries, both a little less sanguine than they were in 1959, still exist here, side by side. Mike Leigh's Thin Man Productions shares a Greek Street staircase with a number of prostitutes. Alan Parker's offices on Lexington Street are within gobbing distance of a drag of peepshows and lap-dancing bars. Walk north up Wardour Street from the Shaftesbury Avenue end and you can track the history of this cohabitation. Pass the dingy row of clip joints that occupies Tisbury Court, cross the junction with Brewer Street, where the neon of the Raymond Revuebar once glowed through a patina of accumulated grime, raise your eyes above the façade of the Las Vegas pool hall, and you'll see the words 'Urbanora House' chiselled into the limestone. Here, in 1908, the American émigré Charles Urban set up his production business and inaugurated the film industry's colonisation of Soho. Next door, at number 84, is the former HQ of Pathé News, where, up on the flat roof, company employees dissolved outdated films in vats of sodium hydroxide. At number 117 is Hammer House, from which Sir James Carreras conducted a bloody and profitable twenty-year reign. Near by are the premises once occupied by the offices of the British arm of Warner Brothers. Beneath your feet, the cellars form a long chain of projection booths and screening rooms, in which film-makers constructed their work and film hacks dismantled it again. And, in rooms on the upper storeys of many of these buildings, the life of a shadow film business was conducted; a world in which Pamela Green and George Harrison Marks were leading figures. Its stars were paid by the hour, and put on performances that their Rank Organisation equivalents would never have countenanced; its productions, shot in small film formats on black-and-white stock, were rarely shown in cinemas; its directors did not receive screen credits.

Little of this work has survived into the twenty-first century. Why would it? These films were unsophisticated sketches intended to provide a solitary form of entertainment. Boredom or guilt consigned them to the dustbin or the incinerator. Their performers were art students, call-girls and teenage runaways who took cash payments to go through some simple comic routine, climb out of their underwear and blink into the lens. Few of the surviving personnel associated with these productions can be persuaded to speak about their experiences – not least because many of them spent time in jail on obscenity charges. Only Mike Free-man, an irrepressible optimist who remains cheerfully committed to the production of a pornographic 'masterpiece', is happy to reminisce about his career in 8mm hardcore, and the sentences he served when the police decided not to extort their customary fee. And yet the collapse of the studio system represented by Korda and Balcon and J. Arthur Rank effected a productive collision between these cinematic cultures, of which *Peeping Tom* is only the most obvious example. We have already seen how independent film-makers were offered new themes by exploitation cinema's lucrative pursuit of violence. The marketable qual-ities of nudity also attracted their attention. They searched energetically for contexts in which naked flesh would be acceptable to the censor, and produced travelogues exploring naturist clubs, documentaries in which men in white coats conducted grave discussions about sexual positions, full-frontal farces. By the beginning of the 1970s, the sleazy sensibility of the stag loop and the blue-movie club had entered the mainstream of British cinema. The listings pages of the local and national press were dense with titles of productions such as *I'm Not Feeling Myself Tonight* (1976), *The Ups and Downs of a Handyman* (1975), *Let's Get Laid* (1978) and – less logically – *Confessions of a Naked Virgin* (1970). At the end of the decade, there was no discernible difference between the two worlds of Wardour Street.

British sexploitation cinema is now a forgotten embarrassment. Par-ticipants who went on to more respectable careers – the composer Michael Nyman, the novelist Justin Cartwright and the musical theatre star Elaine Paige, for example – would probably prefer it to remain that way. Only two small-press books exist on the subject: David McGillivray's *Doing Rude Things* (1992), a pioneering sketch of the genre, authored by a blushing former practitioner, and Simon Sheridan's *Keeping the British End Up* (2001),[1] an attempt to compile the first filmography of sexploitation. A handful of exploratory articles have appeared in scholarly publications and, since 1999, several of the films have been screened on late-night television. The genre, however, remains despised and obscure. 'When they write their monographs on the Cinema of the Twentieth Century,' asserts McGillivray, 'what will historians make of the two and a half decades that produced the British sex film? Not a jot . . . [The] genre will be completely ignored.'[2] The most widely read introductory textbook on British film, *The British Cinema Book* (2001), fulfils McGillivray's prophecy. Even *Come Play with Me* (1977), which remains the most profitable and longest-running film in British history, does not receive a name-check.

It is hard to make the same critical claims for sexploitation cinema as for its bloody twin sister. Its makers, knowing that audiences would be too bashful to bellyache about the shortcomings of the work, rarely felt obliged to pollute it with ideas. It would be wrong, however, to dismiss the genre as historically marginal or unworthy of study. Such productions, irrespective of their poor quality and vulgarity, require restoration to the narrative of our national cinema. This restitution will necessitate a horde of academics sitting down to watch flabby pub studs in towelling Y-fronts trade weak puns and simulate sex with pasty-faced models dressed up as nurses and traffic wardens, but it will be worth it. As much as the films that emerged from Michael Balcon's Ealing, British sexploitation films – *Naked – as Nature Intended*; *The Yellow Teddybears* (1963); *Confessions of a Window Cleaner* (1974); *Emmanuelle in Soho* (1981) – were engaged in the business of projecting Britain, and the British character.

This book began with a search for the last survivors of silent film production in this country, a tiny band of nonagenarians and centenarians. Although the era of sexploitation is comparatively recent, many of its leading participants are already in their graves. Mary Millington – 'the Pamela Green of the Seventies', according to David McGillivray – swallowed a lethal dose of gin and paracetamol in 1979; five years later, one of her leading men, Alan Lake, put a gun to his head; George Harrison Marks's liver finally gave out in 1997; the director Robert Hartford-Davis died in an elevator in 1977. Heather Deeley, who shot five sexploitation features in 1975 alone, was last spotted in a Soho peepshow in the early 1980s. Minah Bird, the only significant black British sex star, suffered a fatal heart-attack in 1995: her body remained undiscovered for several weeks. Barry Evans, the leading man of *The Adventures of a Taxi Driver* (1976), had been reduced to pursuing the same career as his character when he was found dead on his living-room sofa in February 1993, an empty whisky bottle and a spilt container of aspirins – priced before decimalisation – by his side.[3]

David Hamilton Grant, a prolific producer of domestic skinflicks and the first man to give a directing job to Jonathan Demme, suffered the most mysterious fate. For years he kept himself in roulette chips by funding hard- and softcore titles such as *Sinderella* (1972) and *Snow White and the Seven Perverts* (1973). When the bottom fell out of the sexploitation market, however, he switched to video distribution and became the subject of official investigation when he issued Romano Scavolini's notorious slasher flick, *Nightmare in a Damaged Brain* (1981), on VHS and Betamax. A publicity stunt in which he invited punters to guess the weight of a real human brain – procured from who knows where – did not endear him to the tabloids or to the jury at his obscenity trail. He served eighteen months in jail, fled to Cyprus, opened a delicatessen called Mr Piggy, and was expelled from the island in 1988 after assaulting his girlfriend's husband with a spade. In the same year, he was identified by the *Sun* newspaper as a cocaine-dealer and child pornographer. Neither charge was substantiated, nor will they ever be. He is thought to have been the victim of a contract killing in 1991.[4]

It is fortunate, therefore, that Pamela Green, the first British sexploitation star, is still alive to tell her story. Since 1986, she has lived in a modest Victorian villa on the Isle of Wight, crammed with mementoes of her career in modelling, and of her long relationship with the late Douglas Webb, a movie stills photographer and veteran of the Dam Busters raids, who died after a heart attack in 1995. In the 1950s, however, Green rarely left the network of narrow streets on either side of Shaftesbury Avenue. As a student at St Martin's College of Art, she funded her course by removing her clothes in life classes. As a semi-nude showgirl in Norman Wisdom's comedy revue *Paris to Piccadilly*, she acquired a different repertoire of poses. As a dancer in *Latin Quarter* at the Prince Edward Theatre on Old Compton Street, she met her husband, a stage-hand named Guy Hillier, whose fondness for drink, drugs and post-pub assaults did nothing to prolong the marriage. ('Being thrown down the stairs', she says, ruefully, 'gives you the idea that you're not wanted.') As a nude model in dozens of photosets and 'glamour' shorts, she dressed and undressed in a variety of upper-room studios, under the gaze of a Bolex camera.

After Green's separation from Hillier, George Harrison Marks's studio in Gerrard Street offered her escape and employment. Marks, a photographer with a beatnik beard and a vivid imagination, liked to pretend that he was the last of a celebrated music-hall clan, and that he had received training in cinematic technique from Cecil Hepworth. (The publication of Hepworth's memoir *Came the Dawn* in 1951 may have inspired him to construct this fantasy.) He lived on the premises with a menagerie of cats and a mynah bird which had learned to mimic his smoker's cough. Green moved into his bed, became his principal cover girl, oversaw his financial affairs and changed her name by deed poll to match his.[5]

Here, in 1957, the pair launched *Kamera*, a discreet little journal of nude photography which sold out its first print run in a matter of days. Although Marks's name was on the cover, his former partner insists that she was the motivating force behind the publication. ('George was a liability, quite frankly,' she asserts.) She recruited the models, designed and built the sets, colour-checked the prints and retouched the pictures, using a scalpel to marshal the last suggestions of pubic hair from the pages. ('We always shaved,' she recalls, 'and fortunately I was neatly made.') For the sake of profitable variety, Green concocted a number of alternative identities – about whom she speaks in the third person, as if they actually existed in their own rights. Rita Landré was the scarlet-haired temptress who attracted the attention of Michael Powell; Princess Sonmar, despite sounding like a Grimsby herring-lugger, was an equatorial temptress conjured with the liberal application of Max Factor and baby oil. In 1958, with the success of *Kamera* confirmed, these three women, Pam, Rita and Sonmar, became 8mm movie stars. Marks operated the camera and called the shots; Green designed the backdrops, illustrated the title cards and gave the lead performances. Only her diligent preservation of these films has ensured that they have not been lost to history.

The earliest surviving British blue movie was shot by Esme Collings in his studio in Hove in 1896: a simple, casual, one-shot subject in which a woman removes her frock and hat and settles down with a book.[6] Watching Pamela Green's glamour reels from the 1950s is much like viewing early cinema. They share a common silence, a common cinematic grammar, a common disinclination to name their performers. Their textural similarities – caused by the blossom of decay in one case, and the modest width of the format in the other – give the illusion that they might have been made during the same period. *Xcitement* – its title adhering to the eye-catching convention of Val Guest's *The Quatermass Xperiment* (1955) – is a simple striptease reel, in which Green reclines on the attic set reproduced for her scenes in *Peeping Tom*. In *Gypsy Fire*, a Romany violinist scrapes away as Princess Sonmar descends the distinctly rickety steps from her caravan and whirls around the campfire until she has lost her skirts. In *Art for Art's Sake*, Green models for a smocked artist (Jean Spaul), who removes an item of clothing every time she splashes paint on herself. *Witches' Brew* is a more elaborate exercise, in which jump-cuts and pyrotechnics facilitate a wizened necromancer's transformation into Rita Landré. *The Window Dresser* is the *Citizen Kane* of 1950s 8mm pornography. Green takes the leading role as a modern-day highwaywoman in stripy shirt and Zorro mask who steals the wallet of a suited businessman, is pursued by a policeman – who, naturally, stops at every street corner and wipes his forehead with a crumpled hanky – and hides from her pursuers in the window of a boutique, in which she exchanges underwear with a mannequin.

Green and Marks conducted their operations in testing conditions. 'The police were always dropping by for a chat,' she remembers. 'They wouldn't ask for a bribe exactly, but they'd pick up some photographs or a new camera and say, "This is nice," and there was very little you could do to stop them taking it. It was a kind of tax. If you refused, you knew that you were in for trouble.' Sometimes, these gifts were insufficient: Green and Marks found themselves charged under the Post Office Act of 1953 for supplying mail-order copies of *The Window Dresser* – despite the broadcast of its nude scene as part of an ITV documentary. Organised crime also applied unfriendly pressure to their activities. The near-beer joint in their basement became the focus of a battle between two rival

Divorced from their context, these films read like essays in a specialist form of Utopianism: they offer a vision of the Home Counties transformed into a wholesome Polynesia in which clean-limbed young people gather marigolds and play net sports, unencumbered by the guilty association of nudity and sexual voyeurism. For their makers, however, the earnest tone was expedient. It was a way of swinging the censor; of selling pornography to the public in a pristine package. On the screen, there was health and exercise and sunshine. In the darkness of the auditorium, there were the real-life equivalents of Sid James and Bernard Bresslaw, grinding their teeth and staring with dilated pupils at the gentle undulation of the volleyball players. Nobody was fooled. 'While we know perfectly well that the people who make nudist films do so for commercial sex exploitation,' wrote John Trevelyan in 1964, 'we can keep this within reasonable bounds by making them put up the pretence of advocating naturism.'[7] The marketing strategies employed to publicise these pictures, however, tended to expose the pretence. For instance, *The Isle of Levant* was refused a certificate by the British Board of Film Classification, but was passed without comment by the London County Council. 'We had boards made,' recalls Tony Tenser, who managed the film's publicity campaign, 'which said: "The film that has been refused by the censor." They couldn't stop me doing it, because it was the truth.' When the same film was rejected by councillors in Birmingham, Tenser placed the film in a cinema regulated by the more liberal regime in nearby Walsall, and covered the buses travelling between the city and its satellite town with posters advertising its suppression. 'It ran for twelve weeks,' says Tenser, with satisfaction. 'It was a phenomenon.'

Other films posited upon the same hypocrisies soon tripped knicker-less into British cinemas. Anna Karen, a stripper from the Panama Club who would later star as the buck-toothed Olive in the sitcom *On the Buses*, bounced around the Spielplatz in Nat Miller's *Nudist Memories* (1961); Michael Winner made his contribution to the genre in *Some Like It Cool* (1961); Valerie Singleton, a future presenter of the long-running children's magazine programme *Blue Peter*, supplied the po-faced narration for *Nudes of the World* (1961), though it was left to the Hungarian starlet Jutka Gotz to sing the smutty songs around the campfire: 'Slide your trombone, play upon your fiddle, blow the clarinet, ooh la la!'

The disingenuous nature of these pictures was nicely exposed by the directions taken by the careers of their makers after the vogue for such productions had passed. Having spent several years urging their audiences to cast away their bourgeois inhibitions, the principal producers of the genre – Tony Tenser, Michael Klinger, Stanley Long – discovered that there was profit in the adoption of a more censorious, conservative position. The second wave of sexploitation pictures abandoned bracing outdoor pursuits to deliver sermons on social problems familiar from the Sunday newspapers: underage sex, wife-swapping, abortion, prostitution, pornography. Fortunately for their audiences, these films were just as dishonest as their predecessors.

We are used to reading the 1960s through iconoclastic, oppositional, freewheeling sources: films that were made by (or under the influence of) Lindsay Anderson, Tony Richardson, Karel Reisz and John Osborne. In Anderson's *If...* (1968), a gaggle of establishment caricatures are executed in a rain of hot bullets. In Richard Lester's *The Knack... and How to Get It* (1965), Michael Crawford navigates a London so self-consciously hip that you'd imagine he couldn't throw a copy of the *Marat/Sade* across Sloane Square without hitting a Redgrave sister in her white PVC go-go boots. Tony Richardson's *The Loneliness of the Long Distance Runner* (1962) pledges its commitments through Tom Courtenay's resolutely discontented Borstal boy: 'Do you know what I'd do if I had the whip hand?' he asks. 'I'd get all the coppers, governors, posh whores, army officers and Members of Parliament, and I'd stick 'em up against this wall and let them have it. Because that's what they'd like to do to blokes like us.' (Courtenay himself, however, had no sympathy with these sentiments.) Karel Reisz's *Morgan: a Suitable Case for Treatment* (1966), a more thoughtful work than any of the above, argues a sophisticated point: that the governors and posh whores – despite their enthusiastic adoption of kipper ties and mini-dresses and liberal attitude to divorce – had already suppressed the possibility of far-reaching social transformation. These films and their stablemates – *The Entertainer* (1960), *A Taste of Honey* (1961), *Tom Jones* (1963), *Kes* (1969), and the entire back catalogue of Osborne and Richardson's Woodfall Film Productions – are works of unassailable canonicity. They have shaped the way that we look back upon the period in which they were made, leaving us with an impression of a cinematic culture dominated by progressive and uncommercial projects. For that reason, I propose to ignore them here and concentrate instead upon films that will never be released on DVD by the British Film Institute, but which reveal just as much about the ideological texture of their times.

For entirely commercial reasons, the post-nudist sexploitation film argued against either sexual or social revolution. The parade of flesh in films such as *Naked – as Nature Intended* had been legitimised by an insistence upon the desexualised nature of such images. If movie producers, who had no track record of an interest in aesthetic integrity – or, for that matter, no studio backing and a university education – wanted to depict nudity in a sexual context, then their best hope of getting round Trevelyan was to convince him that their films would adopt a cautionary and clinical attitude to their subjects. Tony Tenser was quick to pursue this tactic. After reading in the *News of the World* about a sex scandal in a provincial school, he commissioned a script and rushed it into production at Shepperton.

The climax of Robert Hartford-Davis's *The Yellow Teddybears* (1961) takes place at a meeting of the board of governors in a provincial girls' school. A young teacher, Anne Mason, is being reprimanded for the way she has chosen to deal with the discovery that her sixth-form biology students have been badging their blouses with teddy bears to indicate the loss of their virginity. The film reveals as much evidence of their sexual activities as the certificate will allow: the heroine, Lynn (played by Anne Whitfield with the same spiky vulnerability that she brings to the title role in *Girl on Approval*) befriends a prostitute (Jill Adams), attends a drunken party at which the female guests dance in their flimsies, pays a visit to an illegal abortionist, and attempts to hitch a ride to London in the cab of a sleazy young lorry driver. Instead of condemning the erotic interests of her students, Miss Mason has admitted that she shares them. This does not mean, however, that she approves of their clubbable promiscuity. Treating a sexual relationship too lightly, she argues, is like 'taking a Picasso and using it as a fire-screen'. It is clear that her colleagues would have preferred her to assert the sanctity of sex within marriage, but Mason stands her ground, blaming the media for bombarding young people with sexual images and suggesting that the education system might do more to help them survive in this high-pressure environment. 'We can start by admitting that there's such a thing as sexual desire,' she argues. 'And by explaining the difference between that and love, we can clear up some of the confusion being heaped upon them by exploitative advertising.' Exploitative advertising, perhaps, like the material cooked up by Tenser for *The Yellow Teddybears* – a poster depicting a blindfolded Jill Adams being groped by a blond teenage boy; a newspaper announcement offering free admission to any schoolgirl over sixteen. The latter was denounced by an editorial in *Films and Filming* as 'one of the most cynical, vulgar publicity gimmicks I can remember for a long time'.[8] The film was so successful that its writers were immediately contracted to turn their attention to the social problems of venereal disease (*That Kind of Girl*, 1963) and priapic sailors on shore leave (*Saturday Night Out*, 1964).

These cautionary dramas were played out in featureless suburban lounges, grimy city streets and cheerless hotel rooms. They depicted a Britain of amazing crumminess: the same dowdy world inhabited by the characters of *10 Rillington Place* and *Leo the Last* (1970), in which every bulb was bare, every landlord a Rachman, and every newcomer to the city gulped down like an oyster. Their directors put anonymous actors under flat, unflattering light, emphasising lank hair and bad complexions. With no money to spend on sets, they filled their films with seedy details – sweat soaking the back of a boy's banana-yellow nylon shirt; a pair of hangers-on sharing a ciggie under an abrasive hotel blanket; a bunch of nicotine-stained fingers grasping at a pale breast; a young woman and her pimp drinking mugs of milky tea around a Formica-topped kitchen table.[9] Derek Ford's *Groupie Girl* (1970), for instance, follows a teenage runaway who escapes from a life of provincial boredom by attaching herself to a gang of hippie musicians. (When these boys tire of her, they literally hand her over to another band: 'Hey, wanna floozie?' their lead singer asks, as the screaming girl is hauled between two vans speeding down parallel motorway lanes.) Lindsay Shonteff's *Permissive* (1970) tracks the miseducation of a similar college-age heroine as she learns to be as chilly and self-interested as her rivals. Pete Walker's *Cool It Carol* (1970) sends a pair of rural naïfs (played by Robin Askwith and Janet Lynn) to London, where they are paid sixty quid to take the leading parts in a hardcore loop. ('Make it last, make it last,' urges the director. 'Raise the knee. That's a good girl, that's a good girl.') Walker's picture allows its protagonists to resume their country life, unaltered by their experiences. Ford and Shonteff are not so magnanimous. In the final scene of *Groupie Girl*, we are fooled into believing that the heroine's boyfriend is driving to her rescue. Instead of asking her to climb aboard his cute blue Mini Cooper, however, he simply winds down the window, mutters, 'Thought you might need some bread,' slips her a fiver and screeches off. In the final scene of *Permissive*, Shonteff demonstrates the extent of his heroine's emotional glaciation by depicting her walking calmly from the grubby hotel bathroom in which her former mentor, Coral, is lying in a tubful of blood.

The documentary equivalents of these films were more concerned with pathology than morality, and adapted early precedents. In his memoirs, Vivian Van Damm, the manager of the Windmill Theatre, recalled that when he was a cinema proprietor in the 1910s, a young film renter named Herbert Wilcox persuaded him to programme *The End of the Road* (1919), an educational documentary about venereal disease, made to warn American soldiers about the mortal dangers of sleeping with Frenchwomen. After securing the approval of Sir Kynaston Studd OBE, President of the London Polytechnic, Van Damm gave the picture a long and lucrative run. Fifty years later, a similar strategy was employed by David Grant and Tony Tenser, who persuaded Trevelyan to pass *Love Variations* (1968), a sober guide to sexual positions fronted by a white-coated Harley Street doctor. ('He allowed it with the proviso that they kept their underclothes on and only moved their chests,' Tenser recalls.) According to its makers, *The Wife Swappers* (1970) was similarly successful, though, watching it today, it is hard to imagine why. Derek Ford's film comprises case-history re-enactments of dubious veracity and interviews with members of the public and the Morlocks of the Soho sex industry, linked by the editorialising comments of a suited man behind a mahogany desk, who claims to be an 'eminent London psychiatrist'. The first segment focuses on Ellen (Valerie St John), a thirtysomething housewife with a penchant for Mary Quant flesh-coloured lipstick, who gains her first swinging experience in the arms of a hairy, gap-toothed, middle-aged man (played by Larry Taylor, who, as Captain Bird's Eye, would spend the following two decades doing advocacy work for fish fingers). After this initiation, Ellen is soon submitting to the demands of masked orgiasts in an Anaglypta-papered suburban bedroom. ('Woman's drive for so-called equality', choruses the eminent London psychiatrist, 'means that if a husband finds such activities tempting, she will want to find it equally so.') The audience was sent home with the story of Sheila (Bunty Garland), who, after performing a topless routine in front of her husband's friends, voices her misgivings about group sex. 'You've taken the act of love and dirtied it,' she insists. 'You've taken a private moment and made it a public spectacle.' It's a charge that the makers of *The Wife Swappers* would have found impossible to deny.

The reform of the certification system in 1970 raised the minimum age of admission to an X-rated film from sixteen to eighteen, allowing sexploitation films to mutate into less stentorian forms. It brought the modern sex comedy into being, a bizarre and implacably profitable cinematic genre which put a new and unglamorous generation of British film stars to work on top of a variety of ugly soft furnishings. Its principal actors were Robin Askwith, one of the schoolboys in *If . . .*, who transformed his career by baring his bottom and gurning his simian grin from under a shaggy mop of hair; Mary Millington, a butcher's wife from Dorking whose buoyant enthusiasm for performing in soft- and hardcore sex scenes offered producers some compensation for her inability to deliver a line convincingly; Alan Lake, the third Mr Diana Dors, whose eggs-on-a-plate eyes, flashing medallion and monstrous pubic fuzz contrasted with the pretentious delicacy of his acting style; and Barry Evans, a doe-eyed, boiler-suited slave to the much-mythologised sexual voracity of 1970s housewives, best known for taking the register in the cheerfully racist ITV sitcom, *Mind Your Language*.

Like the medical documentary redeployed to titillate rather than terrify, the sex comedy had its roots in the period before authorities had been formed to regulate the content of films; before managements had persuaded the affluent middle-class public that the picture house was not simply an environment in which amorous couples could secure their 'four penn'orth o' dark'. Percy Stow's *Love and the Varsity* (1913) serves as an example of the form. In this one-reeler, two students don wigs and

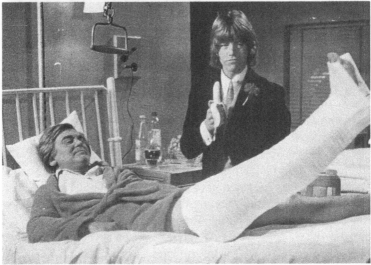

Two scenes from *Confessions of a Window Cleaner* (1974). Above, Robin Askwith shows his appreciation of Anita Graham's collection of oriental art; below, Askwith brings phallic fruit to the bedside of Tony Booth, destined to become the father-in-law of Prime Minister Tony Blair corsets in order to infiltrate the dormitory of a girls' school. The head-mistress, her suspicions aroused by the disinclination of these new students to undress in front of their classmates, peers through the keyhole of their private room and sees two men lounging on the bed in their stockings, smoking cigarettes. (In the final scene of the film, the impostors and their sweethearts abscond to the register office, where all four are married in their best frocks.)

The coming of sound allowed the music-hall tradition of verbal sexual innuendo to be imported to the cinema screen. George Formby smirked and winked as he documented the scopophilic pleasures of window-cleaning and drew attention to his little stick of Blackpool rock. When Albert Burdon gawked through the window at Renée Gadd in *Letting in the Sunshine*, British cinema offered another anticipation of the adventures that Robin Askwith would pursue with chamois and bucket. In *Sabotage* (1936), Alfred Hitchcock gave a founder member of the *Carry On* team his first taste of double entendre, allowing Charles Hawtrey to take his girlfriend to the aquarium at Regent's Park Zoo and lecture her on the sex life of the oyster: 'After laying a million eggs, the female changes sex,' he announces. 'I don't blame her,' she replies.

The *Carry On* films offered the most thorough and dedicated work in this field, and – just in case the gag went over someone's head – ensured that each innuendo was punctuated by a blow to the timpani or a yank on the swanee whistle. 'Fakir, off!' booms Bernard Bresslaw's Bungit Din in *Carry on Up the Khyber*, dismissing the Khasi of Khalibar's resident bed-of-nails man. 'I want you to take my knickers down!' demands Joan Hickson in *Carry on Girls* (1973), as her undergarments flutter on a flagpole in the seaside resort of Fircombe. 'Just a little prick!' twitters Kenneth Williams in *Carry on Screaming* (1966), as he sinks a needle into his Egyptian mummy, Rubbatiti. They saved their best pun until *Carry on Columbus* (1992), an otherwise moribund appendix to the series. Jack Douglas is a crusty old sea dog who warns a young passenger about the proximity of some man-eating sharks. 'Oh my goodness,' she exclaims. 'You don't think they'd eat me whole?' 'No,' counters Douglas, 'I'm told they spit that out.'

For some of their participants, these films were a source of disgust and disappointment: 'The scripts were schoolboy scatology,' concluded Kenneth Williams, 'the most depressing sort of would-be funny rubbish.'[1]For the rest of us, decades of continuous television screenings have made this long run of modest comedies one of our most reassuring national indulgences. Who hasn't spent a rainy Sunday afternoon admiring the mounted underpants of the Queen's Own Third Foot and Mouth, watching suspiciously Caucasian Bedouin salute the great prophet, Mustaphalik, or witnessing the cloacal drowning of Dan Dan the lavatory man? The *Carry On* films offer a comforting, half-recognised encounter with the tradition of working-class humour identified by George Orwell in the Donald McGill postcard, the Max Miller quip, the end-of-the-pier revue. These were cultural artefacts which, in Orwell's words,

stand for the worm's eye-view of life, for the music hall world where marriage is a dirty joke or a comic disaster, where the rent is always behind and the clothes are always up the spout, where the lawyer is always a crook and the Scotsman always a miser, where the newlyweds make fools of themselves on the hideous beds of seaside lodging houses, and the drunken, red-nosed husbands roll home at four in the morning to meet the linen-nightgowned wives who wait for them behind the front door, poker in hand.[11]

The 1970s sex comedies are closely related to the *Carry On* films. They share themes, images, fixations and even personnel. They confer italic status to the same lexicon of trigger-words: *balls, birds, bristols, dumplings, crumpet* and the ubiquitous *it*. The names on their dramatis personae have a common etymology: the *Carry Ons* are populated by W. C. Boggs, Dr Nookey, the Rumpo Kid and Private Jimmy Widdle; their successors by Miss Slenderparts, Mellons the gamekeeper, Peregrine Cockshute and Bob Scratchitt.[12] The archive offers reams of evidence of the cultural and economic importance of these films: photographs of the massive neon marquee for *Confessions of a Driving Instructor* (1976) looming over Piccadilly Circus; box-office figures proving that Robert De Niro in *Taxi Driver* (1975) was outgrossed by Barry Evans in *Adventures of a Taxi Driver* (also 1975); the full-page ad in *Screen International* congratulating Robin Askwith on being named as 'Most Promising Newcomer' in the *Evening News* British Film Awards; the *Guardian* report on the four-year occupation of the Classic Moulin Cinema by *Come Play with Me*, and the film's presence on 1,000 screens nationwide.[13]

They ought to seem familiar, and yet, sitting through a screening of *Adventures of a Plumber's Mate* (1978) or *Can You Keep It Up for a Week?*

(1974) is a baffling, alienating experience. They are neither funny nor sexy. It's hard to believe that they ever made anybody laugh; that the people who bought tickets for them through the 1970s watched in anything but glum resignation. It's harder to believe that they inspired a single lubricious moment. Were they a long series of blow-outs, advertised by posters which promised explicitness that they could not hope to deliver, by which customers consented to be cheated over and over again? Did their original audiences enjoy them? Or were they simply too depressed to walk out of the cinema?

Today, the most surprising characteristic of the post-*Carry On* sex comedy is the large number of cameo appearances by figures familiar from earlier periods of British film production: Diana Dors, a monstrous Zeppelin of blondeness, smoking at the breakfast table in *The Amorous Milkman* (1975), waiting for the title character to inundate her cornflakes; George Baker waving a vibrator in front of the sexology students of *Intimate Games* (1975), and inviting them to document the erotic fantasies of any 'visiting tradesmen' who might call upon them in the summer holidays; Irene Handl, idly improvising her lines as the proprietor of a country-house bordello in *Come Play with Me*; James Robertson Justice and Charles Hawtrey torturing a semi-naked victim in *Zeta One* (1969), as they attempt to force her to spill the secrets of the Angvians, a race of alien Amazons who are said, inexplicably, to live in 'a vast supernatural ant colony'.

What might explain the presence of these players in these films? In the 1970s, sex comedies accounted for the bulk of British production – if a film actor wanted to remain a film actor, then she or he was obliged to take a cheque from David Grant or Tony Tenser. Moreover, events in America briefly suggested that pornography was about to enter mainstream culture. If Sammy Davis Jr was parking his limousine outside New York theatres at which *Deep Throat* (1972) was playing, then Richard Wattis and Joanna Lumley need not feel too ashamed about losing their clothes in *Games that Lovers Play* (1970).

Participants in the terminal phase of British sexploitation – in which a company named Roldvale was the principal operator – can offer fewer pleas for clemency. Roldvale was described in 1989 as a 'dealer in bloodstock and promoter of films, magazines and associated products';[14] in one way or another, sperm was its business. At its head was David Sullivan, a baby-faced pornographer who had made his first million by refusing to overestimate public taste, and several more by refusing to let the truth undermine a smart marketing idea. Sullivan founded Roldvale's film production arm – which operated from offices above a porn cinema on Greek Street – to exploit the talents of Mary Maxted, the favourite centrefold model of his top-shelf titles, and his lover since 1975.

Maxted, a former veterinary nurse, had been a star of illegal 8mm shorts since 1973. (Her first, John Lindsay's *Miss Bohrloch*, had the distinction of winning the Golden Phallus at the Wet Dreams festival in Amsterdam.) Sullivan supplied her new name, Mary Millington – under which she appeared in his magazines and in small roles in a number of British sex comedies – and who decided, in mid-1976, that she deserved promotion from walk-on dolly bird to above-the-title film star.[15] With a satisfying historical symmetry, George Harrison Marks was the man whom he charged with the task.

In 1976, Marks was a jobbing photographer providing sets for Sullivan's *Playbirds* and *Park Lane* titles. Pamela Green had terminated her business relationship with him in 1965, and in the intervening years the photographer's recklessness and fondness for alcohol had lost him *Kamera*, his studio, his Rolls-Royce and an obscenity trial at the Old Bailey. Ignorant of this reversal of fortune, Sullivan offered to fund any film project that Marks might have up his sleeve – on condition that it contained a large amount of nudity and a role for Mary Millington. The result, *Come Play with Me*, was the subject of an extravagantly dishonest advertising campaign in the pages of Sullivan's magazines. Readers were promised footage of unsimulated copulation; the chance to clock 'ten girls being screwed by ten guys at the same time culminating in a group of Hell's Angels coming to an orgy party'.[16] What they got was a musical comedy of gobsmacking technical slackness in which the star attractions were Irene Handl, Alfie Bass and Marks himself, prancing about under a huge square wig suspiciously like the one he wore as a hunchback in *Witches' Brew*. (Millington's appearance is limited to a sauna scene, in which she squats on the back of a paunchy client and offers a hammy simulation of an indeterminate sex act.) Sullivan's ballyhoo, however, ensured that the film's takings were soon attaining levels of obscenity not evidenced by the picture itself.

Roldvale produced eight more features before home video made the 35mm sex film economically unviable – a story since made familiar by *Boogie Nights* (1997). The sleazy vulgarity of these films, the strong impression they give that everyone working on them knew that their audience was simply waiting in the dark for the next pair of floppy bosoms to be loosed from a nylon bra, helps to explain the romantic and conservative nature of many British films of the following decade, their emphasis upon starched wing-collars and tasteful homoerotica. The Roldvale films portray heterosexual desire in a variety of repulsive ways: Marks and Bass in *Come Play with Me*, their huge bellies rolling around in their long johns, going through the motions of a dance routine with a phalanx of bogus nurses; Alan Lake in *Confessions from the David Galaxy Affair* (1979), delivering lines such as 'I would spend the day in the members' enclosure, and the night enclosed in Susan's member,' as if they meant something; John East as a dribbling pornographer in *Emmanuelle in Soho*, his office decorated with a London *Evening Standard* billboard proclaiming, 'London Rape: Shock Figures' and an advertisement for a double-feature presentation of *Playbirds* (1978) and *Violation of the Bitch* (1977). After exposure to these images, who wouldn't want to watch Ian Charleson in a well-upholstered costume drama about athletics, or Rupert Everett sitting pretty in a provincial hotel, gazing across the spotless linen at some boy he fancies, but will never take to bed?

The life and career of John M. East provides a means of understanding this most autocannibalistic phase of film production in Britain. As we saw in Chapter One, East's family history linked him with the beginnings of the British film business. His own career in the late 1970s and early 1980s gave him a ringside seat for its near-annihilation. During the last eighteen months of his life, I spent many afternoons at his home in south London, discussing his researches into silent cinema, listening to his stories about the Edwardian practitioners he interviewed in the 1960s, and examining a tiny fraction of the unique documents in his immense, chaotic collection.

On my first visit, I arranged to take him out to lunch at a nearby pub and, knowing that his mobility had been limited by a stroke, collected him from his house in a taxi. He was waiting for me at the front gate: an emaciated figure, as pale and withered as something the protagonist of an

M. R. James short story might have glimpsed through a grimy fanlight. His physical frailty, however, did not restrain his unconventional taste in small talk. During the three-minute journey, he reminisced about his success promoting surgical penis enlargements. He spoke enthusiastically about the 'third-division model' he paid to attend to his physical needs. He boasted that his friendship with David Sullivan entitled him to receive discounts on the creams, pills and prosthetics stocked in the business-man's chain of sex shops, and asked whether I would like to have a browse in his local branch, where Mary Millington had once worked. The taxi driver, who seemed to be under the impression that John was my grand-father, stared silently ahead.

The venue for our first and only meal together was a shabby one: scuffed carpets, laminated tablecloths, photographic menus bearing the crusty residue of other people's lasagne. With great ceremony, John ordered steak, despite the weakness of his digestive system. Quite unself-consciously, he chewed each forkful of meat to extract its flavour, then used his fingers to scoop out the mulch from his mouth and deposit it on the side of his plate. For pudding, he ordered an enormous serving of vanilla ice-cream. As he worked his way to the bottom of the glass, he dis-cussed his memoirs, which were, he said, nearly finished, and in the hands of his publisher. To whet my appetite, he related a story about an old music-hall comic named Tommy Calden, who, in his last days, worked as a dresser for Spike Milligan. He described how Milligan ordered Calden to go to the café across the road, and bring back a steak and kidney pud-ding. 'When he came back with it,' John related, his voice rising in sudden anger, 'Spike Milligan picked it up and poured it all over his head.' John slammed down his ice-cream spoon and began to bang his fist on the table. 'All the gravy and peas!' he yelled, causing the other diners to stare in our direction. 'He fell down crying . . . that *bastard* . . . that *sadist!*'

David Sullivan was one of the few people about whom John East would hear no criticism. 'Don't write anything bad about him,' he urged me. 'I like him very much; not for his money, for himself. We had a lot of fun making a lot of terrible films together.' East's entry into film production was a consequence of a disagreement between Sullivan and George Har-rison Marks. After *Come Play with Me*, Marks proposed a collaboration on a sequel, *The Reluctant Pornographer*, but made the mistake of asking

Mary Millington bestrides a poster for a Roldvale double-bill, a typical
sexploitation blowout from John M. East and David Sullivan

for an increased budget. Sullivan promptly replaced him with the
improbably named Willy Roe, who wrote, produced and directed *The
Playbirds*, a whodunnit featuring Mary Millington as an undercover
police officer investigating the murders of glamour models from the
pages of Sullivan's own magazine. Millington, nervous about the number
of lines she would be required to deliver, asked Sullivan to hire a dialogue
coach. Sullivan remembered East, a BBC Radio producer who had interviewed him for a series on young British entrepreneurs, recalled that he
had some connection with Elstree Studios, and employed him to give elocution lessons to Millington. The results, as evidenced in *The Playbirds*,
are ludicrous: East has coached her to sound like Irene Handl on her best
behaviour.

John had a number of well-rehearsed anecdotes about Mary Millington, which he would recite on every occasion that we met. He described
the fun they had together working on a depressing striptease picture entitled *Queen of the Blues* (1979); he insisted that she believed in free speech

and the abolition of censorship; that she worked as a high-class prostitute and counted Harold Wilson and the Shah of Iran among her clients; that she was introduced to cocaine by a DJ on a London music station; that her last months were marked by an increase in her kleptomaniac tendencies, which included the theft of a fistful of BBC cutlery and a lamp from the window of Liberty's department store. His favourite and most practised story concerned their telephone conversation on the night that she committed suicide, which he would act out like an odd little play. Mary's voice would always be gruff and brusque: "'I've been arrested for shoplifting again, John. They put me in a cell and beat me. And the tax man is after me. I can't stand it any more.'" His own part, in contrast, was soft and reasonable, even if the words were not: "'Mary, you're ill. You need psychiatric treatment. You're mentally ill.'" After this remark, he said, Millington asked him to sing her favourite song to her. He sang it to me, briskly and without sentiment, impatient to hit his story's melodramatic pay-off line. 'Goodnight sweetheart, sleep will banish sorrow / Goodnight sweetheart, till we meet tomorrow.' Millington, he claimed, cut him short. "'There's going to be no tomorrow, John,'" she said, and slammed down the phone. I rang David Sullivan, but it was too late. She was already dead.' Dead, but not yet incapable of making money. 'I went round the next day,' East said, cheerfully, 'and I filmed the room in which she committed suicide.'

This was an odd boast: John did shoot some footage of the room, but weeks later, after having pitched the idea of a Millington tribute film to David Sullivan and negotiated a £1,000 payment to her widower, Robert Maxted, for permission to take shots in the house. East restaged the scene, disarranging the sheets, scattering them with pills, laying out one of Millington's negligées and her suicide note to David Sullivan, in which she blamed the police and the Inland Revenue for her misery. Perhaps he thought that I would find the idea of straight reportage less ghoulish than this act of theatrical recreation. However, the result of his labours, *Mary Millington's True Blue Confessions* (1980), contains many comparable lapses of taste. A troupe of topless models dances listlessly in the Maxteds' front room as John's voiceover describes Mary's enthusiasm for 'bisexual orgies'. A pair of Alsatians pant on the leather upholstery: 'Mary's dogs still pine for their mistress,' he coos, though Robert Maxted had already disposed of Tippi and Reject, and the animals in the film were borrowed from a friend of David Sullivan. Most dubiously, John hired a glamour model named Marie Harper to play Mary's coffined corpse in a scene shot in Palmer's Green Mortuary. 'What was Mary really like?' the voiceover asks. 'The truth is clouded in so many lies and innuendoes.' John appears at the end of the film, wearing a multicoloured suit bequeathed to him by his guardian, Max Miller, and introducing himself as Mary's last leading man and publicist. 'She always put a charge on this friendship,' he reports, talking sternly into the camera. 'But I can tell you for sure that she always gave value for money.'

After Millington's death, East and Sullivan began to search for a replacement. 'Then,' East recalled, with a hint of resentment, 'Julie Lee, this high-class whore who worked all the hotels on Park Lane, approached Sullivan and said that she'd do a film for him for nothing, on condition that she got the lead role. He agreed, so we were landed with this girl who couldn't act for toffee.' The story of John East, Julie Lee and *Emmanuelle in Soho* forms a bleak little coda to the story of British sex-ploitation. The film began life as a vehicle for Mary Millington entitled *Funeral in Soho*. Over the course of a weekend, East rewrote and retitled the script, assuming the pseudonym of Brian Daly, his grandfather's regular scenarist and greatest friend, dead since 1923. It was not Roldvale's last film. John East brought the sexploitation genre to a close with *Hell Cats – Mud Wrestling* (1983), a documentary in which a troupe of thick-armed American women beat up some ill-organised British opponents in a child's paddling pool filled with grey-green sludge. But *Emmanuelle in Soho* is the firm's last narrative comedy, and a useful navigation-point in the history of British cinema. After this, there was nowhere to go but upmarket.

My viewing of the film has left these pictures in my head: the livid bruise visible on the back of the starlet who half-heartedly simulates sex with Julie Lee; John, with slicked-back hair and teeth as yellow as a sewer rat, licking the nipples of an unfortunate model and gabbling meaning-less smut into the telephone ('I wouldn't handle his prick, never mind his business'); a lifeless dance routine performed by a bunch of third-rate hoofers in transparent PVC raincoats. It is a kind of endgame for British cinema.

As filming progressed, Julie Lee's broad Sheffield accent began to grate on East. He persuaded her to exchange roles with the second female lead, a marginally better actress named Angie Quick. (East renamed her Mandy Miller in the hope that cinemagoers would assume that she was the little deaf girl from the Ealing film, all grown up.) However, once the production had wrapped, the relationship between Lee and East continued on a strange path. John's account of their joint activities was always vague and incoherent, probably in order to disguise the extent of his own culpability. In 1982, he claimed, he was asked to broker a marriage contract between the actress and a wealthy American businessman named Greg. A bizarre photocall took place in the Concordia Restaurant in Bayswater, in which Lee posed with the million pounds she had accepted from her husband-to-be and boasted about the Mercedes that also formed part of their arrangement. Several months later, East asserted, Lee called upon his services again. The fall guy in this scam was an Egyptian millionaire who, unaware of Lee's prior engagement, had agreed to set her

Bill Anderson (John M. East) interviews Paul Benson (Kevin Fraser),
a newcomer to the porn business, in *Emmanuelle in Soho* (1981). Note the
posters on the wall for other Roldvale productions (the polite word for
this is intertextuality)

up in a £400,000 house in Virginia Water – a gated community which Bryan Forbes, Bruce Forsyth and General Augusto Pinochet have, at various points over the years, all called home. 'In the bedroom was a bed on rails,' enthused East. 'And this bed had a motor. And you could drive the bed out on to the balcony and drive it back. Amazing! Never seen anything like it in my life!' The agreement between Lee and her new fiancé was concluded on this bed, but she did not live long enough to enjoy the fruits of her deception. On 4 May 1983, she accompanied East to a beauty contest at Skindles Hotel in Maidenhead, where Ernest Dudley had once monitored the progress of well-to-do adulterers. To her fury, she was placed second. She climbed into her Mercedes and drove back to London. At the junction of the M4 near Datchett, her car careered from the road, smashed into a lamp-post, ploughed through fifty yards of fencing and burst into flames. She died in Wrexham Park Hospital four days later. 'It was a contract killing,' claimed John East. 'One of the men she married put a contract out on her.'

John's own death was clearly not far away, and it was death that we talked about during those afternoons in Norbury. The subject was inescapable. The deaths of Millington and Lee, two women he exploited with professional zeal. The deaths of his heroes, Brian Daly and John Marlborough East. The deaths of the forgotten pioneers whom he sought out when the critical reputation of British silent cinema was at its lowest ebb: Percy Nash, a director whom John discovered in a one-room flat in Brighton, blinded by years of exposure to the glare of the Klieg lamps; Douglas Payne, the silent star who, John insisted, lost his virginity to Oscar Wilde; George Dewhurst, one of Cecil Hepworth's leading men, a talent who diversified into direction and screenwriting, went bankrupt in 1932, and was found by his friends in the 1950s, sleeping rough on Clapham Common. A lost generation whose experiences can never be recovered.

John M. East was a difficult man to like. He was venal, grasping, self-deceiving, temperamental. ('I've led a good life, haven't I?' he would ask me. 'I've never done anyone any harm.') But I admired him for his commitment to the unremembered dead. Now, when I play back my recordings of our conversations, I am struck by the strangulated urgency of his voice as he attempts to pass on every last scrap of information that he thinks I will find useful. Listening to the disc, I can hear him directing me around his study, instructing me to sift through piles of papers for documents and photographs that he wants to show me. He's asking me to find the script of *Shoot to Kill* (1961), a B-picture in which Michael Winner cast him as a Russian spy. (The film is missing from the archive; he performs the lines for me, as if this will conjure it back into existence.) He's indicating the scrapbooks of Hugh Croise, a director at Stoll's Cricklewood Studios in the 1920s, none of whose work survives. He's opening a cardboard box filled with the personal effects of Alf Collins, whose involvement with the British film business began in 1896: here is Collins's visiting card from 1902, upon which he announces himself as 'Producer of Cinematograph Pictures, late of Gaumont'; here is a begging letter from an actor named Benson North, reminding Collins of their work together on a long-lost title. Now John is handing me an autograph book compiled by his aunt, Lottie East, and telling me everything he can recall about the forgotten stars who jotted little messages on its foxed pages: Ambrose Manning, who played opposite Betty Balfour in the *Squibs* films; Dorothy Green, who acted in *The Informer* with Lya de Putti; Matheson Lang, with whom Meggie Albanesi became infatuated on the set of *Mr Wu*. He mourns the loss of this generation, the incineration of their films, the darkening of their stars. And yet he recognises that this loss is a source of melancholy pleasure. He is in love with a world of ghosts. And, as I listen to these conversations, I hear my own thoughts echoed in his voice.

This Is Where You Came In

Lime Grove studios, demolished in 1993

Death has cast a shadow over this book and provided much of its substance: the deaths of reputations, the deaths of careers, the deaths of men and women who put their lives on the screen. Film promises immortality, but for as long as it remains a physical, chemical medium, nature will struggle to reclaim its borrowed elements – camphor, silver, alcohol, sulphur – and return them to their original states. Many of the interviewees who contributed to this book – Patricia Roc, Peter Ustinov, Phyllis Calvert, Anthony Havelock-Allan, Renée Gadd, Joan Morgan, Judy Campbell – have already gone the way of all celluloid. And with the death of John M. East – actor, fantasist, film-maker, pornographer, pimp and cultural historian – its story loops back round to its beginning.

Seventy-nine years previously, his grandfather and namesake – the founder of the first film studios to be built at Elstree – loosed his hold on life in much more difficult circumstances. Forgotten by a cinemagoing public which had once voted him among the greatest of his profession, he was reduced to lumbering around Margate in the bulky costume of Uncle Oojah, the cartoon elephant from the funny pages of the *Daily Sketch*. East was offered the work three days after puncturing his big toe on a rusty nail, but, reasoning that his need for cash was more pressing than treatment for an increasingly septic wound, he signed on the dotted line, climbed into the animal suit and bore the discomfort. In the company of a fellow actor got up as Oojah's sidekick, Snooker the Cat, he spent a day performing a number of slapstick routines on the pier, along the promenade, and between film screenings at the town's cinemas. At the end of the afternoon, septicaemia began to tighten its grip upon him, and children scattered as Uncle Oojah crashed to the pavement in agony. With the aid of a bystander, Snooker the Cat carried his companion to the railway station and made him comfortable in the luggage car of the next train back to Victoria.

Back home at number 14 Iffley Road, Hammersmith, in the tiny top-floor room he shared with his daughter, John M. East watched his leg grow gangrenous, consoled himself by downing an entire barrel of cider and began a brisk slide towards death. His last hours, as narrated by the actor's grandson, were like some black comic sketch from the silent cinema. As John Marlborough East was a sturdy six foot three, the doctor and the caretaker of the lodging-house were obliged to strap him to a kitchen chair and manhandle him down, stair by stair, from the attic room to the ambulance waiting in the street outside. Delirious with pain, he was carted off to Exmoor Street Hospital, where an emergency amputation was performed. We should fade out there, before the ether, before the hacksaw, before the coma's descent: the final frame of another brilliant career in the movies.

Few of East's film performances have made it to the twenty-first century. He appears as the father of H. G. Wells's protagonist in *Kipps* (1921), his face a crumpled mask of disappointment and anxiety. In *The Bargain*, he is an outback lout at the centre of a bar-room brawl. In *Owd Bob* – his last appearance on screen – he is a monstrously bewhiskered shepherd who does little to keep the peace in a less exotic hostelry. The only remaining print of the picture has suffered some serious damage to its last few hundred feet. In the final scene, as he celebrates the hero's victory in a sheepdog trial, John Marlborough East vanishes in a broiling mass of emulsion.

His grandson – whose less distinguished film career has largely escaped the effects of fire and mildew – was fiercely proud of his grandfather's involvement in the foundation of the British studio system. On most of my visits, he would play me a VHS recording of a pub scene from *Owd Bob*, the image fuzzy and striated from having run through the machine so many times. After we'd watched the tape, he would switch off the television and declare that once he had recovered sufficiently, he would take me on a visit to Elstree and point out the last surviving fragment of the old Neptune facilities – the wall of John M. East's office, behind which the scenarios of dozens of three-reel dramas and comedies were crafted by East and his collaborator Brian Daly. We never made the trip, of course – and when I went there by myself I was unable to locate a single brick of it.

Most of the studios in which the stories related in this book were played out have been demolished or depleted by developers and asset-strippers. Only Pinewood remains completely intact. The bulldozers obliterated Denham in the late 1970s. Two housing estates absorbed swaths of Shepperton's backlot in the 1980s. Shepherd's Bush felt the impact of the wrecking ball in 1993. In the same year, half of the Elstree site was sold off to Tesco, and the largest outdoor water-tank in Europe disappeared under the footprint of an enormous supermarket. (A whale-themed mural forms the supermarket's testimony to Gregory Peck's pursuit of Moby Dick through an ocean that flowed over the space across which customers now trundle their trolleys.) The Gainsborough Studios at Islington remained intact until 2002, when they were levelled to accommodate a squadron of apartment blocks.

Don't mourn them. The story of the British film studio system is not legible in its architectural remains. Despite the rich nostalgic power that attends the names of these buildings, walking around the sites that remain is not significantly more evocative than touring a shabby biscuit factory on an idle Sunday. I have walked around Shepperton and seen nothing but a cluster of anonymous hangars. I have stood on the same Ealing sound stage that Basil Dean transformed into a Tyrolean mountainside with thousands of paper crocuses, and seen only girders and corrugated iron. I have peered into the water-tank at Pinewood – in which Roy Ward Baker sank the *Titanic* and John Mills floated in a sea of oil and debris – and seen only whitewashed concrete and rainwater.

In the summer of 1999, I attended a party in the carcass of Gainsborough Studios, thrown to celebrate Alfred Hitchcock's centenary. The rambling complex, used for many years as a carpet warehouse, was loud with the sounds of clinking glasses. Hundreds of guests were heating the large, cool space of the sound stage where once Meggie Albanesi had shimmied around with a yapping lapdog under her arm; where Ivor Novello had used his flick-knife to slit the pencil skirt of Julie Suedo, the better to allow her legs to wrap around his waist; where Stewart Granger had thrown the right hook which sent James Mason sprawling to the floor.

Nobody objected – or noticed, perhaps – when two other guests and I wandered beyond the space marked out for the party and into the unlit area beyond. We passed the monolithic bank of machinery which had once regulated the electricity supply to the studio stage: I ran a finger over chunky translucent switches which would once have illuminated at a flick; tapped at the monstrous dials in black rubber hoods, their needles dead at the zero mark. We walked gingerly down a featureless corridor and through a pair of creaky doors, emerging at the bottom of a stairwell. By now, the noise of the party was far behind us. A cracked sign pointed the way up towards the dressing rooms. What could we do but follow it? Up we went – to a level of the building that no one seemed to have entered for decades. Light poured in through holes in the ceiling. Broken glass snarled under our feet. The tiled floor was obscured by a thick grey stratum of pigeon guano, in which the skeletons of birds lay half-submerged. A dying specimen, one wing snapped, moved in incapable circles. The building told no tales. There was nothing of Novello here.

The real guardians of British studio history were down in the sun-baked courtyard. Shielding his eyes from the light, the veteran cinematographer Bryan Langley perched on a bentwood chair and cast his mind back to the day in 1931 when he arrived for work at Gainsborough as a camera assistant. He recalled seeing Michael Balcon and his brother Shan deep in conversation on Sound Stage 2. He remembered that during the summer, the canal running by the building became clogged with the bodies of dead cats – and that the management refused to ameliorate the smell by paying someone to fish them out. He recalled the moment when a pair of colleagues directed his gaze up into the gloom of the goods-lift shaft and pointed to a tiny pale object protruding from the trellis gate: this, they insisted, was a relic of one Saturday afternoon the previous winter, when fire broke out in the sound recording room on the upper level, and the chief electrician, George Gunn, leapt down the shaft to save his life, leaving a finger behind him. Others, noted Langley, were not so lucky. A young studio assistant, William Shand, was killed in the blaze. He had been performing a task of baffling archaism – using an electric double-boiler to impregnate some wire recording coils with paraffin wax – and had disappeared to lunch without switching off the current. The water boiled away and the paraffin reached its flashpoint. Shand, Gunn and a third volunteer belted from the canteen and returned to the top floor with fire-fighting equipment. When a huge explosion ripped open the doors of the recording room, Shand was nearest to the blast. Though he made his escape down the lift shaft in fewer pieces than Gunn, he did not survive the journey to the studio floor. Michael Balcon's autobiography offers a painful little coda to the story. 'When some members of the studio staff reached us,' he wrote, 'the first words I thought I heard were "Shan is dead." I immediately thought of my brother.'[1] It's only too easy to image Balcon's swift progress from horror to relief to guilt, and how he might have attempted to conceal his thoughts from the employees crowding around him.

This book has followed the lives of British film personnel from the beginnings of the twentieth century, through the growth and dissolution of the studio system and into the tough, cold world of independent exploitation cinema. The beginning of the 1980s seems the logical moment at which to bring its story to a close. By this time, the public appetite for sex and horror had been sated, the old companies had withdrawn from production and the pioneers who founded the industry seven decades previously were deep in their graves. A new form of studio system, in which companies operated without the liabilities of backlots and brick hangars, was about to emerge. Under their auspices, British cinema would spend a decade torn between the arthouse and the country house, before initiating an intense affair with junkies, gangsters and la-di-da Londoners. Danny Boyle, Guy Ritchie, Peter Greenaway, *Four Weddings and a Funeral* (1994), *Absolute Beginners* (1986), the National Lottery and a gang of stripping steelworkers would be identified as the saviours (or murderers) of British film. Three decades of death and resurrection, art and populism – best encapsulated, perhaps, by the moment when John Maybury, writer–director of *Love Is the Devil* (1999), encountered Richard Curtis, writer–director of *Love, Actually* (2003) backstage at the Albert Hall, after a black-tie Robbie Williams concert. 'It's people like you', growled Maybury, grabbing Curtis by the lapels of his dinner jacket, 'who've ruined British cinema for people like me.'

Such stories are beyond the scope of this book. It has dealt with the unknown, the forgotten, the unrecorded – and it would be hard to argue that British cinema since 1980 has remained undocumented, or its participants ignored by researchers. More has been written about the last twenty years of native production than the previous seven decades put together. The expansion of newspaper and magazine coverage has made British film more debated than at any point in its history. Video, DVD, digital television channels and the Internet have ensured that even the most ordinary new releases are granted long, leisurely shelf lives. A sizeable minority of scholars no longer consider contemporary British cinema to be beneath their notice: few would bat an eyelid at being offered a seminar paper on the subject of *The Full Monty* (1997) or *Lock, Stock and Two Smoking Barrels* (1998).

So, fifty years hence, will a sequel to *Shepperton Babylon* be necessary? Is it possible that my mid-century equivalent will one day nibble nursing-home biscuits with Hugh Grant, as he describes how a chance encounter on Sunset Boulevard gave his career an unexpected fillip? Will the nonagenarian Guy Ritchie, forgotten for half a century, share a pot of tea with that same researcher, and tell the story – as if it were news – of how he got a generation of middle-class schoolboys drunk on cockney gangster slang and married the most famous woman in the world? Will Catherine Zeta Jones reveal how she did it? Will Kenneth Branagh reveal where and when it all went wrong? Or will these figures have already told their stories a thousand times in magazine and chat-show interviews, autobiographies and DVD extra features, as well as on the pages of their personal websites? Will the increasingly expansive and archival nature of popular culture ensure that however unfashionable a film-maker or actor becomes, there will always be a small corner of cyberspace where their fame still shines brightly, or a trestle table at a memorabilia fair at which they can charge a small fee for an autographed photo of themselves looking young and clean and optimistic?

Perhaps it is now impossible to be as comprehensively forgotten as a silent-screen star whose career was undone by the talkies. In a culture in which everything is archived and little is truly neglected, the past may never seem as distant as Joan Morgan's memories of galloping across an empty South Africa or playing roulette on the beach at Shoreham. No films may ever be as tantalisingly inaccessible as the missing reels described in the journals of Henry Edwards. No pleasure garden may ever seem as burnished as Ernest Dudley's vision of the movie stars and boxers and cokeheads who rattled the glass tiles of Jack May's illuminated dance floor.

Flesh is not as durable as celluloid, but paper, given the right conditions, can outlive both. Let this book carry these memories a little further into the future, until it, like the figures and films it commemorates, is only so much dust and rumour.

Select Filmography

The listing for each film includes title, date, director, production company and distribution company (where that differs from the production company). Slashes indicate shared credits. For the dating of British films, I have followed Denis Gifford's *British Film Catalogue*, 3rd edition (London: Fitzroy Dearborn, 2000).

10 Rillington Place (1970), Richard Fleischer, Genesis/Filmways/Columbia (Columbia)
The 39 Steps (1935), Alfred Hitchcock, Gaumont
The 39 Steps (1959), Ralph Thomas, Rank (RFD)
Above Us the Waves (1955), Ralph Thomas, London Independent (GFD)
Accident (1967), Joseph Losey, Royal Avenue Chelsea (LIP)
The Admirable Crichton (1957), Lewis Gilbert, Modern Screenplays
Adventures of a Plumber's Mate (1978), Stanley Long, Salon (Alpha)
Adventures of a Taxi Driver (1976), Stanley Long, Salon (Alpha)
Alice in Wonderland (1903), Cecil Hepworth/Percy Stow, Hepworth
Almost a Honeymoon (1930), Monty Banks, BIP (Wardour)
The Amazing Quest of Mr Ernest Bliss (1920), Henry Edwards, Hepworth (Imperial)
The Amorous Milkman (1975), Derren Nesbitt, Lactifer/Lanka (Variety)
Appointment in London (1953), Philip Leacock, Mayflower (British Lion)
Asylum (1972), Roy Ward Baker, Amicus/Harbor (Paramount)
Autobiography of a Princess (1975), James Ivory, Merchant Ivory (Contemporary)
Autumn Crocus (1934), Basil Dean, Associated Talking Pictures (ABFD)
Baby's Playmate (1908), Lewin Fitzhamon, Hepworth
The Bad Lord Byron (1949), David MacDonald, Triton (GFD)
Banana Ridge (1941), Walter Mycroft, ABPC (Pathé)
The Bargain (1921), Henry Edwards, Hepworth
Barnacle Bill (1957), Charles Frend, Ealing (MGM)
The Battles of Coronel and Falkland Islands (1927), Walter Summers, BIF/British Projects (W&F)

Bedrock (1930), Carlyle Blackwell, Piccadilly (Paramount)

Bell-Bottom George (1944), Marcel Varnel, Columbia British

The Belle of Bettwys-Y-Coed (1912), Sidney Northcote B&C (MP)

The Belles of St Clements (1936), Ivar Campbell, B&D/Paramount British

The Bells Go Down (1943), Basil Dearden, Ealing (United Artists)

The Better 'Ole; Or, The Romance of Old Bill (1918), George Pearson, Welsh-
    Pearson (Jury)

The Big Blockade (1942), Charles Frend, Ealing (United Artists)

Big Fella (1937), James Elder Wills, Fortune Films (British Lion)

The Birth of a Flower (1911), Percy Smith, Kineto

Black Beauty (1906), Lewin Fitzhamon, Hepworth

Blackmail (1929), Alfred Hitchcock, BIP (Wardour)

Black Narcissus (1947), Michael Powell/Emeric Pressburger, IP/The Archers (GFD)

Blighty (1927), Adrian Brunel, Gainsborough/Piccadilly (W&F)

Blondes for Danger (1938), Herbert Wilcox, Herbert Wilcox (British Lion)

The Blood Beast Terror (1968), Vernon Sewell, Tigon

Blood on Satan's Claw (1970), Piers Haggard, Tigon/Chilton (Tigon)

Bluebeard's Ten Honeymoons (1960), W Lee Wilder, Anglo-Allied (WPD)

The Blue Lamp (1950), Basil Dearden, Ealing (GFD)

Bonnie Mary (1918), A V Bramble, Master (International Exclusives)

Bonnie Prince Charlie (1923), Charles Calvert, G-B Screencraft

Bonnie Prince Charlie (1948), Anthony Kimmins, London/BLPA (British Lion)

Boots! Boots! (1934), Bert Tracey, Blakely (Butcher)

The Boys in Brown (1949), Montgomery Tully, Gainsborough (GFD)

A Bridge Too Far (1977), Richard Attenborough/Sidney Hayers, Joseph E Levine
    (United Artists)

Brief Encounter (1945), David Lean, IP/Cineguild (GFD)

Brighton Rock (1947), John Boulting, ABPC (Pathé)

Briton vs. Boer (1900), Arthur Cooper, Northern Photographic Works

Broken Blossoms (1936), Hans Brahm, Twickenham (TFD)

Broken in the Wars (1919), Cecil Hepworth, Hepworth

The Brothers (1947), David MacDonald, Triton (GFD)

The Bulldog Breed (1960), Robert Asher, Rank (RFD)

By the Shortest of Heads (1915), Bert Haldane, Barker (LIFT)

Cage of Gold (1950), Basil Dearden, Ealing (GFD)

The Call of the Sea (1930), Leslie Hiscott, Twickenham (Warner)

Can You Keep It Up For A Week? (1974), Jim Atkinson, Pyramid (Target)

The Card (1952), Ronald Neame, BFM (GFD)

Carry on Camping (1969), Gerald Thomas, Adder (RFD)

Carry on Columbus (1992), Gerald Thomas, Island World/Comedy House/Peter
    Rogers Productions (UIP)

Carry on Girls (1973), Gerald Thomas, Peter Rogers Productions (Fox-Rank)

Carry on up the Khyber (1968), Gerald Thomas, Adder (RFD)

Carry on Screaming (1966), Gerald Thomas, Ethiro/Anglo-Amalgamated

The Cause of All the Trouble (1923), Edward D Roberts, Albanian (Globe)

The City of Beautiful Nonsense (1919), Henry Edwards, Hepworth (Butcher)

A Clockwork Orange (1972), Stanley Kubrick, Polaris/Hawk/Warner (Columbia-Warner)

Cocaine (1922), Graham Cutts, Master (Astra)

The Colditz Story (1955), Guy Hamilton, Ivan Foxwell (British Lion)

The Comedians (1967), MGM/Maximillan/Trianon (MGM)

Come On, George (1939), Anthony Kimmins, ATP (ABFD)

Come Play with Me (1977), George Harrison Marks, Roldvale (Tigon)

Comin' Thro' The Rye (1923), Cecil Hepworth, Hepworth

Concerning Mr Martin (1937), Roy Kellino, Fox British

Confessions from the David Galaxy Affair (1979), Willy Roe, Roldvale (Tigon)

Confessions of a Driving Instructor (1976), Norman Cohen, Swiftdown (Columbia)

The Constant Nymph (1928), Adrian Brunel, Gainsborough (W&F)

The Constant Nymph (1933), Basil Dean, Gaumont

Convoy (1940), Pen Tennyson, Ealing (ABFD)

Cool it Carol (1970), Pete Walker, Pete Walker (Miracle)

A Cornish Romance (1912), Sidney Northcote, B&C (Moving Pictures Sales Agency)

The Corpse (1970), Viktors Ritelis, London Cannon/Abacus (Grand National)

Count Dracula (1970), Jess (Jesus) Franco, Hemdale/Fénix/Corona/Filmar/Towers of London

The Crimes of Stephen Hawke (1936), George King, George King (MGM)

The Cruel Sea (1953), Charles Frend, Ealing (GFD)

Cry Freedom (1987), Richard Attenborough, Marble Arch (UIP)

Cry of the Banshee (1970), Gordon Hessler, AIP (MGM-EMI)

Cul-de-Sac (1966), Roman Polanski, Compton-Tekli (Compton)

The Cup Final Mystery (1914), Maurice Elvey, Motograph

The Cut-Ups (1967), Antony Balch, Balch

The Dam Busters (1954), Michael Anderson, ABPC

The Damned (1962), Joseph Losey, Hammer/Swallow (Columbia)

The Dark Eyes of London (1939), Walter Summers, Argyle Productions (Pathe)

David Copperfield (1913), Thomas Bentley, Hepworth (Walturdaw)

Daybreak (1946), Compton Bennett, Triton (GFD)

The Day Will Dawn (1942), Harold French, Niksos (GFD)

Dead of Night (1945), Basil Dearden/Alberto Cavalcanti/Robert Hamer/Charles Crichton, Ealing (Eagle-Lion)

Dear Murderer (1947), Arthur Crabtree, Gainsborough (GFD)

Death in Venice (1971), Luchino Visconti, Alfa (Warner)

Death Line (1972), Gary Sherman, KI Productions (RFD)

The Death of Nelson (1905), Lewin Fitzhamon, Hepworth

The Detective in Peril (1910), Lewin Fitzhamon, Hepworth

Dial 999 (1938), Lawrence Huntington, Fox British

Dick Turpin's Ride to York (1906), Lewin Fitzhamon, Hepworth

Doctor at Large (1957), Ralph Thomas, Rank (RFD)

Doctor in the House (1954), Ralph Thomas, Group (GFD)

The Dog Outwits the Kidnapper (1908), Lewin Fitzhamon, Hepworth

The Dog's Devotion (1911), Lewin Fitzhamon, Hepworth

The Dog Thief (1908), Lewin Fitzhamon, Hepworth

Downhill (1927), Alfred Hitchcock, Gainsborough (W&F)

Down Under Donovan (1922), Harry Lambert, Stoll

Dracula (1958), Terence Fisher, Hammer/Cadogan (Universal-International)

Dumb Sagacity (1907), Lewin Fitzhamon, Hepworth

East is East (1916), Henry Edwards, Turner (Butcher)

Edward II (1991), Derek Jarman, Edward II/Working Title/British Screen/
   BBC (Palace)

Emerald of the East (1929), Jean de Kuharski, British-Pacific/BIP (Wardour)

Emmanuelle (1974), Just Jaeckin, Trinacra/Orphée (Columbia)

Emmanuelle in Soho (1981), David Hughes, Roldvale (Tigon)

Escape (1930), Basil Dean, Associated Talking Pictures (RKO)

Eskimo Nell (1975), Martin Campbell, Salon (Eagle)

Eugenie ... The Story of her Journey into Perversion (1969), Jess (Jesus) Franco,
   Hape Film/Towers of London (Columbia)

The Explosion of a Motor Car (1900), Cecil Hepworth, Hepworth

The Family Way (1966), Roy Boulting, Janbox (British Lion)

Fanny by Gaslight (1944), Anthony Asquith, Gainsborough (GFD)

The Farmer's Wife (1928), Alfred Hitchcock, BIP (Wardour)

The Farmer's Wife (1941), Norman Lee/Leslie Arliss, ABPC (Pathe)

That Fatal Sneeze (1907), Lewin Fitzhamon, Hepworth

Feather Your Nest (1937), William Beaudine, ATP (ABFD)

Fire Over England (1937), William K Howard, London Films/Pendennis (United
   Artists)

The First Mrs Fraser (1932), Sinclair Hill, Sterling

The Fisher Girl of Cornwall (1912), Sidney Northcote B&C (Moving Pictures Sales
   Agency)

The Fixer (1968), John Frankenheimer, Lewis/Frankenheimer (MGM)

The Flag Lieutenant (1926), Maurice Elvey, Astra-National

The Flesh and Blood Show (1972), Pete Walker, Peter Walker/Heritage (Tigon)

Follow a Star (1959), Robert Asher, Rank (RFD)

The Foreman Went to France (1942), Charles Frend, Ealing (United Artists)

For Those in Peril (1944), Charles Crichton, Ealing

Four Dark Hours (1937), William Cameron Menzies, New World (Twentieth Century Fox)

Four Dimensions of Greta (1972), Pete Walker, Peter Walker/Heritage (Hemdale)

A Friend in Need (1909), Lewin Fitzhamon, Hepworth

Frightmare (1975), Pete Walker, Pete Walker/Heritage (Miracle)

The Full Monty (1997), Peter Cattaneo, Channel Four/Redwave (Fox Film Corporation)

Further Adventures of the Flag Lieutenant (1927), W P Kellino, Neo-Art (W&P)

The Galloping Major (1951), Henry Cornelius, Sirius/Romulus (IFD)

Games That Lovers Play (1970), Malcolm Leigh, Border

Gandhi (1982), Richard Attenborough, Indo-British Films/Goldcrest International (Col-EMI-Warner)

Genevieve (1953), Henry Cornelius, Sirius (GFD)

The Ghost's Holiday (1907), Lewin Fitzhamon, Hepworth

Girl on Approval (1962), Charles Frend, Eyeline (Bryanston)

The Girl on the Boat (1962), Henry Kaplan, Knightsbridge (RFD)

The Glorious Adventure (1922), J. Stuart Blackton, J. Stuart Blackton (Stoll)

Goldfinger (1964), Guy Hamilton, Eon/Danjaq (United Artists)

Good-Time Girl (1948), David MacDonald, Triton (GFD)

The Goose Steps Out (1942), Will Hay/Basil Dearden, Ealing (United Artists)

The Great Day (1920), Hugh Ford, Famous Players-Lasky (Paramount)

The Great Rock 'n' Roll Swindle (1980), Julien Temple, Boyd's Co/Matrixbest/Virgin (Virgin)

Green for Danger (1946), Sidney Gilliat, IP/Individual (GFD)

Groupie Girl (1970), Derek Ford, Salon (Eagle)

A Gypsy Cavalier (1922), J Stuart Blackton, International Artists (Gaumont)

The Halfway House (1944), Basil Dearden, Ealing

Hamlet (1913), Charles Raymond, Barker

The Happiest Days of Your Life (1950), Frank Launder, BLPA/Individual (British Lion)

The Hasty Heart (1949), ABPC (Associated British-Pathé)

The Haunted House of Horror (1969), Michael Armstrong, Tigon/AIP (Tigon)

Hell Cats - Mud Wrestling (1983), John M. East, Roldvale (ITC)

Henry VIII (1911), Louis N. Parker, Barker (Globe)

Her Reputation (1931), Sidney Morgan, London Screenplays (Paramount)

Her Son (1920), Walter West, Broadwest (Walturdaw)

Highly Dangerous (1951), Roy Baker, Two Cities (GFD)

High Treason (1928), Maurice Elvey, Gaumont

His House in Order (1928), Randle Ayrton, QTS (Ideal)

Hobson's Choice (1954), David Lean, London/BLPA (British Lion)

Home before Midnight (1979), Pete Walker, Pete Walker/Heritage (Columbia-EMI-Warner)

Horror Hospital (1973), Antony Balch, Noteworthy (Iver)

Hot Enough for June (1963), Ralph Thomas, Rank (RFD)

House of the Long Shadows (1983), Pete Walker, London Cannon (Cannon)

House of Mortal Sin (1976), Pete Walker, Pete Walker/Heritage (Columbia-Warner)

The House of Whipcord (1974), Pete Walker, Pete Walker/Heritage (Miracle)

Hue and Cry (1947), Alberto Cavalcanti, Ealing (GFD)

Hunted (1952), Charles Crichton, BFM/Independent Artists (GFD)

Ice Cold in Alex (1958), J Lee Thompson, ABPC

If . . . (1968), Lindsay Anderson, Memorial Enterprises (Paramount)

I Like Birds (1967), Pete Walker, Pete Walker (Border)

I Met a Murderer (1938), Roy Kellino, Gamma (Grand National Pictures)

In Another Girl's Shoes (1917), G B Samuelson/Alexander Butler, Samuelson

The Informer (1929), Arthur Robison, BIP (Wardour)

Intimate Games (1975), Tudor Gates, Podenhale (Tigon)

In Which We Serve (1942), Noel Coward/David Lean, Two Cities (British Lion)

The Iron Duke (1935), Victor Saville, Gaumont

I See Ice! (1938), Anthony Kimmins, ATP (ABFD)

It Always Rains on Sunday (1947), Robert Hamer, Ealing (GFD)

It's Great to be Young (1956), Cyril Frankel, Marble Arch (Associated British-Pathe)

It's Never Too Late to Mend (1937), David MacDonald, George King (MGM)

Jack Spratt's Parrot as the Artful Dodger (1916), attrib. Toby Cooper, Clarendon

Jack Spratt's Parrot Gets His Own Back (1916), attrib. Toby Cooper, Clarendon

Jane Shore (1915), Bert Haldane/F. Martin Thornton, Barker (Walturdaw)

Jassy (1947), Bernard Knowles, Gainsborough (GFD)

Jericho (1937), Thornton Freeland, Buckingham (GFD)

Jew Suss (1934), Lothar Mendes, Gaumont

Johnny Frenchman (1945), Charles Frend, Ealing (Eagle-Lion)

Josser in the Army (1932), Norman Lee, BIP (Wardour)

Josser Joins the Navy (1932), Norman Lee, BIP (Wardour)

Jubilee (1977), Derek Jarman, Whaley-Malin/Megalovision (Cinegate)

Juno and the Paycock (1929), Alfred Hitchcock, (BIP) (Wardour)

Keep Fit (1937), Anthony Kimmins, ATP (ABFD)

Keep it up Downstairs, (1976) Robert Young, Pyramid (EMI)

Keep Your Seats, Please! (1936), Monty Banks, ATP (ABFD)

Killer's Moon (1978), Alan Birkinshaw, Rothernorth

Kind Hearts and Coronets (1949), Robert Hamer, Ealing (GFD)

Kipps (1921), Harold Shaw, Stoll

Kipps (1941), Carol Reed, Twentieth Century Productions

Kitty (1929), Victor Saville, BIP/Burlington (Wardour)

The Knack .. and How to Get It (1965), Richard Lester, Woodfall (United Artists)

The Ladykillers (1955), Alexander Mackendrick, Ealing (RFD)

The Lady Vanishes (1938), Alfred Hitchcock, Gainsborough (MGM)

The Last Journey (1935), Bernard Vorhaus, Twickenham (TFD)

The Lavender Hill Mob (1951), Charles Crichton, Ealing (GFD)

Lawrence of Arabia (1962), David Lean, Horizon (Columbia)

Leo the Last (1970), John Boorman, Char-Wink-Boor/Calisbury (United Artists)

Letting in the Sunshine (1933), Lupino Lane, BIP (Wardour)

Libel (1959), Anthony Asquith, Anatole de Grunwald/MGM British

Lily of the Alley (1923), Henry Edwards, Hepworth

A Little Bit of Fluff (1928), Jess Robbins/Wheeler Dryden, BIP

Little Dorrit (1920), Sidney Morgan, Progress (Butcher)

The Lodger: A Story of the London Fog (1926), Alfred Hitchcock, Gainsborough (W&F)

London Belongs to Me (1948), Sidney Gilliat, IP/Individual (GFD)

The Loneliness of the Long Distance Runner (1962), Tony Richardson, Woodfall (Bryanston)

The Long and the Short and the Tall (1961), Leslie Norman, Michael Balcon (WPD)

The Long Memory (1953), Robert Hamer, Europa (GFD)

Looking on the Bright Side (1932), Basil Dean, ATP (RKO)

Look Up and Laugh (1935), Basil Dean, ATP (ABFD)

Lorna Doone (1935), Basil Dean, Associated Talking Pictures (ABFD)

The Loss of the Birkenhead (1914), Maurice Elvey, B&C (Ruffell's)

Lost in the Woods (1912), Frank Wilson, Hepworth

Lost People (1949), Bernard Knowles/Muriel Box, Gainsborough (GFD)

Love and the Varsity (1913), Percy Stow, Clarendon

The Love-Ins (1967), Arthur Dreifuss, Four-Leaf Productions (Columbia)

Love on the Spot (1932), Graham Cutts, ATP (RKO)

The Loves of Joanna Godden (1947), Charles Frend, Ealing (GFD)

Love's Old Sweet Song (1917), F Martin Thornton, Clarendon (New Bioscope)

Love Story (1944), Leslie Arliss, Gainsborough (Eagle-Lion)

Love Variations (1968), Terry Gould, Oppidan (Tigon)

A Lowland Cinderella (1921), Sidney Morgan, Progress (Butcher)

The Lure of Crooning Water (1920), Arthur Rooke, George Clark (Stoll)

Madonna of the Seven Moons (1944), Arthur Crabtree, Gainsborough (Eagle-Lion)

The Magic Bow (1946), Bernard Knowles, Gainsborough (GFD)
The Magnet (1950), Charles Frend, Ealing (GFD)
Maisie's Marriage (1923), Alexander Butler, Napoleon
Major Barbara (1941), Gabriel Pascal/Harold French/David Lean, Pascal (GFD)
Malta Story (1953), Brian Desmond Hurst, BFM/Theta (GFD)
Mandy (1952), Alexander Mackendrick, Ealing (GFD)
The Man in Grey (1943), Leslie Arliss, Gainsborough (GFD)
The Man in the White Suit (1951), Alexander Mackendrick, Ealing (GFD)
The Man of the Moment (1955), John Paddy Carstairs, Group (RFD)
The Man Who Knew Too Much (1934), Alfred Hitchcock, Gaumont
The Man Without Desire (1923), Adrian Brunel, Atlas-Biocraft (Novello-Atlas)
The Manxman (1929), Alfred Hitchcock, BIP (Wardour)
Maria Marten; or, Murder in the Red Barn (1935), George King, George King
    (MGM)
Mark of the Devil (1970), Michael Armstrong, Atlas/Hi-Fi Stereo 70
Mary Millington's True Blue Confessions (1980), Nick Galtress, Roldvale (Jay Jay)
Masks and Faces (1917), Fred Paul, Ideal
The Mayor of Casterbridge (1921), Sidney Morgan, Progress (Butcher)
Millions Like Us (1943), Frank Launder/Sidney Gilliat, Gainsborough (GFD)
Miranda (1948), Ken Annakin, Gainsborough (GFD)
Money for Nothing (1932), Monty Banks, BIP (Pathé)
Monique (1970), John Bown, Tigon
Mons (1926), Walter Summers, BIF (New Era)
Morgan: A Suitable Case for Treatment (1966), Karel Reisz, Quintra (British Lion)
Morning Departure (1950), Roy Baker, Jay Lewis (GFD)
Mother Riley Meets the Vampire (1952), John Gilling, Fernwood (Renown)
Mr Drake's Duck (1951), Val Guest, Angel (Eros)
Mr Wu (1919), Maurice Elvey, Stoll
Murder! (1930), Alfred Hitchcock, BIP (Wardour)
Murder by Death (1976), Robert Moore, Columbia/Rastar (Columbia)
My Brother's Keeper (1948), Alfred Roome, Gainsborough (GFD)
Naked – as Nature Intended (1961), George Harrison Marks, Markten/Compton
    (Compton)
Nelson (1918), Maurice Elvey, Master/International Exclusives (Apex)
Next of Kin (1942), Thorold Dickinson, Ealing (United Artists)
Nicholas Nickleby (1947), Alberto Cavalcanti, Ealing (GFD)
Night of the Blood Monster (1970), Jess (Jesus) Franco,
    Fénix/Prodimex/Terra/Towers of London
Night Journey (1938), Oswald Mitchell, British National/Butcher (Butcher)
Nightmare in a Damaged Brain (1981), Romano Scavolini, Goldmine (Screen
    Entertaiment)

The Night Porter (1974), Liliana Cavani, Lotar Films

A Night to Remember (1958), Roy Baker, Rank (RFD)

No Limit (1936), Monty Banks, ATP (ABFD)

Nothing Else Matters (1920), George Pearson, Welsh-Pearson (Jury)

Not Quite a Lady (1928), Thomas Behtley, BIP (Wardour)

Nudes of the World (1961), Arnold Louis Miller, Miracle/Searchlight (Miracle)

Nudist Memories (1961), Arnold Louis Miller/Stanley Long, Searchlight (New Realm)

Number Seventeen (1932), Alfred Hitchcock, BIP (Wardour)

The October Man (1947), Roy Baker, Two Cities (GFD)

Off the Dole (1935), Arthur Mertz, Mancunian

Oh! What a Lovely War (1969), Richard Attenborough, Accord (Paramount)

The Old Curiosity Shop (1921), Thomas Bentley, Welsh-Pearson (Jury)

One of Our Aircraft is Missing (1942), Michael Powell/Emeric Pressburger, British National/The Archers (Anglo)

The One That Got Away (1957), Roy Baker, Rank (RFD)

On the Beat (1962), Robert Asher, Rank (RFD)

Ourselves Alone (1936), Walter Summers/Brian Desmond Hurst, BIP (Wardour)

The Overlanders (1946), Harry Watt, Ealing (Eagle-Lion)

Owd Bob (1924), Henry Edwards, Atlantic Union (Novello-Atlas)

Paper Orchid (1949), Roy Baker, Ganesh (Columbia)

A Passage to India (1985), David Lean, GW Films/HBO (Col-EMI-Warner)

Passage Home (1955), Roy Baker, Group (GFD)

The Passionate Adventure (1924), Graham Cutts, Gainsborough (Gaumont)

Passport to Pimlico (1949), Henry Cornelius, Ealing (GFD)

The Pedlar of Penmaenmawr (1912), Sidney Northcote B&C (Moving Picture Sales Agency)

Peeping Tom (1960), Michael Powell, Michael Powell Theatre (Anglo-Amalgamated)

Penny Paradise (1938), Carol Reed, ATP (ABFD)

Perfect Understanding (1932), Cyril Gardner, Gloria Swanson British (United Artists)

Permissive (1970), Lindsay Shonteff, Shonteff (Tigon)

Piccadilly (1929), E.A. Dupont, BIP (Wardour)

Pipes of Pan (1923), Cecil Hepworth, Hepworth

Playbirds (1978), Willy Roe, Roldvale (Tigon)

A Plucky Little Girl (1909), Lewin Fitzhamon, Hepworth

The Pool of London (1951), Basil Dearden, Ealing (GFD)

Pretty Polly (1967), Guy Green, George-Granat/Universal (RFD)

The Private Life of Don Juan (1934), Alexander Korda, London Films (United Artists)

The Proud Valley (1940), Pen Tennyson, Ealing/CAFAD (ABFD)

The Prude's Fall (1924), Graham Cutts, Gainsborough (W&F)

Psychomania (1973), Don Sharp, Benmar (Scotia-Barber)

Queen of Hearts (1936), Monty Banks, ATP (ABFD)

Queen of the Blues (1979), Willy Roe, Roldvale (Tigon)

Raising a Riot (1955), Wendy Toye, London/Wessex (British Lion)

The Rat (1925), Graham Cutts, Gainsborough (W&F)

Reach for the Sky (1956), Lewis Gilbert/James Hill, Pinnacle (RFD)

The Red Shoes (1948), Michael Powell/Emeric Pressburger, IP/The Archers (GFD)

Repulsion (1965), Roman Polanski, Tekli (Compton)

Rescued By Rover (1905), Lewin Fitzhamon, Hepworth

The Ring (1927), Alfred Hitchcock, BIP (Wardour)

The Road to London (1921) Eugene Mullen, Screen Plays (Phillips)

The Rocks of Valpré (1935), Henry Edwards, Real Art (RKO)

Rome Express (1932), Walter Forde, Gaumont

Room at the Top (1959), Jack Clayton, Remus (IFD)

Roses of Picardy (1927), Maurice Elvey, Gaumont

Rosie Dixon Night Nurse (1978), Justin Cartwright, Multiscope (Columbia)

Rover Takes a Call (1905), Lewin Fitzhamon, Hepworth

Ryan's Daughter (1970), David Lean, Glarus/Faraway (MGM-EMI)

Sabotage (1936), Alfred Hitchcock, Gaumont

Sally in our Alley (1931), Maurice Elvey, Associated Talking Pictures (RKO)

Saloon Bar (1940), Walter Forde, Ealing (ABFD)

Sammy Going South (1963), MBP/Greatshows (Bryanston/Seven Arts)

Sanders of the River (1935), Zoltan Korda, London Films (United Artists)

Saraband for Dead Lovers (1948), Michael Relph/Basil Dearden, Ealing (GFD)

Saturday Night and Sunday Morning (1960), Karel Reisz, Woodfall (Bryanston)

Saturday Night Out (1964), Robert Hartford-Davis, Compton/Tekli (Compton)

The Scapegoat (1959), Robert Hamer, Du Maurier-Guinness (MGM)

School for Secrets (1946), Peter Ustinov, Two Cities (GFD)

School for Sex (1969), Pete Walker, Pete Walker (Miracle)

Scott of the Antarctic (1948), Charles Frend, Ealing (GFD)

Scrooge (1935), Henry Edwards, Twickenham (TFD)

Séance on a Wet Afternoon (1964), Bryan Forbes, AFM/Beaver (RFD)

The Sea Urchin (1926), Graham Cutts, Gainsborough (W&F)

The Servant (1963), Joseph Losey, Springbok (Elstree)

Seven Days to Noon (1950), Roy Boulting, London/BLPA (British Lion)

The Seventh Veil (1945), Compton Bennett, Theatrecraft/Ortus (GFD)

The Sheriff of Fractured Jaw (1958), Raoul Walsh, Apollo (Twentieth Century Fox)
Ships With Wings (1941), Sergei Nolbandov, Ealing (United Artists)
Shooting Stars (1928), A V Bramble/Anthony Asquith, BIF (New Era)
Shoot to Kill (1961), Michael Winner, Border (New Realm)
The Show Goes On (1937), Basil Dean, ATP (ABFD)
Simba (1955), Brian Desmond Hurst, Group (GFD)
Sinderella (1972), Oppidan Films (Border)
Sing As We Go (1934), Basil Dean/Ronald Brown, ATP (ABFD)
The Singer not the Song (1961), Roy Ward Baker, Rank
The Shadow of Egypt (1924), Sidney Morgan, Astra-National
Sixty Years a Queen (1913), Bert Haldane, Barker (Royal)
The Skin Game (1920), B.E. Doxatt-Pratt, Grainger-Binger
The Smuggler's Daughter of Anglesey (1912), Sidney Northcote, B&C (MP)
Snow White and the Seven Perverts (1973), Oppidan Films
The Solitary Cyclist (1921), Maurice Elvey, Stoll
So Long at the Fair (1950), Terence Fisher, Gainsborough (GFD)
Some Like it Cool (1961), Michael Winner, SF Films
Song of Freedom (1936), J Elder Wills, Hammer (British Lion)
The Sorcerers (1967), Michael Reeves, Global/Tigon/Curtwell (Tigon)
Sorrell and Son (1933), Jack Raymond, British and Dominions (United Artists)
Spanish Eyes (1930), G B Samuelson, Julian Wylie-Ulargui (MGM)
The Spanish Gardener (1956), Philip Leacock, Rank (RFD)
Splinters in the Navy (1931), Walter Forde, Twickenham (W&F)
A Stitch in Time (1963), Robert Asher, Rank (RFD)
The Strength and Agility of Insects (1911), Percy Smith, Kineto
Sweeney Todd, the Demon Barber of Fleet Street (1936), George King,
George King (MGM)
Sword of Honour (1939), Maurice Elvey, Butcher
Take off Your Clothes and Live (1963), Miracle/Searchlight (Miracle)
That Kind of Girl (1963), Robert Hartford-Davis, Tekli (Compton)
There Ain't No Justice (1939), Pen Tennyson, Ealing/CAPAD (ABFD)
There was a Crooked Man (1960), Stuart Burge, Knightsbridge (RFD)
They Came to a City (1944), Basil Dearden, Ealing
They Were Sisters (1945), Arthur Crabtree, Gainsborough (GFD)
Things to Come (1936), William Cameron Menzies, London Films (United
Artists)
This Man is News (1938), David Macdonald, Pinebrook (Paramount)
This Sporting Life (1963), Lindsay Anderson, Independent Artists (RFD)
Tilly and the Fire Engines (1911), Lewin Fitzhamon, Hepworth
Tilly's Party (1911), Lewin Fitzhamon, Hepworth
Tilly the Tomboy Visits the Poor (1910), Lewin Fitzhamon, Hepworth

The Titfield Thunderbolt (1953), Charles Crichton/Terry Bishop, Ealing (GFD)

Tower of Evil (1972), Jim O'Connolly, Grenadier/Fanfare/Anglo-EMI (MGM-EMI)

Towers Open Fire (1963), Antony Balch, Balch (Connoisseur)

Town on Trial (1957), John Guillermin, Marskman (Columbia)

A Tragedy of the Cornish Coast (1912), Sidney Northcote B&C (Moving Picture Sales Agency)

The Triumph of the Rat (1926), Graham Cutts, Gainsborough/Piccadilly (W&F)

Trouble Brewing (1939), Anthony Kimmins, ATP (ABFD)

Troubled Waters (1936), Albert Parker, Fox British

Trouble in Store (1953), John Paddy Carstairs, Two Cities (GFD)

Turned Out Nice Again (1941), Marcel Varnel, ATP (United Artists)

Twenty-One Days (1937), Basil Dean, London/Denham (Columbia)

Twisted Nerve (1968), Roy Boulting, Charter (British Lion)

Two Thousand Women (1944), Frank Launder/Sidney Gilliat, Gainsborough (GFD)

Two Worlds (1930), E A Dupont, BIP (Wardour)

Ultus, The Man From the Dead (1916), George Pearson, Gaumont/Victory

Underground (1928), Anthony Asquith, BIF (Pro Patria)

Under the Greenwood Tree (1929), Harry Lachman, BIP (Wardour)

Vagabond Queen (1929), Geza von Bolvary, BIP (Wardour)

The Very Edge (1963), Raymond Stross (Garrick/British Lion)

Victim (1961), Basil Dearden, Parkway (RFD)

The Village Squire (1935), Reginald Denham, B&D/Paramount British

The Vortex (1927), Adrian Brunel, Gainsborough (W&F)

Went the Day Well? (1942), Alberto Cavalcanti, Ealing (United Artists)

What's Good for the Goose (1969), Menahem Golan, Tigon

When the Bough Breaks (1947), Lawrence Huntington, Gainsborough (GFD)

When Tilly's Uncle Flirted (1911), Lewin Fitzhamon, Hepworth

Whisky Galore (1949), Alexander Mackendrick, Ealing (GFD)

White Face (1932), T. Hayes Hunter, Gainsborough/British Lion (W&F)

The White Rose (1923), D.W. Griffith, D.W. Griffith Productions (United Artists)

The White Sheik (1928), Harley Knoles, BIP (Wardour)

Whom the Gods Love (1936), Basil Dean, ATP (ABFD)

The Wicked Lady (1945), Leslie Arliss, Gainsborough (Eagle-Lion)

The Wicker Man (1974), Robin Hardy, British Lion

The Wife Swappers (1970), Derek Ford, Salon (Eagle)

Witchfinder General (1968), Michael Reeves, AIP/Tigon (Tigon)

Wittgenstein (1993), Derek Jarman/Ken Butler, Uplink/Bandung/BFI/Channel 4 (BFI)

The Woman from China (1930), Edward Dryhurst, Edward G. Whiting (JMG)

The World of Wonderful Reality (1924), Henry Edwards, Hepworth
The Years Between (1946), Compton Bennett, Sydney Box (GFD)
The Yellow Teddy Bears (1963), Robert Hartford-Davis, Tekli (Compton)
The Young Mr Pitt (1942), Carol Reed, Twentieth Century Productions
The Yoke (1915), James Warry Vickers, International Cine Corp
Ypres (1925), Walter Summers, BIF (New Era)
Zeta One (1969), Michael Cort, Tigon

Select Bibliography

NEWSPAPERS AND PERIODICALS

Daily Mail; Daily Express; Daily Graphic; Daily Sketch; Daily Telegraph; Hull Daily Mail; Guardian; Independent; London Evening News; London Evening Standard; Listener; News of the World; New Statesman; Observer; South Glamorgan Evening Express; Sun; Sunday Pictorial; Sunday Express; Sunday Times; Time and Tide; The Times

FILM JOURNALS AND TRADE PAPERS

Bioscope; Close-Up; Film Weekly; Films and Filming; Journal of Popular British Cinema; Kinematograph Weekly; Motion Picture Studio; Picturegoer; Picture Show; Sight and Sound; To-Day's Cinema; Variety

UNPUBLISHED AND ARCHIVAL SOURCES

Private papers of Roy Ward Baker, Michael Balcon, Phyllis Calvert, Winton Dean, Ernest Dudley, John M. East, Henry Edwards, Renée Gadd; Michael and Aileen Balcon Collection, Denis Gifford Collection, Ivor Montagu Collection, Mabel Poulton Collection, British Film Institute; Basil Dean Collection, John Rylands Library, University of Manchester

BOOKS AND MONOGRAPHS

Ackland, Rodney, and Elspeth Grant, *The Celluloid Mistress* (London: Allan Wingate, 1954)
Aherne, Brian, *A Proper Job* (Boston: Houghton Mifflin, 1969)
Albanesi, E. Maria, *Meggie Albanesi, by her Mother* (London: Hodder and Stoughton, 1928)
Anger, Kenneth, *Hollywood Babylon* (New York: Dell Publishing, 1975)
Armes, Roy, *A Critical History of British Cinema* (London: Secker and Warburg, 1978)

Ashby, Justine and Andrew Higson, eds., *British Cinema Past and Present* (London: Routledge, 2000)

Askwith, Robin, *The Confessions of Robin Askwith* (London: Ebury Press, 1999)

Attenborough, Richard, *In Search of Gandhi* (London: Bodley Head, 1982),

Babington, Bruce, *British Stars and Stardom from Alma Taylor to Sean Connery* (Manchester: Manchester University Press, 2001)

Baker, Roy Ward, *The Director's Cut* (London: Reynolds and Hearn, 2000)

Balcon, Michael and Ernest Lindgren, Forsyth Hardy, Roger Manvell, *Twenty Years of British Film* (London: Falcon Press Ltd., 1947)

– *Michael Balcon Presents . . . A Lifetime in Films* (London: Hutchinson, 1969)

– *Tinsel or Realism* (London: Workers Film Association, 1943)

Bamford, Kenton, *Distorted Images: British National Identity and Film in the 1920s* (London: I. B. Tauris, 1999)

Bankhead, Tallulah, *Tallulah: My Autobiography* (London: Victor Gollancz, 1952)

Barfe, Louis, *Where Have all the Good Times Gone?: The Rise and Fall of the Record Industry* (London: Atlantic Books, 2004)

Barr, Charles, *Ealing Studios* (London: Studio Vista, 1993)

– English Hitchcock (Moffat, Dumfriesshire: Cameron and Hollis, 1999)

– ed., *All Our Yesterdays* (London: BFI, 1986)

Betts, Ernest, *The Film Business: A History of the British Cinema 1896–1972* (London: George Allen and Unwin Ltd, 1973)

– *Inside Pictures* (London: Cresset, 1960)

Bogarde, Dirk, *A Short Walk from Harrods* (London: Viking, 1993)

– *Backcloth* (London: Viking, 1986)

– *Great Meadow* (London: Viking, 1992)

– *An Orderly Man* (London: Chatto and Windus, 1983)

– *A Postillion Struck by Lightning* (London: Chatto and Windus, 1977)

– *Snakes and Ladders* (London: Chatto and Windus, 1978)

Bret, David, *George Formby: A Troubled Genius* (London: Robson, 1999),

Brown, Geoff, *Launder and Gilliat* (London: BFI, 1977)

Brownlow, Kevin, *The Parade's Gone By* (London: Secker and Warburg, 1968)

Brunel, Adrian, *Nice Work* (London: Forbes Robertson, 1949)

Burnett, R. G. and E. D. Martell, *The Devil's Camera: Menace of a Film-Ridden World* (London: Empworth, 1932)

Burton, Alan and Laraine Porter, eds., *Crossing the Pond: Anglo-American Film Relations before 1930* (Trowbridge: Flicks Books, 2002)

– eds., *Pimple, Pranks and Pratfalls: British Film Comedy before 1930* (Trowbridge: Flicks Books, 2000)

– eds., *Scene-Stealing: Sources for British Cinema before 1930* (Trowbridge: Flicks Books, 2003)

– eds., *The Showman, the Spectacle and the Two-Minute Silence: Performing*

British Cinema before 1930 (Trowbridge: Flicks Books, 2001)

Cardiff, Jack, *Magic Hour* (London: Faber and Faber, 1996)

Caute, David, *Joseph Losey: A Revenge on Life* (London: Faber and Faber, 1994)

Chibnall, Steve, *Making Mischief: The Cult Films of Pete Walker* (Guildford: FAB Press, 1998)

Chapman, James, *The British at War: Cinema, State and Propaganda, 1939–1945* (London: I. B. Tauris, 1998)

Clarke, T. E. B., *This is Where I Came In* (London: Michael Joseph, 1974)

Coldstream, John, *Dirk Bogarde: The Authorised Biography* (London: Weidenfeld and Nicolson, 2004)

Conrich, Ian, 'Traditions of the British Horror Film' in *The British Cinema Book*, 2nd edition (London: BFI, 2001)

Cook, David A., *A History of Narrative Film* (New York: Norton, 1990)

Cook, Pam, ed., *Gainsborough Pictures* (London: Cassell, 1997)

Cowie, Peter, 'The Amoral Ones', *Films and Filming* (December 1962), p. 69

Curtis, James, *James Whale: A New World of Gods and Monsters* (London: Faber and Faber, 1998)

Dacre, Richard, *Trouble in Store: Norman Wisdom – A Career in Comedy* (Dumfries: T. C. Farries, 1991)

Danischewsky, Monja, *White Russian – Red Face* (London: Victor Gollancz, 1966)

Day-Lewis, Sean, *C. Day-Lewis: An English Literary Life* (London: Unwin, 1980)

Dean, Basil, *Mind's Eye: An Autobiography 1927–1972* (London: Hutchinson, 1973)

– *Seven Ages: An Autobiography 1888–1927* (London: Hutchinson, 1970)

Dell, Jeffrey, *Nobody Ordered Wolves* (London: William Heinemann, 1939)

Davies, Russell, ed., *The Kenneth Williams Diaries* (London: Harper Collins, 1994)

Dickinson, Margaret and Sarah Street, *Cinema and State: The Film Industry and the Government 1927-84* (London: BFI, 1985)

Drazin, Charles, *Korda: Britain's Only Movie Mogul* (London: Sidgwick and Jackson, 2002)

Driver, Betty, *Betty: The Autobiography* (London: Granada Media, 2000)

Dryhurst, Edward, *Gilt off the Gingerbread* (London: Bachman and Turner, 1987)

Duberman, Martin, *Paul Robeson* (London: Bodley Head, 1989)

Durgnat, Raymond, *A Mirror for England: British Movies from Austerity to Affluence* (London: Faber and Faber, 1970)

East, John M., *Max Miller: The Cheeky Chappie* (London: W. H. Allen and Co., 1977)

– *'Neath the Mask: The Story of the East Family* (London: George Allen and Unwin, 1967)

Fenton, Harvey and David Flint, *Ten Years of Terror: British Horror Films of the 1970s* (Guildford: FAB Press, 2001)

Fields, Gracie, *Sing as we Go* (London: Frederick Muller, 1960)

Gardiner, Jill, *From the Closet to the Screen: Women at the Gateways Club, 1945–85* (London: Pandora, 2003)

Gledhill, Christine, *Reframing British Cinema 1918–1928: Between Restraint and Passion* (London: BFI, 2004)

Gifford, Denis, The British Film Catalogue, 3rd edition (London: Fitzroy Dearborn, 2000)

Gottlieb, Sidney, *Hitchcock on Hitchcock* (London: Faber and Faber, 1995)

Gray, Dulcie, *Looking Forward, Looking Back* (London: Hodder and Stoughton, 1991)

– *Overture and Beginners* (London: Victor Gollancz, 1973)

Harding, James, *Ivor Novello: A Biography* (Cardiff: Welsh Academic Press, 1997)

Harper, Sue, *Picturing the Past: The Rise and Fall of the British Costume Film* (London: BFI, 1994)

Hennessey, Peter, *The Secret State* (London: Penguin, 2003)

Hepworth, Cecil, *Came the Dawn* (London: Phoenix House, 1951)

Herbert, Stephen and Luke McKernan, *Who's Who of Victorian Cinema* (London: BFI, 1996)

Herzog, Peter, and Romano Tozzi, 'Lya de Putti: Loving Life and Not Fearing Death', *Silent Film Newsletter* 2 (January 1994), supplement pp. 1–8

Higson, Andrew, ed., *Young and Innocent?: The Cinema in Britain 1896–1930* (Exeter: University of Exeter Press, 2002)

Houston, Penelope, *Went the Day Well?* (London: BFI Film Classics, 1992)

Jenkins, Alan, *The Twenties* (London: William Heinemann, 1974),

Kemp, Philip, *Lethal Innocence: The Cinema of Alexander Mackendrick* (London: Methuen, 1991)

Kendall, Henry, *I Remember Romano's* (London: MacDonald, 1960)

Kobal, John, *People Will Talk* (New York: Aurum, 1986)

Korda, Michael, *Charmed Lives* (New York: Random House, 1979)

Kohn, Marek, *Dope Girls* (London: Granta, 1992)

Lang, Matheson, *Mr Wu Looks Back* (London: Stanley Paul and Co., 1940)

Lewis, Roger, *The Man Who Was Private Widdle: Charles Hawtrey 1914–1988* (London: Faber and Faber, 2001)

Low, Rachael, *The History of the British Film 1919–1929* (London: George Allen and Unwin, 1971)

– *The History of the British Film: Film Making in 1930s Britain* (London: George Allen and Unwin/BFI, 1985),

Lukins, Jocelyn, *The Fantasy Factory: Lime Grove Studios* (London: Shepherd's Bush Local History Society, 1996)

McCallum, John, *Life with Googie* (London: Heinemann, 1979)

McFarlane, Brian, *An Autobiography of British Cinema* (London: BFI/Methuen, 1997)

– *The Encyclopedia of British Film* (London: BFI/Methuen, 2003)

McGillivray, David, *Doing Rude Things: The History of the British Sex Film, 1957–1981* (London: Sun Tavern Fields, 1992)

McKernan, Luke, *A Yank in Britain: The Lost Memoirs of Charles Urban, Film Pioneer* (Hastings: The Projection Box, 1999)

Macnab, Geoffrey, 'Looking for Lustre: Stars at Gainsborough', in Pam Cook, ed., *Gainsborough Pictures* (London: Cassell, 1997)

– *J. Arthur Rank and the British Film Industry* (London: Routledge, 1993)

– *Searching for Stars: Rethinking British Cinema* (London: Cassell, 2000)

Macqueen-Pope, W., *Ivor: The Story of an Achievement* (London: Hutchinson, 1951)

Mayne, Xavier, *The Intersexes* (Rome: privately published, 1906)

Mills, Sir John, *Up in the Clouds, Gentlemen, Please* (London: Orion, 2001)

Mitchell, John, *Flickering Shadows: A Lifetime in Film* (London: MHR, 1997)

More, Kenneth, *More or Less* (London: Hodder and Stoughton, 1978)

Morgan, Joan, Backwater (London: Chapman and Hall, 1942)

– *Camera!* (London: Chapman and Hall, 1940)

Morley, Sheridan, *Gladys Cooper* (London: Heinemann, 1979)

– *Dirk Bogarde: Rank Outsider* (London: Bloomsbury, 1999)

Murray, John B., *The Remarkable Michael Reeves: His Short and Tragic Life* (London: Cinematics Publishing, 2002)

Napper, Lawrence, 'A Despicable Tradition? Quota-quickies in the 1930s' in Robert Murphy, ed., *The British Cinema Book* (London: BFI, 2nd edition, 2002)

Neame, Ronald, *Straight from the Horse's Mouth: An Autobiography* (Scarecrow Press: Lanham, Maryland, 2003)

Newton, Michael, *Kind Hearts and Coronets* (London: BFI, 2003)

Orwell, George, *Collected Essays* ii (Harmondsworth: Penguin, 1970),

Owen, Gareth and Brian Burford, *The Pinewood Story* (London: Reynolds and Hearn, 2000)

O'Connor, Gary, *Alec Guniness: The Unknown* (London: Sidgwick and Jackson, 2003)

Parkinson, David, ed., *The Graham Greene Film Reader* (London: Penguin, 1995)

Pearson, George, *Flashback: An Autobiography of a British Film Maker* (London: George Allen and Unwin, 1957)

Perry, George, *Forever Ealing: A Celebration of the Great British Film Studio* (London: Pavilion, 1981)

– *The Great British Picture Show* (London: Pavilion, 2nd edition 1985)

Petley, Julian, 'The Lost Continent', in Charles Barr, ed., *All Our Yesterdays* (London: BFI, 1986), p. 118.

Powell, Michael, *A Life in Movies: An Autobiography* (London: William Heinemann, 1986)

Powell, Violet, *The Constant Novelist* (London: Heinemann, 1983)

Puttnam, David, *The Undeclared War: The Struggle for Control of the World's Film Industry* (London: Harper Collins, 1997)

Richards, Jeffrey, ed., *The Unknown 1930s: An Alternative History of the British Cinema, 1929–1939* (London: I. B. Tauris, 1998)

Rigby, Jonathan, *English Gothic: A Century of Horror Cinema* (London: Reynolds and Hearn, 2000)

Roberts, John Stuart, *Siegfried Sassoon* (London: Richard Cohen, 2000)

Robeson, Paul, Jnr., *The Undiscovered Paul Robeson* (New York: John Wiley, 2001)

Robinson, David, *Chaplin: His Life and Art* (London: William Collins and Sons, 1985)

Rose, Richard, *The World of Ivor Novello: Perchance to Dream* (London: Leslie Frewin, 1974)

Rotha, Paul, *The Film Till Now*, 2nd edition (London: Vision Press, 1949)

Royal Commission on the Press, Minutes of Evidence (London: HMSO, 1948)

Russell, Ken, *The Lion Roars* (London: Faber and Faber, 1994)

Ryall, David, *Alfred Hitchcock and the British Cinema* (Atlantic Highlands, New Jersey: Athlone Press, 1996)

Savage, Jon, *England's Dreaming: Sex Pistols and Punk Rock* (London: Faber and Faber, 1991)

Sheridan, Simon, *Come Play with Me: The Life and Films of Mary Millington* (Guildford: FAB Press, 1999)

– *Keeping the British End Up: Four Decades of Saucy Cinema* (London: Reynolds and Hearn, 2001)

Shute, Nerina, *Come into the Sunlight: The Story of My Edwardian Mother* (London: Jarrolds, 1958)

– *The Escapist Generations: My London Story* (London: Robert Hale, 1973)

– *Passionate Friendships; Memoirs and Confessions of a Rebel* (London: Robert Hale, 1992)

Sinden, Donald, *A Touch of the Memoirs* (London: Hodder and Stoughton, 1982)

Slide, Anthony, *Silent Players* (Lexington: University Press of Kentucky, 2002)

Smith, Alison, ed., *Exposed: The Victorian Nude* (London: Tate Publishing)

Smith, Dodie, *Look Back with Astonishment* (London: W. H. Allen, 1973)

Spoto, Donald, *The Dark Side of Genius: The Life of Alfred Hitchcock* (London: Collins, 1983)

Swanson, Gloria, *Swanson on Swanson* (London: Michael Joseph, 1981)

Tennyson, Charles, *Life's All a Fragment* (London: Cassell, 1953)

– *Penrose Tennyson* (London: A.S. Atkinson, 1943)

Thomson, David, *The New Biographical Dictionary of Film* (London: Little, Brown, 2002)

Threadgall, Derek, *Shepperton Studios: An Independent View* (London: BFI, 1994)

Trevelyan, John, *What the Censor Saw* (London: Michael Joseph, 1973)

Trimble, Marion Blackton, *J. Stuart Blackton: A Personal Biography by His Daughter* (Metuchen, New Jersey: Scarecrow Press, 1985)

Ustinov, Peter, *Dear Me* (London: Heinemann, 1977)

Van Damm, Vivian, *Tonight and Every Night* (London: Stanley Paul and Co. Ltd, 1952)

Wakelin, Michael, *J. Arthur Rank: The Man behind the Gong* (Oxford: Lion Publishing, 1996)

Walker, Alexander, *The Celluloid Sacrifice* (London: Michael Joseph, 1966)

Warren, Patricia, *British Film Studios: An Illustrated History* (London: Batsford, 2001)

– *Elstree: The British Hollywood* (London: Elm Tree Books, 1983)

Wilcox, Pamela, *Between Hell and Charing Cross* (London: George Allen and Unwin, 1977)

Williams, Hugo, *Collected Poems* (London: Faber and Faber, 2002)

Williams, Philip Martin and David L. Williams, *Hooray for Jollywood: The Life of John E. Blakeley and the Mancunian Film Corporation* (Ashton-under-Lyme: History on Your Doorstep, 2001)

Williams, Michael, *Ivor Novello: Screen Idol* (London: BFI, 2004)

Wise, Damon, *Come by Sunday: The Fabulous, Ruined Life of Diana Dors* (London: Sidgwick and Jackson, 1998)

Wright, Basil, *The Long View: An International History of Cinema* (London: Secker and Warburg, 1974)

Ziegler, Philip, *Diana Cooper* (London: Hamish Hamilton, 1981)

Notes

INTRODUCTION Strange England

1 See Charles Barr, 'Writing Screen Plays: Stannard and Hitchcock', in Andrew Higson (ed.), *Young and Innocent?: The Cinema in Britain 1896–1930* (Exeter: University of Exeter Press, 2002), pp. 227–8.

2 Paul Rotha, *The Film Till Now* (London: Vision Press, second edition, 1949), pp. 313–14.

3 Roger Manvell, *Film* (Harmonsdworth: Penguin, 1950), p. 223.

4 Victor Perkins, 'The British Cinema', *Movie* 1 (1962), p. 3.

5 François Truffaut, *Hitchcock* (London: Panther books, 1969), p.140.

6 Roy Armes's *A Critical History of British Cinema* (1978) was the master-text of this ideological position. In prose flavoured by the critical theory of the Frankfurt School, it damns the British film business for failing to create 'an adequate working context for those who wish to question the dominant stylistic approaches or provide stimulus for social change, with the result that there has been virtually no avant-garde filmmaking and no effective militant cinema in Britain' (Roy Armes, *A Critical History of British Cinema* (London: Secker & Warburg, 1978), pp. 3–4).

7 Julian Petley, 'The Lost Continent', in Charles Barr (ed.), *All Our Yesterdays* (London: BFI, 1986), p. 118.

CHAPTER ONE The Silent World of Lilian Hall-Davis

1 'Film Favourites on the British Screen', *Film Weekly* (28 July 1923), p. 18.

2 Some time later the Pembertons emigrated to South Africa, where, in a grim repetition of history, Grosvenor took his own life.

3 'Long Shots', *Kinematograph Weekly* (2 November 1933), p. 4.

4 'Afraid to Act for the Talkies', *London Evening News* (26 October 1933), p. 1.

5 'Tragic Twilight of Screen Beauty', *News of the World* (29 October 1933), p. 16.

6 Taylor sued over an article by Cecile Leslie, 'British Films in the Making', *Film*

Weekly (5 March 1932), in which the studio doorman was reported to have said to an extra, 'That was Alma Taylor. She was a big star once. Bigger'n you'll ever be.' Taylor maintained that she had come to Elstree to pick up some photographs and have her hair cut ('Film Actress's Libel Action', *The Times* (11 May 1933), p. 4). There were many similar casualties. The prolific character actor Robert Vallis – who was, according to one acquaintance, 'always willing to jump off any Thames Bridge for £3' – spent his last years as a car-park attendant in Brighton, where he died, penniless, in December 1932 ('Bob Vallis Dead', *Kinematograph Weekly* (10 May 1934), p. 39). Estelle Brody was working as a typist the year after she starred in *Kitty* (1929) ('From Film Star to Typist', *Film Weekly* (29 March 1930), p. 4).

7 Jack Cardiff, *Magic Hour* (London: Faber and Faber, 1996), p.11.

8 Correspondence with Cora Goffin, 8 July 2003.

9 Joan Morgan, *Camera!* (London: Chapman & Hall, 1940), pp. 23, 266, 268.

10 *Pictures and Picturegoer* (January 1924), p. 50.

11 Quoted in John M. East, *'Neath the Mask: The Story of the East Family* (London: George Allen & Unwin, 1967), p. 329.

12 'Northcote Again Charged with Fraud', *Motion Picture Studio* (8 December 1923), p. 7

13 Rome described his unwilling work on this early sound film in an interview recorded for BBC Radio in the 1960s (see BFI Special Collections).

14 David A. Cook, *A History of Narrative Film* (New York: Norton, 1990), p. 61. Later editions soften the assertion: 'Griffith did more than any single individual to establish the narrative language of cinema' (*ibid.*, fourth edition, 2004, p. 51).

15 A number of scenes have not survived: an establishing shot of gypsy caravans rolling by the riverside under the weeping willows; a scene in which Rover leaps over a bush; a tension-increasing sequence in which the dog, after crossing the brook, momentarily loses the scent.

16 For a defence of Hepworth's pictorialism, see Christine Gledhill, *Reframing British cinema 1918–1928: Between Restraint and Passion* (London: BFI Publishing, 2004), pp.95–100.

17 Cecil Hepworth, *Came the Dawn* (London: Phoenix House, 1951), p. 139.

18 In 1896, the French showman François Xaintrailles shot a short scene of Fitzhamon tipping his hat outside the Middlesex Music Hall, but this proved too scratchy to project (Denis Gifford, 'Fitz: The Old Man of the Screen', in Barr (ed.), *op. cit.*, p. 314). Gifford's interviews with Fitzhamon are the principal source of biographical information on the director.

19 *Pictures and the Picturegoer* (7 March 1914), p. 69. 'Many others beside the Hepworth Company', keened a rival journal, 'will deplore the death of this old favourite' (*Bioscope* (26 February 1914), p. 873).

20 Hay Plumb claimed that when his leading actress, Gladys Sylvani, was kept back by the Gaiety for extra rehearsals, he did not abandon filming, but took the rest of the cast to the Walton barber's shop, pored over dog-eared back numbers of *Chips* and *Comic Cuts*, plagiarised a few promising ideas, and concocted *Wife for a Day* on the lawn of the Red Lion pub in Shepperton. The cast comprised Johnny Butt, Thurston Harris, Harry Buss, Harry Gilbey and Jack Raymond (Hay Plumb, 'Those Were the Days', *Picture Show Annual* (1948)).

21 His stage name was 'Whimsical' Walker.

22 'Chrissie White', *Picture Show* (16 August 1919), p. 8; 'Henry Edwards', *Picture Show* (13 September 1919), pp. 12–13.

23 Babette, 'Hero and Heroine Come to Life', Hull *Daily Mail* (14 February 1929), p. 6.

24 'Back to the Stage', South Glamorgan *Evening Express* (8 November 1924), p. 10.

25 Quoted with permission of Henryetta Edwards.

26 Joan Morgan, *Backwater* (London: Chapman and Hall, 1942), p.176.

CHAPTER TWO The Pleasure Garden

1 'Dancing Her Way to Fame', *Picture Show* (13 May 1922), p. 9.

2 See 'After Their Record Climb', *The Times* (27 July 1922), p. 14.

3 Flora Le Breton, 'What I Know of Drowning', unidentified cutting in her file at the BFI.

4 The script indicates that Rob is a pianist; the pressbook says that he is a violinist (BFI Special Collections).

5 See Marek Kohn, *Dope Girls* (London: Granta, 1992), p. 99.

6 'Victims of the Drug Habit', *Daily Express* (7 December 1918), p. 1.

7 For Jack May and Billie Carleton see 'Miss Carleton's Death', *The Times* (17 January 1919), p. 8. For Belcher's heroin consumption see 'Miss Carleton's Death', *The Times* (8 March 1919), p. 4. For Belcher's cross-examination at the trial see 'Face to Face', *News of the World* (19 January 1919), p. 1.

8 'The "Cocaine" Ban', *Kinematograph Weekly* (18 May 1922), p. 42.

9 A. Jympson Hauman, 'The Film World', London *Evening News* (20 May 1922), p. 6.

10 Ernest Dudley, 'Pipe of Dreams', London *Evening News* (10 November 1956), p. 4.

11 W. Macqueen-Pope, *Ivor: The Story of an Achievement* (London: Hutchinson, 1951), p. 116.

12 Richard Rose, *The World of Ivor Novello: Perchance to Dream* (London: Leslie Frewin, 1974), p. 34.

13 *Ibid.*, p. 30.

14 James Harding, *Ivor Novello: A Biography* (Cardiff: Welsh Academic Press, 1997), p. 17; Ivor Novello, 'Life Romance of Ivor Novello', *Picture Show* (4 April 1925), p. 8; May Herschel Clarke, 'Music and the Movies', *Picture Show* (7 January 1922), p. 22.

15 Douglas Warth, 'The Picture that was Never Taken in Real Life', *Sunday Pictorial* (11 March 1951), p. 7.

16 Sheridan Morley, *Gladys Cooper* (London: Heinemann, 1979), pp. 95–6; 121–2.

17 Donald Sinden, *A Touch of the Memoirs* (London: Hodder & Stoughton, 1982), p. 126.

18 See Harding, *op. cit.*, p. 143, for the melancholy details.

19 John Stuart Roberts, *Siegfried Sassoon* (London: Richard Cohen, 2000), pp. 176–7.

20 *Ibid.*, p. 199. Glen Byam Shaw – the son of the Edwardian painter John Byam Shaw – lived long enough to get his revenge: he played Major Redfern in the film of *Look Back in Anger* (1958), the play that proved a nail in the coffin of Novello's style of theatre.

21 Harding, *op. cit.*, p. 142.

22 Herschel Clarke, *op. cit.*, p. 22.

23 Macqueen-Pope, *op. cit.*, pp. 87–8.

24 Harding, *op. cit.*, p. 71.

25 Dandolo, it strikes me, is also the name of the cat zapped into the ether by Vincent Price in Roger Corman's *The Fly*.

26 *Picture Show* (30 May 1925), p. 18.

27 Graham Cutts, 'Secrets of a Film Director', *Picturegoer* (October 1926), p. 9.

28 See Donald Spoto, *The Dark Side of Genius: The Life of Alfred Hitchcock* (London: Collins, 1983), p. 61. I am grateful to Christine Gledhill for advice on the chronology of the production of *The Prude's Fall*.

29 *New York Times* (11 June 1928), p. 27.

30 Michael Balcon, *Michael Balcon Presents . . . A Lifetime of Films* (London: Hutchinson, 1969), p.26.

31 Adrian Brunel, *Nice Work* (London: Forbes Robertson, 1949), p. 132.

32 Alan Jenkins, *The Twenties* (London: William Heinemann, 1974), p. 174.

33 Violet Powell, *The Constant Novelist* (London: Heinemann, 1983), p. 78.

34 Nerina Shute, 'Two New Lovers', *Film Weekly* (2 August 1930), p. 10. The same correspondent joked that Bentley had been reported to address a mosquito as 'darling' (Nerina Shute, 'On the Road to Fame', *Film Weekly* (16 August 1930), p. 10).

35 Mabel Poulton Collection, BFI Special Collections,, item 3.

36 Michael Balcon, *Michael Balcon Presents . . . A Lifetime in Films* (London: Hutchinson, 1969), p. 24.

37 Brunel, *op. cit.*, p. 135.

38 P. L. Mannock, 'About Basil Dean', *Picturegoer* (May 1928), p. 11.

39 *Variety* (21 March 1928), p. 18.

40 See Geoffrey Macnab, 'Looking for Lustre: Stars at Gainsborough', in Pam Cook (ed.), *Gainsborough Pictures* (London: Cassell, 1997), p. 102.

41 'Are you peculiarly fond of Wagner?' was a test-question for sniffing out sexual deviance (Xavier Mayne, *The Intersexes* (Rome: privately published, 1906)).

CHAPTER THREE Shute the Journalist

1 Rebecca West, 'Books of the Day', *Daily Telegraph* (30 January 1931), p. 7.

2 For *The Viking* see *Kinematograph Weekly* (27 August 1931), p. 31; 'First for Starret', *Classic Film Collector* 45 (1974), p. 43; 'Seal Hunters', *Hollywood Spectator* (29 August 1931), pp. 24–5.

3 Nerina Shute, '"Dead" Man as Studio Executive', *Film Weekly* (14 October 1929), p. 11.

4 See Rachael Low, *The History of the British Film 1919–1929* (London: George Allen & Unwin, 1971), pp. 190, 188.

5 See 'A Film Actor's Affairs', *The Times* (15 January 1931), p. 5.

6 Ronald Neame, interview with the author, 27 October 2002.

7 For the Molly Wright case see *Kinematograph Weekly* (20 November 1930), p. 33, and (27 November 1930), p. 36. The details of the assault were supplied by Geraldine Chaplin and Betty Tetrick.

8 Nerina Shute, 'Talkie Tests for Henry Ainley and Nelson Keys', *Film Weekly* (8 July 1929), p. 13. Sidney Gilliat's views were more representative. When he recalled Mycroft in 1977, it was as 'one of the most disliked people in films' (Geoff Brown, *Launder and Gilliat* (London: British Film Institute, 1977), p. 22).

9 Shute, '"Dead" Man as Studio Executive', *op. cit.*, p. 11; Nerina Shute, 'Doubling for Elstree's Famous Parrot', *Film Weekly* (1 February 1930), p. 13.

10 Nerina Shute, 'Lya de Putti Surrenders', *Film Weekly* (17 May 1930), p. 12.

11 See Peter Herzog and Romano Tozzi, 'Lya de Putti: Loving Life and Not Fearing Death,' *Silent Film Newsletter* 2 (January 1994), supplement pp. 1–8.

12 'Leaving Poverty Behind', *Film Weekly* (28 June 1930), p. 12.

13 Nerina Shute, 'Behind the Film Scenes with Nerina Shute', *Film Weekly* 6 February 1932), p. 8.

14 An observation made by Tony Richardson, when he directed her on Broadway in *The Milk Train Doesn't Stop Here Anymore*, relayed to the author by Rupert Everett.

15 Public Records Office File HO/382/9. Bankhead later admitted that she had been 'on the brink of wedlock' with the nineteen-year-old Tony Wilson, and that she had taken the boy, his two brothers and a fourteen-year-old classmate

for tea on the Thames at Bray (Tallulah Bankhead, *Tallulah: My Autobiography* (London: Victor Gollancz, 1952), p. 137).

16 See P. L. Mannock, 'New Star Signed up', *Kinematograph Weekly* (19 November 1931), p. 57.

17 Hugo Williams, 'Shelf Life', in *Collected Poems* (Faber and Faber, 2002), pp. 118–19.

18 A relapse occurred on the set of *The Good Companions* (1933) (see 'Edmund Gwenn Succeeds Henry Ainley', *Kinematograph Weekly* (27 October 1932), p. 44).

19 Sir John Mills, *Up in the Clouds, Gentlemen, Please* (London: Orion, 2001), p. 170.

20 See 'Stage Girl Burnt to Death: Actor's Story of the Film Studio Horror', *News of the World* (6 April 1930), p.1; 'The Film Studio Fire', *The Times* (7 April 1930), p. 8.

21 Nerina Shute, 'Beauty in the Bath!', *Film Weekly* (26 April 1930), p. 19.

22 'Donald Calthrop Plans to Return to Films', *Daily Mail* (1 June 1937), p. 4.

23 'A Splendid Farewell!', *Bioscope* (7 May 1930), p. 27. See also 'Tubby Phillips', *Kinematograph Weekly* (8 May 1930), p. 32.

24 'Donald Calthrop', *Picture Show* (14 April 1934), p. 9; unidentified cutting (21 October 1935); Nerina Shute, 'Elstree's Most Annoying Man', *Film Weekly* (21 June 1930), p. 18.

25 Nerina Shute, 'Elstree's Most Annoying Man', *Film Weekly* (21 June 1930), p. 18.

CHAPTER FOUR A Short Chapter about Quick Films

1 Rachael Low, *The History of the British Film: Film Making in 1930s Britain* (London: George Allen & Unwin/British Film Institute, 1985), pp. 33, 115.

2 Basil Wright, *The Long View: An International History of Cinema* (London: Secker & Warburg, 1974), p. 138.

3 Ernest Betts, *Inside Pictures* (London: Cresset, 1960), pp. 6–7.

4 William K. Everson, programme notes to accompany MOMA's Powell and Pressburger season (20 November 1980 to 5 January 1981).

5 McLaughlin played another Oriental villain in Twickenham Studios' remake of *Broken Blossoms* (1936).

6 Edward Dryhurst, *Gilt off the Gingerbread* (London: Bachman & Turner, 1987), pp. 174–80.

7 Margaret Dickinson and Sarah Street, *Cinema and State: The Film Industry and the Government 1927–84* (London: British Film Institute, 1985), p. 42.

8 Balcon, *op. cit.*, pp. 92–3.

9 *Kinematograph Year Book* (1938), p. 216.

10 'Alleged Evasion of Quota Act', *Kinematograph Year Book* (1932), p. 173.

11 David Puttnam, *The Undeclared War: The Struggle for Control of the World's Film Industry* (London: HarperCollins, 1997), p. 162.

12 George Perry, *The Great British Picture Show* (London: Pavilion, second edition, 1985), p. 65.

13 Charles Drazin, *Alexander Korda: Britain's Only Movie Mogul* (London: Sidgwick and Jackson, 2002), p. 18.

14 'Quota "Quickies" for Half-Wits', *Kinematograph Weekly* (15 October 1936), p. 30.

15 Interview with Roy Ward Baker, 30 January 2003.

16 Quoted in Lawrence Napper, 'A Despicable Tradition? Quota-quickies in the 1930s', in Robert Murphy (ed.), *The British Cinema Book* (London: BFI, second edition, 2002), p. 45.

17 See 'Leslie Fuller Wins Salary Claim', *Kinematograph Weekly* (4 February 1937), p. 37.

18 See 'Boreham Wood's Plight', *Kinematograph Weekly* (24 February 1938), p. 21.

19 Geoffrey Toone, interview with the author, 10 May 2002.

CHAPTER FIVE Our Father, which Art in Ealing

1 Interview with Victoria Hopper, 2 April 2002.

2 John Galsworthy, foreword to E. Maria Albanesi, *Meggie Albanesi, by Her Mother* (London: Hodder & Stoughton, 1928), pp. 8–9.

3 Basil Dean, *Seven Ages: An Autobiography 1888–1927* (London: Hutchinson, 1970), p. 223.

4 See George Pearson, *Flashback: An Autobiography of a British Film Maker* (London: George Allen & Unwin, 1957), pp. 74–5.

5 Albanesi, *op. cit.*, p. 93.

6 Dean, *op. cit*, p. 197.

7 Henry Kendall, *I Remember Romano's* (London: MacDonald, 1960), p. 71.

8 Letter from Basil Dean to E. M. Albanesi (3 February 1928), Basil Dean Collection, John Rylands Library, Manchester, item 1/1/37.

9 Basil Dean, *Mind's Eye: An Autobiography 1927–1972* (London: Hutchinson, 1973), p. 109.

10 Basil Dean Collection, 1/1/464$^{1/2}$.

11 Interview with Winton Dean, 28 June 2002.

12 See Gloria Swanson, *Swanson on Swanson* (London: Michael Joseph, 1981), pp. 425–8.

13 Basil Dean, *Mind's Eye*, p. 184.

14 Eltham Palace is located in south-east London, where visitors can marvel at its vast circular entrance hall, its centrally powered vacuum-cleaning system, and the cage which was once home to the Courtaulds' pet ring-tailed lemur.

15 Dodie Smith, *Look Back with Astonishment* (London: W. H. Allen, 1973), p. 177.

16 Dean, *Mind's Eye, op. cit.*, p. 222.

17 Letter from Reginald Baker to Basil Dean (24 August 1934), Basil Dean collection 4/3/29.

18 *Mind's Eye*, p. 225.

19 Basil Dean, undated confidential memo to Stephen Courtauld, Basil Dean Collection 4/3/47.

20 Gracie Fields, *Sing as We Go* (London: Frederick Muller, 1960), p. 76.

21 *Ibid.*, p. 46.

22 Dean, *Mind's Eye, op. cit.*, p. 134.

23 *Ibid.*, p. 157.

24 Confidential memo from Basil Dean to Stephen Courtauld (1935), Basil Dean Collection.

25 Balcon, *op. cit.*, p. 118; David Bret, *George Formby: A Troubled Genius* (London: Robson, 1999), p. 35.

26 See Betty Driver, *Betty: The Autobiography* (London: Granada Media, 2000), pp. 39–40. Driver believed that they were never filmed, though a print of *Boots! Boots!* recovered in 1998 retains her scenes.

27 Quoted in *George Formby: A Troubled Genius*. I have been unable to trace the original article.

28 Interview with Googie Withers, 10 July 2002.

29 'Secret Weddings of Actor and Sister', *Daily Mail* (3 March 1936), p. 3.

30 Letter from Virginia Courtauld to Basil Dean (undated), Basil Dean Collection, 4/3/57.

31 Letter from Virginia Courtauld to Basil Dean (19 July 1936), Basil Dean Collection 4/3/54

32 Interview with Winton Dean, 28 June 2002.

33 Interview with Stuart Freeborn, 19 September 2002.

34 Letter from Alexander Korda to Basil Dean (undated, 1937), Basil Dean Collection 4/4/10.

35 Letter from Stephen Courtauld to Basil Dean (14 April 1938), Basil Dean Collection 4/3/47.

36 Letter from Basil Dean to Stephen Courtauld (30 June 1938), Basil Dean Collection 4/3/99.

37 Letter from Stephen Courtauld to Basil Dean (21 July 1938), Basil Dean Collection 4/3/34.

38 Letter from Basil Dean to Stephen Courtauld (30 June 1938), Basil Dean Collection 4/3/99.

39 Letter from Basil Dean to Stephen Courtauld (3 August 1938), Basil Dean Collection 4/3/91.

40 *To-Day's Cinema* (16 September 1938), p. 1.

CHAPTER SIX Balconisation

1 See 'BBC Booked Julie Andrews for Doomsday', *Sunday Times* (11 July 1999),
   p. 3; Peter Hennessey, *The Secret State* (London: Penguin, 2003), pp. 149, 218;
   additional information from interview with Peter Hennessey.

2 Alexander Walker, 'The Ealing Comedies', in *British Greats* (London: Cassell,
   2000), p. 63.

3 Ken Russell, *The Lion Roars* (London: Faber & Faber, 1994), p. 40.

4 Jonathan Coe, 'Political Comedy at Its Best', *New Statesman* (22 August 1997),
   p. 40.

5 'Another Golden Age that Never Was', *Guardian* (9 October 1993), p. 24.

6 Tom Harris, MP for Glasgow (Cathcart), *Hansard* (25 March 2003),
   col. 178.

7 Waller, Robert, and Byron Criddle, *The Almanac of British Politics*, 7th edn
   (London: Routledge, 2002), p. 667.

8 David Irving, 'We Have Lost Our Sense of Destiny', speech to the Clarendon
   Club, 1990.

9 A sentiment not lost upon Guy Hamilton, the film's director: 'I was always
   pushing to remind people that James Bond was Commander Bond, RN,' he
   told me. 'He was a member of the establishment. I spent a long time, for
   instance, persuading Roger Moore to get his hair cut short.'

10 Charles Barr, *Ealing Studios* (London: Studio Vista, 1993), p. 165.

11 Michael Balcon, 'Film Comedy', in Peter Noble (ed.), *British Film Yearbook
   1949–50* (London: Skelton Spelling? Robinson, 1949), pp. 25–8.

12 Monja Danischewsky, *White Russian – Red Face* (London: Victor Gollancz,
   1966) p. 127.

13 Sean Day-Lewis, *C. Day-Lewis: An English Literary Life* (London: Unwin,
   1980), p. 186.

14 Evill was played by the Ealing actor Michael Redgrave in Guy Hamilton's *The
   Battle of Britain* (1969).

15 Sid Cole estimated that the studio's directors spent £300 a week at the bar of
   the Red Lion pub on Ealing Green.

16 Charles Crichton and Douglas Slocombe, for instance, were responsible for
   the famous montage sequence in *Whisky Galore!*; Aileen Balcon hit upon the
   subject of *The Captive Heart*; a family friend of Douglas Slocombe came up
   with the founding conceit of *The Lavender Hill Mob*; Sid Cole and Charles
   Frend formulated *Dead of Night*, though did not work on the project officially; the projectionist at the studio's screening room suggested that that film
   should conclude with a repeat of the first reel; and, according to his family,
   Balcon himself came up with the initial idea for *Passport to Pimlico*, after
   making a rare journey on the London Underground.

17 Letter from Michael Balcon to Alberto Cavalcanti (28 January 1947), Aileen and Michael Balcon Collection, BFI.

18 Douglas Slocombe, interview with the author, 22 February 2002.

19 To Balcon's embarrassment, Baker broke the terms of his bail. When the disgraced MP emerged from prison, however, Balcon signalled his willingness to donate funds to a committee for prison reform which Baker intended to establish (Peter Baker, *Time out of Life* (London: Quality Book Club, 1962), p. 245).

20 John Ellis, 'Made in Ealing', *Screen* (Spring 1975), pp. 118–19.

21 See *Between Hell and Charing Cross* (London: George Allen & Unwin, 1977)

22 Information from Stephen Poliakoff. Montagu's wife retained her terminal 'e'; Montagu dropped his, thinking that it looked too aristocratic.

23 Interview with Michael Foot, 22 August 2003.

24 Michael Balcon, *Tinsel or Realism* (London: Workers Film Association, 1943), pp. 4–5.

25 *Ibid.*, p. 5.

26 See George Perry, *Forever Ealing: A Celebration of the Great British Film Studio* (London: Pavilion, 1981), p. 8. Ustinov was recruited from the Army Kinematograph Unit, in which, he says, his most significant achievement was a film entitled *Tanks: Best Use of Smoke, Number 4*. 'It was shot in Richmond Park and it was absolute balls,' he told me. 'When all the films were made, a general came to see them. At the end we all stood up sheepishly to be congratulated, and the general walked past us, opened the door of the projection booth and congratulated the projectionist.' Sir Peter Ustinov, interview with the author, 22 June 2002.

27 Charles Tennyson, *Penrose Tennyson* (London: A. S. Atkinson, 1943), p. 12.

28 *Ibid.*, p. 99.

29 Charles Tennyson, *Life's All a Fragment* (London: Cassell, 1953), p. 193.

30 Information from Googie Withers.

31 Tennyson, *Life's All a Fragment, op. cit.*, p. 218.

32 The slogan 'Eat Here and Keep Your Wife as a Pet' also appears on the wall of an Italian restaurant patronised by Dirk Bogarde in *Accident* (1967).

33 We first meet the old boxer Harry in a café, where he is accused of looking at pornographic postcards – they're actually a set of his own shots, when he was a boxing champion in 1904. Later, Dot accuses him of being jealous of her, when she kisses Tommy during his post-match rub-down.

34 'Paul Robeson's Ideals', *Jewish Chronicle* (4 November 1938), p. 58.

35 See Paul Robeson Jr, *The Undiscovered Paul Robeson* (New York: John Wiley, 2001), p. 331.

36 See Martin Duberman, *Paul Robeson* (London: The Bodley Head, 1989), pp. 231–3.

37 *Royal Commission on the Press, Minutes of Evidence* (London: HMSO, 1948), paragraph 1909.

38 *Ibid.*, paragraph 4919.

39 *Ibid.*, paragraph 8622.

40 Interview with Michael Foot, 22 August 2003.

41 Judy Campbell, interview with the author, 27 June 1999.

42 George Orwell, *The Lion and the Unicorn* (London: Secker and Warburg, 1941), p. 12.

43 'There was a poetic quality inherent in Tennyson which sought expression in the new medium of films,' he wrote. 'He was preoccupied with social problems . . . and I am sure that it was on these lines that his work would have developed' (Michael Balcon, letter to *The Times* (22 July 1941), p. 7).

44 Danischewsky, *op. cit.*, p. 139.

45 Balcon, *Michael Balcon Presents, op. cit.*, facing p. 202.

46 *Ibid.*, pp. 8, 9, 10.

47 Walker, *op. cit.*, p. 62.

48 There is some confusion in the script as to whether Wilsford is an English traitor or a Nazi sleeper placed in Bramley End some years before the action takes place (see Penelope Houston, *Went the Day Well?* (London: BFI Film Classics, 1992), pp. 27–9).

49 Two bizarre footnotes to the production of this film. Location work was carried out in the Buckinghamshire village of Turville, where the Ealing crew drained the local pub of every last drop of alcohol. Wartime restrictions prevented the landlord from replenishing his cellar: deeply upset by the complaints of his regulars, he committed suicide. Back in London, it was discovered that wind noise had marred a scene in which the captain of the Bramley End Home Guard chatted with the Nazi commander (Basil Sydney) about the best places to site his machine-gun posts. Re-recording of the dialogue was hampered when Basil Sydney announced that he was a member of a religious sect whose members were forbidden to look upon their own images (see *ibid.*, pp. 50–1).

50 Quoted in Barr, *op. cit.*, p. 60.

51 Philip Kemp, *Lethal Innocence: The Cinema of Alexander Mackendrick* (London: Methuen, 1991), p. 51.

52 See 'A World Safe for Science', *The Times* (1 December 1945), p. 6.

53 Kemp, *op. cit.*, p. 46. Some were also caricatures of Ealing personnel: Patric Doonan's shop steward is a sketch of Sidney Cole; Ernest Thesiger's vulture-like industrialist a parody of Ealing's musical director, Ernest Irving; Cecil Parker's indecisive factory boss an affectionate lampoon of Michael Balcon.

54 T. S. Eliot, *The Cocktail Party* (London: Faber & Faber, 1950), p. 34.

55 Kemp, *op. cit.*, p. 51.

CHAPTER SEVEN They Were Sisters

1 James Mason, *Before I Forget* (London: Sphere, 1982), p. 110–11.

2 Pamela Mason, Obituary, *The Times* (6 July 1996), p. 25.

3 Quoted in Geoffrey MacNab, 'Odd Man Out', *Guardian* (30 October 2003), G2 section, p. 10.

4 'Patricia Roc Fined £25 for Shoplifting', *Daily Mail* (13 February 1975), p. 3.

5 Information from Judy Campbell.

6 See 'Star Saved by Housekeeper', *Daily Mirror* (26 April 1954), p. 2.

CHAPTER EIGHT Breaking Rank

1 Geoffrey Macnab's *J. Arthur Rank and the British Film Industry* (London: Routledge, 1993) makes an excellent case against Rank's detractors.

2 R. G. Burnett and E. D. Martell, *The Devil's Camera: Menace of a Film-Ridden World* (London: Epworth Press, 1932), opening dedication, quoted in Macnab, *op. cit.*, p. 11.

3 See Michael Wakelin, *J. Arthur Rank: The Man behind the Gong* (Oxford: Lion Publishing, 1996), p. 47.

4 Interview with Ronald Neame, 19 October 2003.

5 Interview with Peter Ustinov, 22 June 2002.

6 Roy Ward Baker, interview with the author, 30 January 2003.

7 'Wife's Standard of Living', *The Times* (25 October 1966), p. 7.

8 At the risk of labouring the point, other remarks made about Davis by my interviewees include: 'he was a complete shit' (Jonathan Balcon); 'I haven't a good word for him' (Patricia Roc); 'he was an evil spirit' (Michael Foot).

9 See Richard Dacre, *Trouble in Store: Norman Wisdom – A Career in Comedy* (Dumfries: T. C. Farries, 1991), p. 98. Would *The Exorcist* have been possible, I wonder, if William Friedkin had already made a comedy of demonic possession?

10 'Use Wisdom Wisely', *Picturegoer* (30 August 1952), p. 5.

11 See Gareth Owen and Brian Burford, *The Pinewood Story* (London: Reynolds & Hearn, 2000), p. 65.

12 See Macnab, *op. cit.*, p. 223.

13 Edward Goring, 'Wisdom's US Film Deal Scrapped', *Daily Mail* (28 March 1957), p. 5.

14 She was a viscose-wrapped siren with a thing for Borodin – a composer surprisingly popular on the Jupiter of *Fire Maidens from Outer Space*.

15 Kenneth More, *More or Less* (London: Hodder & Stoughton, 1978), p. 55.

16 *Ibid.*, pp. 183–4.

17 *Ibid.*, p. 184.

18 A footnote on Tony Forwood's sexual life: in the mid-1930s, Forwood and

Googie Withers were marooned in a remote bed-and-breakfast,after fog had halted their drive to a joint engagement. There was only one bed left. They climbed into it. As soon as Withers began to make advances, she felt a bolster fall down between them like a portcullis.

19 Quoted in John Coldstream, *Dirk Bogarde: The Authorised Biography* (London: Weidenfeld and Nicolson), p. 122.

20 Dirk Bogarde, *Backcloth* (London: Viking, 1986), p. 110.

21 See Dirk Bogarde, 'The right to die with dignity', *Daily Telegraph* (16 July 1991), p. 15.

22 Dirk Bogarde, *Snakes and Ladders* (Harmondsworth: Penguin, 1988), p. 170.

23 John Behr, the Pinewood publicity manager, informed Baker on 26 February 1960: 'we have got a slightly disgruntled Dirk on our hands because of today's *Daily Mail*'. He then wrote a grovelling letter to Bogarde: 'I cannot say how sorry I am about the very unfortunate headline in today's *Daily Mail*. I have spoken to Shirley Flack but she says she arrived at that figure from some cuttings of some years ago, and she added the difference in time between the cuttings and today's date' (letter from John Behr to Dirk Bogarde (26 February 1960), personal files of Roy War Baker, Singer Not the Song (SNS) File 1. In reality, Flack's error was Bogarde's own fault: his *Who's Who* entry, for which he supplied the information, overestimated his age by two years.

24 *Snakes and Ladders*, p. 188.

25 Dirk Bogarde, *Snakes and Ladders* (London: Penguin, 1988), p. 180.

26 Letter from Laurence Pollinger to Roy Baker (18 August 1959), SNS File 1; letter from Malcolm Arnold to Roy Baker (25 March 1960), SNS File 1.

27 Letter from Roy Baker to Richard Widmark (14 December 1959), SNS File 1.

28 Letter from Roy Baker to Dirk Bogarde (31 December 1959), SNS File 1.

29 Letter from Earl St John to Peter Finch (4 January 1959 [*sic*: year should, of course, be 1960]), SNS File 1.

30 Telegram from Dirk Bogarde to John Davis (3 February 1960), SNS File 1.

31 Letter from Roy Baker to Audrey Erskine Lindop (8 March 1960), SNS File 1; letter from Hugh French to Roy Baker (22 February 1960), SNS File 1.

32 Letter from John Behr to Roy Baker (3 April 1960), SNS File 1.

33 John Mills, *Up in the Clouds, Gentlemen, Please* (London: Orion Books, 2nd edn, 2001), p. 415.

34 '*The Singer Not the Song*, Summary of Discussions of the Pre-Production Publicity Meeting held at Victoria on 30 April, SNS File 2.

35 Not everyone is so reticent: 'Dirk Bogarde', Richard Todd told me, 'was always a vicious little sod.'

36 Clancy Sigal, 'The Winter of My Discontent', *Time and Tide* (13 January 1961), p. 57.

37 Penelope Gilliat, 'Death Wish on the Left Bank', *Observer* (8 January 1961), p. 27.

38 Alexander Walker, 'I'm Not Easily Shocked, but Really This Film!' *Evening Standard* (5 January 1961), p. 10.

39 Letter from Nigel Balchin to Roy Baker (18 February 1960), SNS File 1.

40 *Ibid*.

41 Letter from Roy Baker to Mylene Demongeot (28 December 1960), SNS File 2.

42 Postcard from Dirk Bogarde to Roy Baker (8 May [1965?]), SNS File 2.

CHAPTER NINE No Future

1 Interview with Siân Phillips, 15 July 2002.

2 In John Frankenheimer's *The Fixer* (1968), these generations were also cast against each other: Dirk Bogarde plays Bibikov, a progressive Russian magistrate acting on behalf of Yakov Bok (Alan Bates), a Jewish migrant who has fallen foul of the Kiev authorities. Bibikov is a man too implicated in a regime he despises to offer explicit opposition to its inhumanities; Bok is a shaggy-haired figure from the counter-culture, willing to suffer any indignity rather than confess to the child-murder for which he has been framed. Bibikov pleads his client's innocence to the man with real power, Count Odeovsky (David Warner). Warner, wrapped in white fur, lounges on a chaise longue and listens impassively to Bogarde's case. Frankenheimer shot the scene with Warner in a single day, and, with time running out, asked his stills photographer to take shots only of the younger actor. As the photographer snapped away, Bogarde burst into tears. 'I suppose I'm just an old has-been,' he whimpered.

3 Harold Conway, 'Richard Todd Wants to Give up His Pot Boilers', London *Evening Standard* (17 October 1953), p. 9.

4 *Daily Graphic* (29 September 1953), p. 10. See also Walter Hayes, 'Hollywood Picks the Little Guy Again', *Daily Sketch* (19 November 1953), p. 10.

5 Ian Conrich, 'Traditions of the British Horror Film', in *The British Cinema Book* (London: BFI, second edition, 2001), p. 231.

6 Until *28 Days Later* (2002) loosed its slavering zombies on to the streets of a deserted London, and *My Little Eye* (also 2002) offered a gruesome satire on reality television, work of this kind was produced only sporadically, and when it did appear, it provoked little response.

7 'Ridiculous ... dull ... poorly executed ... cast who apparently treated the whole affair with the reverence kids usually reserve for a school play' was Alexander Stuart's verdict on *The Wicker Man* (1974) ('The Wicker Man', *Films and Filming* (April 1974), p. 47). In the same issue, Stuart offered a glowing report and 'highly recommended' two-star rating to Robert Stevenson's *Herbie Rides Again* (1974).

8 Richard Attenborough, *In Search of Gandhi* (London: The Bodley Head, 1982), p. 147.

9 See Robert Mighall, *A Geography of Victorian Gothic Fiction: Mapping History's Nightmares* (Oxford: Oxford University Press, 1999), pp. 210–47.

10 Christopher Lee, interview with the author, 20 February 2002.

11 Herbert Wilcox had attempted to film the same story in 1934, but the objections of the censors squashed the project (see '"The Hanging Judge" Ban', *Kinematograph Weekly* (14 June 1934), p. 51).

12 'Herschell Gordon Lewis', *Son et image* (April 1978), p. 22.

13 Herschell Gordon Lewis, interview with the author, 13 June 2001.

14 R. F. Delderfield, 'Build-Up of Horror', *Daily Telegraph* (2 October 1958), p. 8.

15 Frank Baker, 'Horror Films', *The Times* (8 October 1958), p. 11.

16 See Alexander Walker, 'Who Killed Peeping Tom?' *Evening Standard* (21 November 1997).

17 Peter Cowie, 'The Amoral Ones', *Films and Filming* (December 1962), p. 69.

18 Interview with Guy Hamilton, 14 May 2002.

19 See Peter Noble, '"Why I Surrendered" – Producer Towers', *Screen International* (13 December 1980), p. 30.

20 In *Eugenie*, Lee's participation in scenes of rapacious sadism has been achieved through clever editing. However, he does share one shot with the teenage heroine, in which she appears in a transparent negligée clutching a bloodied instrument of torture.

21 David McGillivray, *Doing Rude Things: The History of the British Sex Film, 1957–1981* (London: Sun Tavern Fields, 1992), p. 129.

22 Compare the opening of *Cul de Sac* with his short *The Mammals* (1962), and you'll see how strong the influence was.

23 Interview with Roy Hudd, 11 February 2002.

24 The best friend was played by Victor Henry, a star of the Royal Court who was hit by a bus two years after making *The Sorcerers* and remained in a coma for seventeen years. He was pronounced dead in November 1985.

25 John Russell Taylor, 'Horror and Something More', *The Times* (11 May 1968), p. 19; Alan Bennett, 'Views', *Listener* (23 May 1968), p. 657.

26 Piers Haggard, 'The Importance of Being Honest', *Screen International* (25 October 1975), p. 21.

27 Audiences who had witnessed Hayden's performance as Luci, the orphaned teenager who brings sexual chaos to the middle-class household of the Michael Klinger production *Baby Love* (1968), had already been asked to consider a similar question.

28 Weldon describes her work on the picture in *Auto da Fay* (London: Flamingo, 2002), pp. 114–15.

29 Jon Savage, *England's Dreaming: Sex Pistols and Punk Rock* (London: Faber and Faber, 1991), p. 122.

30 Philip French, 'Garbo's Farewell to Europe', *The Times* (6 December 1974), p. 15.

31 Ian Christie, 'If You Like This – Have Your Brain Examined', *Daily Express* (6 December 1974), p. 12.

32 'Walker's "Confessional"', *Photoplay* (August 1975), p. 24.

33 See 'Mr Walker Wants to Know', *Kinematograph Weekly* (10 August 1939), p. 11; 'Film Copyright Action', *Kinematograph Weekly* (17 August 1939), p. 7.

34 Walker knew Rice-Davis through his association with the Condor, a Wardour Street night-club owned by her boyfriend, Peter Rachman, and fronted by Tommy Yeardye, a former stuntman briefly married to Diana Dors.

35 See Fergus Cashin, 'What Are Stars Like These Doing in Trash Like This?', *Sun* (7 December 1974), p. 12.

36 The name of Keith's character in the *The House of Whipcord* is Walker: Alfred Shaughnessy, who scripted *The Flesh and Blood Show*, suggested that the character was sufficiently sadistic to be named after the picture's director.

37 Roger Ebert, who scripted the Russ Meyer version of the Pistols film, remembers giving a lift to Johnny Rotten after a meeting. 'As we drove him home,' Ebert recalls, 'he complained bitterly that McLaren had the band on a salary of eight pounds a week, borrowed five pounds from Meyer and had us stop at an all-night store so he could buy a six-pack of lager and cans of pork and beans. Rotten was the victim of a razor attack while walking the streets of London; McLaren not only failed to provide security, he wouldn't pay taxi fares.'

CHAPTER TEN The Oldest Living Sexploitation Star Tells All

1 David McGillivray, *Doing Rude Things* (London: Sun Tavern fields, 1992); Simon Sherdian, *Keeping the British End Up* (London: Reynolds and Hearn, 2001).

2 McGillivray, *op. cit.*, p. 19.

3 As his credit cards were missing, his phone line cut and his car had been driven on the day of his death, the coroner returned an open verdict.

4 Not everyone came to a sticky end. Anna Bergman, the star of *Intimate Games* (1975) among many others, returned to Sweden at the beginning of the 1980s to play a small part in her father's *Fanny and Alexander*. Justin Cartwright, director of *Rosie Dixon, Night Nurse* (1978), went to work as a PR man for the Liberal Democrats, and eventually won the Whitbread Prize for Fiction. Angela Grant, who stripped off in *Zeta One* (1969) and Derek Ford's *What's Up . . .* series, became a fundraiser for the Tory Party. Tony Booth, Robin Askwith's sidekick in all the *Confessions* pictures, became the father-in-law of the British Prime Minister, Tony Blair.

5 Though not quite: Green adopted his real name, Harris Marks, which was the source of confusion to a number of hotel registrars.

6 See Alison Smith (ed.), *Exposed: The Victorian Nude* (London: Tate Publishing), p. 180

7 John Trevelyan, *What the Censor Saw* (London: Michael Joseph, 1973), p. 98.

8 'In Camera', *Films and Filming* (September 1963), p. 6.

9 The later sex comedies also exhibit an interest in squalor. *The Adventures of a Plumber's Mate* (1978), for instance, opens with a shot of Barry Evans's filthy bedsit, in which a soot-coloured mouse is scurrying over a plate of last night's chicken and chips.

10 Russell Davies (ed.), *The Kenneth Williams Diaries* (London: HarperCollins, 1994), p. 762.

11 George Orwell, *Collected Essays*, vol. ii (Penguin: Harmondsworth, 1970), p. 194.

12 Kenneth Williams played W. C. Boggs in *Carry on at Your Convenience*; Jim Dale was Dr Nookey in *Carry on Again, Doctor*; Sid James made the Rumpo Kid flesh in *Carry on Cowboy*; and Charles Hawtrey was Private Widdle in *Carry on Up the Khyber* (1968). Irene Handl played Miss Slenderparts in *Confessions of a Driving Instructor* (1976); Anthony Kenyon and Jack Wild were Mellons and Cockshute in *Keep It Up Downstairs* (1976); Hughie Greene was Bob Scratchitt in *What's Up Superdoc?* (1978).

13 *Screen International* (15 November 1975), pp. 11, 17.

14 See *Mr David Sullivan and the Bristol Evening Post plc: A Report on the Proposed Transfer of a Controlling Interest as Defined in Section 57(4) of the Fair Trading Act 1973* (London: HM Stationery Office, 1990), section 2.2.

15 Before *Come Play with Me*, Millington played a choirgirl in *Intimate Games*, a scullery maid in *Keep It Up Downstairs* , and a champagne-proffering prostitute in *What's Up Superdoc?*

16 Simon Sheridan, *Come Play with Me: The Life and Films of Mary Millington* (London: FAB Press, 1999), p. 79.

CONCLUSION This Is Where You Came In

1 Balcon, *Michael Balcon Presents, op. cit.*, p. 46.

Index of Films

General Index